Management and Labour in Europe

The Industrial Enterprise in Germany, Britain and France

Christel Lane

Lecturer in Sociology
The Business School
University of Aston

EDWARD ELGAR

Published by
Edward Elgar Publishing Limited
Gower House
Croft Road
Aldershot
Hants GU11 3HR
England

Edward Elgar Publishing Limited
Distributed in the United States by
Ashgate Publishing Company
Old Post Road
Brookfield
Vermont 05036
USA

Reprinted 1992

British Library Cataloguing in Publication Data
Lane, Christel
  Management and labour in Europe: the industrial
enterprise in Germany, Britain and France
  1. European Community countries. Industries.
  Organization structure
  I. Title
  338.7'094   5660002153

Library of Congress Cataloguing-in-Publication Data
Lane, Christel.
    Management and labour in Europe: the industrial enterprise in
  Germany, Britain, and France/Christel Lane.
      p. cm.
    Includes bibliographical references.
    1. Industrial management—Germany (West) 2. Industrial
  management—Great Britain. 3. Industrial management—France.
  4. Business enterprises—Germany (West) 5. Business enterprises—
  Great Britain. 6. Business enterprises—France. 7. Industrial
  relations—Germany (West) 8. Industrial relations—Great Britain.
  9. Industrial relations—France. I. Title.
HD70.G2L36 1989
331'.094—dc20   89–17070
                                                    CIP

ISBN 1 85278 058 4
     1 85278 208 0 (pbk)

Printed in Great Britain by
Billing & Sons Ltd, Worcester

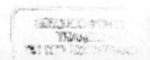

Contents

Tables

Figures

Acknowledgements

The advice and help of several European colleagues have contributed to the completion of this work. German colleagues at the Institut für Sozialforschung in Munich, Professor Norbert Altmann and Dr Werner Sengenberger gave ideas and material for Chapters 6 and 7. Professor Wolfgang Streeck and Dr Arndt Sorge, of the Research Unit Labour Market and Employment at the Wissenschaftszentrum Berlin provided stimulation and practical help during a visit to the WZ. In France, Professor Françoise Piotet of the Institut d'Etudes Politiques and Professor M. Berry of the Centre de Rercherche en Gestion at the Ecole Polytechnique generously responded to appeals for literature for Chapter 7. Special thanks are due to my English colleagues at Aston University: to Dr David Podmore, for reading and commenting on several draft chapters, and to Dr Linda Hantrais, for valuable advice on some aspects of French society. Last, but not least, I owe thanks to my Aston students on the International Business Management course who, by their questions and comments, have frequently alerted me to the need for further elaboration and clarification of arguments.

Christel Lane
August 1988

Introduction

Britain, France and the Federal Republic of Germany (hereafter Germany) are highly developed capitalist industrial societies, displaying substantial similarities in terms of population size, endowment with natural resources, industrial development as well as in political and cultural heritage. The organization of industrial enterprises is structured along similar lines, and the activities and concerns of both industrial management and labour are oriented towards the same kinds of goals. Their common membership of the European Economic Community (EEC) has not only served to homogenize many business practices but has also presented industrial concerns in the three nations with similar economic and social opportunities which have latterly increasingly become comparable constraints and problems. The growth of multi-national corporations, not only in Britain but recently also in France and Germany, is commonly held to have advanced even further a process of homogenization of enterprise organization and culture.

Yet a closer investigation of the industrial enterprise in the three societies reveals that there has occurred relatively little convergence towards a common European type, but that superficially common structural arrangements hide enduringly distinctive national ways of going about and organizing industrial production. These diverse ways of tackling the tasks of industrial organization, manifested in different structural arrangements and social identities of both management and labour, have been shaped by the continuing diversity in the societal and political institutional framework in which industrial enterprises are embedded. Management and labour, and their constant interaction in the process of industrial production, have been socially constituted and thus bear the distinctive marks of the societies in which they are situated. The capitalist and advanced industrial nature of all three societies has acted to create many common patterns in business organization – and these should not be belittled or ignored – but they have not obliterated national distinctiveness. The unique character of the British, French and German manufacturing enterprise is both reflected in the general economy and reflects its historical development and present state. The following section will therefore be devoted to a general

1

overview of postwar economic and, to a lesser extent, socio-political development of the three European societies. Such a survey provides the general context in which to situate the development of individual firms, as well as the activities of managements of labour.

ECONOMIC PROFILES OF FRANCE, GERMANY AND BRITAIN

France

The industrial development of France occurred later and much more slowly than that of its main European competitors. Although development started around the 1870s and significant advances were made in a few industrial sectors, overall economic development and population growth stagnated up to World War I and did not accelerate greatly in the interwar period. An advanced industrial economy, oriented towards international trade, emerged only from the late 1950s onwards after the formation of the EEC.

Whereas a German 'economic miracle' during the early postwar decades has become a well established cliché, it is less well known that France achieved a similarly impressive economic transformation and growth within a short timespan. During the 1960s and early 1970s the French economy was transformed from a traditional type – it possessed a large agrarian sector,[1] together with an industrial sector dominated by small to medium-sized, family-owned firms – into an advanced industrial one with a significant large-scale corporate sector. France moved from a highly protectionist economy, oriented mainly to the internal market, to an open one, attempting increasingly to compete on a world market. Between around 1955 and 1970 France's economic growth rate surpassed that of most OECD countries, excepting only Japan. France reached an average annual growth rate of 5.7 per cent which was almost twice as high as that of the UK during the same period (Barker et al., 1984: 69). Export earnings became a rapidly growing component of the GNP, and French export share in manufacturing outstripped that of Britain during the early 1970s but remained only half that of Germany. (Figures quoted by Telesis, 1986: 12, Figure 7). Although its net trade balance from manufacturing[2] was lower than that of the UK, it was maintained at a much more constant level during this early period (ibid.: Figure 8). By the early 1970s, France had overtaken Britain as regards the level of industrial labour productivity and the standard of living (ibid.: 12f; Barker et al., 1984: 70). Both the population and the labour force expanded significantly during 1958–73, and the level of general education surpassed that of both the British and the German population.

This impressive economic growth and transformation is widely attributed to government economic planning and intervention. Government intervention in the size and distribution of investment effected not only a rationalization of production and trade by developing the large-firm sector but also a modernization of industrial specialization and a spurt of technological advance. Appealing to a spirit of economic nationalism, the state managed to harness and develop the productive energies of the French population. At the same time, the relatively large size of the agrarian sector in the early 1960s provided a larger scope for economic growth than was the case in either Germany or Britain. The result was the transformation to an advanced corporate economy, specializing in such modern sectors as aerospace, weapons technology and energy development.

At the same time, however, the corporate sector has remained less significant in proportional terms than in Germany and, more so, in Britain, and a large sector of small, family-owned firms was largely left intact. The modernization of economic capacity was not accompanied by the emergence of a more modern management style, and the system of industrial relations saw only very modest and piecemeal reforms. The whole period was characterized by poor management–labour relations which erupted in the 1968 general strike and widespread political unrest and in the more localized industrial unrest of the early 1970s. But labour productivity remained relatively high, and stability in macro-economic and social policy was guaranteed by a succession of Conservative governments. Overall, French economic performance and the improvement in the level of material well-being was impressive by international standards, and the early postwar decades (1945–75) became known, in the words of the economist Jean Fourastié, as 'les trentes glorieuses' (Telesis, 1986: 5).

During the 1970s, French economic performance began to deteriorate. But, taking most indices, it still remained superior to that of the UK, although France steadily lost ground compared with Germany. (For details of French–British economic indices at the turn of the 1970s, see Table 1.1). The growth rate declined to just under 3 per cent per annum, and unemployment had risen steadily from 2½ per cent during the early 1970s to 8 per cent in the early 1980s (Barker et al., 1984: 69–70). Between 1968 and 1979 exports still continued to grow (Piotet, 1984: 243). But increasingly sharp competition on world markets began to show up the weaknesses of France's more traditional industrial

Table 1.1 *French, British and German economies compared in the 1980s*

	1980–1981			1983–1985			
	France	UK	Germany	France	UK	Germany	
Population in 1980	53 mill	56 mill	61.6 mill	55 mill	56.5 mill	61 mill	Population 1984
GDP per capita (In US $) at PPP in 1980	9.150	7.730	9.435				
Percentage employed in industry in 1980/81	35.3	35.9	44.1				
Export shares in manufacturing in 1980	9.1	8.4	18.2	8.5	7.7	18.5	Export shares in manufacturing in 1983
				7.7	8.5	14.5	World export shares of technology – intensive products in 1984
Value-added in manufacturing as % of GDP in 1979	27.0	25.8	33.8	25.4	22.6	32.3	Value-added in manufacturing as % of GDP in 1984/5
Labour productivity: output per man-hour	70	37	82				
				57.7	49.5	96.4	Industry-financed R & D per capita in $ in 1983
Rate of unemployment in 1981	8.0	10.5	5.5	11.0	10.2	8.7	Rate of unemployment in 1987

Sources: Barker *et al.* 1984: 68, table 1; Roy 1982; Patel and Pavitt 1987: 72; Streeck 1987, table III; Duchêne and Shepherd 1987: 36; *Key Data* 1987: 7; *The Economist* 10–16.10.87: 111; Mayes 1987: 49.

sectors (steel, shipbuilding, textiles, leather goods and machine tools), as well as the vulnerability of its large corporations. The latter, being largely the result of state-directed mergers and acquisitions, had never properly rationalized their productive activities and consequently lost cost-competitiveness in both international and home markets (Telesis, 1986: 132f). Between 1974 and 1982, according to Soulage (1985: 169), France did not significantly improve its competitive position in any industrial sector.

During the 1980s, the negative trends of the late 1970s intensified, fuelled partly by the world recession of the early 1980s and partly by the increasingly sharp competition from both low-wage countries (in low-skill product sectors) and more efficient OECD countries (in high-quality/high-tech product sectors) (Telesis, 1986: 31f). The misconceived attempt by the socialist government in 1981 to revive the economy and bring down unemployment served to worsen performance and led to a dramatic increase in foreign debts (Hall, 1986). Generally during the 1980s, government intervention in industry has become less extensive and detailed, and it is also no longer credited with its earlier effectiveness (see the discussion in Adams and Stoffaës, 1986).

During the 1980s, GDP growth rates suffered a further decline and, from 1982, fell below those of the UK (Barker et al., 1984: 69). Net exports as a percentage of GDP also decreased (*National Institute Economic Review* 1987; 121: 29, for the later 1980s). Unemployment continued to rise and in 1987 surpassed the high level reached in the UK.[3] Also, the gap in labour productivity and living standards between the two societies has become progressively smaller, although France probably still maintains a slight superiority in these areas (Barker et al., 1984: 81), as well as in the level of investment (Telesis, 1986: 10), industry-financed R & D (Patel and Pavitt, 1987: 72) and training (see Chapter 3).

Despite the larger pool of highly skilled engineers in France, as compared with Britain, French industry is not much more technologically sophisticated, if at all.[4] As in Britain, too many manufacturing enterprises in the consumer and producer goods sectors have remained in product areas of low technological sophistication and skill intensity (Barker et al., 1984: 72). Although France can still point to several industrial sectors with a high international reputation, these are now mainly sectors which are dependent on state support for R & D, procurement policy and export diplomacy, such as nuclear energy, aerospace, weapons technology and electronic communications (Stoffaës, 1986: 44). In sectors, such as consumer electronics, textiles, leather goods, chemicals and machine tools, French firms have slipped badly behind (Soulage, 1985: 169). The latter is also true of the all-important car manufacturing sector where French competitiveness has dipped dramatically during the 1980s (Telesis, 1986: 9) although it has not yet reached the parlous state of the British car industry.

These weaknesses of the French economy during the 1980s are mirrored in the declining fortunes of a significant proportion of the large corporations. Many have shown declining profits or even overall losses, as has been true of Renault, Peugeot and Michelin (Telesis, 1986: 7, 9, 65). Conversely, France has few star performers among the large corporations, i.e. firms which can compete in traded world markets and show both a high level of return on invested capital and a high value-added per employee. Particularly notable is the very small number of stars in the export-oriented high-tech sector. The main areas of French economic success are either in traditional French goods, such as food and drinks, e.g. Bongrain, Danône, Perrier, and beauty products, e.g. L'Oréal, or they are in the oil industry (ibid.: 59f, 80f, 98). Unlike Britain, France also has an insufficient number of widely-implanted multinational companies which are more likely to weather downturns in individual areas of the world market.

Although state support to business remains vital, France's return to industrial competitiveness in changed world conditions now depends more crucially on manufacturing industry itself and particularly on the management of its large corporations. France is still seen as 'Europe's second most powerful engine' (Telesis, 1986: 299), and it remains to be seen whether management can overcome the weaknesses outlined and develop its strengths sufficiently to repeat the earlier success story.

Germany

Germany industrialized between 1830 and 1860 and on the eve of World War I had already become a powerful economic rival to Britain, leading in such industries as steel, machinery and chemicals. In the interwar period Germany lost some ground, but during the National Socialist period its industry gained fresh momentum and developed some more modern sectors. The destruction of industrial capacity during World War II was made good during the 1950s, and by the early 1960s a revitalized and modernized German economy began to overtake both France and Britain in terms of the size of its GNP (Stocks, 1983: 1).

The period of the late 1950s to the middle 1970s, which became known as the 'German Economic Miracle', established Germany not only as the strongest economy in Europe but also as one of the leading manufacturing countries in the Western world, after the USA and, later, Japan. During that period of the postwar boom the German economy and pattern of industrial production developed all the distinctive features which, with only a few adaptations, still persist today. Given its poor supply of natural resources, the German economy became geared to the production and export of goods which aimed to compete by offering advanced technical design, high quality and good 'after sales' service. These could be ensured by the relatively high level of industry-financed R & D, the pragmatic engineering skills of German management and the generally high level of technical skill and disciplined working methods of the whole industrial labour force. Although large enterprises dominated in many industries, Germany also retained a thriving sector of small to medium-sized and largely owner-managed enterprises.[5] The dominant industries in the early period were chemicals, electrical goods, steel, shipbuilding, cars and the producer goods of mechanical engineering.

The steadily increasing proportion of exports from these sectors led to high economic growth rates which, together with high levels of labour productivity, pushed up the German standard of living well above that of its major European competitors. Although German workers enjoyed relatively high levels of wages and social benefits by European standards, their equally high labour productivity meant that overall production costs were no higher than in Britain. The growth of manufacturing output and export also received a boost from a generally stable economic environment, a low level of inflation, an undervalued currency, as well as from political stability and a high degree of social consensus. Stocks (1983: 1) sums up the early period of postwar successes as follows:

> The weight of the country has become such that sustainable economic growth in much of Western Europe – and indeed also in Eastern Europe – is now virtually impossible without a similar out turn in West Germany, the locomotive of the European economy.

From the mid-1970s onwards, the effects of the oil shock and of the general world recession left their mark also on Germany which, as a highly open economy, inevitably became affected by the declining economic strength of its customers. But the late 1970s also brought to light internal industrial weaknesses. Although Germany was much better placed than France and Britain to accommodate the changes in world demand for high value-added goods (see Chapter 7), Germany, too, had not restructured its manufacturing sector sufficiently from traditional to modern sectors, required by a changed international division of labour and demand on a world market. The competition from Japan, constituted by its ability to combine lower-cost production with a faster rate of technological innovation, became particularly threatening to Germany. It became evident that, in the area of consumer electronics, Germany had lost the initiative to Japan and that penetration by Japanese imports and even production units had become a *fait accompli* (Stocks 1983). At the same time, development of industrial capacity in low-wage countries in such areas as steel production, shipbuilding, textiles, etc., caused a world overcapacity. This forced Germany, in the same way as it did Britain and France, to cut back severely capacity in these sectors and in petrochemicals, as well as develop and expand the manufacture of speciality products, such as galvanised steel or high-value pharmaceutical goods.[6]

These difficulties from both external sources and internal tardiness of structural adjustment were further exacerbated by changes in the world currency system. These resulted in a more highly valued DM and thus in higher prices for export goods. The social and political stability became disturbed by the emergence of Citizens' Initiatives and of the Green Party. Their supporters questioned the desirability of Germany's economic and social model and demanded political measures to limit, hedge in and make more costly production in industries, perceived to be a threat to the human and natural environment. But a comparatively high degree of industrial peace and general economic stability remained a feature also of this period.

The early 1980s thus saw Germany reach the lowest point of its economic fortunes. The problems outlined manifested themselves in some undercapacity, in reduced rates of GDP growth – an average of 2.1 per cent during the early 1980s, and in the persistence of a relatively high level of unemployment – 5.5 per cent in 1981, which stayed, however, well below levels in France and Britain. But even in the early 1980s one quarter of GNP came from the export of manufactured goods (Stocks, 1983: 27).

By the middle 1980s, however, German manufacturing industry appeared to have weathered most of the earlier problems (*The Economist*, 16 December 1986: 19), and most performance indicators showed that it was fundamentally healthy and had remained highly competitive (OECD, 1986a: 7, 59; Telesis, 1986: 42). Although one could no longer talk about an 'economic miracle' and not all problems had been solved German industry remained, in most respects, a model of efficient performance. Germany has remained the world's second largest exporter. Manufacturing industry's competitive edge, through strength of design, quality, reliability and innovativeness, was kept up in most core industries. Opinions are divided over whether or not competition on price has become more problematic after the DM revaluation (Stocks, 1983: 54; *The Economist*, 16 December 1986: 1a).[7] Exports increased considerably in 1982–85 (OECD, 1986a: 132). Moreover, in contrast to the situation in France, German exports go predominantly – to 75 per cent – to advanced Western countries and are thus less vulnerable to the greater economic and political instability of the developing countries (Telesis, 1986: 42). The balance of payments remained healthy and inflation has been kept at a relatively low level. By 1985 company profitability was restored to the level of the early 1970s and has sustained investment growth. Capacity utilization, on average, approached the pre-recession peak of the late 1970s (OECD, 1986a: 32). Employment has started to grow again but, due to a simultaneous growth in the labour force, has not brought down unemployment. GNP growth in 1982–85 stayed below the 3 per cent level (ibid.: 7, 8, 32).

The car industry, which has particularly important multiplier effects, remained competitive, as did production of most chemicals and the mechanical and electronic producer goods industries (Telesis, 1986). Germany's medium-sized firms showed themselves to be particularly adept in exploiting the potential of microelectronics in engineering (*The Economist*, 6 December 1986: 19). Germany has retained more star performers among its large manufacturing companies in terms of both returns on capital and value-added per employee, than either France or Britain (Telesis, 1986: 69), and many of its medium-sized firms have also shown themselves very innovative, adaptable and able to compete on world markets (*The Economist*, 6 December 1986). In short, despite greater problems than in earlier postwar decades, Germany still outperforms France and Britain, as well as maintaining a relatively strong position in the EEC and on the world market.

If, however, the comparison is extended to take in Japan, some of the German strengths become less convincing. For example, Germany's industry-financed R & D of 96.4 dollars per capita in 1983 looks less impressive against Japan's 116 dollars per head (Patel and Pavitt, 1987: 72, Table 1), as does its overall level of investment and its employment record (OECD statistics, quoted by Telesis, 1986: 10). Thus Germany, too, needs to improve its industrial performance, but its policy-makers and industrialists are unlikely to find many models in either France or Britain.

Britain

Britain's post-war economic decline is widely seen to have long historical roots, going back as far as the middle of the last century. A general loss of industrial dynamism from that time onwards is attributed to the fact that Britain was the first and, for a long time, unchallenged industrial power, and to the way it became insulated from competition by access to its captive colonial markets. Here is not the place to discuss this complex process (for details see Landes, 1969; Wiener, 1981; or Gamble, 1985), except to indicate that Britain entered the postwar economic race from an already weak starting position which became more evident during the 1960s and 1970s. A relatively low rate of investment, low labour productivity and an insufficient development of technically skilled manpower, allied to an unstable macro-economic environment (the stop–go monetary policy), a high level of inflation, and conflict-ridden industrial relations, resulted in relatively low rates of growth or even decline in existing industries, as well as in a failure to restructure manufacturing industry towards newer and technologically more advanced branches. (An average overall growth rate of 2.6 per cent in 1950–79 may be contrasted with Germany's rate of 5.3 per cent for the same period (figures quoted by Jacobi, 1985: 55).) Britain's share in world manufacturing output fell from 9.6 per cent in 1960 to 5.8 per cent in 1975 (Blackaby, 1979: 24). Although Britain remained a politically influential nation, its economic ineffectiveness and the population's standard of living had moved it almost to the bottom of the European league table. The real extent of industrial decline, however, remained partially disguised by the facts that material wealth had increased substantially during the postwar period and that those in employment were still enjoying a rising standard of living.

The nadir of industrial decline was reached in 1981–82 when widespread business failure, cutbacks and a record level of unemployment (around 13 per cent) led to fears of deindustrialization, i.e. of an absolute decline in industrial capacity and employment. The Thatcher government had come to power in 1979 with the promise to cure Britain's industrial ills and put the country back on the road to economic health. From 1983 onwards, there began to occur some encouraging changes. These have led to government claims that recovery has begun and that Britain is regaining competitive strength. A close examination of manufacturing industry is therefore in order to see whether this optimistic evaluation of recent trends can be sustained.

Clear signs of recovery from the lowest point at the turn of the decade are certainly indicated by an above average (for the EEC) rate of output growth and by significant increases in labour productivity. Thus a growth rate of an average of 3 per cent during 1980–85, a modest employment growth since 1983, an increase in profits (18 per cent of GDP in 1984 as compared with 13 per cent in 1980), a rise in exports since 1983 (OECD, 1986b), as well as considerable productivity gains (a rise of 25 per cent in manufacturing industry between 1981 and 1986, according to Rudolph, 1987), all look encouraging. A much reduced level of industrial action has further enhanced public confidence.

But a closer examination of economic trends raises doubts about whether these changes are sufficient for a regeneration of manufacturing industry. By the middle of 1985 output was still 6 per cent below its average level in 1979 which, in turn, had been below the peak level in 1973. Furthermore, recovery has been concentrated in only a few industrial sectors and a significant proportion – one-fifth – of output growth came from North Sea oil production. A growth in services, too, was far more marked than one in manufacturing. Around 50 per cent of firms were still working below normal capacity in 1985. Similarly, employment growth has been more strongly concentrated in the service sector and had by 1986, not advanced employment beyond the 1981 trough (OECD, 1986b: 37–9). There is still a negative trade balance which is forecast to last until the end of the decade (Oxford Economic Forecast, *The Guardian*, 13 November 1987), and the deficit on manufactured goods has even increased since 1983 (OECD, 1986b: 44). Lastly, the superficially impressive growth in output must not disguise the fact that, in 1982, per capita real GDP in Britain still was 75 per cent below that enjoyed by the German population (Jacobi, 1985: 58).

The increases in productivity also have to be interpreted with care. They started from such a low level, by international standards, that Britain is still significantly behind its competitors in advanced industrial countries. More importantly, rising labour productivity is largely attributed to cyclical developments, i.e. to the shake-out of inefficient and overmanned firms during the last decade of industrial recession, and is not connected with fundamental restructuring of business organization (Jacobi, 1985: 56; Rudolph, 1987), although more research would be needed fully to substantiate this claim. But the more general suggestion that only higher levels of R & D spending and of investment[8] generally, more technological innovation and a more efficient exploitation of potential advantages given by innovation can restore British firms and manufacturing industry to an internationally competitive position must be regarded beyond doubt (Freeman 1979; Hall 1986; Lisle-Williams 1986; Patel and Pavitt 1987).

Similar to the situation in France, Britain's problems today stem from the overspecialization in product areas of low skill intensity and technological sophistication and a tardy reorientation of manufacturing towards new industries and products, corresponding to the demands resulting from the international division of labour. An examination of

British large firms in the manufacturing sector shows that Britain has few stars or world-beaters (Goldsmith and Clutterbuck, 1984). Two of the three stars – British Petroleum and Shell – are in the energy rather than the manufacturing industry so that ICI remains the only internationally competitive company of any size (Telesis, 1986: 71). The complete absence of even moderately successful firms in the sectors of mechanical and electrical engineering and the all-important car industry is striking. (For a more detailed analysis of export performance of the various industries see Mayes, 1987: 55).

A careful analysis of overall performance of British manufacturing industry in the 1980s thus demonstrates that a less sanguine interpretation of the significance of recent signs of recovery is in order. To catch up with its continental competitors, and particularly with Germany, and to regain competitiveness in manufactured goods on world markets requires further drastic internal reorganization of enterprises. Given the scale of the problem still to be confronted, it might be argued that it would be wiser to concentrate efforts in the field of services where Britain has a more successful record and to stop investing resources and talent in manufacturing industry. It is, therefore, important to address the question of how important a role manufacturing industry plays in the British economy.

DOES MANUFACTURING INDUSTRY MATTER?

A recent article by Mayes (1987) explores the complex issues raised by this question. Mayes surveys a number of arguments which attribute to manufacturing a central role in the economy. He attributes validity only to one line of reasoning which was also pursued by the 1984 House of Lords Committee on Overseas Trade. According to this argument, the inability of manufacturing industry to compete cannot be sufficiently compensated for by other sectors. Hence it becomes difficult to generate the foreign exchange necessary to pay for desired imports. In these circumstances the balance of payments acts as a brake on economic growth. Given that economic sectors such as agriculture and oil production are expected to make a declining contribution to national income in the foreseeable future, the importance of manufacturing for the whole economy may even increase over the next few years.

In conclusion, a vigorous manufacturing sector is a crucial contributor to overall economic health, and manufacturing industry's level of performance is determined by all the enterprises which constitute the sector. Hence a comparative analysis of differences between European industrial enterprises and of the levels of economic performance associated with them remains an important object of study.

OBJECTIVES OF THE BOOK

The initial impetus for undertaking a comparative study of the industrial enterprise in the three European societies came from a desire simply to describe and explain sociologically the nationally diverse responses to the similar challenges, facing European industrial undertakings during a period of rapid economic and technological change. The comparative approach was adopted to highlight the distinctiveness of each national pattern and to arrive at a better understanding of the unique way in which each has been constructed. The use of comparison to aid explanation and to enhance understanding of social phenomena has always been recognized as a valuable tool of social scientific research and hence as an end in itself.

Those approaching the analysis of the business organization from a more practical 'business' or 'management' point of view, however, have not always seen the need to extend their interest in the functioning of business organization beyond the confines of their own national environment. But students of business studies and practising managers cannot obtain an adequate grasp of the opportunities and constraints of industrial production if they confine themselves to a study of business organization within British national boundaries only. Britain has always produced for international markets. Since joining the Common Market in 1973, Britain has increasingly become oriented towards Europe. Not only do British enterprises find some of their main customers and competitors on the continent – exports to the EEC amounted to 49.2 per cent of total export in 1986, as compared with only 14.3 per cent of exports to the American market (*The Economist*, 28 November 1987: 25) – but British managements also face similar opportunities and constraints, as do their German and French opposites. The high degree of economic integration within Europe means that the economic well-being of each European nation depends on that of each major EC partner (Stocks, 1983; Duchêne and Shepherd, 1987). Just as Britain's success in climbing out of the recession depends on the economic recovery of France and Germany, the latter cannot achieve high levels of economic prosperity without at least a moderate performance of its main European trading partners. The formation of a single European market in 1992 will further increase the degree of integration and of competition. A knowledge of the strengths and weaknesses of the main European competitors will become indispensable to British managements.

Such a focus on Europe does not intend to distract awareness from the fact that the USA and, more so, Japan should be regarded as important industrial rivals. It merely tries to redirect interest towards the historically and contemporarily close economic ties between the three nations which have often been forgotten in the current excessive fascination with Japan, which has replaced the equally faddish interest in US corporations in the previous decade. Consequently, a comparative analysis of the business enterprise in the three major European societies compels also the attention of students and practitioners of management.

The initial intention of this three-sided comparison was to avoid an evaluation of differences between the national business organizations in terms of superior or inferior coping with the tasks of profitable industrial production. But it soon became evident that such an objective analysis cannot be sustained and that descriptive accounts inevitably assume also an evaluative and hence prescriptive character. The industrial enterprise in capitalist society is first and foremost a social structure oriented towards the achievement of economic performance targets. These in turn shape national industrial and overall economic vigour, health and even viability, as well as the condition of labour and the general societal level of material and social well-being. The marked differences between the three societies in industrial performance during the postwar period and, particularly, the alarming relative and absolute industrial decline of Britain during the last decade, could not be left out of account and were, indeed, illuminated by the study of industrial activity at enterprise level. The focus will be exclusively on the manufacturing enterprise. Although the manufacturing sector has been declining in proportional size in all three societies, it is still the case that a thriving economy cannot be attained without a successful manufacturing industry.

If the resulting evaluation and implicit ranking of enterprise structures and social relations in terms of performance criteria is to go beyond a negative, exposé-type account of Britain's industrial problems, a further step has to be taken. One has to venture into the problematic field of suggesting lessons which could be learnt by management and labour from studying best practice in the other European societies. In many cases, such a learning process is equally necessary for policy-making élites in government. But such a didactic approach has remained a minor objective of this study and opportunities to learn from good practice elsewhere have been merely implied rather than explicitly recommended. It would be wrong to suggest that a relearning process is only required on the part of British business, union and governmental decision-makers. Business enterprises and related institutions in all three societies have found in recent years that major adaptations in manufacturing organization have been called for and that time-honoured practices no longer succeed in these times of head-on world competition.

It has been pointed out that the comparative approach adopted consists of both showing how the various elements, which constitute the manufacturing enterprise, hang together and how they have historically evolved in interaction with other societal institutions, such as the system of education and training or the pattern of state–business relations, to name only a few. Such an emphasis on the interconnectedness of industrial and general societal structures implies, of course, certain limitations on transferring elements from one society to another. The problems and opportunities of learning from the experience of foreign business organizations will be more fully discussed in the Conclusion. Here it suffices to say that, although this theoretical approach precludes a recommendation of piecemeal borrowing from other national contexts, it does not exclude a learning process which is sensitive to different national cultures. Any transplant of elements of foreign business organization must, therefore, view them in their social context and adapt the domestic institutional environment accordingly. Hence the initiation of change in the institutional framework impinging on business organization usually goes beyond the capabilities of individual or even groups of firms and concerns national policy-makers as much as business leaders.

Inertia under the weight of history is inevitably greater than the inclination to change. But one need not assume that each nation's industrial structures and culture are therefore immutable and policy-makers completely impotent. Institutions which have been constructed by human agents must also be amenable to sensitive adaptation by these very same agents. It would be misguided to assume as, for example, does Hall (1986: 27, 45) that because of the long history of British industrial development, British management is completely constrained by historically formed institutions and thus could not have performed any better than it has. This is not to deny that efforts to initiate fundamental structural change in various sub-systems of society face tremendous obstacles and that initiation of change may require a special, externally imposed impetus. It is suggested that the combined circumstances of severe economic recession and the emergence of a new crossroads in industrial development (see Chapter 7) may just provide such an impetus for Britain.

GENERAL APPROACH AND CONTENT OF THE STUDY

This book aims to fill an important gap in the literature by providing a comparative study of the manufacturing enterprise in Europe which covers most aspects of business organization and which consistently situates the business organization in its social context. It is addressed to both student and academic readers. Despite abiding interest in the comparative analysis of European business enterprises by social historians, social scientists and more policy-oriented researchers, there exists, as yet, no such comprehensive study. The recent comparison of French and German manufacturing organizations by Maurice and Sellier (1986) and of British and German ones by Sorge and Warner (1986) have laid a thorough groundwork on aspects of the internal organization of production units. These books have not attempted to analyse systematically social and political institutions which are important influences on business organizations, such as banks or the state. Also both teams of authors primarily address themselves to scholars and would prove inaccessible to student readers. Other recent comparative studies of manufacturing industry, in contrast, have focused *only* on the business environment, particularly on state activity in the area of industrial policy and on financial institutions. They have analysed industrial change at the macro-economic rather than at enterprise level. (See, for example, the excellent studies by Cox, 1986; Hall, 1986; Duchêne and Shepherd, 1987; Wilks and Wright, 1987). In addition to these wideranging books, there exists a multitude of specialist studies – many of them in the form of articles in a wide range of scholarly and management journals – which deal with selected aspects of management, labour or business organization. Many of these have not been published in English.

This book has drawn on this widely dispersed literature and has sought to integrate accounts from British, German and, to a lesser degree, French social science, management and statistical sources, as well as consulting some of the more popular journals written for practising managers. While source material in some areas, e.g. industrial relations or industrial policy, has been abundant, other aspects, such as comparative studies of the work of managers, have remained very underdeveloped.

This study constitutes an attempt to integrate a social science perspective with one informed by management studies. The text is addressed to academics and students, working in the areas of comparative sociology, sociology of work and/or industry, management or business studies and European studies. Students will derive greater benefit from the book if they have already studied some of the basic concepts in the social sciences and/or management studies. It is hoped that the book will also appeal to practising managers and other policy-makers.

The first chapter introduces readers to the various theoretical approaches to the comparative study of business organization and discusses in greater detail the cultural/institutional perspective. The second chapter undertakes an analysis of social interaction at work and how this shapes business organization. It debates such aspects as overall organizational structure and its impact on spans of control, horizontal and vertical integration and processes of communication. The close interrelation between organizational configuration and the level and kind of vocational/professional expertise possessed by categories of employees at different hierarchical levels is further explored in Chapter 3, which gives an overview of training and qualifying practices and institutions in the three societies. It considers these practices not only in relation to manual workers but also to technical workers, foremen and engineers. Chapters 4 to 7 are devoted to the study of management and its relations with labour. In Chapter 4 an overview of management education and career patterns is linked to a discussion of management style in the three societies. This explores management behaviour in terms of the typologies of 'employee-vs. production-oriented' style and 'democratic vs. autocratic' style and suggests explanations for national variation in terms of historically evolved institutional and cultural patterns. The all-important management function of control receives detailed attention in Chapter 5 where particular attention is given to control as a process of planning, coordinating and checking processes of resource utilization at both top and lower management level. Chapters 6 and 7, in contrast, are more oriented towards management control over the labour process and towards management–labour relations in the process of work organization. Whereas Chapter 6 surveys the situation in the earlier postwar decades up to the middle 1970s, Chapter 7 is concerned to analyse recent transformations in work organization and their relation to change in other areas, such as technology and product and labour markets. Chapters 8 and 9 deal with the systems of industrial relations and of industrial democracy and explore their impact on the general functioning and performance of the three national business organizations. Chapter 10 discusses the different ways in which government and industry have interacted in the three societies and draws out some of the implications of industrial policy for the development of manufacturing industries in the three societies. Chapter 11 explores the role of the state in the area of employment policy. It summarizes the movement in the last decade or so from welfare to free market capitalism and traces the impact of the policy changes, implied by these broad terms, on the quantity and quality of employment. The book concludes with a summary and discussion of findings and explores what lessons can be learnt from studying 'good practice' in other societies. In all chapters, themes are systematically analysed in the form of a three-sided comparison, although the data on France have not always been as plentiful as those on the other two societies. A constant endeavour has been to provide a rounded picture of what it means to organize, and work in, a manufacturing enterprise the German, British or the French way.

NOTES

1. The proportion of the working population in agriculture declined by 23 per cent between 1946 and 1975 (Hantrais, 1982: 22).
2. The net trade balance in manufacturing is calculated by subtracting manufactured imports from manufactured exports and considering it as a percentage of manufacturing output.
3. In August 1987 the unemployment rate was 11.0 per cent in France, 10.2 per cent in the UK and 8.7 per cent in Germany, (*The Economist.* 10–16 October 1987: 111).
4. The evidence on this is ambiguous, with some sources imputing French superiority in some areas (Northcott et al., 1985; Stoffaës, 1986: 44) and others claiming it for Britain. (Booz Allen and Hamilton, 1984, quoted in Patel and Pavitt, 1987: 73; Sharp, 1985).
5. In the mechanical engineering sector, for example, around 80 per cent of enterprises employ less than 300 workers (Stocks, 1983: 61).
6. Germany had, however, initiated product and process changes in steel and chemicals earlier than its two European competitors, and the chemical industry never entered a real crisis situation (Stocks, 1983; Telesis, 1986: 113).
7. According to a study by the Dresdner Bank, reported in *The Economist* (6 December 1986: 26), the highly-paid German worker is still cheaper per unit of output than any other European worker, excepting only the Spaniards.
8. In 1986, German manufacturers invested £700 more per employee than British ones, resulting in an annual investment gap of almost £4 billion (Banham, 1988: 24).

1 Business Organization in Comparative Perspective: The Theoretical Debate

This book looks at the modern business organization, and the human resources deployed within it, from a comparative perspective. Comparison focuses on the interplay between societal settings on the one hand and organizational forms and processes on the other. Depending on the goals and interests of the analyst, comparison can be oriented towards underlining the degree of similarity of organizational structures and processes found in different societies, i.e. it identifies processes of convergence, or it can emphasize the divergence in this respect between societies. But the researcher does not necessarily have to make a hard-and-fast choice between these alternative theoretical orientations. An overall emphasis on convergence can nevertheless admit distinctive arrangements in certain areas, and a perspective dwelling on national divergency need not exclude convergence in certain respects or at some higher levels of generality. This work does not seek to deny the utility of approaches stressing the growing uniformity of structural arrangements but holds that our understanding of different national business organizations is much more enhanced by an approach dwelling on the enduring distinctiveness in national ways of organizing and carrying out industrial work. Consequently, the following discussion of the various theoretical frameworks for making comparisons will devote more space to approaches emphasizing national divergency. This book is concerned to show to what extent, how and why organizational structure and behaviour varies between three different European societies – Britain, France and the Federal Republic of Germany (hereafter Germany).

What is to be gained from making such comparisons? At a theoretical level, comparison gives a framework for judgement. Understanding of a given social phenomenon is greatly increased if we can analyse it, and observe variation, in different social contexts. We learn that, although certain tasks, such as recruiting and training a labour force or obtaining capital, have to be accomplished in all modern business organizations, they can be handled in a variety of ways and with differing results. We can, for example, grasp more readily why a British business organization is constituted, and functions, in certain ways if we know from comparison the unique constellation of social environmental factors which have shaped it.

At a more practical level, we gain an understanding of how business organizations are structured and operate in other societies which can be useful in a number of ways. We learn how foreign business partners (suppliers, customers) and competitors operate. As potential members of a multinational business organization, we become familiar with either foreign local conditions and 'human resources' problems to which the top management of a British-owned company needs to adapt, or with foreign top management assumptions and practices, if the foreign-owned organization is based in Britain. (For an example of the latter, see the study by Millar, 1974.) Most contentiously (see the discussion in the Conclusion), we can learn from more efficient/effective foreign organizational structure or behaviour and transfer aspects of this to our own national organization.

Before we can examine actual organization structures and behaviour in the three societies, however, we need to acquire a theoretical framework which guides comparative analysis and explanation of business organization. Several competing theoretical approaches, based on different basic assumptions, suggest themselves: contingency theory; an approach from 'political economy' or, more narrowly, from 'capitalism'; a perspective stressing the central importance of national culture and an approach from national institutions. Although each of these approaches has some strengths this book gives preference to a cultural/institutional approach and thus will devote considerably more space to a discussion of the latter. But this preference does in no way suggest that the other approaches can be discounted. On the contrary, it is suggested in the concluding section of this chapter that they can usefully complement each other.

Studies in the first and the second paradigm both stress universal factors and adopt a 'culture-free' approach whereas the third and fourth theoretical framework dwell on particularism and favour a 'culture-dependent' approach. Theorists of the first and, to a lesser extent, the second persuasion, therefore, believe that there can be a supra-national theory of organization whereas those focusing on national culture or institutions stress the uniqueness of different national business organizations. They thus put a limit on theorizing at a very general level.

The two approaches which postulate convergence of salient features of business organizations in different advanced societies – the contingency theory and the approach from capitalism – are derived from, or are part of, broader social theories about the development of advanced societies. The contingency approach shares basic assumptions with the theory of industrialism as formulated by C. Kerr et al. (1960), and the approach from 'political economy' is part of the Marxist theory of the development of capitalist society. Both theories are concerned to identify long-run economic and social processes and postulate an end-stage towards which advanced societies will converge, and in both cases productive technology is considered a motor of change. But the theories differ fundamentally over how they view ownership relations and the process of capital accumulation and consequently postulate a radically different process of societal transformation, leading to a different end-stage.

INDUSTRIALISM AND THE CONTINGENCY PERSPECTIVE

C. Kerr et al. have formulated a theory of industrial society which postulates that there are imperatives intrinsic to the industrialization process. These lead societies, regardless of their different starting conditions, to the same end-point – industrialism, the concept of a fully industrialized society, which is characterized by a number of common basic economic and social structural features. At the time of their writing no advanced society had reached industrialism and, depending on the nature of national industrializing elites and the resulting differing processes of industrialization, industrial societies were seen to differ from each other in terms of both culture and political economy (socialist or capitalist). But these differences, Kerr et al. claim, would eventually be swept away by industrialism and one homogeneous type would remain. The underlying force which drives all societies towards this end-point is said to be productive technology. The constant development of science and the resulting creation of more and more highly developed forms of technology and production processes set in motion a whole number of processes of social and political change (Kerr et al., 1960: 33f).

The epicentre of societal change is the business organization, and it is the postulated emergence of a new universal type which is of interest to this study. The abovementioned process of rapid and far-reaching technological change requires the creation of a wide range of skills and professional competencies and hence an educational system geared to turning out a highly skilled labour force. The diversity of tasks and skills found in the modern business organization demands ordering through the establishment of hierarchy, distinguished by different levels of authority and by specialization of function. Authority and specialization are said to be necessarily associated with large scale. Large scale and specialization of business organization, in turn, require extensive coordination of both managers and managed. The problem of coordination is solved by the development of a web of rules which regulate conditions of employment, recruitment and promotion. This web of rules is shaped not only by the degree of complexity of technology employed, of scale and specialization but also by market and budgetary constraints (ibid.: 39–42). Although the main rule-making power under industrialism lies with management it becomes shared with other agencies in a constitutional manner. Agencies such as trade unions and the government increasingly limit or regulate managerial authority, and constitutional management becomes the norm (ibid.: 147f).

The theory of industrialism thus makes a number of sweeping generalizations. The most important ones are the claim that technology determines organizational structure and behaviour and that the resulting organizational characteristics will be stable across nations, regardless of any differences between industrial nations in culture or forms of ownership of productive resources. Whereas most comparative studies of national business organizations emphasize the enduring importance of the way in which a country has come to industrialization, the theory of industrialism discounts the powerful impact of history.

The *contingency perspective* takes over several of the central assumptions of the theory of industrialism, but it puts forward much more limited claims concerning only the structure of business organization and not of whole societies. It also eschews its technological determinism and sees technology as only one of several factors in the business environment which shape a more limited number of structural factors. But the contingency approach shares with the theory of industrialism the assumption that countries at similar stages of development adopt the same approach to the design of their business (and other) organizations, and it posits the existence of a rationality, transcending national or cultural peculiarities.

The contingency approach posits that a limited number of contingencies in the immediate environment of the business organization – contingencies such as scale or size, degree of dependence and/or of market stability, production technology – impose a logic of rational administration on the organization. Irrespective of the culture, economic and political system of a society, this logic must be followed to ensure the survival of the organization. If, for example, we take the contingency of scale, theorists of this persuasion would argue as follows:

when a business organization reaches a certain scale, defined by the number of employees, it becomes imperative to introduce functional specialization, i.e. to separate, for example, the management of production from that of research and development and/or design. Greater functional specialization means that knowledge about the various business functions becomes dispersed and that overall control becomes more problematic. To coordinate and control these separated functions, each function needs to be organized in a more formal way, i.e. according to precise written rules, procedures and instructions. Consequently more staff are needed to engage in supervision and coordination. Thus, to recapitulate, large scale leads to functional specialization which, in turn, causes greater formalization as well as further expansion in size. Often these processes are also accompanied by a greater centralization of authority to handle increased problems of control, although this correlation has not been consistently established. Less frequently, the environmental contingency of production technology is related to the structure of work organization. But the evidence on the link between technology and structure is uneven. According to a study by Hickson et al., (1969) technology only influences structural features, linked to the work-flow itself.

In this approach, then, a limited number of environmental contingencies are isolated. The most thoroughly researched ones are the size of operational unit or of its parent, the degree of dependence on either a parent company (internal dependence) or on customers or suppliers (external dependence) (see Hickson et al., 1979: 37). Environment is thus narrowly conceived as the immediate task environment, and the wider social, political or economic environment is deliberately ignored. These contingencies of the task environment have an impact on a limited number of organizational structural characteristics, such as specialization, formalization, and centralization of authority. Relationships between contingencies and aspects of organization structure are constant in direction but not necessarily the same in magnitude. For example, in all societies increases in the size of organization bring increases in formalization, but not necessarily the same degree of increase. Hickson et al., (1979: 38) summarize their theoretical claims as follows:

> all the world over the biggest industrial units in the biggest parent groups are the most bureaucratised in formalisation and specialisation of structure and centralized, too, if they are heavily dependent not only on that parent group but on large suppliers and customers.

This theory thus makes no predictions about actors' attitudes or behaviour although it is usually implied that structure will then mould organizational behaviour. The emphasis is on rational design, on the adaption of structure to contingency, in order to ensure high levels of performance. These theorists posit merely a stable relation between contingencies and structure across different societies. They do not maintain that organizations in different countries are alike because the distribution of contingencies still varies across societies, e.g. Britain has more large-scale corporations than France, or German companies manufacturing machine tools have greater market certainty than British ones. Contingency theorists do not totally deny the impact of culture. They merely claim that contingency constraints override it in those limited respects outlined above. Contingency theorists see an approach from culture as complementary to their own in as far as they suggest that an explanation from culture might explain the varying magnitude of correlation coefficients, i.e. of the mathematical value calculated for the relationship between a contingent factor and a structural property of an organization. Thus, for example, the degree of formalization may uniformly rise with the increase in organizational size but it rises more steeply in some national contexts than in others (Hickson et al., 1979: 39).

The contingency approach was developed by the so-called 'Aston School' from the 1960s onwards and is associated primarily with the names of Hickson and Pugh (see Hickson et al., 1974, 1979). They also operationalized the various dependent and independent variables so that they can be quantified and measured in a precise way. As their theory is simple and their methodology highly standardized they were adopted in numerous national and cross-national empirical studies around the world. These yielded results of remarkable consistency, for the social sciences, across societies at least for *some* of the variables. These strengths gained the contingency approach considerable influence, and for a long time it displaced the approach from culture which had remained both theoretically and methodologically unsophisticated.

But the contingency approach also has numerous weak points and blind spots. Child and Tayeb (1982–83) point out that although this theory can show the consistency and strength of correlation between the two sets of variables it has never provided an adequate rationale for measured associations and the theoretical status of contingencies has remained uncertain. Are they imperatives or do they merely have the force of implications if a certain threshhold is overstepped? Jamieson (1982–83) comments that the theory is not as free from economic-political context as it claims. It is built on assumptions about 'coping effectively' which are clearly oriented towards the goals of the capitalist enterprise and not towards a universal type of business organization. This criticism is also echoed by Child and Tayeb (1982–83: 34) who, in addition, envisage differences in performance assumptions between capitalist societies, depending on the degree of market dominance.

The contingency approach only elucidates properties of *formal* structure and remains insensitive to informal structures within this formal framework. For example, German business organizations usually come out as highly centralized. However, when relations of superiors to subordinates are analysed in detail it turns out that autonomy of works from staff is actually greater than in Britain and France (see details in Chapter 2). This shortcoming is due to the fact that the theory focuses only on structure -- moreover on only limited aspects of the latter – and completely leaves out of the picture human agents and informal interaction between them. It thus operates at a high level of abstraction and generality. It imparts a very limited amount and kind of information to the analyst which does not take her/him very far in trying to understand the functioning of actual business organizations in different societies. More importantly, as Horvath et al., (1981) point out, this culture-free theoretical framework can only be maintained *because* the actor is left out of the picture. Formal structures may indeed be remarkably alike across societies, but different national actors perceive, interpret or live with them in very different ways, due to deep-rooted cultural forces.

It may be argued that the validity of the contingency approach becomes most apparent when applied to the study of multinational enterprises which tend to be very similar in structure across a whole range of developed and developing capitalist societies. But, as the study by Hofstede (1980) of a prominent multinational has shown, similar control structures may be interpreted in fundamentally different ways by actors. As staff below the level of top management are recruited locally they bring with them indigenous values, attitudes and expectations and thus modify the way in which formal structures are interpreted.

THE APPROACH FROM CAPITALISM

This approach also presupposes transnational influences on organization structures. It differs from the preceding in that cross-national contextual similarities are seen to be due to common location in the world capitalist system which causes similar pressures and contradictions. This approach follows Marx in attributing to capitalism, as a mode of production, the following characteristics: private ownership of productive capital, competition between capitals and production of commodities for profit. Profit is derived from the appropriation of surplus value from labour, i.e. from paying labour a wage which is lower than the value of goods produced. The compulsion continually to increase capital accumulation, due to competition between capitals, entails the need for employers to reduce their unit cost of labour and to develop and maintain systems of control over labour which enable them to achieve this end. Alternatively employers may invest in technology to displace labour or to utilize technology in such a way as to simplify and cheapen labour. In either case the interests of employers stand in conflict to those of the employed. The latter try at least to maintain levels of pay and to protect the skills which give them a measure of control over their work. The Marxist analysis of the business organization is thus concerned with the underlying principles which structure the relation between capital and labour. As such it constitutes a theoretically more sophisticated approach than the contingency perspective which can explain uniformities in business organization by pointing to the underlying dynamic. The latter, conceived of as the conflict between capital and labour, will initiate a process of transformation which will eventually lead to socialism, i.e. a form of society in which capital is in common ownership and labour is no longer organized according to the profit motive.

In this perspective the focus shifts from very general structural characteristics of the organization to the management–labour relation. One example of this approach is the recent spate of work on the labour process. Cross-national changes in the management–labour relation identified in such work have been increasing managerial control over work, deskilling and the cheapening or displacement of workers (see Braverman, 1974). It is further suggested that the ideological and financial commitment to capitalism is shared by all social institutions in capitalist society. Although business and other elites may respond to system pressures in nationally distinctive ways they are still driven by the same forces to achieve the same goals. Cross-national uniformity is considered of primary significance, and national distinctiveness is seen as being of secondary importance. Any differences in organizational behaviour between organizations or countries are explained by reference to different location within the world capitalist system, e.g. differences in relation to capital flow, or access to cheap labour.

In contrast to contingency theory the approach from capitalism thus lends itself to the identification and explanation of both transnational commonalities and national specificities. In practice, though, with a few notable exceptions (e.g. Littler, 1982), Marxist approaches have in the main confined themselves to stressing the uniformity of structural arrangements across societies. This is partly due to ideological motives in that attention is to be focused on the world-wide nature of the capitalist system and the common oppression of labour across national boundaries. But the neglect of national distinctiveness can also be ascribed to methodological difficulties, encountered when applying a relatively abstract and narrowly focussed theoretical framework to the explanation of complex, historically evolved national structures. Although the Marxist framework has been relatively successfully applied in 'grand sweep' analyses of differences between capitalist societies at a macro-level it lends itself less well to the analysis of meso-level peculiarities, such as differences in structural arrangements of business organisations. This methodological shortcoming of narrowly Marxist analyses may be attributed to the fact that the actor and his/her perception and manipulation of organizational relations tends to disappear from sight.

THE APPROACH FROM CULTURE

There is a 'commonsense' realization that, despite growing cross-national uniformity in organizational structure and behaviour and/or management labour relations, national diversity and distinctiveness have remained pervasive and thus vital to an understanding of individual business organizations. This has led to a revival during the last decade in comparative studies focusing on cross-national diversity and trying to account for it in terms of nationally/culturally specific features. Although it is now widely accepted by both social scientists and practitioners that nationally specific factors play an important role in explaining differences in business organization, there exists as yet little agreement on how such features are best conceptualized and operationalized in empirical studies.

Culture is a very vague and general concept which has been defined in a great variety of ways. The study of organizations from a culturalist perspective can usefully be divided into two broad, analytically distinct perspectives which have been lucidly discussed by Child and Tayeb (1982–83: 41f). The first is a tradition which sees cultures as 'ideational systems', i.e. it focuses on the ideas, values, norms and meanings shared by members of a social entity. Ideationalists see culture transmitted through primary socialization in the family and local community, and they tend to focus on cultural dimensions at the level of the personality. Researchers in this tradition are primarily interested in identifying norms and values, and they regard values as a general disposition to act in certain ways.

The second tradition sees culture as 'adaptive systems', that is as a total way of life by which communities have adapted in their ecological settings. In this perspective culture may take the form of artifacts or, more commonly in organization studies, of institutions. Institutions are conceived of as socially transmitted behaviour patterns. Organization studies adopting the institutional approach show a concern with how the nature of organizations reflects the institutional features of the society in which they are located. Institutions are regarded as tangible expressions of value orientations which have historically evolved within a given society. While some scholars adopting the institutional perspective acknowledge its close connection with the notion of culture as an ideational system and do, indeed, identify a constant and complex interplay between the two (e.g. Dore, 1973; and Gallie, 1978), others see the institutional perspective as a theoretical approach in its own right and avoid the label 'culture' altogether, e.g. Hall (1986). This study does not wish to deny the complex interdependencies between culture and institutions but will, for the sake of analytical precision, distinguish an institutional approach from an ideational or culturalist perspective.

THE CULTURALIST PERSPECTIVE

A belief in the importance of culture as an explanatory variable is often coupled with the conviction that national business organizations are unique configurations and as such cannot be compared across national/ cultural boundaries. This extreme stance, as Przeworski and Teune (1970: 8) point out, is not justified. The problem can be overcome by substituting names of variables for names of social or ideational systems. The culture of a particular society thus is seen as a unique pattern of a set of variables, each of which is applicable across societies.

Studies favouring this approach from culture are confronted by major problems of both a conceptual and a methodological nature. The questions of what is culture and of how it can best be studied have received a great many different answers, and as yet no one best practice has emerged. (It is beyond the scope of this book to review the different studies in this field. Readers are referred to the article by Roberts, 1970.) Instead, some of the major problems confronting scholars committed to a culturalist approach are outlined. The first step in a culturalist analysis is to adopt a definition of culture and to specify at the outset with a reasonable degree of precision which elements of national culture are seen to influence aspects of business organization. Unless this step is taken – and a surprisingly large number of studies never take it – culture becomes a 'black box' catch-all term to which all observed variation becomes ascribed.

The second and probably most difficult step demands that the researcher lays bare the roots of these designated elements in the national culture. He/she has to demonstrate their centrality to the national culture and show that they still have saliency at the present time. Unless this task is confronted the scholar runs the risk of perpetuating national stereotypes. This danger is particularly acute in the case of a society which has undergone dramatic change, as has been the case in Germany. To establish such a link between the elements of culture, influencing the business organization, and the general societal culture requires an attitude survey of a representative sample of the national population or, at least, a fairly detailed historical study, going beyond the confines of the organization. Not surprisingly, these tasks are rarely undertaken.

Thirdly, the researcher needs to show how those factors, designated as elements of national culture, *actually* influence organizational structure and/or behaviour. In other words, they have to be shown to be organization-relevant. (For greater detail about these points and a generally lucid introduction to the problems, surrounding the 'culturalist' approach, see Child, 1981; and/or Child and Tayeb, 1982–83.)

Another problem at the conceptual level is that most definitions of culture do not consider the fact that not all members of a given society share the same values and beliefs or that, if they share them, they are not equally strongly affected by them. The approach from culture often ignores the well-established fact that members of different social classes perceive their society differently. Some may hold to oppositional values challenging the notion of a supposedly consensual social order. (For an example of a study which articulates this problem at a theoretical level, see Dubois, 1981; for empirical studies illustrating this lack of value consensus see Gallie, 1978 and 1983.)

The ideational approach is also very difficult to operationalize. It is hard for researchers to identify values and norms to be studied cross-culturally without imposing their own cultural bias. For example, the prevalence of a strong achievement orientation in American society may lead American researchers to formulate an interview schedule probing the degree of development of this orientation in different societies which may be quite meaningless in societies with a different social ethos. To overcome this problem researchers formulate their conceptual framework at a level of generality which is high enough to avoid cultural bias. But instead it may become so general as to be void of meaning in any specific society. Another problem of the ideational approach is that it only probes beliefs and not behaviour, and it is well known that individuals can display considerable divergence between the two (see Hofstede, 1980: 18). This problem is particularly acute in organizational studies of management attitudes, as exemplified by the studies of Horovitz (1980) or Budde et al. (1982), to be reviewed in Chapter 4. One way to check whether management values are reflected in behaviour is to probe attitudes at the lower levels of the hierarchy in order to establish how managerial style is perceived by subordinates. This was successfully done in the study by Hofstede (1980).

To illustrate the problems and opportunities involved in the study of business organizations from a culturalist perspective a brief examination of a recent, highly acclaimed study in this tradition may be useful. Hofstede's (1980) book, *Culture's Consequences*, can be taken to be representative of the 'ideational' tradition. Hofstede's research design was inspired by a concern to demonstrate cultural difference across a wide spectrum of both industrialized and industrializing societies. He views culture in terms of values and norms and refers to it as 'collective programming of the mind' which distinguishes the members of one human group from another (Hofstede, 1980: 25). He examines the subsidiaries of one parent company in 40 countries and interviews the native employees and managers at various levels of the organizational hierarchy at two points in time, during 1967–69 and again during 1971–73. Instead of focusing on structural features, Hofstede is interested in how people at different levels of hierarchy perceive structural arrangements. He formulates four complexes of cultural values and norms which can be seen to be relevant to organizational behaviour at a high level of generality – Power Distance, Uncertainty Avoidance, Individualism, Masculinity. The results of a carefully worded standardized questionnaire are utilized to construct indices for each country with reference to each of the four cultural complexes. Lastly, an attempt is made to explain the emerging country differences by correlating country scores with a number of variables of an economic, geographic, political and social nature.

It can be seen that Hofstede's study is very exact at identifying and operationalizing the elements of culture seen to be relevant to business organization. It avoids cultural bias but is forced to formulate the elements at such a high level of generality that some, though by no means all, become vacuous. The study is not able to locate these elements in their cultural systems but mainly assumes centrality and saliency. Although Hofstede is extremely careful in matching his research method to his theoretical perspective he does not, as Sorge and Warner (1986) point out, fully succeed. He infers values from preferences expressed in replies to his questionnaire. Although his theory posits that values direct behaviour *ex ante* his method probes not only loose preferences but also *ad hoc* rationalizations *after* the act and basic values which are morally charged and consciously referred to in actual behaviour.

Hofstede's work points to institutional arrangements which have shaped cultural values in a *post hoc* fashion by establishing correlations between intra- and extra-organizational variables. This exercise remains very schematic. It is able to deal with broad patterns, distinguishing between advanced Western industrial societies and developing oriental ones. But it is unable to explain, for example, why an advanced Western country like France has to be grouped with Oriental countries in terms of its score on power distance. (Power distance is the difference between the extent to which A can determine the behaviour of B, and vice versa.) Lastly, Hofstede does not adhere to a consensual view of culture but assumes that organizational structures are interpreted in different ways at different hierarchical levels.

THE INSTITUTIONAL PERSPECTIVE

This perspective has been popular both among industrial sociologists and among scholars engaged in organization studies. Scholars in this tradition focus either on structural features of business organization, such as the division of labour between different levels of the hierarchy or the representation of worker interests, or on attitudinal dimensions, such as attitudes to authority or social justice, and explain these by reference to institutional arrangements in the social environment in which the business enterprise is embedded. They see the business organization as socially constituted and thus reflecting national distinctiveness in institutional arrangements. Scholars taking this approach are more inclined to stress the historical evolvement of societal institutions and are thus able to consider the crucial differences in the way in which different nations came to industrialization. Among the institutions singled out for study are the system of both general education and of vocational education and training, industrial relations, the state, the employment system, the system of social stratification, to name only a few.

The approach from institutions makes it easier to avoid the conceptual and methodological problems associated with the approach from culture, and it is the most successful of all the approaches reviewed in identifying the nationally distinctive features of business organizations.

It is, therefore, the approach favoured in the remainder of this book. The more detailed conceptual and methodological assumptions entailed by this approach vary between scholars and can best be made clear by short reviews of some of the best studies in this tradition.

The two most outstanding recent sociological comparative studies of business enterprises adopting an institutionalist perspective are those by Dore (1973) and Gallie (1978, 1983). Dore's work is also a good example of how several theoretical approaches to comparative study can be combined in an imaginative way. Dore's comparison of a British and a Japanese corporation is characterized first and foremost by a perspective which links an institutional with a cultural approach. But, at the same time, Dore gives validity to a universalist type of explanation, namely the theory of late development (for details, see Dore, 1986 or Dore, 1973: 404), and posits a limited degree of convergence between the British and the Japanese large business organization (ibid.: 419f). Dore's work is valuable for probing the relation between cultural values and institutional arrangements. It is able to show how an institution, such as the Japanese employment system, is partly an adaptation of earlier pre-industrial institutional patterns, partly a conscious attempt to create new arrangements consonant with dominant cultural values, and partly the result of borrowing elements from other industrial nations (ibid.: 375f). Dore thus draws attention to the fact that institutions are perpetuated or created by powerful actors in accordance with their interests and cultural orientations. He implies that we need not necessarily regard individual actors as prisoners of inert institutions, handed down to them by their forebears. Lastly, when Dore tries to explain why the British business enterprise became institutionalized in one distinctive way and the Japanese in another, he again falls back on a universalist explanation. He stresses the way in which each country came to industrialization and points to the economic and social circumstances of the historical period which shaped the consolidation of industrial organization in each case.

Gallie's comparisons of French and British working-class consciousness are, at the same time, valuable studies of important aspects of business organization in the two societies. Gallie's first book, *In Search of the New Working Class*, makes a comparison of two oil refineries each in France and Britain, matched according to size, location and production technology. It is concerned to demonstrate the inadequacy of explanations of social consciousness, framed in the universalist mould of either 'industrial society' or Marxist theory. The work shows convincingly that technology cannot be regarded as the critical variable affecting the degree of working-class subjective integration into society but that its impact is mediated by the different institutional arrangements found in the two societies. Of these the structure of managerial power and the nature of the trade union movement are singled out as particularly important.

In the first book Gallie posits a close connection between institutions and cultural values. Institutions are said 'to be moulded in significant ways by the values and beliefs of those in key positions' in them, and 'they will embody the strategies by which these groups seek to obtain their goals' (Gallie, 1978: 36). In addition, actors are said to be socialized into 'the more enduring cultural traditions of the wider social groups to which they belong' (ibid.). Both values and institutions are seen as having been shaped by broader patterns of historical/societal development.

Gallie's second book, *Social Inequality and Class Radicalism in France and Britain*, is devoted to the study of the broader historical developments which have shaped influential institutions. It repudiates the idea that national cultural tradition has shaped current institutional arrangements and ideological dispositions in the business enterprise (Gallie, 1983: 205). Gallie's attempt to establish historical causation is successful in showing why radical parties of the left remained influential in France but not in Britain but the persistence of authoritarian management structures in France, but not in Britain, is explained in an ahistorical and much less satisfactory way. It must be said in Gallie's defence that the demonstration of historical causation is an arduous and complex task which few social scientists ever undertake.

The comparative method of both Gallie and Dore thus falls half-way between the cultural and the institutional perspective. Although they advance explanations in cultural terms they are careful to link values and attitudes to an institutional base. This approach is able to take cognisance of the fact that cultural values within the business organization and, even more so, within society are heterogeneous and may stand in conflict with each other. They also emphasize that institutions are shaped by the interests and values of key actors and that the latter may engage in more or less conscious attempts to adapt or change them. Both authors acknowledge that institutions have evolved in a complex historical process. This kind of critical and historical awareness as well as sensitivity to the creativity of social actors is lacking in the institutional approach of scholars in the tradition of organization studies.

Such an institutional perspective is, above all, connected with the work of the French Aix group, led by Marc Maurice. (See the work of Brossard and Maurice, 1976; Maurice et al., 1986) and their erstwhile German and British collaborators Sorge and Warner (Maurice, Sorge and Warner, 1980); Sorge and Warner 1986). In the following, I shall briefly outline the theoretical and methodological approach of the Aix group as it has guided empirical work, and then introduce the more explicit and fully articulated theoretical approach worked out more recently in the book of Sorge and Warner (1986).

Maurice and his associates describe their theoretical orientation as the 'societal effect' approach. They posit that the structures of organizations reflect the institutional arrangements of their societal environments. The business organization is viewed as an institution within society and the boundaries between the two are seen as fluid. Hence they plead that the organization–environment distinction be abandoned. The focus of all their studies is on work and on the different ways people go about it in the three societies. They examine such structural elements of organization as interaction of people at work, work characteristics of jobs, systems of recruitment, the level and nature of qualifications, remuneration, industrial relations and the interrelation between these areas. The authors point out that, although organizational goals in these areas do not differ across organisations, courses of action towards reaching these goals do, because action is socially constructed and hence shaped by culture as manifested in societal institutions. Their meticulous studies of the interrelationship between three blocks of variables – organizational configuration (size of the various components of the labour force and the relations between them); work structuring and work coordination; qualification and career systems – show convincingly that there are nationally divergent manufacturing cultures.

It can be seen that the theoretical framework offered by the Aix group remains somewhat vague and ambiguous. There is, in fact, no theory in the conventional sense, i.e. the explanatory variables are never specified nor is the exact relation between culture as institutionalized patterns of action and the business organization ever explicated. The recent book by Sorge and Warner (1986) outlines the theoretical assumptions they see implied by the 'societal effect' approach, as practised so far. The Anglo-German team come up with a sophisticated and original theoretical framework which is given a complex methodological underpinning on the nature of human action and is presented as superseding all other theoretical approaches to the comparative study of organization. It is also carefully related to empirical findings for reciprocal clarification and substantiation. The following short summary of their theoretical orientation cannot do justice to its complexity and completely disregards the philosophical underpinnings elaborated in the first part of the book. Finally, it must be said that despite the valiant efforts by Sorge and Warner to clarify the theoretical assumptions underlying the 'societal effect' approach, for this author they still remain elusive and raised new questions as they answered old ones.

Institutions, in this approach, are viewed as patterns of habitualized reciprocal social action. They do not only delimit possible forms of behaviour for actors, but actors also modify institutions as they reproduce them. Within a given society institutions exist in different functional areas, e.g. economic institutions or educational institutions. Although each possesses functional autonomy there is coherence between them. There occurs what Sorge and Warner (1986: 44) term 'reciprocal conditioning' of institutions which overarch different functional spheres. Such conditioning does not only take place when institutions are patterned in harmonizing fashion, i.e. they are similar, but also when patterning is countervailing, i.e. diametrically opposed patterns obtain.

The starting-point for comparative organizational research following the 'societal effect' approach is the fact that the generation and utilization of qualifications, expressed in the design of work and hence in organizational configurations, is marked differently by institutional patterns in the three European societies. Sorge and Warner explore the questions of what these institutions are and what is the nature of the relationship between the various variables. They propose that the differences between these three European societies cannot be explained by reference to one factor only: 'we do not tend to privilege one primary cause. Rather ... there appears to be a close interaction between factors in different spheres of society which follows a logic upon which the identity of a particular society is built' (ibid.: 184). The authors put particular stress on the fact that interaction or reciprocal conditioning occurs between societal institutions, on the one side, and what they term 'material conditions for the survival and well-being in society' (ibid.: 126) or 'economic parameters' (ibid.: 193), on the other. To illustrate this they refer to the example of the engineering profession in Britain and Germany. The contrasting education and industrial deployment of the engineer in these societies is both a response to the different opportunities in terms of status and material rewards available to members of this profession in the two societies and serves as a reinforcement of the different patterns. In sum, institutional spheres are thus seen as evolving to match each other and must be regarded as forming a syndrome.

The relationship between various factors is not posited in terms of dependent and independent variables. There exists a fuzzy relationship of mutual interaction between a whole number of variables of both a social and an economic kind. It does not become clear to this author whether the resulting syndrome then determines the dependent variable

– the design of work, reflected in the organizational configuration – or whether this relationship is again one of mutual adaptation. The societal effect' approach gives the researcher the task of identifying correspondences between different institutional spheres and to highlight the contrasts in these correspondences between societies. The researcher explores and makes evident the common logic of all or most of the contrasts identified (ibid.: 124). They concede that the 'societal effect' approach is not a theory in the conventional sense and that it does not identify variables which can be described as 'cultural'.

The methodological approach of the 'societal effect' approach – common to all national teams – differs significantly from that of the Aston School. They argue for the collection of data both relative to firms *and* relative to the society in which the firm is located. Their approach is that of comparing carefully matched pairs in the different societies, controlling for such well-known constants as size, product and dependency. This method gives a relatively small, non-randomly chosen sample and hence dictates a more qualitative and 'in-depth' study which aims to develop sensitivity to unexpected variation. They are not as selective and precise in their variables and they do not aim to quantify them. The results obtained convincingly demonstrate that it is imperative to consider national variation, and they give a very full and sophisticated account of what it means to achieve the goals of a business organization the British, the French or the German way. They provide enough concrete information to ponder the question of whether any practical lessons might be learnt from the example of any one national type of organization by the others. But they are careful not to introduce any explicit judgements as to superior or inferior performance into their analysis although, as Rose (1985) points out, such judgements are often strongly implied.

It can be seen from the preceding outline of the 'societal effects' approach that the latter is much better at avoiding the pitfalls of culturalism outlined above. It clearly identifies the elements of culture which are hypothesized to have an effect on the structure of business organizations. This perspective is much better equipped to avoid ethnocentric bias in cross-national comparison. It taps culture relative to actions, and it is safer to hypothesize that certain actions have to be performed in all business organizations than it is to make presumptions about value orientations. Lastly, this theoretical orientation also avoids the assumption that culture is a separate causal factor to be distinguished from economic factors. It acknowledges that the two are both products of history and hence have become inextricably interwoven.

If there are any shortcomings in this approach it is the implicit suggestion that choices in the adoption of certain courses of action are *only* structured by national culture and that constraints connected with the capitalist nature of these societies are presumed rather than made explicit. This perspective makes the tacit assumption that the institutional arrangements of capitalist societies embody the values of all social classes and does not consider that institutions are predominantly shaped by the powerful in society. To overcome this problem the 'societal effect' research method needs to be supplemented by interview techniques which attempt to clarify how organizational structures are viewed by organization members at different levels of the hierarchy. Although Maurice and his collaborators frequently refer to actors they have, as Rose (1985: 79) points out, only minimally consulted the actors themselves. The 'interview' as a research instrument has played a very subordinate role. Interviews were not conducted at the lowest levels of the hierarchy and the content of questions was not designed to elicit responses as to individual or group perceptions of societal institutions.

It is now appropriate to answer questions posed at the beginning of this chapter as to how the different theoretical approaches are to be evaluated. I do not see one of these four approaches to the cross-national study of organization supersede the others but view them as complementary, to be used in combination. Although the cultural and the institutional approaches have been presented as analytically separate, in practice they have been successfully combined. If the cultural perspective is committed to an examination of the historical emergence and perpetuation of cultural values it is bound to acknowledge the important role played by institutions. Conversely, if institutions are conceived of as concrete manifestations of societal values and norms, then it appears logical to specify what values and norms are seen to be congruent with given institutional structures. Lastly, it is important to remember that institutions are shaped by the values and interests of powerful social actors. The approach from capitalism underlines the fact that power within the business organization is very unevenly distributed. Hence, the approach adopted in this book is to give priority to the institutionalist perspective but to supplement it occasionally with an 'ideationist' focus if this enhances the explanatory power.

Given that this book is primarily concerned with highlighting the differences in business organization between three European capitalist societies, the value of the two universalist approaches has been underplayed. But most studies from a cultural/institutional perspective tacitly utilize the insights of contingency theory. Hickson et al., (1974: 29) underline the contribution contingency theory can make when they point out that 'we can only start to attribute features to culture when we have made sure that relations between variables, e.g. between size and degree of specialisation, are stable between cultures.' Contingency theory thus permits the researcher to highlight cultural or societal differences by controlling for the stable relationships identified. This means that the researcher selects his/her cross-national sample in such a way that units of analysis are carefully matched according to certain factors. Size, degree of dependency, and production technology or product are the variables usually matched in a comparison of business organizations in different societies.

The fact that all three societies are of the 'capitalist' type also means that the main features of this system – the pressure to maintain profit and the ensuing conflict of interests between employer and employed – can be held constant. This recognition does, however, not imply that this relationship is actually perceived in this homogeneous way in the three societies. On the contrary, the preoccupation of this book will be to show how these common underlying pressures become moderated by the impact of 'societal effects'. The impact of capitalism will not be ignored and business organizations are examined in such a way, to quote Jamieson (1982–83: 96), to reveal 'the tensions between "demands" of capitalism and the influence of culture'. Culture, in this approach, is not viewed as something separate from economic and/or political structures and relations but is regarded as inextricably intertwined with them. Thus, the approach adopted in this book will take on board some of the 'universalist' assumptions of both contingency and Marxist theory and will, indeed, utilize the findings of these approaches to highlight national distinctiveness and place the latter at the centre of attention.

2 Work in the Business Enterprise: The Organizational Structure of European Business Enterprises

The structure of a business organization, understood as 'regularities in activities, such as task allocation, supervision, and co-ordination' (Pugh and Hickson, 1968: 374), can be viewed as a means for attaining organizational goals and objectives as defined by management. The more appropriate the design of the organization structure to the attainment of designated goals and objectives the more effective will be the business enterprise. As indicated in the discussion of organization theory in the previous chapter, the structure of a business organization is shaped by a number of factors in its environment. It is, therefore, highly variable between organizations within a society and even within a given industrial sector or group of companies similar in size. But numerous pieces of research have shown that, if certain contingencies, such as size or technology/product, are controlled for, the structure of business organizations on a societal level displays such a degree of consistency that clear national patterns can be discerned.

This chapter will compare the differing structures of British, French and German business enterprises and connect structural features with business behaviour. The emerging distinctive patterns are seen as shaped by national culture as reflected in, and perpetuated by, societal institutions. Cultural factors, expressed in such institutional arrangements as training and promotion systems and industrial relations structures, have been found to be the most prominent environmental influences. But features such as the relationship between financial and industrial capital and the structure and tradition of the state – particularly legal and regulational practices – have also had some influence, particularly at board level. Although the design of organizational structure has to take account of environmental factors managers can usually exercise a degree of choice between alternative designs. Such choice can be influenced by knowledge about alternative and more effective designs of organizational structure. This chapter is intended to provide such knowledge. The problems of borrowing elements of structure across national/cultural boundaries will be discussed in the Conclusion of this book.

In the first part of this chapter the focus is on the structure of production units in the three societies, whereas the second part will be devoted to a comparison of the company structure at board level. The following aspects of organization structure will be considered in a comparative manner: the division of work tasks into their component elements; their distribution among the various positions in the enterprise hierarchy; and the processes of coordinating and supervising the execution of tasks. This entails a consideration of the design of jobs, of the differing nature of hierarchy and spans of control. The horizontal grouping of activities into sections and departments and the necessary forms of communication and modes of integration are also important aspects of structure. Finally, a discussion of control procedures and reward systems to facilitate task performance and coordination is necessary. This chapter will give a general overview of the various elements of organizational structure and of their interconnections. In later chapters selected aspects will be treated in greater detail. Chapters 4 and 5 deal with aspects of management, particularly management style and management control and the various devices adopted to achieve it. Chapters 6 and 7 are devoted to job design and work organization at operative level.

THE SHAPE OF ORGANIZATIONS

The following discussion of work structuring and shape of organizations has benefited greatly from the work by Maurice, Sorge and Warner (1980). This work is the result of a comparative survey of nine production units in Britain, Germany and France, carefully matched according to a number of contingent factors. In all three societies we find organizations divided according to task performance into the same categories of employees, arranged in the same hierarchical manner. A basic division of labour between 'staff' and 'works', between those who engage in conceptual work and those who merely execute these plans, and between those who control and those who submit to control, is widely seen as an indispensable feature of the capitalist enterprise. Further horizontal division of labour developed with the increasing complexity of the capitalist enterprise. These common structural features are illustrated in Figure 2.1.

But the size of each category, relative to the other categories, differs significantly between the three societies. This indicates important

Figure 2.1   A basic organizational configuration

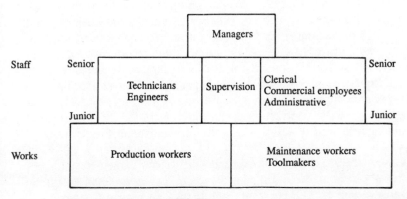

Source: Maurice et al. (1980:67).

differences in the division of labour and in the allocation of tasks to positions. It is expressed in the following detailed features:

1. The relation of 'works' to 'staff' differs significantly between the three societies. Germany has the highest 'works' component, reaching an average of 71.8 per cent of all employees. France has the lowest, with an average of 58.4 per cent, and British organizations, with an average of 63 per cent of 'works', take an intermediate position. (Averages are calculated from the separate proportions for various production methods, cited by Maurice et al., 1980: 66, Table 2.) This finding is supported by a study of matched (according to output) German and British factories by Finlay (1981), who also found that the German plant employed far less (39 per cent less) people altogether.
2. The same national patterns persist if we look at the ratio of supervisory staff (foremen) to 'works', with French enterprises having the highest, German the lowest ratio and British again occupying an intermediate position (ibid.: 67, Table 3).
3. If, however, all managerial/supervisory staff (i.e. all staff positions with authority over other employees) are considered in relation to

the 'works' component, British business organizations in the research have the least and French the most, while German organizations occupy an intermediate position (ibid.: Table 4). This result is due to the fact that in German enterprises there is no strong distinction between those in supervisory/managerial positions and those with 'technical staff' status. Consequently many of those in authority positions are at the same time technical experts. In Britain, in contrast, this distinction is strong and technical experts are rarely found in supervisory/managerial positions. The French–German difference is also brought out by Lutz's (1981: 74) comparative study contrasting a German ratio of 20 supervisory/managerial staff to 450 workers with an equivalent French ratio of 40:450.

4. Lastly, the study by Maurice et al., (1980: 68, Table 5) establishes that the ratio of technical staff to 'works' is the lowest in Germany (an average of 12.8 per cent), the highest in France (31 per cent) and medium-high in Britain (21 per cent).

WORK STRUCTURING AT 'WORKS' LEVEL

The different organizational configurations resulting from the staffing ratios outlined above under 1–4 reflect different national ways of structuring and coordinating work. German business organizations manage with a relative low overall staffing level because of the way jobs are designed and supervised. Among German manual workers, both skilled and semi-skilled, a high proportion have a relatively high level of skill, have received an 'all-round' training and display self-motivation. They do not exercise union control over the allocation of tasks. Consequently they can be utilized highly flexibly, with operators rotating between all the jobs in the plant, thus blurring the distinction between maintenance and production. Also German workers (chargehands) carry out many supervisory tasks themselves. Together with their foreman they exercise greater discretion than their European counterparts on how jobs are carried out, referring to 'craft' judgement and making informal arrangements. Technical staff, therefore, have a less prominent role on the German shopfloor.

In British, and even more in French enterprises, in contrast, worker autonomy as regards works structuring is less, and direction from 'staff' departments more entrenched. The more rigid division of labour between 'works' and 'staff' in these two socieites, particularly where separation of conception from execution is concerned, also means deficient communication and more disputes and hence more time spent on resolving labour disputes and grievances (Maurice et al., 1980: 72). The lesser degree of autonomy among manual workers in both societies is partly explained by generally lower levels of skill, both by the workers themselves and by the foremen directing them. But British workers, in their everyday performance in jobs, enjoy a much higher degree of freedom from supervision than French workers. Maurice et al., (1980) explain these differences purely in 'qualification' terms. The very high degree of supervision of French workers, it seems to this author, is also attributable to the organizational culture. Bad worker–management relations have reduced worker self-motivation and have, in turn, engendered low trust from the management side (see Gallie, 1978, 1983). Worker flexibility, due to training methods, is not as developed in France and Britain as it is in Germany. In this respect there is, however, an important difference between the British and the French way of labour utilization. In Britain, but not in France, the craft unions have retained a large degree of control over labour recruitment and deployment. Through the practice of job demarcation, they maintain a rigid division of labour both between maintenance workers and operators and between the various maintenance crafts. The negative consequences of this rigid division in terms of labour productivity have been explored in detail by the comparative study of Dubois (1981). Although these job demarcations and associated restrictive practices have been under sustained attack from management since the late 1970s and are beginning to be eroded they are still a significant phenomenon at the time of writing. (For details, see Brady, 1984: 29f; Daniel, 1987: 168f). Thus, all in all, shopfloor workers are most economically deployed and workers enjoy the highest degree of autonomy in Germany. British workers occupy an intermediate position (excepting only the practice of demarcation) whereas French workers are the most highly directed and supervised of all three.

These different modes of structuring the work of manual labour have, of course, repercussions for task allocation at other levels of the hierarchy as well as affecting horizontal differentiation and integration at all levels. They are also reflected in the shapes of organizational hierarchy and spans of control[1]. In France, we find quite clearly the tallest organization structures and the narrowest average spans of control. Maurice et al., (1980: 71) found at least two, but sometimes three, layers of supervision and also numerous layers of management in France. Lutz's (1981: 74) comparative study of French and German firms of similar size contrasts the eight hierarchical levels of managerial/ supervisory staff of the French firm with only three in the German one.

Gallie (1978), too, speaks about the massive concentration of supervisory staff confronting French workers.

The case of British organizations is less clear-cut. Although the ratio of staff to works and the ratio of supervisory labour to works are greater in Britain than in Germany, the ratio of managerial/supervisory staff taken together is lower. Thus spans of control must get wider as we ascend the management hierarchy. As far as worker experience is concerned the span of control at the lower end of the hierarchy is most salient. Maitland (1983: 26), comparing the overall span of control in a British with that in a German enterprise, found it to be significantly narrower in Britain than in Germany.

The shape of German organizational structures is generally said to be flat with wide spans of control, particularly at the supervisory level (Maurice et al., 1980; Lutz, 1981; Finlay, 1981). Despite these wider spans of control, disputes and grievances were largely sorted out at this level between foremen, workers' representatives in unions and works councils and the workers concerned. In Britain and France, in contrast, the larger contingent of supervisory staff nevertheless referred the resolution of a high proportion of disputes and grievances up the line to managers (Maurice et al., 1980: 72). The bypassing of British supervisory staff by management in decision-making about control problems is also highlighted by Maitland (1983: 92).

WORK STRUCTURING AT THE LEVEL OF INTERMEDIATE STAFF

As promotion from works to staff is extensive in all three societies the weaknesses and strengths respectively in both degree and content of worker training become perpetuated at staff level. Important and inter-related differences between the three societies in work structuring at staff level are: the relatively high proportion of staff in technical services in France and Britain but not in Germany; the weak horizontal division of labour between staff and line management in Germany but not in France and, even less, in Britain; the high degree of technical expertise of German line management not found in Britain and France. A concomitant of easy interchange between 'staff' and 'line' in Germany is a greater hierarchization of technical staff. The much higher degree of technical expertise of both supervisory staff and line management in Germany, particularly as compared with British, and somewhat less, with French enterprises is both a reflection of the training received and a consequence of relatively frequent mobility from 'skilled worker' status to technical and supervisory staff.

The different kind and degree of competence and the resulting role of the foreman in the three national business organizations has wide-ranging repercussions for organizational structure and performance. This role is singled out as a pivotal difference by many authors.[2] German foremen must possess a foreman's certificate (*Meisterbrief*) which indicates the successful passing of an examination, granted after attendance of a two-year (part-time) training course which teaches mainly technical competence. This technical competence is passed on to workers in his role as the chief teacher of apprentices. British and French foremen, in contrast, rarely receive such formal technical training. If they receive any training it prepares them mainly for their supervisory role. In Britain there exists a relatively high proportion of staff without any formal qualification, even among technical staff. This is not to deny that they often receive considerable informal 'on-the-job' training. But the finding by Maitland (1983: 94) that supervisory staff were mainly 'back injuries' and 'dermatitis cases' is, unfortunately, not an atypical one for British enterprises.

Whereas the British foreman and the French *contremaître* have mainly supervisory duties and have to refer technical matters either to higher managerial or technical staff, the German *Meister* is competent to take on both supervisory/administrative and technical tasks. He performs the combined roles of the British foreman and superintendent (found only in larger British firms) and is, in his degree of qualification and in his duties, closer to the latter than the former. (Bessant and Grunt, 1985: 251, find the organizational responsibilities and autonomy of the *Meister* closer to those of British lower management than to supervisors.) The German *Meister* differs from the British superintendent in his greater degree of shop floor experience (Sorge and Warner, 1986: 101) which affords him a better understanding of, and communication with, workers.

The French foreman, in contrast, is increasingly restricted to executing only administrative tasks and both technical functions and the teaching of new workers and industrial relations problems have been transferred to specialists in a parallel hierarchy. Two new types of worker-technicians, the so-called master workers and demonstrators, are respectively charged with technical supervision and technical troubleshooting tasks, and they enjoy levels of status and remuneration comparable to those of the foreman. Their presence undermines the foreman's authority and creates 'dual authority' problems of communication and control (Maurice et al., 1986: 74f). Although the foreman is meant to deal with 'industrial relations' issues, his authority in this area is too restricted to permit him to perform this role satisfactorily.

Demands by the unions have to be referred to the personnel office or directly to higher management. All this casts the foreman in a very ambiguous role and does not permit him to perform the same integrating function between staff and works as his German counterpart. While he is technically part of management, he is not accepted as one of them in practice, and the emphasis on his positional authority has alienated him from the shop floor workers (ibid.; 109f).

In contrast to the French and British foreman, the German *Meister*'s qualifications and experience assign him a role which provides him with a foothold in both the managerial and the worker camp. It makes him an extremely important 'link' person in the business organization who keeps communication between works and staff flowing. The *Meister* sorts out a lot of organizational and industrial relations problems which in France and Britain go up the line and seriously deflect production management from their task of organizing production. But the *Meister* also remains close to his men who respect him for his technical competence and who, under his guidance, execute tasks with a higher degree of autonomy than their British or French counterparts. British and French foremen do not form a team with workers. In both countries the foreman is set above the work group, and his exclusively supervisory role puts him in a position where workers regard him with suspicion or even hostility. In many British firms, according to Dore (1973: 250), he may relate to workers only via the shopsteward. The *Meister* is also a strategic person as far as horizontal lines of communication are concerned. He mediates between production, technical support and personnel departments. Such a mediating role is precluded for his French or British counterparts due to their narrow expertise and competence. This fact explains the more informal, yet disciplined and integrated pattern of organization on the German, as compared with the French or British, shopfloor. The wide scope of the *Meister*'s competence is often linked with the fact that there is less managerial/supervisory staff in German than in British or French firms, and his important 'link' role is seen to contribute to the greater organizational flexibility of the German as compared with the British or French organization (e.g. Bessant and Grunt, 1985: 264).

The lack of technical expertise on the part of British and French foremen has become regarded as more problematic during the 1980s by many managements in both societies. The increasingly high level of technical sophistication of computer-controlled machinery and, particularly in France, the increased level of qualifications among young workers deprives these technically unskilled foremen of authority *vis-à-vis* subordinates. In France it is gradually becoming a practice to make

Figure 2.2 National organizational configurations

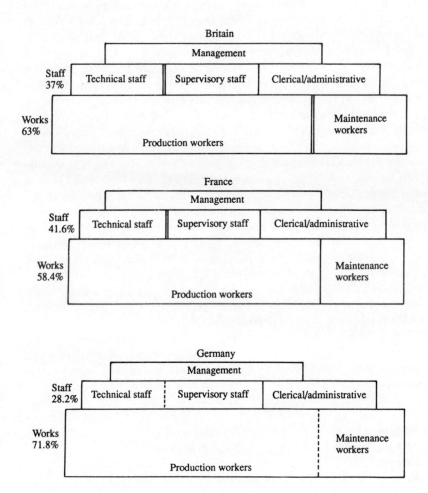

Lines of horizontal differentiation: ══════ Distinction is strong
-------- Distinction is blurred
────── Distinction exists

outside appointments of people with a diploma, rather than promoting workers from the shopfloor (Delamotte, 1986: 78–9).

These differing national ways of structuring and coordinating work result in different organizational configurations which are summarized in Figure 2.2. A high degree of division of labour along both vertical (between staff and works) and along horizontal lines (staff and line) creates problems of integration and communication. In France, it has been shown, features of organizational structure are both the large number of hierarchical layers and the compartmentalization along horizontal lines. In Britain high horizontal differentiation between operators and maintenance, staff and line, production and technical services is the outstanding feature. In Germany, in contrast, a relatively flat organizational structure and a blurring of horizontal differentiation are the norm. The relatively high degree of horizontal differentiation in both British and French business enterprises, compared with German ones, expresses differing overall conceptions as to the centrality of the production department and the roles other departments play in relation to it. In Germany the production department is central, and the other departments are considered to be at its service. Boundaries between departments are fluid and the relation with maintenance and technical services is one of mutual interaction and support and of close cooperation. In Britain and France, in contrast, greater specialization and compartmentalization between departments has led to a state where production is often dominated by technical services and relations are characterized by competition for resources and conflict. These differing structural features of the three national sets of business organizations indicate different kinds and scales of organizational problems.

ORGANIZATIONAL SHAPES AND ORGANIZATIONAL FUNCTIONING

The French business enterprise emerges as the epitome of the bureaucratized and highly formalized business organization. Formalization is the corollary of a rigorous division of labour coordinated by hierarchical means. Such a form of organization creates heavy administrative overheads, a bypassing of supervisory staff, serious problems of communication, and a lowering of employee morale, particularly at the lower levels. Disaffection with the high degree of formalization is expressed in the following worker comments, quoted by Gallie (1978: 109):

'It's the century of red tape. To get anything you have to go somewhere to get hold of a form, and then you've got to go and get the signature of two or three chaps. You lose hours because of paperwork.'

'There are heaps of useless papers. We had to ask for a year for a slide rule. There are so many bits of paper for a tiny repair. I think it's something special to France.'

Gallie (1978) also expresses well how excessive hierarchization has undermined the communication process, with written documents re-placing direct communication. Poor communication has created both cold and distant management–worker relations and has led to frequent misunderstandings and, paradoxically, a feeling by workers that there is a *lack* of information (ibid.: 116). Communication is further impaired by a lack of consistency and continuity in the nature of professionality between 'works' and 'staff', particularly higher management. The latter is due to the particularly stark differences in social origin and education in France (see Chapters 3 and 4), and it is further reinforced by the most pronounced pay differentials between 'works' and 'staff' among our three societies.

Does the tall organization structure have any advantages either for business efficiency or for the welfare of organization members which compensate for the many problems it creates? In the context of French employment and promotion policy, a long and finely graded hierarchy becomes an essential precondition. This policy puts prime emphasis on 'on-the-job' training and an internal labour market. It favours gradual progression from job to job and career mobility *within* the enterprise. A tall hierarchy thus secures better career prospects for organization members and enables management to reward selectively those who display the desired behaviour characteristics. It secures management the motiva-tion and commitment to the enterprise by individual members in the context of a collective worker ideology detrimental to such incorporation.

The heavy reliance on supervision and control, despite its many negative consequences for employee morale, does, however appear to achieve some of its purpose. Studies by Gallie (1978), Dubois (1981) and Grünberg (1986) find that efficiency and productivity in matched British and French plants are clearly superior in the latter. However, the heavy costs of this achievement in terms of a much greater employee disaffection cannot be ignored.

In British business organizations, in contrast, poor lateral integration and communication seems to be the greatest problem. This has, in turn, some negative repercussions for vertical integration. The problem starts at the base of the organization with the deficient integration between operatives and maintenance and between the various crafts within the maintenance sector. It reappears in the middle of the hierarchy in pronounced form between technical staff and line and, lastly, between the various management functions. Bessant and Grunt (1985: 316) connect the divisions and barriers in large British enterprises with over-specialization and pigeon-holing and point to the ensuing conflict between functional groups which prevents the smooth working together in the production process of the many functional subsections. The consequences of lack of integration at the base of the production unit are extensively discussed in other chapters. Here I only want to point out that negative consequences could be mitigated by superior manage-ment planning and supervision. This is, however, not forthcoming. Maintenance workers in Gallie's (1978) study see management fall short on planning while operators accuse management of 'failing in its job of supervision of idle and careless craftsmen' (ibid.: 111). The rigid division of labour between staff and line creates problems of 'dual authority' which in turn generates problems of communication. This results in the high level of grievance and dispute on the shopfloor (reported in Chapter 8). In addition, the separation of technical competence from authority characterizing British supervisory staff undermines their ability to exercise their 'control' function effectively. Their bypassing in the event of any serious control problem further reinforces their lack of authority. The resulting widespread disaffection among foremen and other supervisory staff has been documented by Child and Partridge (1982). A negative impact on the quantity and quality of production seems highly likely.

The lack of lateral integration between the various functional depart-ments in British business organizations finds its most dramatic express-ion in the notoriously poor delivery and 'after-sales' service perform-ance by British firms (Turnbull and Cunningham, 1981). While this is caused by a number of factors lack of integration between sales, production and purchasing departments must rate as an important cause. Although friction between the various functional departments is probably found in all business organizations the level of non-cooperation is certainly higher in the British than the German business enterprise. Child (1984: 120) mentions the additional problem, pronounced in Britain, of coordinating the various 'technical services' and making them available to production on a reliable basis. The failure on the part of management to ensure a smooth flow of production is also quoted as a prominent complaint of workers by Maitland (1983) and Gallie (1978). This could be attributed to the less holistic and more departmentalized British concept of business organization as well as to the lesser degree of cohesion between production and other staff, due to an absence of a common socialization experience through training. It is clear from the preceding that, although more and better management 'integrative mechanisms' could overcome some of this lack of horizontal integration (as recommended by Child 1984: 127), most of it can be reduced to the qualification structure and to resulting professional and industrial relations system and occupational identities and thus has deeper roots.

In German business organizations problems of communication along both vertical and horizontal lines seem to be least developed. The relatively flat structure of business enterprises means that bureaucratization and formalization are least developed. Contrary to the stereotype of a highly bureaucratized and formal German organizational style, the study by Maurice et al., (1980: 72) finds it the most personal. This is also supported by Lawrence's (1984: 16) finding that German negotiators spend more time in *ad hoc* discussions, rather than formal meetings with colleagues and subordinates, than do British ones. A loose homogeneity of qualifications, technical knowledge and experience lessens problems of communication both along vertical and horizontal lines of division of labour. Maurice et al. (1980) emphasize the high degree of lateral integration between operatives and maintenance workers at works level and between technical staff and line at the staff level. The relatively smooth relations between different departments providing services to production is underlined by Lawrence (1980: 143). Lawrence (1984: 593) also emphasizes the lesser differentiation between different functional departments and its positive impact on achieving *Termintreue*, i.e. faithful adherence to deadlines promised to customers. Finally, it can be stated that this flat and flexible organization structure poses few problems for career mobility. The functioning of German

Table 2.1 Overall view of administrative structures

	Low	Medium	High
Tallness of hierarchy	G	GB	F
Functional differentiation	G	GB	F
Share of staff employees as part of total workforce	G	GB	F
Supervisory span of control	G	GB	F
Administrative and commercial personnel/works	G	GB	F
Authority positions/works	GB	G	F
Authority positions/staff	GB	F	G

G = Germany
GB = Great Britain
F = France

labour markets, where certified credentials can be traded on external occupational labour markets, does not disadvantage organization members who, with their high level of qualifications, are less dependent on a given employer.

The contrasting features of organizational structures in France, Britain and Germany, outlined on the previous pages, have been usefully summarized in Table 2.1, based on Sorge and Warner (1986: 80).

EXPLAINING DIFFERENCES IN NATIONAL ORGANIZATIONAL SHAPES

How do we account for the striking differences in work structuring and coordination and the resulting organizational shapes between business organizations in our three societies? Maurice et al., (1980) answer this question by pointing to the different ways and degrees to which workers and staff are qualified and promoted in the three countries. They also emphasize the ways in which they may progress through the organizational career structure. The French authors speak about the degree of *professionality* with which tasks are accomplished by the various organizational groupings. By this they mean the formal knowledge base, mastery of practical skills, and formal recognition of qualifications. This concept draws our attention to the fact that education and training of workers is as vital as that of staff and should be given more emphasis in both social science writing and in organizational/governmental planning. The foregoing discussion has, indeed, demonstrated that the degree and kind of professionality achieved through the training system has a far-reaching effect on all aspects of the organizational structure. This key status of occupational/professional training demands a more detailed examination of the various national practices as well as their impact on organizational effectiveness. This will be provided in Chapter 3.

But the shape of organizational structure is also influenced by other societal factors not made explicit by Maurice et al. The first of these is union organizational strength and control orientation. This will be discussed in Chapter 8. The second factor is the organizational culture. Organizational culture refers to the values, attitudes and expectations held by both management and employees about their role in the organization and, particularly, about mutual relations. This culture is shaped by a number of factors but is particularly strongly influenced by the societal industrial relations system and by the skill profile of the labour force. Both the German and the French legal framework for industrial relations express a unitary conception of the firm. Strong emphasis is put on the harmonious resolution of conflict and on the representation of the works community as a whole, as exemplified by the works council. Although there has not been an unbroken German tradition, accepting the idea of a works community, this ideological conception of the business enterprise as a corporate unit has become a reality during the postwar period. It can be regarded as a stable and widely accepted idea among both workers and employers. But it needs to be realized that this acceptance is of a very pragmatic and instrumental kind. It is based on the realization that the good of the community can coincide with the good of the individual member. As one worker expresses it very vividly: 'The fatter the cow we are milking the more milk we get' (quoted by Weltz, 1978: 115). Thus it is quite clear that this conception of the works community entails no notion of 'a higher good' for which the individual must sacrifice himself but is, instead, combined with a strong dose of self-interest. Cooperation is called forth, and is rewarded, by worker participation is some areas of company decision-making and by high levels of material reward. In this situation, relations of mutual trust could develop between management and labour in a large proportion of German enterprises.

The unitary conception of the firm is also supported by the skill profile of the German industrial labour force, as was already indicated in the main part of this chapter. Both the high level of occupational skill possessed by employees at all levels of the hierarchy and its homogeneity mean that workers, technical, supervisory and managerial staff see themselves as a professional community, united around particular work tasks and committed to common standards of achievement – the German *Leistungsbereitschaft*. The feelings of a common purpose, generated in the professional community, appear to exist side by side with an awareness that employers and labour may have conflicting interests in the distribution of surplus.

In France, in contrast, the legal conception of the enterprise as a community is a relatively new phenomenon which has not organically developed out of worker–employer relations. Consequently, it has remained a legal fiction which is regarded with cynicism by the workers. Paternalist or authoritarian management and widespread worker alienation are so deeply ingrained that mutual distrust and hostile confrontation have remained the norm. These differing organizational cultures in German and French business enterprises have inevitably affected worker motivation, effort and self-discipline in different ways and hence must have a bearing on the supervision levels applied.

The situation in British business enterprises in this respect is much less clear-cut. There exists no legal framework promoting a managerial ideology of the works community. Any attempt to introduce such an ideological framework would go right against the grain of British industrial culture and would meet with the same lack of resonance among workers as in France, albeit for different reasons. There is not, in Britain, the stong anti-capitalist worker culture found in France. The very informal system of worker–management relations is based on the notions of negotiation, compromise and worker participation at the workplace. At the same time worker self-motivation is relatively low and effective coordination of effort is deficient. Yet this has not called forth a high concentration of supervision by line management. Nor has deficient performance prompted the development of a new training strategy to increase skill, autonomy and self-direction, despite ample indications that both quantity and quality of output are being affected adversely. (For details see Chapter 3.) The suggestion by Maitland (1983) of a lack of government in British enterprises has some plausibility. (See also Chapter 5.)

Fox (1983) explains this state of affairs in a sophisticated way, pointing to long-established cultural dispositions which have shaped worker and management responses in a reciprocal way. He traces the roots of present interpersonal relations structures and general attitudes back to the origins of industrial development and places them in the philosophical context of individualism and the contractual view of industrial labour. English individualism stresses the rights and privileges of the individual as against the wider group or the state. These individualistic impulses received expression in many English practices and institutions and came finally also to define the view of individuals towards the employment relationship. They gave rise to contractualism – 'a stance which treated the worker as a contracting agent in a purely economic relationship which involved no obligations beyond the "cash nexus". The result was the "us and them" syndrome: a posture of wary mutual inspection by two parties who ... pursued a zero-sum game within an essentially adversary relationship' (ibid.: 22–3). In the absence of any sense of cooperation and common interest the concept of 'works community' could not gain hold. The idea of a 'corporate community' to which the individual must submit appears an alien idea in an individualistic culture emphasizing minimal commitment and the pursuit of sectional interest.

Although it was realized already at the close of the last century that this culture had a very negative impact on the competitiveness of British industry and individual employers tried to reverse the trend, no state support could ever be gained for this. A second explanation for employer inertness, cited by Fox (ibid.: 28), is the public school leadership ideal which has proved inimical to a thrusting, aggressive entrepreneurship and an uncompromising attack on restrictive shop-floor practices.

During the 1980s, however, several developments have served to change the relationship between management and labour. On the one side, the Thatcher government has given both legal and moral support to managers' assertion of the right to manage and, on the other, the economic recession and increased market competition have convinced both management and labour that greater coopera-tion is necessary. Management, at least in the larger firms, has tried to gain greater commitment towards organizational goals by fostering worker involvement through increased communication and consulta-tion. (This is well documented in the Warwick survey of factory managers, reported by Edwards, 1987.) It is too early to determine whether this change signals the first step towards the establishment of a more unitary conception of the British enterprise and a more enduring cooperative organizational culture, or whether this move towards employee involvement will only last until the end of the recession. (This issue will be taken up again in Chapters 8 and 9.)

So far the discussion has mainly focused on the bottom and middle levels of the organizational hierarchy and their coordination by top management. In the following section, the structure at the top of organizational hierarchies will receive consideration. At this level, factors such as differing institutional frameworks for 'human re-sources' development and for handling industrial relations are not important influences. Instead, nationally divergent relations between industrial capital on the one side, and financial capital and/or the state on the other, have become important structuring variables. (For greater details on this see Hall, 1986; and Cox, 1986.)

STRUCTURES OF BUSINESS GOVERNANCE

This section is concerned to show how decision-making of a strategic kind, i.e. the kind affecting the overall and long-term development of the enterprise, is distributed between legally defined administrative entities or informally constituted groups at the top of the enterprise hierarchy. It is merely indicating some of the consequences of different structural arrangements and is in no way intended to be a full treatment of the complex problem of where strategic control of the business enter-prise is located. The latter would require a much broader investigation of the relations between business enterprises and external agencies which is beyond the scope of this chapter. Readers wanting to peruse this issue are referred to the comparative work of Scott (1985).

Whereas German and French companies can have either a two-tier or a unitary system of administration, depending on size and legal status, British companies know only the unitary system. In the two-tier system there is both a supervisory and a management board with no overlap in membership, and the former is designated to exert control over the latter. In the unitary system executive and non-executive directors sit together on one board. The argument in favour of the two-tier structure claims that effective control over management can only be exerted if the non-executive directors are formally separate and independent from managers (e.g. Prais, 1981: 51). Critics of the two-tier system contend that members on a separate supervisory board remain too remote from the work of senior management (e.g. Mills, 1985: 100), or that this system leads to confusion in top management and slows down the decision-making process (Vogl, 1973: 69). Analyses of the three national patterns will show that such simple judgements are not sustainable.

In Germany, the unitary system is associated with smaller (less than 500 employees) private limited companies (the GmbH type), whereas the two-tier system is found in larger private and public limited companies (AG or *Aktiengesellschaft*). The single-tier board consists of the company managers (*Geschäftsführer*) and of the directors, elected by the shareholders. In the two-tier system the supervisory board (*Aufsichtsrat*) is made up, in varying proportions, of shareholders' and of employee representatives. (For greater detail on varying proportions see Chapter 9 on 'Industrial Democracy'.) Dyson (1986) points out that the two-tier system was instituted in Germany in 1870 to give recognition to the close relations between industry and banking and to provide bank representatives with an organ of control. Bankers are, indeed, still on the supervisory boards of a large proportion of large corporations but the control relationship, it will be shown below, is more complex than the formal structure indicates. The composition of the supervisory board tends to be a mirror of the company's business relationships. Besides bankers, it consists of other industrialists whose firms are either customers or suppliers. Lawrence (1980: 36) points out that there is none of the status lenders on German boards, favoured by many top British companies. The management board (*Vorstand*) consists solely of 3–15 top managers (Dyas and Thanheiser, 1976: 106). The management board alone is charged with the management of the company and represents it *vis-à-vis* third parties. The German system of management is a collegiate system where members bear collective responsibility for the company. There is no managing director, only a chairman who is considered *primus inter pares*, but in practice the degree of power wielded by the chairman may depart considerably from this ideal. The technical director on the *Vorstand* usually carries more influence than managers specializing in other areas.

The supervisory board is the legally designated organ of control over the management board and is given extensive formal powers. It appoints and dismisses top managers, determines their remuneration and supervises their activity. It advises on general company policy and can specify which kind of management decisions require its prior consent. The work of the IDE Research Group (Wilpert and Rayley, 1983: 45, Table 4.2) shows that organizational members perceive the actual exercise of control to correspond closely to that formally designated by law. The management board, according to this study, is seen to run the company without much interference from either the supervisory board or any outside bodies, such as banks. An impression of lack of interference from banks may arise from the lending habits of the latter. Unlike British and French banks and individual shareholders, German banks tend to take a long-term perspective and do not press business enterprises for short-term returns on invested capital.

Dyson (1986: 130), too, claims that the supervisory board has changed from an organ of control to one of administration and that a close community of interest between members of the two boards has developed. Bank representatives are greatly valued as supervisory board members as they provide a broader sectoral or even macro-economic perspective, offer an unrivalled consultancy service, can mobilize capital and have good government contacts (ibid.: 131). Industrialists, in turn, serve on banks' supervisory boards. Thus Mills' (1985) charge of remoteness from the concerns of management appears unjustified. Other evidence, however, shows that, in certain conditions, the supervisory board may wrest control from top management and actively participate in, or dominate, key decision-making (Vogl, 1973; 35 Streeck, 1984a;). The fact that top management is on five-year contracts which have to be renewed by the board certainly gives the latter considerable potential power. Dyson (1986: 132) mentions two recent cases (Gutehoffnungshütte in 1983 and Thyssen in 1984) where the bank representatives removed the chairman of the management board because his performance was considered unsatisfactory. Many recent restructuring exercises of individual companies (e.g. Krupp and AEG) have also shown the power of the banks in whose sphere of influence the given company is situated. The legal provision that 25 per cent of share ownership (banks can vote their own and their clients' shares) is enough to veto certain board decisions gives the banks a convenient instrument to assert control.

In limited companies (the GmbH type) and family-owned businesses the *Geschäftsführung*, in all but the smallest companies, is again said to practise collegial management. Bessant and Grunt (1985: 322) found that the *Geschäftsführung* usually consists of three to four people – the MD (Geschäftsführer), being the owner or chairman, the technical director, and the commercial director. The latter function is sometimes split between two managers – one focusing on sales and marketing, the other on administration. Although theoretically they manage collectively, the technical director is invariably more powerful than the commercial director, highlighting the central importance of production in the German enterprise.

In Britain there is no such clear division of power at the top of the enterprise hierarchy. The board of directors, consisting of both executive and non-executive directors, is formally the supreme decision-making body. It has a counselling rather than just a supervisory role. It is said to be the institutional focus of strategic control, although it is not necessarily the unified *agency* of control. A top management meeting in Britain, in contrast with Germany, is a board meeting (Horovitz, 1980: 63). Non-executive directors may be both representatives of share-owners and non-stakeholders who are present to provide expertise or lend status. There are no employee representatives on the board. Some of the directors are full-time employees of the company and form its top management. According to Horovitz (ibid.), a majority of board members (69 per cent in his sample) are insiders. In a high proportion of large British companies the managing director is at the same time the chairman of the board. The actual exercise of strategic control varies from company to company. It can lie either entirely with top management, with the board merely acting in a councelling capacity and rubber-stamping their decisions (this is relatively rare), or the board can be, to varying degrees, actively involved in strategic policy making. According to the data collected by the IDE Research Group (Wilpert and Rayley, 1983: 45, Table 4.2), the board is considered more influential in relation to top management than is the case in German companies. Although there is no collegiate management in British companies and the chief executive or managing director has ultimate responsibility for the conduct of company affairs, delegation of responsibility to other managers is extensive. The chief executive is elected and can be dismissed by the board.

Financial organizations, particularly pension funds, have in recent decades become important as shareholders, and banks have begun to play a more prominent role as providers of credit, but neither have the same close relationship with industrial companies as identified in Germany. Although financial organizations exercise control in the broadest sense, by virtue of the fact that they can withdraw capital, they are not as prominently involved in individual enterprises as German banks. They neither exercise control nor provide an early warning system in times of crisis, and they do not lend the extensive support and advice, considered highly beneficial by German top management. In the words of Scott (1985: 112), financial institutions have the power of constraint but they do not exercise deliberate and overt intervention. Thus it is not necessarily the existence of the unitary form of board but the absence of *any* external control agency which leaves the British business enterprise more vulnerable to the unchecked development of crises.

In France the articles of a company determine whether a single-or two-tier board is to be established. According to Mills (1985: 277f), the vast majority of large limited companies (*Société Anonyme*, SA) have a single-tier board. This board (*conseil d'administration*) consists of 3–12 directors (*administrateurs*), presided over by an elected *Président Directeur-Général* – PDG (chairman and managing director) to whom extensive powers are delegated. (For details on employee representation on the board, see Chapter 9.) The PDG is often the only management representative on the board (Horovitz, 1980: 63). In smaller SAs it is not unusual for the board to meet only once a year to approve the accounts. In larger companies the functions of the PDG and the *Dirécteur-Général* are usually separated. The latter is then responsible for running the day-to-day operations. The SA must have its accounts inspected once a year by an external *Commissaire aux Comptes* (auditor) (Vickery, 1986: 47–8). In the two-tier alternative, according to Mills (1985), there is a supervisory board (*directoire*). The former appoints and supervises the directors on the management board. Private limited companies which are usually owner-managed (*Société à responsibilité limitée*, SARL) do not usually have a board but merely managers (*gérants*) with powers and responsibilities similar to members of the *directoire*. The French board is thus more akin to the British board in that company policy is not usually monitored by an independent supervisory board. The very infrequent meeting of the *conseil d'administration* must give comparatively greater power to the managing director (PDG) than is enjoyed by his British or German counterpart.

There is insufficient information on the origins and implications of structural arrangements at board level in French business organizations.

Nearly forty of even the largest 200 industrial companies were still family-controlled (majority-controlled) during the early 1980s and another sixty appeared to be dominated by the owning family (Syzman, 1983: 113), but the extensive nationalization programme of the early 1980s must have changed this picture to some extent. The situation in the remaining large companies is complex. As in Germany, the stock-market is underdeveloped and shares in larger companies are held mainly by other financial and industrial companies which are often loosely linked together as holding companies (Scott, 1985: 131f). As in Britain, deposit banks have not become prominently involved as providers of industrial capital/long-term loans. Instead, capital is pro-vided by a few investment banks, large financial intermediaries, such as Crédit National, and by para-public equity financing agencies (Green, 1986: 85f; Syzman, 1983: 112f). The state – both through its extensive ownership and its supervision of financial institutions[3] – plays a promin-ent role in determining the allocation of investment funds. (A more detailed description of the French financial system and of its relations with industry is provided in Chapter 10.) Morin (1977: 33, quoted by Scott, 1985: 138) has described this situation as one where control is not determined on the basis of economic property but is exerted in a technocratic manner. This phenomenon is well summed up by the French phrase *l'état-entrepreneur*. The prominence on French boards of former high civil servants (the system of *pantouflage*) reflects this technocratic control and the strong involvement of the state in industrial life (Marceau, 1977: 147, 150). Civil servants, through their extensive experience in state administration of industry and their financial expertise, can be said to play the same supportive role on company boards that was associated with bankers on German supervisory boards. Smaller French firms tend to remain under-capitalized rather than risking the loss of financial independence and of strategic control by the patron and his family (Green, 1986).

Chapter 2 has provided an overall view of the organizational structure of European business enterprises as well as examining organizational roles and role relationships at various levels of the enterprise hierarchy. These structural arrangements, it was emphasized, reflect the way in which work is divided, allocated and controlled. More detailed analyses of managerial roles, practices and relationships with subordinates will be provided in later chapters. Throughout the first part of Chapter 2, the pivotal importance for the organization of work of the system of vocational education and training has been emphasized. A closer examination of the different national systems and of their widespread ramifications for industrial organization will be undertaken in the following chapter.

NOTES

1. The term 'span of control' refers to the number of subordinates responsible to a manager. A narrow span exists when this number is small, and a wide span denotes the opposite.
2. For details, see Bessant and Grunt (1985: 250f); NEDO (1981: 5, 11); Maurice et al. (1986: 74f); Sorge and Warner (1986: 101); Lawrence (1980).
3. During the 1980s, state-owned corporations in the financial sector accounted for 87 per cent of bank deposits and 81 per cent of credits in metropolitan France (Green, 1986: 83).

3　Vocational Education and Training

We saw in Chapter 2 that differences in relative availability of skill at various levels affect the organizational structure of a firm – the number of levels of control, the span of control, the degree of delegation and supervision. These, in turn, it is suggested by various authors, have a strong bearing on a firm's overall productivity, flexibility and rate of innovation and even on a country's macro-level economic performance.[1] The nature and quantity of skill of a given labour force does not only have a positive impact on the overall efficiency of the firm but also has a strong bearing on workers' chances in the enterprise and in the labour market and hence on their level of work satisfaction, overall income opportunities and mobility chances (for details on this see Sengenberger, 1984a).

The nature, quantity and distribution of skill in industry are mainly determined by a country's system of vocational education and training (VET), i.e. by all institutions which systematically lead to the attainment of occupational skills and qualifications. These institutions can be part of the education system, of industry or the result of joint initiatives. Vocational training (VT) is generally divided into initial, further and advanced training. Initial VT, occurring at the beginning of a person's occupational life, is the most widespread in all three societies. Further or continuing training, which may also include retraining, occurs during work life and updates, augments or changes existing skills. Due to increasingly rapid industrial change further training has become more prevalent in recent years. Advanced training prepares trainees for technical or supervisory work. Vocational education and training not only conveys knowledge and competence in certain technical areas but also imparts, implicitly or explicitly, attitudes to work which promote effective performance. Pride in the quality of output, self-reliance and the ability to adjust flexibly to new situations are often mentioned. The technical content of vocational education and training can be specific to a narrow area of expertise, or it can be more general, permitting flexible employment. In recent decades the high rate of technical and occupational change has made a wide training for flexible deployment very important for both employers and workers.

What then are the characteristics of the French, German and British systems of vocational education and training, and how do they differ? A general outline of the main features of each system will be followed by a more detailed description of the various components of the system. The German system, being the most highly developed of the three, is also the best documented in the literature. This fact is inevitably reflected in the amount of space devoted to each system in this chapter. In France – which has the most highly educated population of the three – there is a consistently strong emphasis on general education and a relatively weak one on vocational education, except at the level of the *Grandes Ecoles*. Most of the formal vocational education is provided within the state-controlled education system and is of a systematically planned and standardized nature. The theoretical aspect of vocational education is always more prominently developed than the practical aspect, and there is insufficient continuity from one level of the vocational education system to the next. There exists a particularly large gap between the high level of vocational education possessed by the managerial elite and the sparse and unsystematic vocational education received by manual workers.

In Germany, in contrast, both general and vocational education are equally strongly developed and confer similar levels of prestige. Vocational education caters for many occupational groups, not merely the manual craftworkers. This education has a strong practical component at all levels without, however, neglecting the theoretical aspect. Vocational education at the higher levels builds on that at the lower levels. Hence there is a very high degree of homogeneity throughout the system. Vocational education has been developed and shaped in a corporatist manner, with the state and the two sides of industry cooperating. The strong guiding role of the state has meant that vocational education is conducted in a highly standardized and formalized manner throughout the country. The system is very much designed to meet the varying demands of technical change in a planned fashion.

In Britain vocational education was developed relatively late in a 'feast and famine' pattern and has never been of the same importance as general education. It is felt that there exists a confusing variety of training and validating bodies, that there is wasteful overlap between them and insufficient continuity between different levels of VET. The report of a recent working party on the subject of VET, sponsored by the DES and the MSC, concludes that 'there is no effective national system for vocational qualifications' and that urgent steps need to be taken to remedy the situation (*Review of Vocational Qualifications 1986*). The weaknesses of the British system are now widely recognized.

The whole system is at present under review, and many changes have already been introduced during the last decade.

The apprenticeship system, which caters for a comparatively small section of the working population – concentrating mainly on the traditional crafts – is probably still the most important component of VET for industrial occupations. It usually develops both theoretical and practical competence and can involve both the employer and vocational education institutions. Until recently, the state has deliberately kept out of vocational education, leaving it a matter for employers and unions, with the latter preserving a large measure of control over various matters of apprenticeships. More recently, however, the state has taken the initiative in remodelling the system of VET, and new training courses have developed under the auspices of the MSC. Furthermore, in Britain, in great contrast to Germany and France, the general education system appears to be much weaker in providing the lower ability groups with an educational base on which subsequent vocational training could build. This was demonstrated in meticulous detail in a German–British comparison for such subjects as mathematics and other subjects with a vocational slant in a study conducted by Prais and Wagner (1985). There is no equivalent comparative study covering France but it is likely that French general education, with its strong emphasis on mathematics, also provides a better base on which VET can build.

INITIAL VOCATIONAL EDUCATION AND TRAINING

Germany

In Germany there are two major institutional forms of initial vocational training. By far the most important is the apprenticeship of mainly young workers within the dual system. In addition, vocational education is being acquired in an elaborate system of specialized vocational or professional schools and colleges (*Berufsfachschulen*) (for details, see Figure 3.1). Institutes of higher education, particularly the polytechnics (*Fachhochschulen*), also have a strong vocational slant. During the early 1980s over 65 per cent of the relevant age cohort entered the dual system or studied in full-time vocational schools, and another 20 per cent entered higher education. Thus we find in Germany a very high participation rate in post-secondary vocational education, the highest of our three countries. It is a characteristic of the German system that apprenticeships are also served by older people who want to add this highly marketable qualification to their more academic ones. In recent

Figure 3.1   The system of vocational education and training in Germany*

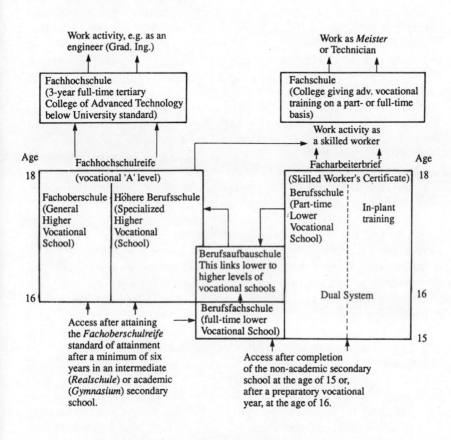

Indicates possible routes of progression through the system.

* This system exists parallel to the general education system and interchange at all levels is possible but decreases in numerical importance the higher up the scale a student ascends.

years a growing proportion of people with 'A' level (*Abitur*) and a degree have gone on to do an apprenticeship (Institute of Manpower Studies (IMS), 1984: 13).[2] The apprenticeship system is derived from the medieval guild system although the foundations for its present form were laid mainly after World War I. It has spread from the still strongly developed small enterprises of the artisan or handicraft (*Handwerk*) sector to the larger, modern factories in all sectors of industry, as well as into trade and administration, and to newly emerging occupations in all sectors (for details see Sengenberger, 1984a). The legal obligation on employers to release all young people for vocational education – and the strong impetus this gave to the system – is of relatively recent date, namely 1938 (CEDEFOP), 1984: 115). Major legislation in recent decades under the Vocational Education Act (*Berufsbildungsgesetz*) of 1969 and the Federal Training Promotion Act (*Bundesausbildungsförderungsgesetz*) of 1969 and 1976 further strengthened German vocational education. They also ensured that those undertaking vocational education would receive similar financial support to those in academic education.

The organization of the dual system of vocational education and training is undertaken through the common efforts of employers, unions and the state. Whereas the more theoretical part of VET in vocational schools is the responsibility of, and is paid for by, the state (mainly the *Länder* governments), the practical 'in-firm' training is organized in a tripartite manner although the employers, who are largely responsible for finance, are the most influential party. The training content for a given occupation is worked out at national level by the Federal Institute of Vocational Education in consultation with the social partners. The Institute is responsible for all the laws and regulations governing training. It also systematically collects statistical information on, and initiates research into, VET and undertakes periodic reviews of, and makes the necessary adjustments to, occupational profiles. In addition, general training policy is a matter for negotiation between the social partners in collective bargaining and through the works council. The training is supervised and examined at local level by special committees of the Chambers of Industry, Craft (*Handwerk*) and Commerce. At this level employers are by far the most influential party, and union attempts to correct the balance have been unsuccessful. The implementation of training occurs at the level of the firm, with works councils monitoring faithful adherence to the training contract incorporating national guidelines. The costs of the dual system are shared between the state and employers, with the latter paying the lion share – two-thirds, according to Roberts (1986: 111). It must be pointed out, though, that trainees receive only a low training allowance, in contrast to the relatively high proportion of an adult wage received by apprentices in Britain and France (ibid.).

Alternatively, students can attend a vocational school (*Berufsfach-schule*) on a full-time basis. They offer training programmes for a recognized occupation that may later be credited in a recognized training programme, or occupational certificates that are only available in these colleges. A recent report (CEDEFOP, 1987: 93) considers them more as a supplement rather than as an alternative to the dual system.

Apprenticeships form the backbone of vocational training in all economic sectors. Not only have a large proportion of manual workers served them but also many technical, commercial, supervisory and managerial members of staff. Besides the full apprenticeship of three years there is also a two-year variant for semi-skilled workers, and progression from this to the higher level is possible. An apprenticeship consists of three years' practical training in the company and of a more theoretical education in a vocational school (*Berufsschule*), run by the education authorities on a weekly day-release basis. The training imparts not only technical knowledge and skills, but apprentices in industry also learn about costs, design, and the planning and administration of production. Both apprentices and semi-apprentices (*Anlehrling*) are trained by systematic exposure to the whole spectrum of work situations and problem-solving tasks in an ascending order of difficulty. In recent years, supra-plant training centres have often come to supplement training at the plant level as individual firms no longer contain all the work settings a trainee must be familiarized with. At the end of three years the apprentice is examined on both theoretical and practical competence and receives his certificate (*Facharbeiterbrief*) only if he has passed both.

In Germany industrial training is regarded as a matter of public interest and as a valuable societal resource (CEDEFOP, 1987: 84) which should not be left to the economic interests of isolated firms. The apprenticeship system is highly valued by all involved. Employers feel that their considerable financial investment in this area ensures them ample returns. Not only do they gain a labour force with a high level of technical skill but also workers with positive work habits and attitudes. They are particularly concerned to maintain the German reputation for high-quality products and services which has ensured German enterprises such a strong position in exports markets. This they link directly with the system of vocational education (IMS, 1984: 13). In recent years another purpose of this system has received a growing emphasis: the ability to develop a flexible approach to change (ibid.: 12). Lastly, German employers train not only for current needs but also for stock.

For German workers the apprenticeship system has also very positive consequences. The Skilled Worker's Certificate (*Facharbeiterbrief*) gains them not only a high and steady income but also responsibility and autonomy at work. This certificate is a highly valued passport for promotion throughout the country. The high degree of standardization and formalization of certification allows German workers to seek promotion on a *national* labour market and there is no danger of being confined to the intra-organizational one. This has obvious implications for the degree of worker dependence and for their bargaining strength. German unions also give full support to a system of vocational education and training, but they would like it to be more geared to workers' long-term employment needs rather than employers' current production needs. In this respect, two criticisms have been levelled at the German system in recent years: too much training is oriented towards occupations without a future; and adjustment of training profiles to changing industry needs has been too slow at the present time of rapid technological change.

France

Initial vocational education/training may be gained either through an apprenticeship or in full-time state education. At the present time apprenticeship training for industrial occupations is very uncommon although it does still cater for the artisan sector of the economy. The low degree of importance of the apprenticeship system in industry has its roots in the events of the French Revolution. The abolition of the guilds at that time greatly weakened the system, and it never managed to penetrate industrial training in later centuries. Apprentices receive their training partly on the job and partly in apprentice training centres. Their in-firm training is regulated by a training contract, and the final certificate is the *Certificat d'Aptitude Professionelle* (CAP). Apprentice-ships are very much regarded as an option for the less able, and their reputation in French society is low (CEDEFOP, 1984: 220). The system is financed by an apprenticeship tax on employers (ibid.: 221).

Consequently, the bulk of initial VET occurs in full-time state education institutions which were developed in the late 1950s. (Figure 3.2 gives an overview of the whole system of initial and advanced VET.) Young people can transfer to a vocational school (*Lycée d'Enseigne-ment Professionel* (LEP)) at the age of thirteen and complete a three-year course for the CAP, or they can start the course after the end of compulsory secondary education, at the age of fifteen. At this later stage there is also the possibility to sit for the Vocational Studies Certificate (*Brevet d'Etudes Professionelles* (BEP)). The CAP gives young people

Figure 3.2   The system of vocational education and training in France

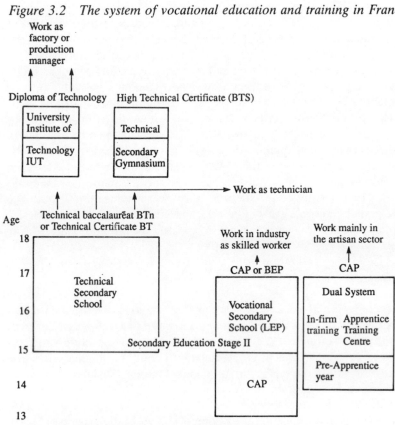

Based on data in CEDEFOP (1984: 218); NEDO (1987: 61f).

the status of a skilled worker whereas the BEP prepares mainly for work in the tertiary sector (CEDEFOP, 1984: 219).

Initial VET is completely school-based, and industry is involved only in an advisory capacity in determining its content. Students receive instruction in basic technical principles and have occupation-oriented curricula. In-firm vocational training is received only after the school-based course has been completed and the young person has taken up employment. It is referred to as 'continuing training' and is neither systematically developed nor necessarily related to initial VET. French industrialists are not satisfied with the nature of the training imparted by schools. A survey of 3000 leading industrialists in 1986 established that 72 per cent of them considered that the French educational system does not equip young people for working life (Oechslin, 1987: 653).

Initial VET is acquired only by a minority of young people – 23 per cent transfer to a LEP at the age of fifteen, and a further 12 per cent have transferred at the age of thirteen (NEDO, 1987: 61). Although the level of those taking the Vocational Proficiency Certificate (CAP) has fallen significantly in recent years the proportion of those possessing a CAP or equivalent is still three times higher among those who entered the labour force in the early 1980s than among those who left it (Piotet, 1984: 240–1). The majority – 38 per cent – now study for a general or technical baccalauréat, and around a third of young people enter work without any formal qualifications (ibid.; Volz, 1983: 27). Few of the students who have taken the CAP proceed to the technical education schools to acquire a more advanced technical training (CEDEFOP, 1984: 219). It is notable that French secondary education at both the first and the second cycle puts a strong emphasis on mathematics, a subject usually considered a good base for technical training of any kind.

Britain

In Britain, initial vocational training has traditionally received a low emphasis, and vocational education is imparted in a number of different institutional settings: it can be part of a traditional apprenticeship or it can be received in the further education sector, the higher education sector or, more recently, on a Youth Training Scheme (YTS). In contrast to the situation in Germany, a very high proportion (around two-thirds) of young people have until recently gone straight into employment after finishing their compulsory secondary schooling without receiving any vocational education at all (IMS, 1984: 6, 69). The authors of the latter report do not only bemoan the insufficient quantity of vocational education imparted but also criticize objectives. There is insufficient emphasis on imparting general competencies, such as flexibility, the desire to learn and self-reliance, which they see as necessary for effective performance at work as the possession of technical skills. The organization and finance of initial vocational education varies according to the scheme. Whereas the apprenticeship training is financed by employers and the state is hardly involved in it, vocational education in further education colleges is organized and financed by the state through the local authorities. The state wants employers to take a more active part in VET and accuses them of displaying both insufficient initiative in this area and of getting inadequate results from existing inputs (ibid.). A recent quasi-governmental (NEDO and MSC) report, inquiring into the reasons for employers' low input into training, established that the latter did not link it directly with profitability and competitiveness and tended to regard it as an overhead to be cut when profits are threatened. This short-term perspective is partly due to the fact that training is often a decision left to line management] (*A Challenge to Complacency*, 1985).

The apprenticeship training system, like the German system, dates back to the pre-industrial guild system. It shares other similarities with the German system but its differing features are probably of more importance for its general development and its weakening position at the present time. Only a small proportion of workers are covered by it as apprenticeships are oriented mainly towards the maintenance trades and much less to work in production. The practical in- firm training is not necessarily examined and certified. There are no training plans stipulated and monitored by outside bodies, and there is no legal obligation on employers to release apprentices for attendance at college. Lastly, the terms of the apprenticeship in industry are negotiated between employers and unions. The optional theoretical instruction received during an initial year at college or under an Industrial Training Board (ITB), followed by day-or block-release, may be examined by the London City and Guilds examination authority but an examination is not obligatory. Semi-skilled workers receive only short (about two months), firm-specific induction courses so that a progression from semi-skilled to skilled status is precluded. Thus the bulk of the workers are confined to the intra-firm labour market. Their search for improvement and/or promotion becomes curtailed, and their fate becomes tied up with the one employer.

Whereas in Germany employers have retained the greatest influence over shaping the training system in Britain the unions have wielded strong control in this area. The apprenticeship system may be characterized as giving workers the right to undertake a particular set of tasks within the work process, and these tasks come to form a 'job territory' for given skilled workers. This feature has made the British system insufficiently responsive to changing production conditions and is said to have contributed to its decline in recent years. The inflexibility of the apprenticeship system to meet changing needs has led to a situation where production skills have become more and more firm-specific and where supply of skills depends greatly on individual employers' training policy. This fact, as Marsden and Saunders (1981: 178) point out, has made the British system evolve in the direction of the French. The unions' insistence that apprentices be paid between 50 and 100 percent (depending on age and firm) of an adult's wage also makes apprentices very expensive to employers and explains some of the reluctance of

British employers to increase their training efforts (Roberts, 1986: 111). The recent decline in apprenticeships is not merely a consequence of recession but is also an attempt to move vocational training out of union control.

In the late 1970s the focus of the debate on training shifted from skill shortages to restrictive work practices and the role of the trade unions in training (Vickerstaff, 1985: 60). The 1981 Government White Paper on training demanded the reform of the apprenticeship system and made the MSC the agency to execute this reform. The propensity of craft unions to cultivate narrow and inflexible skill profiles is seen as being irreconcilable with the achievement of the hybrid (or mixed) skills said to be needed in connection with the new technology. Joining an enhanced Youth Training Scheme or staying on in full-time education are now regarded as preferable alternatives to the traditional apprenticeship (IMS, 1984: 6–7.

Besides acquiring initial vocational education and training through an apprenticeship it can be gained by attending courses of varying length and degrees of difficulties at further education colleges. More recently, courses organized by the Manpower Service Commission have added further opportunities for initial vocational training. These will be discussed below.

The rather patchy development of the British system of vocational education is largely due to the fact that until the middle 1960s the state denied all responsibility for training. British voluntarism in industrial affairs shaped also the development of vocational training. A partial break with this attitude was indicated by the passing of the Industrial Training Act (ITA) in 1964. This signified the recognition that voluntarist policies could not overcome the problem of skill shortages which were connected with poor economic performance in the postwar period. The ITA set up an advisory Central Training Council, composed of equal numbers of employer and union representatives and initiated the founding of statutory Industrial Training Boards (ITBs). The operation of a levy-grant system by these boards was designed to induce employers to give training a higher priority. Although the ITBs have effected great improvements they have been unable to make good the great lag in British technical training relative to some of its continental competitors. They were criticized, both by the CBI and, in 1968, by the Donovan Commission (on Trade Unions and Employers' Associations) for their lack of progress in reforming apprenticeships. It was pointed out that the Act had not introduced a centrally planned and directed training system and had not satisfied the economy's need for a more flexible, trans-sectoral training policy. In the early 1980s the majority of the ITBs were closed down. Exchequer financing of the remainder was phased out. They have greatly reduced their intake of craft or technical trainees (Daly et al., 1985: 60). Whereas in 1979 100,000 apprentices were recruited, by 1983 recruitment had fallen drastically to only 40,000 (IMS, 1984: 70).

During the 1970s and, more so the 1980s, the necessity fundamentally to reform the system of initial VT became widely accepted at government level, and a large number of initiatives towards this end were adopted. In 1974 the Manpower Services Commission (MSC), again composed of equal numbers of trade union and employer representatives, was founded to plan training on a national level. The MSC was made responsible to the Department of Employment, and state expenditure on training was greatly increased. During the 1970s, however, the MSC did not succeed in enforcing the adoption of its many recommendations at enterprise level and was unable to make fundamental changes to the structure of training. The deepening recession made employers less willing to spend money on training. The growing number of the unemployed meant that the MSC had to devote a high proportion of its resources to their particular training needs. During the 1980s expenditure on Youth Training Schemes has been greatly increased, and there exist now both one-year and two-year schemes (the latter since 1986) which aim to provide all 16-year-old school-leavers with some training. Criticisms of the schemes are, however, still strong. It is said that there is insufficient monitoring of standards and a lack of rigorous examination. Although training is examined and certified, much of it enjoys, as yet, only a low level of prestige and of recognition from employers. This loose outside monitoring tempts some employers to use youths as cheap labour without giving them useful training. The two-year scheme has been hailed as a great advance for initial VT by the MSC, and it has had the approval of both the CBI and the TUC (*Employment Gazette*, February 1986). Although the scheme is filling an important gap, it must remain doubtful whether it will be sufficient to close the skill gap between Britain and its continental competitors.

More generally, criticism has been levelled at the wide variety of training schemes existing in Britain and the absence of coordination between them (Channel 4 Inquiry, 11 May 1986). The MSC has emphasized the need to rationalize and simplify training provisions, standards and examining bodies into a unified national scheme and to put the funding of such a system on a more secure base by returning to a comprehensive levy-grant system for employers (*CEDEFOP News*, 4 1986).

Other new state-sponsored developments are the introduction, on an experimental basis, into schools of a one-year course for 14-to 16-year-olds, leading to the acquisition of the Certificate of Pre-Vocational Education (CPVE) (since 1985) and the Technical and Vocational Education Initiative (TVEI), introduced in 1982 by the MSC. The former concentrates mainly on business studies. The main objective of the latter scheme is to offer full-time four-year courses of a general, technical and vocational nature in schools which will lead to recognized qualifications. It aims to introduce young people to the world of work and to facilitate the transition from school to work. By 1986 the TVEI had been introduced into 9 per cent of schools, and generally it has been considered successful by both pupils and employers. But it is uncertain whether and when the TVEI can be introduced into all schools in its present form ('Inquiry' programme on Channel 4, 11 May 1986).

FURTHER VOCATIONAL EDUCATION AND TRAINING

Rapid technological and industrial change in recent decades has made it more important to provide further/continued training or retraining to increase or to adapt the level/kind of skill of employed adults or of those seeking to re-enter employment.

Germany

In the FRG further VET is considered to be of similar importance as initial VET, and considerable investment into this kind of training is made. Further training may take the form of in-firm training or it may be organized by outside public agencies, such as the Chambers of Commerce and Industry or the Trade Union Federation (DGB) or by private institutions. The largest part is probably of the in-firm type. It is organized and financed by employers to answer their own needs and is not subject to the high degree of regulation as initial VET. Certification is not as common as for initial VET. Although the larger employers are more active in providing further and re-training, in the early 1980s there were nevertheless more than 50 per cent of firms involved in it (CEDEFOP, 1984: 172). During recent decades expenditure on this kind of training has greatly increased. Much of it has been devoted to familiarizing workers with the new microelectronic technology and to broaden their skills to increase flexibility of deployment. (For further details, see Chapter 7.)

Since the late 1960s the state has assumed a more prominent role in this field. The reduction of capacity in many of the traditional industries and the obsolescence of many industrial processes/skills has called for a greater effort in retraining those people displaced by these processes of change. In 1969 two important Acts[3] were passed extending and improving the provision of further VET, and the state has stepped in with financial assistance to both trainees and the organizations providing retraining. But the initial goal to transform the area of further training into a fully-fledged public training system has been abandoned (CEDEFOP, 1987: 102).

France

In France, too, the state has increased provision for further and retraining in recent decades. Two Acts of the early 1970s (1970 and 1971) make provision for certain groups in the communities to be (re)integrated into employment and for occupational advancement. Firms themselves are obliged to provide a certain amount of training and must spend at least 1.1 per cent of their total wage bill on further training activity, as well as provide written accounts of their training effort. Nearly 40 per cent of this sum, however, goes towards trainees' salaries (NEDO, 1987: 71). Further or continuing training is jointly regulated by the union and employers' federations, and funds are set up to help the smaller enterprises to fulfil their training obligations. But it must be noted that, although French firms' expenditure on further training has been rising, only a small proportion of it is spent on manual workers. The lion share in firms of all sizes goes towards the training of office, technical/supervisory and managerial staff (NEDO, 1987: 70, Table 11).

Firms can spend their 1.1 per cent on further training either by providing it in-firm or by engaging an external training body. In 1984 in-house training was the most popular, with 24.5 per cent of training being accomplished in this way (NEDO, 1987: 72). In-firm training, according to Maurice et al. (1986a), is geared towards the elaborate French system of positions graded according to skill requirement, and gives workers a fairly narrow and specific training. This confines them to narrowly defined tasks and their skills are not tradeable on the external labour market. Workers become familiarized with jobs successively, through promotion from one job to another. Promotion, in the French system, depends on good behaviour and seniority in the firm and not on formal qualifications. Maurice et al. (1986a: 72) claim that the level of skill possessed by a French skilled worker (skill categories OP1 and OP2) is often no higher than that of a German semi-skilled worker. More recently, however, efforts have been made to train a small elite of workers to relatively high standards. They are provided with a wider training which allows employers to introduce some flexibility into the fairly rigid French system of job grading and narrow task definition. Another impetus to further training has come from a law obliging employers to grant every employee a paid training leave and to undertake a course of his/her own choice, but this facility is not widely taken up – by 44,000 people in 1984 (NEDO, 1987: 69).

Britain

Further vocational training and retraining is mainly carried out by employers. Although there has been an increase in this kind of training in recent years, it is still being considered as insufficient in relation to continental competitors. No comprehensive national statistics on the extent and cost to employers of such training are available, but it is assumed that in this area, too, Britain lags behind Germany (IMS, 1984: 88). A recent MSC survey (1986) of British employers in all economic sectors on attitudes and practices in this area established that private sector employers invested an average of £200 per employee per year in such training, amounting to 0.15 per cent of turnover. The survey also found that 24 per cent of establishments had provided no training of any kind during the preceding year and that 69 per cent of employees had received no further training. Where training is provided it can occur either in-firm, particularly in the larger firms, or it can occur on external courses at further education colleges which keep a close liaison with local industrialists on matters of course content.

An important part of further training has concentrated on broadening the skills and spheres of competence of existing craftsmen and training multiskilled craftsmen, competent in two or more different areas. Such retraining has to overcome the resistance of craft unions and only moderate progress has been made in this area (Brady, 1984; Daniel, 1987).

ADVANCED VOCATIONAL EDUCATION AND TRAINING

Germany

To move into a technical or supervisory position it is necessary to be both an experienced skilled worker with a *Facharbeiterbrief* and to attend further part- or full-time courses in institutes of vocational education. These courses are examined and certified and develop both theoretical and practical competence. Aspiring technicians attend a vocational school (*Berufsfachschule*) or a vocational college (*Fachschule*) on a part-time (2–3 years) or a full-time basis respectively. The course for *Meister* is taken part-time over two years at a *Fachschule*. The curriculum is particularly strong on the technical side, but the future *Meister* also acquires organizational/administrative competence as well as receiving some pedagogical instruction in relation to his training function in the enterprise.

France

Pupils aiming for a technician's certificate (*Brevet de Technician*, BT), or a Technical Baccalauréat (BTn), take a three-year course at a technical secondary school, without release into industry. The number of young people choosing this course is again relatively small but has risen significantly in recent years (Piotet, 1984: 241). Those in possession of either a General or a Technical Baccalauréat can go on to acquire a Higher Technical Certificate in a short course (*Brevet de Technicien Supérieur* (BTS) or in a long course at a university or *grande école*, leading to an engineering qualification. (This account is based on CEDEFOP, 1983.) Since 1969 there exist also the University Institutes of Technology (IUT) which offer short, specialized and scientific and technical courses to satisfy the rising demand for highly qualified technicians. Some 54,000 students attended full-time in 1982–83 (NEDO, 1987: 62). The increase of students in tertiary technical education has been particularly marked in recent years (Piotet, 1984: 241).

The training of intermediate staff is infrequent and fragmented. Whereas in Germany 70.2 per cent of foremen have a qualification above the *Facharbeiterbrief*, in France only 11 per cent have a training above the CAP, and 50 per cent have no training at all (Maurice et al., 1986a: 113), but it is becoming customary now in some industries to fill foremen's posts with young people with technical qualifications. There is a lack of continuity in training between the different levels of the hierarchy. It is uncommon, for example, for workers with a CAP to go on studying to acquire a BT or a Technical Baccalauréat (ibid.: 160), and there appears to be no opportunity to become a technician later on in one's working life.

Britain

Traditionally, technicians in British industry have often been craftworkers, promoted into the technical department without further formal training. Only during the early 1980s was a framework worked out by the Engineering Council which systematized the development of technical and engineering education and laid down standards of certification. The Council distinguished between a technician engineer (T.Eng.) and an engineering technician (Eng.Tech.). The first requires the completion of an HNC/HC or HND/HD and the second that of an ONC, as well as several years of work experience in both cases. Courses are validated and examined by the Business and Technician Education Council. The lower certificate can be used as a base for acquiring the higher one, and technician engineers can also, after further training, advance to the status of Chartered Engineer (C.Eng). These bridging provisions are very useful although the British system provides insufficient continuity between the training of workers and technical staff. It is said that the British system of VET blocks the occupational advancement of workers and leads to the freezing of career paths at a very early age.

At the present time, the number of young people completing these technical training courses is still very small and is generally held to be very inadequate to fulfil the increased need for technical skill, brought about by the introduction of the new technology. According to a recent government report (IT Skills Shortages Committee, 1985), the supply of technicians in the area of information technology is particularly inadequate. An increase in recruits to technical training courses, depending on a good base in mathematical school education, is going to be very slow in Britain. Compared with the situation in France and Germany, this shortage of technical skill at intermediate level will greatly handicap British manufacturing industry's position in the new technology-based market competition.

Foremen are not required to attend any further outside training courses, and in many industries they have not even served an apprenticeship. Any in-firm training they receive emphasizes the supervisory rather than the technical aspect of their work. Superintendents, the higher British supervisory grade, always have a technical or management training but there are relatively few of them. Although this lack of technical skill among foremen is now becoming recognized as a serious problem in high-tech firms, measures to ameliorate this situation have not yet been initiated in Britain.

THE TRAINING OF ENGINEERS

Engineers form a group which bridges the divide between technical and managerial staff as well as between practice- and theory-oriented staff.

They must be considered a key group in the manufacturing enterprise, supplying the technical ingenuity which has become a *sine qua non* in the competitive struggle in a world market where technological advance and sophistication have become a decisive weapon.

The historical development and present social, educational and industrial profile of the engineering profession differs decisively between France and Germany on the one side, and Britain on the other. Professional engineers evolved first of all in France where institutions for their education and training, dedicated to the development of expertise for designing installations for military purposes, evolved already in the eighteenth century. Germany began to copy the French system of technical education and the *écoles polytechniques* in the early decades of the nineteenth century when polytechnic institutes were founded in Karlsruhe and Berlin. France stayed in the lead until 1869 after which Germany began to overtake it in its output of professional engineers. By the eve of World War I, Germany had left France far behind and had developed a high reputation in Europe for the quality of its engineering institutions and engineers. (The historical account is based on Ahlström, 1982: 29f). In both countries, there arose from these early beginnings a technical university system which could rival the rest of the higher education sector in degree of academic excellence and social status.

In Britain, in contrast, the idea of a scientific education for those in technical occupations gained acceptance at a much later date. Although lower-level technical education had evolved at the beginning of the nineteenth century in Mechanics' Institutes these did not develop sufficiently high academic levels to create the basis from which an engineering profession could emerge. It was only after the 1851 Great Exhibition in London – which demonstrated the technical superiority of Britain's continental rivals – that a beginning in the scientific education of engineers was being made. But the number of professional engineers, their level of expertise and their social status, have never come to equal those in France and Germany. Whereas on the Continent the term 'engineer' was defined and protected by the state and referred to as a profession, in Britain it remained a more ambiguous term, encompassing a range of occupational positions from the grease-covered mechanic to the graduate engineer sitting mainly at a desk (Gerstl and Hutton, 1966: 5). In Britain, until the 1980s, the routes leading to the title engineer have been very diverse, and there has not been such a clear distinction made between the graduates of the educational/training institutions on the different tiers.

These differing historical developments still leave their imprint today on the training, level of competence and resultant status of the industrial engineer in the three societies. In both Germany and France the engineer is regarded as a very prestigious occupation, and the salary of a senior engineer in Germany is higher than that of senior civil servant or university professor. Consequently, there is no shortage of people wanting to qualify in engineering. In both countries there exists a two-tier structure for training engineers. In addition to the universities and *grandes écoles* turning out the *Diplomingenieur* or *Ingenieur Diplomé* (graduate engineers) in five to six years of study, there are the polytechnics (*Fachhochschulen, formerly Ingenieurschulen*) and *écoles d'ingénieur* which train the lower-level engineers during three to four years of study. In contrast to the situation in Britain, French and German engineers are clearly marked off from lower technical staff in qualification terms. In France, in addition, there is also a strong social distinction as engineers enjoy *cadre* status and the various social privileges associated with it (Whalley, 1986: 189). Although French technicians can cross the cadre barrier and become an *ingénieur maison* this status is only firm-specific and non-transferable (ibid.). It is said that engineering in French and German universities is both independent from, and equal in status to, science whereas in Britain it is very much a poor relation of science. The training at both French and German universities is said to be highly theoretical. German employers, in particular, complain both about the lack of practical training and the fact that university training is not sufficiently attuned to the great technological changes which have occurred in industry (IMS, 1984: 19). The engineer trained at a *Fachhochschule* is much more popular among German employers because his/her training is more practice-oriented. In 1979 there were three times as many engineers from polytechnics as from universities in employment (ibid.: 25, Table 2.12). References in the non-German literature to German engineering training do not always distinguish between the two kinds but the predominance of engineers from polytechnics leads to the assumption that they must set the tone. Sorge and Warner (1986: 115), for example, contrast the more practical bent and greater orientation to industry of German engineering positively with the British discipline which is taught as 'engineering science'.

In Britain, until recently, only a small minority of engineers were trained in universities whereas the majority were former craftworkers and technicians who studied on a part-time basis in technical colleges and polytechnics for Higher National Certificates and Higher National Diplomas (Lee, 1986: 3, 6). This made them as eligible for the title of Chartered Engineer as are university graduates. Probably the big weight of these engineers with relatively low qualifications gave Bessant and Grunt (1985: 318) the impression that the qualifications of German engineers tend to be higher than those of their British colleagues. The low status of engineering in the universities and of engineers in society has meant that an insufficient number of high calibre students has been attracted on to engineering courses (Glover and Kelly, 1987: 104). More recently, British engineering education has been extensively reformed in an effort to raise standards and status and to make it more relevant to industry. A three to four years university degree has now become the normal entry route for aspiring engineers and is a precondition for the status of Chartered Engineer (C.Eng.). Since 1984 an effort has also been made to meet employers' criticisms that graduates are not immediately useful and to make training more industry-oriented (Glover and Kelly, 1987). Although there has been an increase in engineering graduates their proportion remains small in comparison with graduates in arts and social sciences subjects. Furthermore, only a minority of engineering students specialize in, or aspire to go into, production management, and the more theoretically-oriented R & D specialism is the most popular (ibid.: 27, 104). Consequently, there is still a shortage of engineers in production, particularly at the senior engineer level and in the area of product design involving microprocessors (Brady, 1984: 64), and, in contrast to French and German firms, engineers remain exceptional in management positions. Finally, in all three societies engineers are employed both as technical staff and in managerial positions. Hence what has been said about engineering education in this section is also relevant to the introduction to management education in Chapter 4.

SKILL PROFILES AND ORGANIZATIONAL EFFECTIVENESS

Now that we have a picture of the three national systems of vocational education and training we can examine their impact on the skill profiles of the working populations of the three societies. Prais (1981b) provides a very detailed German–British comparison, while Lutz (1981) makes a more limited contrast of the situation in Germany and France.

If we take vocational training at all levels, then 69 per cent of the German working population, but only 29 per cent of the French, possessed it at the beginning of the 1980s. If we take those with an apprenticeship qualification only, the German proportion becomes 62 per cent and the French a mere 20 per cent (Lutz, 1981: 77). More recent NEDO (1987: 62) figures state that 54 per cent of the French 16–18 age group stay on at school for some further general or vocational education. Prais (1981b) divides the working populations of Britain and Germany into those having university-level education, those having intermediate qualifications - apprenticeships, technician and foreman qualifications, and those having no qualifications at all. He gives figures for the various economic sectors as well as for the whole working population. The following figures concentrate on the manufacturing sector. Taking university-level education we find very similar proportions of the respective working populations possessing it – 3.5 per cent in Germany and 3.3 per cent in Britain. At the intermediate level, however, the discrepancy becomes vast – 60.8 per cent of the German working population but only 28.7 per cent of the British have formal qualifications. This then leaves 35.7 per cent of Germans in the manufacturing sector without qualifications and a staggering 68.0 per cent in the British. The deficiencies in Britain are greatest at the level of technician, foreman, office clerk and a little less, though still considerable, at the level of manual workers.

The picture on qualifications is further filled out by figures on school-leavers' destination in recent years, provided by Roberts (1986). In 1980 50 per cent of German young people went into apprenticeships and 18 per cent were in full-time vocational education. Comparable figures for French young people in 1978 were 14 per cent and 40 per cent, respectively, and in Britain in 1977 the figures were 14 per cent and 10 per cent (Roberts, 1986: 110, basing himself on figures provided by Bernard Casey of the Policy Studies Institute). Since then, however, the introduction of Youth Training Schemes in Britain has dramatically decreased the number of young people going straight into employment or unemployment without any vocational education. Lastly, it must be pointed out that a significant proportion of young people in Germany who gain an apprenticeship cannot find employment at equivalent level afterwards because employers, particularly in the artisan (*Handwerk*) sector, train more than they can subsequently employ.

To pull even with Germany and, to a lesser extent, with France, Britain needs to improve both the quantity and the quality of vocational education for staff and workers at all levels of industry. A more systematic and homogeneous system of vocational education and training needs to be developed. Such efforts are urgently required because of the widespread ramifications of the system of vocational education and training on many aspects of the industrial organization. Some of these were already highlighted in Chapter 2. Others, with a direct bearing on overall efficiency and productivity, as well as worker satisfaction, will be reviewed below.

Productivity levels in different countries are difficult to compare, and it is particularly problematic to pinpoint the factors which determine differences. A recent book on productivity in British manufacturing industry (Nichols, 1986) points to the host of influences which have to be considered and demonstrates that the relatively poor British productivity record is not, as the popular cliché maintains, solely connected with industrial relations, nor is it due mainly to attitudinal shortcomings on the part of British workers. Two central theses of Nichols' book – that education and training of the workforce are important determinants of productivity and that management is as much responsible for levels of productivity as workers – are also upheld in this work. The first of these will be discussed in the following pages, and the impact of management on production organization will be considered in greater detail in Chapters 4 and 5.

Despite the problems of making accurate comparative measurements of productivity, the existence of a large British productivity gap is not in doubt. There exist a whole number of meticulous comparative studies of matched plants which show convincingly the vast differences in both labour and investment productivity between British and German plants. According to Prais's study of matched plants in 1976 (1981a: 56) for example, output per employee was about 50 per cent higher in Germany than in Britain, and the study by Daly et al. (1985: 51) established an average differential of about 63 per cent. Pratten (1976: 81–105) notes that labour productivity per hour is also lower than in France, and this finding is confirmed by other, more broadly-based matched comparisons of firms (Gallie, 1978; Dubois, 1981; Grünberg, 1986). During the 1980s, however, worker productivity in Britain has greatly increased, due to the partial elimination of restrictive practices but also to the drastic decline in manufacturing capacity which has swept away the weaker and probably less efficient firms. But the gap with Germany, although diminished, has not been closed (Daly et al., 1985: 48, footnote 1).

Worker productivity is affected by a number of factors, such as insufficient investment in modern technology, industrial relations problems, managerial incompetence and low level of skill and motivation in the labour force. It is difficult to separate out the importance of the various factors, but there is now a large body of opinion which holds the skill level of the labour force to be a crucial impact on productivity.

The link between training and productivity can occur in a number of ways. Daly el al. (1985) have emphasized strongly the great importance of technical skill in relation to choosing, installing, handling and maintaining production machinery as well as for buying material. Skilled technical and managerial staff are vital for choosing the right kinds of machine. They are better able to assess the risks and potential of new machinery, and they are more likely to buy technologically more advanced products. The comparative study of new (microelectronics-based) technology in manufacturing industry by Northcott et al. (1985: 2, 6) found that, although Germany is only slightly more advanced than Britain and France in the percentage of factories using the new technology in production processes and products, it is far more ahead in the rate of enterprises using the technically most advanced processes and machinery, such as CAD, CNC machine tools and flexible manufacturing systems. The purchase of the right raw materials by skilled staff, too, has important consequences both for the number of rejects produced and for the quality of the finished product. Once the new machines are installed, skilled technical staff and workers are more resourceful and successful in repairing them and keeping them well maintained. Maitland (1983), for example, points out that workers in the German plant of his matched pair engaged in routine weekly cleaning sessions of their machines whereas British workers neglected cleaning and generally misused machinery. If workers themselves can handle small repairs there will be less machine down-time and loss of production. A body of skilled technical, supervisory and manual workers will also enable a firm to produce more technically sophisticated products and to adapt products more easily and quickly in response to market changes. Sengenberger (1984a: 30) connects worker versatility, acquired through systematic exposure to different work stations during the period of training, with the higher rate of productivity and international competitiveness of German industry. German employers themselves, too, connect the high quality and technical sophistication of German goods with the high skill profile of their labour force (IMS, 1984).

Underqualified staff and workers, in contrast, use new machines below capacity or cause frequent breakdowns. If staff and workers possess narrow skills the resulting high degree of division of labour between various categories of technical and supervisory staff and workers will often result in large numbers working in parallel. This causes wasteful disputes and longer machine down-times. A last negative implication of a national industrial labour force with a low skill profile is the poor availability of home-produced sophisticated machinery which, in turn, has obvious implications for repairs and machine down-times. Daly et al. (1985) find all these positive and negative consequences related to the respective skill structures of the matched samples of German and British firms, Although they concede that skill structure may not be the only factor affecting productivity, they nevertheless regard it as a highly important one.

The nature of the training system also affects the ease with which employees adapt to technical change. The German system, being geared to life-long training and to progression from lower to higher stages of training, is considered to be well adapted to fast technical change and the accompanying human capital depreciation (Weiermair, 1986: 5). The French and British systems, in contrast, provide far less chances for older workers to acquire a new type of initial training or to progress to higher levels of skill. These differences between the training systems go some way towards explaining the faster adoption of the most sophisticated new technological devices/processes by German as compared with French and British industry (see the data by Northcott, 1985). They also explain the marked superiority of German over British firms in export markets for products with high-technology components (e.g. cars, machine tools). The German advantage over France in this respect is less striking, probably due to the high degree of engineering expertise in the latter country.

Improvements of the skill structure do not only increase overall efficiency and competitiveness but they also have positive consequences for individual workers and staff. Raised skill levels increase the degree of work satisfaction, the opportunity for further occupational advancement and the degree of employment security. The latter is particularly important at the present time when rapid technological change and consequent structural reorganization are affecting manual workers to a high degree. Skilled workers are more likely to adapt to new job demands and can be redeployed more flexibly within a changed organizational structure, provided unions do not practise demarcation. Greater certainty of their continued usefulness rids skilled workers of fears of job and earning losses. This, in turn, benefits the organization in that it is less likely to be confronted with resistance to change. A more homogeneous skill structure will also reduce some of the social divisions and social distance between workers and staff and improve communication and cooperation between different levels of the hierarchy.

NOTES

1. See Mant (1978); Glover (1978); Prais (1981b); Sengenberger (1984a); Daly et al. (1985); NEDO (1984); Wiener (1981).
2. At the beginning of 1986 12 per cent of trainees had qualified for admission to university or an institution of equivalent status (*CEDEFOP News*, 4, 1986).
3. The Work Promotion Act (*Arbeitsförderungsgesetz* – AFG) was to lay down a set of standards for determining what forms and subjects of further training were to be most useful in the context of labour market policy objectives. The Vocational Training Act (*Berufsbildungsgesetz* – BBiG) created the framework for structuring and organizing the subjects of further training (CEDEFOP, 1987: 102).

4 Managers and Management Style

Management must be viewed as the key source of any business organization's success. One of the reasons for the poor performance of British industry in the postwar period is widely held to be the low quality of British management in relation to its continental competitors. This chapter is concerned to establish the processes which have moulded the social identity and self-image of managers in the three European societies and to indicate how the latter, in turn, have shaped management style, i.e. the way managers approach the tasks which constitute their job.

Definitions of a manager/managerial work abound. Managers' work is so varied and fragmented that it is extremely difficult to compress it into simple definitions (see Mintzberg, 1973). Definitional problems become magnified in a comparative study which includes countries outside the Anglo-Saxon cultural tradition. The following definition is intended as an introductory, rough approximation which will be further elaborated in the country comparisons of managers/management style. Managers occupy positions of leadership within an organization, and they are required to carry out some or all of the following functions:

1. to formulate policy for, and plan the development of, the organizational unit for which they are responsible;
2. to organize and co-ordinate work and allocate responsibility; and
3. to check that performance is according to plan, i.e. to exercise control.

The emphasis on leadership, as well as on the three broad functional areas, will differ according to position in the managerial hierarchy as will the scope of managerial responsibility. Whereas the top manager is responsible for the whole organization and concentrates disproportionately on the tasks outlined under 1, middle and lower/junior management lead organizational/functional sub-units and deal mainly with the tasks detailed under 2 and 3. Junior managers differ from middle managers by the lesser scope of responsibility and the fact that they have no other managers reporting to them. But this tripartite division is not adhered to in all empirical studies, nor is it always made clear where management stops and supervisory levels start. Differences in this respect are often indicative of national organizational differences, and they will be indicated in the country comparisons.

The management functions outlined above – also referred to as the management process – and the managerial hierarchy established around it exist in similar form in all three European societies. But the *way* these functions are carried out – the so-called management style – has been found to differ significantly between these societies. It is shaped by a number of factors: the pattern and pace of national industrial development and the way this has moulded the institutional framework impinging on the business organization; the political culture of the wider society; and last, but not least, the social origins and pre-entry education of managers. (Post-entry management education/development is seen as less formative in its impact, though by no means unimportant, and, for reasons of space, will not be covered in this book.) Because social origin and, more so, education determine to a large extent how managers view themselves and how they are perceived by their society, these factors are particularly important influences on management style. A detailed comparative study of these management characteristics and of the way they shape self-identity and status in society will therefore precede the analysis of management style.

MANAGERS IN COMPARATIVE PERSPECTIVE

The word 'manager' is of Anglo-American origin and has entered French and German usage only in recent decades. In France and Germany the term still coexists, and competes with, indigenous titles which have different social and organizational implications. It is interesting, though, that the term 'manager' and the American connotations attached to it have been more easily accepted in France than in Germany, contrary to the stereotype of the Americanization of German society and business culture perpetuated by some authors (e.g. Berghahn, 1985).

In *France* managers are referred to by the collective term *cadres* who constitute a legally defined group enjoying certain common privileges, e.g. in the areas of insurance and collective bargaining. The term *cadres* is understood in both a wide sense, which includes other groups with professional expertise, such as doctors, civil servants, etc., and in a narrow sense, referring to managers only. But this grouping together is significant in as far as managers and civil servants tend to have gone through the same educational process and, often, early professional socialization. They adhere to a similar bureaucratic ethos which is preoccupied with hierarchy and discipline and not primarily with profit-making (Levy-Leboyer, 1980: 133). The French *cadre* of managers is more exclusive and clearly defined than is the group of managers in Britain where the term often includes anyone who supervises an operation or a person. Management status and pay are graduated as precisely as in a military context – a stark contrast to the informal and loose British system. The French terms *cadres dirigeants*, *supérieurs* and *moyens* can be taken to be rough equivalents of top, higher and middle management. Another less formal indigenous French term, 'patron', referring originally to the owner-manager, is also used more widely and indicates a distinct management style.

In *Germany* the word 'manager' still competes with *Unternehmer* (entrepreneur)[1] when reference is made to the top of the business hierarchy, i.e. to the *Geschäftsführer* in smaller GmbH companies or to the chair of the management board or the whole board in AG-type companies. Most small to medium-sized companies do not use the term 'manager' at all. The persistence of the term *'Unternehmer'*, with its connotations of economic risk taking and creativity, is indicative of the long survival of owner managers in the many medium-sized and even in several large enterprises[2] as, for example, in the firms of Siemens, Thyssen and Bosch. All managers below this top level are referred to by the administrative term *Leitende Angestellte* (leading employees) which includes both line and staff. The less formal and more widely used title for managers, however, is the word *Führungskräfte* – the word *Führung* indicating the German emphasis on leadership in defining the management role. Many studies of German management operate with only two levels of authority below board level, i.e. head of division (*Hauptabteilungsleiter*) and head of department (*Abteilungsleiter*), and lower management is rarely mentioned. This may be indicative of the shorter organisational hierarchy which has been commented upon in Chapter 2.

SOCIAL ORIGINS OF MANAGERS

Top and higher managers in all three societies are recruited from relatively high social strata and infrequently come from working-class origins. But a social élite appears to be more prominent among British and French than among German managers.[3] In Britain the public school system and Oxbridge attract and recreate a social élite, and titled members are still prized and prominent in boardrooms. In France the *grandes écoles* recruit form, and turn out, a similarly exclusive social group which is, however, at the same time an intellectual élite. In Germany, in contrast, a social élite (aristocracy) was destroyed by the two world wars, and the education system has no equivalents to the French and British élite institutions. Finally, in all three societies managers, particularly at top and middle levels, are overwhelmingly of male sex. Despite the recent influx of women into management education, senior managers in both France and Germany have remained at the 4 per cent level and are unlikely to be higher in Britain (*Manager Magazin* 11, 1986: 342; NEDO, 1987: 75). In 1984 women constituted only 2.51 per cent of members of the British Institute of Management (Equal Opportunities Commission, 1986). Management below board level is more diverse in terms of social origins, and men of working-class origins have been able to work their way up the hierarchy in all three societies. The proportion of managers who started their occupational lives in a manual occupation is particularly high in Britain. Thus a recent survey of general managers in large firms (Edwards, 1987: 41) established that 38 per cent – the single largest category – could be classified in this way.

MANAGEMENT EDUCATION

In all three societies the larger companies now choose their future top and higher managers predominantly from among graduates, but the differences in level and kind of education possessed by European managers remain profound between France and Germany, on the one side, and Britain, on the other. This is partly a legacy of past practice in that French and German firms have chosen their managers from among graduates for a much longer period than have British companies, but even at the present time significant differences in management qualifications remain. Comparative data from the 1970s and early 1980s, collected by NEDO (1987: 2, Table 1), suggest a sharp contrast between the British proportion of only 24 per cent of graduate managers and the French and German proportions of 65 and 62 per cent, respectively.

In *France* industry and profit-making have long been disparaged, but more recently attitudes have changed considerably. Business executives, particularly of large companies, now enjoy a higher prestige, and companies have no problem attracting management recruits of the highest academic calibre from the élite *grandes écoles*. Graduates are also recruited from the universities and the technical institutes below university level which have, in recent years, become more oriented towards the needs of industry. But by far the highest proportion of all managers in all age groups come from the *grandes écoles* (NEDO, 1987: 7). Although managers also come up from the ranks – the *autodidactes* (self-made men) – the latter are mostly former technicians whereas men of worker origin are now a rarity in the larger companies. According to INSEE (the French National Statistics Office) (1985) statistics on *cadres d'entreprises* (industrial cadres, including staff and line), 69 per cent have at least the *baccalauréat* or bac and a further 37 per cent have the bac + 4/5, i.e. four to five years higher education (NEDO, 1987: 64). These latter figures are for managers in all size categories of enterprises, and they reflect the fact that managers even in SMEs are relatively highly educated in France. Vickery (1986: 24) reports that in the early 1980s nearly half of chief executives in SMEs in all economic sectors had a higher education qualification.

Among managers with tertiary education, the majority have an engineering qualification, usually from a *grande école*. The strong bias towards engineering has a long tradition in French society and was present among military leaders and civil servants before it penetrated industry. Among younger managers (25–35 year old) engineers constituted 74.3 per cent, of which nearly 50 per cent came from a *grande école* (NEDO, 1987: 7, Table 2). Most of the others had a background in law or business economics, also predominantly acquired in one of the élite institutions. Graduates with a pure arts background have no chance to enter management in France.

As education from the *grandes écoles* has this predominant influence on French managers it is pertinent to examine its content. The emphasis in these institutions is on mastery of quantitative techniques, rapid problem-solving and abstract/analytical reasoning. Whereas some commentators see this education as broadly relevant to the work managers do within large organizations, e.g. Glover (1978: 176), others regard French managers as having an excessively theoretical cast of mind. Rose (1985: 72), for example, described managers from engineering *écoles supérieurs* as follows:

> Higher managers . . . may well be capable of deploying their abstract expertise with brilliance to those problems reserved for their attention. But these generals of the industrial army would never be able to base any claim to lead 'the charge with the spanner' upon their experience of tightening nuts.

This criticism of managers' lack of practical understanding is echoed widely at the present time and is often added to the charge that top managers lack interpersonal skills and have an insufficiently developed international orientation. In recent decades American ideas of management have begun to have a strong impact. They have caused some higher schools to move away from a narrowly technical emphasis and to give more emphasis to qualities of personal leadership and decision-making (NEDO, 1987: 67).

It is also due to American influence that business schools have now become prominent in France. A comparative study by Whitley et al. (1981) found that, in comparison with British business schools, the French recruit students from a significantly higher social background and that course content is more practically oriented. Lastly, it is notable that attendance of top American business schools has been gaining ground and that it has become a passport for gaining access to the most coveted jobs in industry.

In *Britain* a career in industry has also traditionally been held in low esteem, and many graduates have gone into industry as a last resort. More recently, attitudes of graduates have begun to change, but many of the ablest students from the top universities still disdain a career in industry. Although British industry recruits from élite schools and universities it does not attract the ablest products of these institutions. Of the three societies, Britain has the lowest proportion of graduates both among top management – 24 per cent – and among all management (NEDO, op. cit.). The very low figure of only 12.5 per cent of all managers with a first or higher degree, given by the 1985 British Labour Force Survey, must be understood in the context of the British loose definition of 'manager' and as such is not strictly comparable to the more exclusive continental categories. British managers, at all levels, are more likely to have a professional qualification, gained in part-time courses at colleges of further education or from professional institutes, such as ONC/OND, HNC/HND, (NEDO, 1987; Lee, 1981). A sizeable proportion of British managers have come up from the ranks and possess no post-school qualifications at all (ibid.). Lastly, only a small proportion of managers – 10 per cent – have a 'craft' qualification (*Labour Force Survey*, GB, 1985; Lee, 1981: 55). The proportion of managers with no post-school qualifications at all appears to be particularly high in small and medium-sized firms, but it is by no means insignificant even in large firms. Of the owner-managers of Britain's top 100 owner-managed firms, a mere five per cent have a degree and 91 per cent have qualifications of O'-level standard or below (*The British Entrepreneur 1988*, quoted in *The Independent*, 29 December 1988).

When we examine the content of the degrees held by British managers, a stark contrast with continental patterns emerges. In the 1970s less than a third of graduate managers had an engineering degree, and managers with an arts background were common (Glover, 1978). In recent years, there has been a steady increase in the intake of graduates with a management/business degree. Also more people with engineering and science qualifications have moved into industry. But these remain very often in staff positions and relatively rarely make it into top management posts. In contrast to the situation in France and Germany, British engineers, according to Glover and Kelly (1987: 28), are employed as technical specialists 'whose assumed lack of wider knowledge and social skills makes them ineligible for promotion to top management posts'. Although the under-representation of engineers at top level has been widely criticized (e.g. by the Finniston Report in 1978), change in this respect has been slow. (For a lively discussion of the problems of engineers in gaining access to management positions, see Armstrong, 1987.) In this context it is interesting to note that the most recent report on management education (Constable and McCormick, 1987: 12) does not mention engineering at all when it examines university programmes which qualify for management work. In the British context, a degree in accounting is held to be an ideal qualification for a top management post. Generally, it remains true to say that the promotion to top level posts of 'gifted amateurs' remains a uniquely British phenomenon. Lastly, since the middle 1960s Britain has followed the American example of founding business schools which provide a general management education at a high level.

In *Germany*, executive jobs in manufacturing industry have for a long time enjoyed a high prestige,[5] and firms have no problem in attracting highly-qualified staff. The Anglo-Saxon concept of management as a unified profession is still not accepted. Consequently, there exists no general management education in Germany. Executive staff see themselves primarily as specialists in a certain field – as *Techniker* or *Kaufmann* (on the technical or commercial side) – who have taken on extra responsibility by executing some of the management functions outlined in the introduction. Promotion in the German enterprise follows this functionally specialized route and retraining across functions is relatively rare. But it must be remembered that this functional specialization occurs relatively late in the educational system and that university entrants have a broad educational base on which to build. In addition to functional responsibility, a top manager also takes on responsibility for a geographical area. The latter is meant to keep him/her in touch with the more mundane aspects of management work (*The Economist*, 15 October 1988: 108). Managers may still come up from the ranks, but top and senior managers in large firms are now predominantly graduates from either a university or a polytechnic (*Fachhochschule*).

The majority of graduates possess a degree in engineering which has a strong vocational component and includes a 'practical' in industry, particularly at the *Fachhochschule*. Although the latter type of engineer (Ing. Grad.) is very popular among German employers, the university-educated Dip. Ing. is more likely to reach the top level in large firms. Those with engineering qualifications also command the highest salaries in all types of firms (*Manager Magazin*, 11, 1986: 343). To enable them to move into top management positions engineers and scientists (in the chemical industry) often receive in-firm training in basic economics, accounting and EDP. A second widely-read subject is business economics, and law is also regarded as a useful qualification. There appears to be a shift away from the strong focus on engineering among younger managers. Thus a survey of 4360 young actual or aspiring managers, competing for the title of 'Manager of Tomorrow', established that 51.9 per cent had studied economic sciences (*Wirtschaftswissenschaften*) and only 24.2 per cent engineering (ibid.: 340). Among the economic sciences, business economics (*Betriebswirtschaft*) is by far the most frequently read subject, and, during the 1980s, it has gained greatly in popularity. As the name indicates, this subject focuses on the various business functions, rather than being concerned with management or the process of managing. It is generally very practically oriented. A more detailed breakdown of the level and, to a lesser extent, kind of education of top, higher and middle managers in the early 1980s is provided in Figure 4.1.

A high proportion (over 50 per cent) of top managers have a doctorate, usually in science or engineering (NEDO, 1987: 2, Figure 1). Many managers at all levels have also served an apprenticeship (Lawrence, 1980), and a vocational qualification, in contrast to the situation in France, is highly valued by employers. A recent survey of younger managers brought out that those with an apprenticeship and/or a doctorate commanded the highest salaries. Managers with a first degree and an apprenticeship received higher salaries than those with a business school diploma. (*Manager Magazin*, 11, 1986: 343). Generally speaking, qualificational levels are appreciably higher on the technical than on the administrative or commercial side (Lawrence, 1980). A post-graduate management education is uncommon. Because the concept of management is still not fully accepted in Germany there exist no business schools. Although German firms encourage an internationally-oriented outlook – fluency in a foreign language and a spell of study or work abroad are highly thought of – Germans are notable for their absence at top American business schools (NEDO, 1987: 46). But MBAs are sought after by the large multinational companies, and a minority of younger managers are beginning to acquire this higher degree.

Figure 4.1 The educational qualifications of top, higher (senior) and middle management in Germany (%)

	University	Poly-technic (economic studies)	Poly-technic (technical studies)	'A' level	'O' level	'CSE' level	No reply
Managing directors	46	6	10	11	16	6	5
First level (e.g. head of division)	34	7	14	9	23	9	3
Second level (e.g. head of department)	21	5	18	7	26	14	9

Sources: Institut der deutschen Wirtschaft, 1985 and Kienbaum Vergütungsberatung, 1984, quoted by NEDO (1987: 45)

The long educational preparation (German university courses last on average between five and six years, and longer if a doctorate is pursued), the obligation to do national service and, frequently, the serving of an apprenticeship mean that German managers are in their late twenties when they enter a firm and usually 30 before they begin to wield managerial authority. Promotion after this is still mainly internal and slow. There is little hope of reaching the *Vorstand* level before the age of 40 and, more often, managers have to wait until they are between 50 and 60 years of age (*Capital*, 7, 1987: 114).

In conclusion, how do the three societies grow and cultivate their managers? Which qualities and qualifications are looked for and secure promotion in European industrial enterprises? Despite some improvement in recent years, *British* managers continue to appear under-educated in comparison with their continental competitors. British companies still put a stronger emphasis on pragmatism rather than professionalism (NEDO, 1987: 10). Personal qualities and background appear to be given a disproportionate emphasis. A recent enquiry about qualities and attributes deemed desirable in good managers, conducted by Mangham and Silver (1986), bears out this claim. It established that a vague leadership quality/motivating ability received the most frequent mention, both in relation to top and middle managers, whereas more functional attributes received only a low emphasis. Where managers are highly qualified for their work a generalist management education is the norm. Promotion in British firms occurs at a much younger age than in Germany, and it is usually gained by moving between firms rather than by long-term loyal service to one company. Here it is interesting to note, though, that nearly all the 23 companies, deemed to be Britain's best by Goldsmith and Clutterbuck (1984: 77f), adhered to the continental pattern of promotion from within. Chief executives of the firms argued that such internal promotion and long-term service was the only way to secure internalization of the company culture and to evoke a close identification with its objectives.

German firms also put a high value on individual qualities, such as leadership ability, but they demand these in addition to a high professional standard in a functional area. Here it is notable that professional virtuosity in engineering is prized above all and that desirable management candidates must be strong in terms of both theoretical and practical competence. Promotion is according to professional merit and loyalty to the firm.

In *France*, too, managers are first and foremost selected for their educational qualifications. In contrast to German firms, practical competence is undervalued, and the British emphasis on interpersonal skills has only been taken on board very recently. Management remains a somewhat rarified and remote social and educational élite. Promotion to top positions in large firms is largely confined to this élite, and access through in-firm mobility of recruits from other backgrounds is precluded in large companies.

MANAGEMENT STYLE

Analysts of management style have examined management–employee relations by applying a variety of typologies ranging from highly sophisticated ones with many different types (e.g. Purcell and Sisson, 1983) to simple dichotomous, i.e. two-type ones. (Types do not necessarily correspond to empirically observable phenomena but contain a bundle of logically related attributes, abstracted from reality, which are then used to analyse social phenomena.) In the case of dichotomous typologies, positions on a continuum between two extreme poles are envisaged. Alternatively, managerial style can be considered to be less exclusive and elements of both types can be held to be present in the behaviour of a given group of managers, depending on the context. The following tripartite comparison of national management style, drawing on a range of dispersed secondary data, has to confine itself to the use of simple dichotomies. Such simple dichotomies cannot encompass the large variety in styles within societies, differing between industries, firms, hierarchical levels and functional areas, and should only be regarded as pointing towards dominant national tendencies which express broad value orientations. In the first part, a distinction will be made between the styles of 'social sensibility' and 'production emphasis' which have also been called 'employee-centred' and 'job-centred' styles. The two sets of terms will be used interchangeably. In the second part the 'democratic-autocratic' management style dichotomy will be applied. As was made clear at the beginning of this chapter, these kinds of management style are *not* being connected with personality traits or equally vague national characteristics but are viewed as the result of typical nationally specific institutional constraints and educational characteristics, which are themselves socially determined.

Employee vs. Job-centred Style

An employee-centred style characterizes managers whose behaviour is orientated towards needs and relationships. They are approachable and helpful; listen to subordinates' suggestions and try to get their consent;

and they give recognition to good performance. Managers with a 'production' emphasis are task-oriented. They emphasize production and the achievements of organizational goals, plan ahead and decide how things are going to get done; they make expectations clear, emphasize deadlines and the achievement of objectives; and they expect subordinates to follow instructions closely. This management outlook does not necessarily imply an absence of concern for employees but can stimulate enthusiasm to achieve objectives as well as encouraging and helping employees to get the work done.

This typology of management style is implicit in a lot of writing contrasting German and British management behaviour. It has not been systematically referred to in the analysis of French management behaviour. Isolated comments (e.g. Dyas and Thanheiser, 1976: 38; Levy-Leboyer, 1980: 153; Telesis, 1986) suggest that French management style is closer to the German than British pattern but that it nevertheless differs in crucial respects. Due to lack of data, the discussion of French management style in the framework of this typology will have to be brief and summary.

A comparative study by Budde et al. (1982), examining the goals and objectives held by top German and British managers during the late 1970s, implies such a typology, although the authors themselves draw out slightly different implications. Thus they hypothesize that British managers display greater concern for the well-being of subordinates and their personal development than German ones, whereas the latter make greater use of procedures to minimize control loss than do their British counterparts (Hypothesis VII) (ibid.: 10). They see Hypothesis VII confirmed by their finding that (a) British managers see high profitability as more important for attracting good managers, providing a larger cake for everybody, and maintaining a high morale among the workforce; (b) British managers explain their emphasis on growth by giving employee-related and personal benefit reasons whereas German ones relate theirs more to the company future, emphasizing the pay-off of growth for product and capital market position (ibid.: 14–15). Most revealing are the replies Budde et al., (ibid.) received to the question as to what gives managers most job satisfaction. British managers certainly rate employee-centred reasons consistently much higher but most of the time they are focusing on the benefits to *themselves*, rather than to subordinate groups: high income, promotion prospects and personal prestige inside and outside the company. German managers, in contrast, focus much less on their own development, but give the greatest emphasis to task-related sources of satisfaction. They display a high level of agreement with such suggestions as 'intrinsic interest derived from solving problems and dealing with the complexity of your job'; 'ability to influence important events within your company'; 'satisfaction you give to your customers' (ibid.: 17, Table 6).

Some of these differences might be explained by the different national approaches to promotion. The German pattern of in-firm promotion and long assocation with one firm is said to be conducive to the development of long-term business horizons and of loyalty to the firm and its objectives (NEDO, 1981: 14; Bessant and Grunt, 1985). In Britain, in contrast, the more frequent external promotion and the attendant changes of job make managers more intent on achieving short-term financial gains to further their own career and impede a strong identification with the firm's longer term goals.

Budde et al. (1982) appear to relate the British managerial responses to the concept of an employee-centred management style, but they do not counterpose a German job-centred style. Instead, they label the German style as authoritarian, implying that authoritarianism is necessarily the other side of the coin of a job-centred style. Generally, these authors can be said to perpetuate rather uncritically the popular stereotypes that 'British management is good at handling people' and 'German management is authoritarian', ignoring any evidence which might contradict these claims, such as the relatively poor British record in handling industrial relations (see Chapter 8). Whether or not a job-centred and an authoritarian management style are logically inseparable and whether the label 'authoritarian' is still illuminating when applied to German management style will be investigated in more detail below. First, evidence will be adduced from other sources to show that the less value-laden employee versus job-centred dichotomy is useful for the analysis of British and German management behaviour. It will be further suggested that a production-centred style does not preclude a concern for employees' welfare but, on the contrary, can be successfully combined with it.

Strong support for the idea that a production emphasis is highly developed in Germany, but not in Britain, and that it cannot be equated with authoritarianism, comes from the work of Lawrence (1980 and 1988). Lawrence brings out clearly how the basic function of a manufacturing organization – to design and manufacture high-quality and reliable products – is still central to German management concerns and consistently informs management style. Such a production-orientation is inculcated by education and training at all hierarchical levels and thus is diffused right through the enterprise. Hence it has no negative consequences for management–employee relations. On the contrary, it provides an integrating mechanism which is so often absent in British enterprises. A strong task-orientation generates a sense of common purpose and of shared responsibility for production. A production-orientation also implies a product-orientation, i.e. a concern for, and pride in, a high-quality product with which the firm becomes identified. It thus evokes a deep loyalty to, and proprietary instincts about, the firm. Analysts from a different cultural background are liable to misinterpret this worker–management relation in terms of managerial authoritarianism and worker submissiveness. Although this loyalty of a skilled man to a skilled team and pride in both product and firm can also be found in the best British firms (see Goldsmith and Clutterbuck, 1984) it remains an exception rather than the rule. Lawrence's observation of German managers' interactions with subordinates in meetings convinced him that, in comparison with Britain, the tone of meetings was less deferential. He experienced vigorous and outspoken contributions from junior participants, including foremen, and noted the prevalence of direct criticism of superiors and its ready acceptance by them (Lawrence, 1988: 104).

That a strong production-orientation in German enterprises does not exclude a concern with human relations is confirmed by many sources. Bessant and Grunt (1985: 322) point out that corporate identity, particularly of SMEs, often has two focal points: a strong product orientation and a family ideology. This is supported by Millar (1974) who concluded from her German–British comparison that 'German management appeared to be *more* concerned about "human relations" or "people issues" than their UK counterparts. This concern revealed itself in a greater preoccupation with the quality of working life on the shop floor' (ibid.: 56, 57). This aspect of management style will receive further consideration in the discussion of paternalism in the second part of this chapter.

These different orientations of British and German managers are expressed in different professional identities. Whereas British top business executives see themselves in generalist terms as managers, German ones describe themselves first and foremost as specialists in certain fields who have taken on more responsibility than their colleagues (Glover, 1978: 170). These different professional identities also find expression in divergent conceptions of authority at all levels of the managerial hierarchy. Whereas German managerial–supervisory staff base their authority on knowledge and expertise in a given field (what Lawrence, 1980, calls 'sapiental' authority), their British counterparts claim 'positional authority', i.e. authority based merely on management status. The latter is clearly a more precarious basis for securing subordinates' compliance and hence necessitates greater efforts in building up relationships.

It is, of course, not implied by the foregoing that a task orientation is absent among British managers, only that it is not primarily a production orientation. Instead, we find a strong concern with financial performance which, because it is a top management task, does not have the same total impact on management styles as it is expressed in management–employee relations. This difference in priorities of British and German managers is aptly summarized by Lawrence (1980: 142) when he says: 'British managers think industry is about making money: Germans that it is about making three-dimensional artefacts.' The higher importance accorded to the financial task in Britain and the production task in Germany also receives clear expression in the differential status and career prospects associated with these two specialisms in Britain and Germany respectively (for details see Lawrence, 1984: 46f).

At this point it is appropriate to explore briefly whether the typology contrasting a production orientation with a style characterized by social sensibility can be used to analyse French management style. It will be obvious from earlier references to French management–employee relations that a steep hierarchy and cold and distant relations are incompatible with the 'social sensibility' style. According to a study of French corporate strategy by Telesis (1986), a production orientation is also underdeveloped. Background and education induce management to cultivate a technology rather than a production orientation. French managers' highly theoretical engineering education makes them pursue brilliant invention and conceptually excellent design, regardless of overall costs, as typified, for example, in the design and production of Concorde. Conversely, their training causes them to disdain the more mundane and practical tasks of the production engineer, and implementation of strategy is often poor (*The Economist*, 15 October 1988: 107). The French engineer's quest for technological breakthrough may be contrasted with his German colleague's interest in the commercial application of inventions. Very few of the *grandes écoles* even teach production management, and French firms generally do not reward this function very highly. This lack of a production orientation among French managers has resulted in a relatively low interest in skill development for the entire labour force (ibid.: 45). Thus, although French management can base their authority on technical excellence, they do not use their knowledge and skill to integrate subordinates around a common task.

These basic differences in management orientation, coupled with the German and French tendency to place engineers in top management positions and the British to favour accountants, has been explained in a variety of ways. Armstrong (1987) connects the British pattern with the lack of integration between industrial and financial capital and the consequent problems of management to raise investment capital and ascribes the German productionist orientation to the ease with which management has been able to obtain capital, due to the close connections between industry and banking. But such an explanation ignores the fact that a concern for technical expertise exists at all levels of the German business enterprise and a disdain for it at all levels of the British enterprise (as well as in the civil service and the whole system of education) and that it is not merely a characteristic of management. This explanation also breaks down when the French case is included in the comparison. In France we find the same strong emphasis on engineering as a management qualification as in Germany but not the same close cooperation between banking and industry. A more persuasive historical explanation is offered by Landes (1969: 53). Speaking about Britain in the eighteenth century, Landes states that 'this readiness to . . . place profit above craft pride . . . implies a certain separation of the producer from production, an orientation to the market instead of the shop.' He links this orientation to the early opportunities in Britain to produce for large 'captive' colonial markets which generated pressures to put quantity before quality. In Germany and in France, in contrast, such market pressures did not exist at the beginning of their industrialization processes.

These contrasting management styles are the expression of different values and attitudes which have been shaped over a long period of history and which have been acquired by those in management positions through socialization and education. The process of education, in particular, is of central importance in reproducing not only technical skills but also basic value orientations. The strong technical bias in German and French but not British education is of a long standing and precedes the rise of corporate employed managers as a 'mass' occupation. A top management position in German non-family firms is strictly the reward for prolonged high performance (members of the *Vorstand* are usually between 45 and 60 years old). British boardrooms, in contrast, are still populated by a significant proportion of members of a social élite who owe their positions to the social skills they are believed to possess and the status they lend. Their ideas of leadership, acquired in the élite schools, have not only had a significant impact on management–employee relations, they have also influenced the priorities adopted in the larger British enterprises. The public school ethos, with its 'minimal concept of government' which traditionally saw 'the ruler as a guardian rather than an innovator' and which reacted to any threat to the old order by accommodation (Wilkinson, 1964: 4, 62, in Fox, 1985) set the tone in industry also for those who came from a different background (see also Wiener, 1981). Dore (1973: 251) draws out the implications of management's social image and languid aristocratic style for the legitimacy of the authority system, as perceived by subordinates. He speaks of resentment against management based on the belief that the latter are overprivileged, inefficient and owe their jobs to influence rather than merit. In the smaller British enterprises, in contrast, the social ethos of the 'self-made' man who has risen from the shopfloor is often dominant. In such enterprises, as Bessant and Grunt (1985) have shown, the management style is often much closer to the German pattern although the emphasis is less professionalist and more on 'learning by doing'.

The earlier review of British top managers' education has emphasized that it is infrequently a technical education and that a large proportion of British managers possess no higher educational qualification at all. The promotion of 'amateurs' to top level, who often possess no more than a vague quality of leadership, is hardly conducive to the development of a production orientation and a task-centred style.

A large minority of top managers are, of course, not 'gifted amateurs' but possess a solid management education. Whether or not these 'generalist' managers are well qualified for a top management job and are perhaps even better prepared for their wideranging responsibilities than their German counterparts with a more specialist qualification in engineering is a complex issue. It may be argued that functional specialization in engineering makes German managers too narrow and that a British generalist manager has a much broader vision. Moreover, he can always draw on the technical expertise of those below him. But reality is not as simple as this. German managers who reach board level either have received extra training in business economics or, in the collegiate system, share top management responsibility with a colleague who possesses a business education. British top managers, in contrast, often totally lack support at high level from a technically skilled colleague. Research by Maurice Sage, quoted by Goldsmith and Clutterbuck (1984: 120), has shown that enterprises in the forefront of technological innovation usually have a chief executive directly involved in the innovation process. These authors therefore argue convincingly that the best solution is that a high proportion of managers begin with a thorough technical knowledge and then develop generalist skills. Alternatively, generalist British chief executives ought to take more trouble than is taken at present to work in close harness with a technical expert who is placed in an appropriate position in the managerial hierarchy to make constant influence likely.

At present the educational profiles of British and German managers remain expressed in distinct management styles. Mant (1978: 75) sums this up when he says that 'on the continent the manufacturing tasks forms the basis of role relationships [whereas] British managers see themselves in a 'generalist' management role, somewhat detached from production.' He concludes bluntly, 'a concern with human relations is not a substitute for competence. An extrinsic task assumption leads to phoney interpersonal relations, an intrinsic one to limited, but authentic ones' (ibid.: 76). German standards of performance, it is often suggested, can only be reached at the price of authoritarianism whereas the relatively poor British performance may be the price we pay for democratic management. But the analysis so far has indicated that, far from implying a neglect of human relations, the production-oriented German style has an inbuilt integrating focus which provides a common basis for relationships and encourages cooperative attitudes. The absence of such a task-oriented style in the British enterprise, in contrast, necessitates a conscious effort to work at building and maintaining good relations. The following section, examining the 'democratic vs. autocratic' management style typology, will further investigate the claim that an authoritarian management style necessarily follows from a strongly developed production-orientation.

Democratic vs. Autocratic (and/or Paternalist) Management Style

The following section investigates what qualities of management–employee relations are implied by this dichotomy; how prevalent they are in our three societies; whether this typology can be taken as synonymous with the one dealt with on previous pages; and, lastly, what influences may have shaped these styles. The terms 'autocratic' and 'authoritarian' are used as synonyms in the literature, and this practice will also be followed here. The 'democratic' style is also referred to as 'participative' or as 'semi-constitutional' style, and the three terms will be used interchangeably here, too. A democratic or participative managerial style prevails when subordinates are consulted in decision-making and are given wide opportunity to exercise discretion in their work. People practising participative management are said to believe that subordinates are motivated to do jobs well. They have developed a relation of trust. An authoritarian style, in contrast, is characterized by the belief that subordinates are indolent and/or uncooperative and that they require strong direction and control if discipline and efficiency are to be maintained. Consequently, good human relations are felt to be irrelevant to getting work done.

An authoritarian management style often appears in the literature in close association with a paternalist style. Although the latter contains some elements of the former, they are *not* synonymous. A paternalist management style is characterized by a belief that subordinates are less capable than their superiors and have to be treated like children. The owner/manager has to protect his employees not only from the hazards of life but also from their own weaknesses. But paternalism implies a benevolent employer attitude, emphasizing the reward of good be-haviour, usually by the provision of good working conditions and a range of welfare facilities. This generosity is motivated by the belief that it will secure subordinates' attachment to, and dependence on, the firm and thus elicit good work performance. Paternalist managers will listen to their subordinates but insist on retaining full management discretion. It is clear from these definitions that both authoritarian and paternalist mana-gers eschew delegation of authority and participation in decision-making by subordinates because the latter are not seen as equals. But whereas the authoritarian management style is essentially seen as malevolent because it completely disregards the needs of subordinates, the paternalist style is informed by a concern for their welfare. These two styles are obviously closer to each other than each is to the participative style. In practice, they are often merged as when rewards are used to manipulate the work behaviour of subordinates. Hence paternalism will also be considered in this section. A more sophisticated contemporary paternalism has moved closer to a participative style. This variant no longer emphasizes the 'father–children' relationship but merely utilizes the cultivation of an unbroken firm tradition, of diffuse relationships and personal ties, and the generous provision of benefits to secure attachment and loyalty to the firm. Such firms are not necessarily anti-union although they may prefer consultation to collective bargaining (Edwards, 1987: 142).

How prevalent have these three styles been found to be in the business organizations of France, Britain and Germany? There is a strong consensus in the literature about the nature of French and British management style, whereas the evidence concerning typical patterns of German management behaviour is more contradictory and is in need of closer analysis. As managerial style varies, depending on the level of the hierarchy and on functional area at which interaction takes place, it is useful to analyse styles accordingly.

French Management Style

French management style is commonly characterized as being predomi-nantly autocratic and/or paternalistic. Of the three national business organizations, the French one is said to have the strongest degree of centralization of authority, with the chief executive frequently monopolizing decision-making power on a wide spectrum of issues (Horovitz, 1980: 67; Dyas and Thanheiser, 1976: 246). The Président-Directeur Général enjoys an exalted staus in the company which is unparalleled in Britain and Germany (ibid.). His status is clearly above that of other top management and his authority is completely unquestioned. Strong management control is favoured at all levels of business organization down to the shopfloor.

The management style adopted in relation to shopfloor workers has been well documented by Gallie (1978). He portrays it as a mixture of autocratic and paternalist elements. Management eschew any participation of workers in decision-making and insist on management prerogative on nearly all important issues. There is an unwillingness to involve subordinates in decision-making in any meaningful sense and a low level of concern for gaining the consent of those affected by decision-making. This results in management by fiat or decree, regardless of the consequences in terms of human relations. Management attitudes to workers are characterized by mistrust and coldness and the realization that worker commitment to the achievement of organizational goals is low. The exceptionally high degree (within Europe) of social distance between management and subordinates in the French business enterprise is reflected in great power distance between them, as has been demonstrated by Hofstede's (1979) comparative work. His calculations of Power Distance Indices (PDI)[6] established that the French index is considerably above those calculated for German and British business organizations and closer to the PDIs of developing industrial societies, such as Hong Kong, Columbia and Turkey (ibid.: 105, Table 6.3).

To gain the necessary degree of cooperation in this context of worker disaffection, French management has adopted a two-pronged strategy: first, to limit worker discretion in task performance and to apply detailed and close supervision (see Maurice et al., 1980); secondly, to reward good performance in a highly individualistic way and to make sure that such rewards are clearly seen to be entirely within management's discretion (Gallie, 1978: 182f). An important element of this latter approach is a pay and promotion policy which rewards 'seniority in the family' and good behaviour. Conversely, bad behaviour in the eyes of management, such as the participation in strikes, is punished on an individual basis by a withdrawal of rewards in terms of merit bonuses or promotion chances. The above applies particularly to larger enterprises. In small and medium-sized enterprises employer–employee relations are more direct, and the paternalist approach comes more strongly to the fore. To conclude, the French managerial style is thus

portrayed as being fairly consistent. It is described as basically authoritarian with elements of paternalism. These are, however, applied in a
highly manipulative way which lacks the essentially benevolent attitude
to workers implied by the pure paternalist type of managerial style.
There is fragmentary evidence, though, that this autocratic style is
coming under attack in some quarters. The greater concern in recent
years to develop top managers' interpersonal and communication skills
and the work, within the employers' association CNPF, of a group of
young progressive managers towards the improvement of work organization on the shopfloor (Jenkins, 1981) point towards the emergence of
new and more liberal orientations also in France.

Explanations of why this style has come to prevail in French business
organizations usually point to the historical pattern of industrial development in France. This has been characterized by a much greater and
longer-lasting preponderance of small to medium-sized firms, frequently
under family ownership. Such firms are generally associated with an
extreme degree of centralized control by the owner-manager, opposition to unions and close (in the sense of direct) relations with employees
which take either a paternalist or an authoritarian form. Although the
'large business' sector in multiple ownership has expanded significantly
in France since the late 1950s, owners of small to medium-sized firms
have nevertheless retained a disproportionate amount of influence at
national level. Their management philosophies have frequently prevailed even in those firms where the structural framework is no longer
congruent with this style. The autocratic management style has also
been reinforced by the bureaucratic ethos fostered by the *grandes écoles*
and has been maintained by the system of '*pantouflage*', i.e. the
interlocking of élites from civil service and business hierarchies.

Authoritarian management style is, of course, continually reinforced
by the ideology and policy of the major union federations (see Chapter
7). Such reinforcement is of two kinds. First, the open rejection by these
unions of management goals and of the management hierarchy set up to
achieve them hardens managerial resolve to prevent the achievement of
meaningful worker participation. Secondly, the weakness of the unions
in both numerical and organizational terms convinces management that
they can continue their authoritarian behaviour with impunity. The
exceptionally high degree of social distance in terms of social origins,
status and educational attainment between top management and subordinates further exacerbates the cold and distant quality of human
relations inherent in an authoritarian management style. Lastly, the
general political culture in French society, shaped by the long and
uninterrupted hold on government by Conservative parties (with the

exception of the short socialist interlude of 1981–86),[7] has exerted little pressure on managers to abandon this management style.

British Management Style

The following account describes management style as it has been portrayed up to the early 1980s. More recent changes are not yet sufficiently documented in the literature and can only be briefly referred to at the end of this section. There is wide agreement that control in British business organizations is relatively dispersed and that subordinates are allowed to participate in decision-making at all levels. Top management displays a willingness to delegate to lower management which is supposedly based on trust that the latter will execute tasks to the expected standard. An examination of strategic decision-making by senior managers in British and West German firms by Budde et al. (1982: 23–6) found that, on strategic issues, such as investment decisions, delegation was notably stronger in Britain. Horovitz's (1980) comparative study of top management control found a significantly stronger tendency to delegate across the board among British managers. Most of the production and sales decisions were delegated to local subsidiaries. The latter were also given some leeway in the capital expenditure area (ibid.: 70). Both studies established a much greater willingness to delegate among British as compared with German top managers where operational and personnel categories of decision-making are concerned.

At shopfloor level British management is concerned to achieve the consent of workers to decisions which directly affect their work, (e.g. manning levels) and their terms of employment (Gallie, 1978: 183–4). Until the early 1980s, worker participation in, and, some would even say, worker domination of decision-making at this level has been widespread and at a higher level than in the other two societies. (For details see Wilpert and Rayley, 1984: 45.) But whether this participatory style is based on a feeling of greater trust in workers by management, as Budde et al. (1982) infer, is debatable. The greater separation between conception and execution and the higher degree of supervision of shopfloor workers practised in British as compared with German business organizations (Maurice et al., 1980) hardly bears out a high degree of trust. Also the evidence on evaluation of management style by subordinates gathered by the IDE Research Group (Wilpert and Rayley, 1983: 74), shows a lower estimation of management style in a work relation by British than by German workers. The prevalence of an 'adversarial' style in British industrial relations is difficult to reconcile with a 'trust' relation between management and workers. The claim of a more democratic British managerial style is also roundly rejected by Millar's (1979) comparative study. Millar concludes that 'German management showed more awareness of the role and significance of genuine participation' than their British colleagues. This manifested itself for Millar in the fact that German managers would go to meetings with workers with an open mind and prepared to take their suggestions on board. British managers, in contrast, practised pseudo-participation in as far as consultation with workers did not influence their decision-making. Lastly, it should also be remembered that participation in decision-making on the part of workers has always been confined to the level of the work place, and participation at board level has consistently been resisted.

A traditional paternalist style is now infrequently encountered in British manufacturing but an updated and more sophisticated paternalism appears to be more prominent. This style prevails particularly in family-dominated firms, upholding the social ethos of religious dissent (e.g. Cadbury-Schweppes, Clarks Shoes) but can also be found in other contexts. This kind of paternalism has dropped the master–servant notion, allows for some pluralism of interest and makes generous welfare provision as 'a practical response to the need to create a positive working environment' (Goldsmith and Clutterbuck, 1984: 84). It is also concerned to establish diffuse social relations between management and employees rather than the usual narrow and functional mere employment relation. These authors found that a sophisticated paternalism runs through most of the highly successful British companies they studied, regardless of size (ibid.: 83). Edwards (1987: 139), too, in his study of general managers found that a sophisticated paternalist style was being cultivated in a significant minority (15 per cent) of the large firms in his sample.

A number of reasons for the alleged prevalence of the democratic managerial style in British business organizations come to mind. The higher degree of delegation on the part of British, as compared with German, top management, must partly be a result of the peculiar patterns of growth, experienced by British companies in recent decades. These have led to a very distinctive organizational structure. Whereas German companies have grown organically through expanding activities by direct investment in capital equipment, British companies have grown through mergers. This pattern has created large firms, consisting of a number of small subsidiaries, which have not undertaken a thorough rationalization of production activity. Such a structure would necessitate a more decentralized mode of decision-making, regardless of what sentiments top management have on this matter.

But participative management style at all levels of the hierarchy is more often explained in cultural terms. The political culture of the wider society, renowned for its long tradition of accommodating opposition through partial incorporation, has also set the tone in the industrial enterprise. Achievement of objectives through a compromise between opposing parties and gaining the consent of the governed are the guiding motives in politics and industry alike. A further influence on managerial style in dealings with shopfloor workers is exerted by a perception of union power. The relatively strong position *vis-à-vis* management of British unions and stewards, at least until recently, has made the maintenance of a democratic management style advisable. The close association between the Trades Union Council and the Labour Party has, for long periods of time, ensured the unions of state support for their demands for far-reaching participation rights.

Recent change in the economic situation and the ensuing shift in the balance of power in favour of management has shown that a democratic style did not indicate an active legitimation of worker participation but merely passive acquiescence to a situation management was powerless to change. In many British enterprises the right of worker participation in determining working conditions has unilaterally been withdrawn. Although there has occurred no attack on shop stewards' organizations, a change in the management approach to labour has been widely discerned. The emphasis has shifted from negotiation with representative bodies to persuasion of individual workers to support management policy. The now prevalent stress on greater worker involvement does not signal a readiness to grant workers greater participation in decision-making (Edwards, 1987: 115f).

The relative rarity of a paternalist management style can be explained both in terms of contingencies arising from economic development and in terms of culture. Unlike France and, to a lesser degree, Germany, Britain has experienced a pattern of economic development during the postwar period which favoured the creation of large firms and militated against the reproduction of small firms. This has led to a situation where Britain has the most underdeveloped 'small firm' sector of the three societies, both in terms of employees and of share of production. As paternalism thrives particularly in the smaller, family-owned firm the British pattern of economic development has not provided a fertile soil for its perpetuation. A paternalist managerial style has also been undermined by the early acceptance of a contractual approach to labour, dictating a 'minimalist involvement' relationship between management and labour. A 'contract ideology', suggests Fox (1974: 195), 'purges the employment relationship of all personal and particularistic bonds, considerations, and sentiments'.

Management Style in German Enterprises

Many writers on the German business organizations still label management style as unambiguously authoritarian (e.g. Child and Kieser, 1979; Horovitz, 1980; Budde et al., 1982). Here it will be argued that the evidence supporting this claim is not strong and that a more differentiated analysis of German management style needs to be made. Such an analysis will establish that there is not one predominant type but that a number of different types coexist, reflecting the tremendous changes in both political and industrial culture, experienced in Germany since 1945.

An authoritarian management style, it was pointed out above, is not only characterized by tight centralized control but also by strong direction of subordinates, and both are based on the belief that the latter are indolent and/or uncooperative. Proponents of the 'authoritarian management style' thesis, however, have only demonstrated that control in German business organizations is more centralized and exerted more energetically than in British enterprises. Maurice et al. (1980: 72) point out, however, that on many operational matters control is not, in fact, as highly centralized as formal assessments of organization structure would make us believe. Conversely, British control is not always as decentralized as management intend it to be because lower management is often bypassed in situations of disputes which occur relatively frequently (Maitland, 1983: 88). These authors have not been able to show a link with the managerial *beliefs* outlined above nor have they provided strong evidence to sustain their claim that human relations are being regarded as irrelevant. Budde et al. (1982: 8–9), for example, quote in support of their claim empirical data on German general cultural traits from studies such as Almond and Verba (1963), which are, by now, very dated and cannot do justice to the tremendous changes which occurred in the FRG from the 1960s onwards. A later comparative study on childrearing practice, for example, found that the level of authoritarianism has greatly decreased and is only slightly higher in Germany than in Britain and much lower than in some other European countries (Lupri, 1970).

Although there is consistent evidence that control is more highly centralized in German business organizations this could be explained by reference to their patterns of growth and their organizational structure rather than by reference to a general societal culture supporting authoritarianism. The less haphazard organic growth of companies has made for a pattern of more integrated production units, and individual plants tend to have flatter organization structures. In this situation centralized control can be operated very effectively. A high degree of centralization is not *per se* a negative feature but only becomes one if it leads to managerial overload, poor communication and employee disaffection. There is no evidence in the literature that any of these are more common in German enterprises. On the contrary, relations are generally said to be informal and are evaluated relatively positively by subordinates.

Evidence which can be cited against the claim that an authoritarian managerial style is pervasive in German business organizations comes from a variety of sources. A lesser separation between planning and execution and a lower level of supervision on the shopfloor, as well as larger spans of control throughout the organization – all features identified by Maurice et al. (1980: 70–1) – would indicate a higher, rather than a lower level of trust in subordinates on the part of German, as compared with British, managers. This higher degree of discretion granted to both shopfloor workers and their foremen is also underlined by Lawrence (1980). The findings of the Industrial Democracy in Europe (IDE) Group on management control, as perceived by subordinates (see Wilpert and Rayley, 1983: 73), are also difficult to reconcile with the notion of authoritarianism. The IDE Group examined the relation of subordinates to superiors in task-related relationships and focused on such features as the degree of absence of authoritarian hierarchical interaction patterns. They found that German workers and chargehands evaluated the style of their superiors more positively than both British and French workers. They voiced relatively high levels of agreement with such statements as 'superior will explain decisions' (65 per cent) but were less satisfied with levels of delegation (42 per cent) (ibid.: 74–5). These findings are consistent with those of Hofstede (1979) who constructed a Power Distance index (PDI) from answers to questions, similar to those above. (For details see note 6.) Hofstede found that power distance between superiors and subordinates was relatively low in Germany by international standards. It was, in fact, equal to that established for Britain (ibid.: 101, 105). The findings by Maurice et al. (1980: 72) that German production units are run along the most personalized lines and by Lawrence (1980: 107) that there is less hierarchical distance between managers and workers are difficult to reconcile with the claim about a low concern for human relations, contained in the 'authoritarianism' thesis. The lesser social distance between managers and subordinates, indicated by a lower proportion of managers from an upper-class social origin and by a greater homogeneity in terms of VET, would point in the same direction.

There is further evidence from German sources that an authoritarian ' management style is no longer the predominant pattern. A recent survey of younger managers found that a majority (67 per cent) of those in top and middle management positions expressed a preference for a task-oriented style (*sachlicher Stil*) but also that an authoritarian[8] style found more support among top managers (43.9 per cent) than among departmental managers (32.3 per cent) (*Manager Magazin* 11, 1986: 344). An empirical study on change of leadership style (Grünwald und Lilge, 1981) concluded that 'a change in the predominant leadership style in West German enterprises towards a cooperative-participative form is evident' (ibid.: 721). The authors concede, though, that attitudes are in advance of behaviour. Generally then, the evidence does not suggest that a participative style has become the dominant one among all German managers but merely that it is becoming more important in large companies. In small to medium-sized firms, in contrast, where owner-managers still prevail, authoritarian and paternalist styles have endured much stronger.

A rough indication of the incidence and distribution of the various styles is afforded by Kotthoff's study (1981: 115f) of participation in 491 German enterprises of varying size. A participative style was practised by managers in 51 per cent of the larger medium-sized and large enterprises (ibid.: 153, 193). These managers held a pluralist model of open-minded social partnership. They conceived of society as consisting of interest groups, holding opposing but not antagonistic interests and expressed expectations that conflicts between management and works councils/unions can be resolved in a manner acceptable to both sides. Kotthoff suggests, however, that attitudes are not always converted into behaviour in the field of industrial relations. This indicates perhaps that a participative style is not yet as securely established as it is in Britain.

Kotthoff detects an authoritarian style in about 20 per cent and a paternalist ('patriarchal' in his book) style in about 35 per cent of his sample of firms (ibid.: 78). The latter appears to be the dominant style in small to medium-sized enterprises. Managers are said constantly to emphasize 'the human element' in their dealings with subordinates and their care and responsibility for the welfare of all the employed. The enterprise is seen as a communal structure. Humane care is offered in exchange for performance, discipline, and compliance (ibid.: 115–20).

The prevalence of a paternalist style in small to medium-sized, mainly owner-managed enterprises is attested to by other authors (e.g. Bessant and Grunt, 1985: 322f) who further elucidate the special quality of this style. It appears to be closely connected with the ideology of a 'craft community', i.e. a notion of skilled men working side by side towards the achievement of common technical goals (e.g. NEDO, 1981). This orientation infuses management style with democratic impulses absent from the traditional definition of paternalism. The picture is further complicated by the fact that a generous welfare policy is now often presented in the modern guise of a *Sozialpolitische Verpflichtung*, i.e. an obligation imposed by the ethos of co-determination (see Chapter 9). Other sources (Perrow, 1970: 168; Zürn, 1985: 55) emphasize the loyalty of workers – sometimes over several family generations – to their firm and their pride in the product produced by it. These latter claims are made also in relation to large firms, such as Bosch, BMW and Mercedes.

This analysis of management style in Germany has shown that it is much more diverse than indicated by some sources. To continue writing only about authoritarianism is to ignore the tremendous changes that have occurred in recent decades. Also, to answer the question posed earlier in this chapter, it is not valid to equate a job-oriented style with an authoritarian style, nor should it be assumed that a production orientation necessarily implies the surrender of a concern for human relations. Such an orientation constitutes merely a different approach to motivating workers which, moreover, has proved highly effective in the German context.

How can one explain this diversity of management styles in German business enterprises? One important explanatory variable must be the pattern of industrial development and the present-day structure evolved from it. Germany industrialized later than Britain but slightly earlier than France, and, in contrast to the situation in the other two societies, industrialization occurred at a fast pace within a relatively short time-span. The later development, together with a state policy protective towards small businesses, has meant that small, family-owned 'craft'-type enterprises have survived much longer than in Britain and are still today a dominant feature of the industrial structure. In contrast to the development in France, however, a substantial 'large firm' sector evolved already during the industrialization period, creating a more, even distribution of firms according to size than in the other two societies. Size and type of ownership of firm are strongly correlated with certain types of management styles. This would provide one explanatory strand for the diverse patterns of management style found in Germany.

Another explanatory variable is the political culture of the wider society. Germany has experienced a much greater hiatus in the development of this culture between pre- and postwar experience than have the other two societies. This change occurred not only in the political realm but also on the social and industrial front. A fascist dictatorship became replaced by a parliamentary democracy; the old social élites – the *Junker* – lost their place and influence in German society, and the war had effected a general social levelling, at least during the early postwar years; and from 1951–2 onwards, industrial democracy of a relatively far-reaching kind (see Chapter 9) was introduced into all but the smallest business organizations. All these changes have endured and have now been institutionalized for over 30 years. Their impact on both political and industrial culture has been considerable, as can be seen from the data on changes in public opinion, assembled by Noelle-Neumann (1981). But German culture has been shaped by conservative forces over centuries, and genuine change will be a slow and uneven process. Hence it is not surprising that paternalist and authoritarian styles are still to be found in industrial enterprises side by side with more progressive ones.

Management style is also influenced by the perception of the power possessed by the opposite side and by the ideological stance adopted by the working-class movement. German unions emerged from the last war as a morally strong force which, in contrast to many large employers, was not tainted by the charge of collaboration with Hitler's regime. Consequently during the late 1940s/early 1950s, backed by the Allies, they found themselves in a sufficiently strong position to launch a major offensive on employer prerogatives and to secure legislation on co-determination. The institution in the early fifties of co-determination at company board level and, more importantly, of works councils, further strengthened the position of the working class *vis-à-vis* employers (for details, see Chapter 9). The generally cooperative stance of these bodies and the evolving concept of *Sozialpartner* all contributed to the fact that workers' representatives had to be treated as responsible negotiating partners rather than as mere subordinates. Although the concept of *Sozialpartner* is clearly an ideological device the creation of such devices nevertheless gradually comes to constrain behaviour in a way that precludes too blatant deviations from the norms implied by the concept. In this situation, authoritarian and/or paternalist managerial styles have become increasingly incongruous although, as Kotthoff (1981) indicates, not eliminated.

These analyses of management styles have shown that there are still considerable differences between the three societies, and that features of national economic and political development have had a strong impact on institutional structures/cultural orientations shaping management styles. The following chapter indicates how these differing styles become expressed in the exercise of one management function – control.

NOTES

1. Thus a recent German survey of ten external courses for management development included five which used the word manager in their title, four which referred to *Unternehmer* and one to *Kader* (cadres) (*Capital* 5, 1987: 288).
2. Thus in the 1970s 47 large companies were still family-dominated in that more than 25 per cent of stock was family-owned (figures quoted by Scott, 1985: 128).
3. For details see Maurice et al. (1986a: 116–17); Levy-Leboyer (1980); Marceau (1977); Fidler (1981); Lawrence (1980); NEDO (1987: 61). In the early 1970s 29 per cent of the German industrial élite came from a lower middle class social background (Bolte and Hradil, 1984: 187).
4. The German figure appears to include graduates from a *Fachhochschule*. The latter is considered to be below university level in Germany although it might be argued that its diploma is equivalent to a degree from a British polytechnic. This indicates that comparisons based on nationally collected figures can be problematic and that they should only be taken as rough approximations. But a wide gap between the three societies has nevertheless repeatedly been confirmed.
5. May (1974: 5) points out that, up to the 1920s, work in industry was despised by social élites in the same way it has been in Britain and France right into the 1970s. In the 1920s there occurred a large influx of aristocrats into industry, due to their loss of landed property. This gave industry a new prestige and brought about a change in social ethos.
6. The Power Distance Index (PDI) is constructed from answers to three questions on a scale from 0 (low power distance) to 100 (high power distance). The PDI is high if:
   (a) a large proportion of subordinates describe their superiors' decision-making behaviour as either autocratic or paternalistic;
   (b) respondents state that employees are frequently afraid to disagree with their manager;
   (c) subordinates do *not* prefer a 'consultative' decision-making in their superior (Hofstede, 1979: 102).
7. The attempt by the Mitterrand government to change the quality of industrial relations will be briefly discussed in Chapter 8.
8. Managers were deemed to prefer an authoritarian style if they sometimes utilized authoritarian means to achieve their goals.

5 Management Control

Control is said by many to be the single most important management function; it is even claimed that management in all its aspects is a 'control' function. It is also the most complex to understand both from a theoretical and a practising manager's point of view because its meaning differs according to context. Thus, as Buchanan and Huczynski (1985: 453) point out, control has connotations of both order, predictability, reliability *and* of coercion, domination and manipulation. The definition of 'management control' as 'the process of ensuring that performance is according to plan' makes it appear a neutral, technical activity which is economically necessary to secure the efficient utilization of business resources. Such a view implies that control is mainly a task of coordinating the efforts of different groups towards the achievement of objectives about which there is general agreement.

This interpretation is, however, based on a faulty analysis of the business organization. Although there is no doubt that control, as defined above, is economically necessary in complex organizations it is naive to assume that it is a neutral process, i.e. a process with equally beneficial results for all involved. In capitalist societies, management, i.e. those working on behalf of capital, and labour have objectively opposed interests and, therefore, different objectives, even if the protagonists are not always subjectively aware of this. The goals and objectives adopted for business organizations are defined by management, usually without any consultation with labour. In order to secure the agreement of workers to work towards the achievement of management objectives the latter have to exert the power they possess by virtue of their management position. Exercising control is, therefore, a *political* process in which various means are used by those in dominant positions to get the compliance of those in subordinate positions. Although this objective conflict of interest does not touch on every area of organizational decision-making and is not usually at the forefront of management–employee relations, most management objectives are imposed in such a political process.

To understand how managers have come to possess the power which

116

enables them to exercise control over the production process we need to focus on another kind of control which managers exercise as the representatives of capital. This is control over the means and methods of production, i.e. control over decision-making in areas such as expansion or contraction of business capacity, replacing old with new types of production technology or choosing new markets or new production sites. This is generally referred to as 'strategic control' and needs to be distinguished from 'operational control'. The control by capital and its managers over material resources and strategic business decisions enables them to refuse employment to those who question the way these resources are utilized. This strategic control secures control over the production process, i.e. the power to determine *how* subordinates perform their work. This aspect of strategic control will not be examined in this chapter, nor will the question of the locus of strategic control be touched upon. (For a consideration of the latter, see the work of Scott, 1985.)

Management control, it has been pointed out, has two faces: a mainly technical aspect emphasizing the coordination of effort towards the achievement of specified objectives and a political aspect, focusing on asymmetrical power relations between management and subordinates and on the domination and/or manipulation of the latter by the former. Although in practice one aspect is generally connected with the other, at a theoretical level the two have mainly been analysed separately. Whereas management writers have concerned themselves predominantly with the former, sociologists and industrial relations analysts have almost exclusively analysed the latter. This book will steer a course between these two extreme positions and consider both faces of control, albeit as analytically separate problems. Chapters 6 and 7, being concerned with work organization on the shopfloor, will explore the political aspect. This chapter, in contrast, will study control in various areas of enterprise activity and will emphasize the technical aspect, i.e. control as a coordinating exercise. It will be concerned to establish to what extent and how management in the three societies try to determine the overall development of their company; how they go about procuring the instruments and materials of production and make them available to workers on a reliable basis; and, lastly, how production is coordinated with marketing of produced goods. Such an emphasis on the more technical rather than the man-management aspect of production is justified when one considers that in a sample of British plants during the 1980s only 18 per cent of the cost structure of finished products was attributable to direct labour costs (New and Myers, 1986: 7).

The focus will not only be on the control process itself. An attempt will also be made to show how the nature of the control process is linked with business performance and to throw some light on why the degree of effectiveness in this respect differs between the three societies. Effectiveness can be influenced by many factors and is thus difficult to measure in any one country, let alone compare between countries. The following discussion can do no more than present a general, largely qualitative picture.

Effectiveness can be assessed by utilizing some or all of the following economic or more qualitative indicators: profit in relation to the value of net resources owned and rate of growth of assets and sales (Child, 1969: 85); on-going investment in equipment and training; or by assessing reputation as a leader within a given industrial sector (Goldsmith and Clutterbuck, 1984: 1). If the study of control is centred on production labour productivity may be taken as an indicator but, to assess general effectiveness, productivity needs to be calculated in relation to overall employment costs. Different measures yield different results but the general conclusions on a rank order of manufacturing performance in our three European societies are nevertheless remarkably consistent, although France is less often included in comparisons. German firms are said to outstrip the other two in the degree of effectiveness obtained and Britain usually comes a poor third.[1] Since the 1980s the superiority of French firms has, however, become less clear-cut.

An examination of the technical aspect of control can start with the following definition: to control is to ensure that objectives are as near as possible to plan. To this end, management is required to engage in the following activities: to translate organizational goals into operational standards; to measure performance; to compare actual performance with stipulated standards; and to undertake the necessary corrective action to bridge any gaps between specified standards and achieved performance. Figure 5.1 below sets out the process of management control in graphic form.

Figure 5.1 illustrates the importance of feedback of the information derived from monitoring performance in order that goals and standards may be adjusted as required. This is referred to as the cybernetic view of control.

The systematic comparative study of management control in Europe is very underdeveloped, particularly as far as top management is concerned. Horovitz's (1980) book stands alone in this latter field. Consequently Horovitz's study, despite some serious limitations, will form the nucleus of the following assessment. It will be supplemented by, and contrasted with, data from other studies, touching on this

Figure 5.1   The process of management control

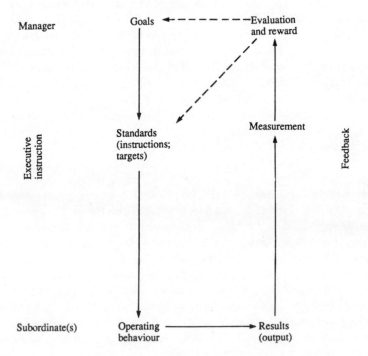

Source: Child (1984: 141, Figure 6.1).

area. Data are more plentiful when we move to operational control, particularly production control below the level of top management. First a short outline of the scope and limits of Horovitz's study is in order.

Horovitz adheres to the cybernetic view of control outlined above. He examines the nature of control exerted by chief executives and functional senior managers in 52 matched (by size, type of ownership and economic sector) companies in France, Britain, and Germany. The focus is on the areas of general management, finance, production, and marketing. Horovitz is concerned to establish how the characteristics of control practices – such as degree of formality, centralization, etc. – differ between these three countries. He also explores on what element control bears, how much and how frequently it is exerted in different functional areas, as well as by whom (i.e. at what level of the hierarchy) it is exercised. Horovitz studies control only as it is viewed and measured by top management itself and also checks on how it is formally defined by control manuals. He does not investigate how it is actually exercised, let alone how it is perceived by those subject to this control. Effectiveness of control is assessed by management itself in terms of the achievement of plans rather than by reference to performance indicators. The study reveals that managers do not always check whether performance deviates from stipulated standards and hence their views may not give a very reliable assessment of actually achieved performance.

PLANNING AS A PRE-CONDITION FOR EFFECTIVE CONTROL

The definition of control used emphasizes its close interrelationship with planning. Hence in the following a short review of planning in the three national business organizations will be undertaken. A distinction needs to be made between long-range and short-term planning. Long-range planning, according to Horovitz (1980: 70f), appears to be most systematically developed in Britain, tends to cover a five-year period, and involves a relatively large number of people at both group and unit organizational level. In Germany, long-range planning is also widely adopted, but often covers fewer years, is less formalized and tends to involve a smaller number of people. In France, long-range planning is only haphazardly developed, covers shorter timespans and is the least formalized of the three. In both Germany and France planning is mainly operational and uses quantitative standards whereas in Britain it tends to be more strategic in nature and less quantitative. British chief executives, it is widely claimed, refuse to become involved in the planning and control of manufacturing operations (e.g. New and Myers, 1986: 45). Corporate strategy is not necessarily better explicated in Britain as it consists merely of an aggregation of unit strategies. In all three countries, the bottom-up approach indicates for Horovitz a lack of corporate strategy, i.e. of an overall development plan.

With respect to short-term planning there exists a fundamental difference between the German and the other two national business organizations. Horovitz (1980: 77) reports a very high degree of participation in the one-year planning cycle in Germany, with every work group acting as a cost centre. Budget and task planning appears to be highly integrated. Detailed, quantified targets are set for every work group in the enterprise which generate definite commitment to task fulfilment. Generally, short-term planning in quantitative terms is most developed in Germany, least in Britain, and unevenly in France.

Horovitz's findings on planning are borne out by other studies, particularly for Britain and Germany, although the British planning process generally receives a more negative evaluation. Freeman (1979: 70f) sees the difference in focus of British and German long-term strategic planning as being very pronounced and crucial in its consequences for competitiveness. Whereas German top management puts a strong strategic emphasis on product design and development and on process innovation – backed up by considerably higher inputs in R & D expenditure – British top management concerns itself with these objectives only in exceptional cases. The less operations-oriented nature of British long-term planning has given some analysts the impression that long-term planning is inadequately developed in comparison with German practice. Thus Budde et al. (1982: 21) note the 'greater tendency for West German management to adopt a proactive and long-term view of business opportunity'. A NEDO (1981: viii) study of one industrial sector observes that British management, in contrast to its German counterpart, does not adopt a sufficiently long-term perspective in the areas of investment, development and training. The lack of forward planning in the field of training by British companies and the negative consequences for effectiveness were already highlighted in Chapter 3. It is recognized, however, that this lack of a long-term perspective is partly caused by the restricting lending practices of British banks. Lawrence (1984: 46), too, notes the British reluctance to long-term commitment of resources when he speaks of 'a strong vein of profit now rather than technical excellence in ten years' time in British business culture'. Lawrence (1984: 93) generally finds forward planning more developed in Germany and also notes a superior capacity to anticipate, and make contingency plans for, difficulties.

All the above findings are difficult to reconcile with Horovitz's identification of a well-developed British long-term planning system. One is led to conclude that the formal properties of the British planning system identified by Horovitz remain ineffective because they address themselves insufficiently to the relevant issues – they remain too narrowly focused on finance and thus do not generate clear objectives to be pursued by management at the lower levels. The latter may be partly due to the underdeveloped and loose nature of British short-term planning which is unfavourably contrasted with

German precision and thoroughness in this area by several authors. The importance of good short-term planning for the quality of long-term planning is underlined by Bessant and Grunt (1985: 272).

Like Horovitz, most of the above mentioned authors deduce clear consequences for control from the planning patterns identified. But they are more explicit in connecting the British vagueness at the planning level with laxity in the area of management control, particularly operational control. The French commitment to quantitative operational short-term planning, other sources suggest (Gallie, 1978; Dubois, 1981), appears to outweigh some of the disadvantages for the exercise of control implied by the unsystematic and haphazard nature of French long-term planning. In short, a focus on operations-oriented short-term planning is held to be a very important pre-condition for effective control.

THE NATURE OF TOP MANAGEMENT CONTROL

Chief executives' views on the use of control in general are found to differ significantly between the three societies (Horovitz, 1980: 80f). The British and, even more strongly, the French do not believe that control does and should ensure that actual performance comes close to plan and that corrective action can be taken. They thus do not accept the cybernetic view of control shown in Figure 5.1. This view is consistent with the French lack of faith in long-term planning. It also reflects the great difficulty of maintaining control in the large corporations which resulted from the frenzied merger activities of the 1960s and 1970s. They are described by Telesis (1986: 132–3) as 'agglomerations of largely unrelated businesses' which have turned headquarters into rather passive holding companies 'with little control over divisional strategies/performances'. In the British case, in contrast, where long-range planning is more accepted this view is indicative of an ideological preference for a managerial style which provides loose guidance rather than viewing control as an instrument for correcting employees' errors. In Germany, in contrast, there is a high degree of consistency between the highly detailed planning practice and top management's faith in the cybernetic view of control. This leads Horovitz to conclude that 'in Germany, the control systems appear to be much more stringent and oriented towards corrective action than in France or Great Britain.' Computers are used to collect and analyse the profusion of detail needed to monitor performance. Goldsmith and Clutterbuck (1984: 8, 47,

53), writing only about Britain's most successful companies, show that these *are* strongly committed to tight control, albeit only in a few areas held to be crucial by them, and that monitoring of performance is not eschewed.

The differing views on control of chief executives are reflected in/ reflect the differing control strategies as indicated by structural arrangements of companies found in the three societies. Most British companies are holding companies organized by product market subsidiaries. They are highly decentralized and maintain a relatively small central staff who deal with policy decisions and exert mainly financial control. Many other decisions are delegated to management at subsidiary level. Goldsmith and Clutterbuck (1984: 29) found not a single example of a highly successful British manufacturing company with a heavily centralized organization. German companies are organized by division or function. Decision-making is highly central-ized. The companies employ a large central staff who maintain control over many operational as well as financial matters but also offer support activities and services to local units. In France, where Horovitz (1980: 55) finds most companies to be organized by func-tions, centralization of decision-making is also very pronounced, and a large central staff is maintained. Centralization is, in some ways, even more extreme than in Germany in as far as chief executives often monopolize decision-making. In Germany, in contrast, the 'team' approach is widely established.

Next Horovitz (1980: 83) probes what procedures are involved in exercising control, i.e. whether there is an emphasis on checking procedures, getting as much information as possible and on looking over subordinates' shoulders to see if they make errors. He finds that the procedures followed are entirely consistent with the view of control held by chief executives in the British and the German case. The French, however, are inconsistent in emphasizing the use of these procedures despite their strong rejection of the cybernetic view of control. Thus Horovitz is probably correct in interpreting the French use of control as a 'policing device'. But he is not justified in applying this same label to German control procedures which appear to this author as an integral part of control strategies. The fact that, of the three national business organizations, control in Germany is least used to evaluate performance with a view to reward or punishment also casts doubt on the interpretation of control as a policing device. Finally, the information passed up to the chief executive does, in any case, not lend itself to checking up on individual employees but is presented in aggregated form to document achievement in functional areas, such as quantities produced, sales, orders, or for cost centres.

In all three societies, control by chief executives is exerted with varying degrees of intensity over the different business functions although there are national differences on which functions assume prominence. The British overwhelmingly give pride of place to finance whereas the Germans and French give priority, albeit less consistently, to production with finance coming a close second. Although all three put relatively low emphasis on Research and Development (R & D), it is nevertheless significant that it was held to be very important only among a few German chief executives (Horovitz, 1980: 91–2). Comparative figures on industry-financed R & D show that investment in R & D is significantly higher in Germany than in both Britain and France (see data presented by Freeman 1979: 63). Goldsmith and Clutterbuck (1984: 47) reveal that even among Britain's most successful companies only a small proportion have tight controls on technology. Horovitz, quite plausibly, explains these different emphases both in terms of diffuse vs. centralized organizational structures and by reference to the lesser or greater expertise of top management in the technical field.

Control involves the collection and evaluation of information. A more precise picture of the nature of control is obtained if it is ascertained what kind of information is collected at what intervals and how this information is used. In this area Horovitz (1980: 93f) finds sharp differences between the British and the Germans. British managers receive and look at information less often, information is more often in qualitative form and frequently oriented towards future performance. The content is heavily biased towards financial control. German managers, in contrast, receive information – mostly about past performance – very frequently. It is presented in quantitative form by central staff and tends to be operations-oriented. The overwhelming importance of the gathering and use of detailed information on performance at *all* levels of the German business organization is also underlined by NEDO (1981: 3). It is seen as one element responsible for greater business effectiveness, as measured by comparing economic indicators. A similar pattern of information gathering and utilization is found by Horovitz in French enterprises, although monitoring is carried out with less automation and rigour. Thus, to sum up this section, whereas the information supplied to German and French chief executives is used for purposes of control, for British chief executives it is more of a steering and/or early warning device.

The British literature on management control constantly emphasizes that the efficiency of large companies depends on decentralization of control and a delegation of decision-making to subsidiary level. The literature reviewed above, particularly the observations on German control practices, implies that the matter is more complex than that. It would seem to suggest that tight central control in *some* areas aids rather than hinders successful performance but that it needs to be exerted in an environment which encourages flexibility and initiative in other respects. The selection of areas for a more stringent central control depends on which aspects of strategic decision-making are believed to be crucial to the economic success of an enterprise at any given time. It would seem that the concentration on purely financial objectives by most British companies is insufficient at this juncture of economic and technological development. (For a further discussion of this matter, see Chapter 7.)

OPERATIONAL CONTROL: PRODUCTION AND MARKETING

The emphasis, it must be repeated, will be primarily on control as the process of coordinating the various activities of the firm rather than on the exercise of managerial authority over workers. Production control, it is claimed by Horovitz (1980: 129f), is most formal in Germany, least formal in France, with Britain taking a middle position between the two. As this finding is contrary to interpretations of other studies (e.g. Maurice et al., 1980) which emphasize the low degree of formality in German production, as compared with that in Britain and France, Horovitz's results need closer analysis. Formalism in his work takes a different form in each society. In Germany it consists of the use of more specific criteria for the evaluation of performance and of closer supervision whereas the application of rules is not very pronounced. Performance is also clearly linked to rewards. In France and Britain, in contrast, rules are more frequently applied in production, but criteria for performance evaluation are less specific, supervision is not as close and links with rewards are more infrequent. Even if one takes into consideration Horovitz's differentiated approach to the analysis of formalism, his results are difficult to reconcile with those of other studies (Gallie, 1978; Maurice et al., 1980; Lawrence 1980; Lutz, 1981; Bessant and Grunt 1985) which show that the span of control is relatively wide in Germany and narrow in France. Maybe control is more sharply focused and hence more effectively wielded in German production, but it is certainly not as formal as in France if extent of supervision is taken as an indicator. (See the discussion in Chapter 2.)

Horovitz's overall conclusion, however, that managerial grasp in production is tightest in Germany and loosest in Britain (France falls between) is borne out by other studies. Several studies, going beyond managerial self-assessment of effectiveness, fill out this picture with more details. Whereas British managerial performance is characterized by poor systems of production control, lack of attention to methods of production and capital utilization and excessive waiting times, German management is generally seen to excel on all these fronts (e.g. Mant, 1978; Maitland, 1983; Lawrence, 1984). In Germany much greater attention is also devoted to the control of the purchasing function (Daly et al., 1985). The importance of such control – bought materials and components may amount to over 50 per cent of product costs – is underlined by New and Myers (1986: 7) who also bear out the general lack of purchasing effectiveness on the part of British management. NEDO (1981: 19) attributes the lower degree of management control in British production to the more frequent turnover of managerial staff, the poorer communication between management and shopfloor and the insufficient utilization of performance information. The lack of skilled intermediate staff also makes the British production manager's lot a difficult and hectic one. According to Lawrence (1988: 106) he is 'gang boss, trouble-shooter and instant fixer' whereas his German counterpart is less pressurized and can make more inputs in terms of technological understanding and creativity. French production management is seen to have similar shortcomings to those found in Britain: a disproportionate effort to control wage costs rather than the much more substantial overhead costs in such areas as materials handling, inspection, internal transport, etc. Accountability in cost performance, as in Britain, has been hampered by a quick turnover in management (Telesis, 1986: 136f).

Maitland (1983: 1) goes as far as equating this loose grip in production with a complete lack of government on the part of British management. He compares the exercise of operational control in matched British and German plants as follows:

> Resistance to, and subversion of, managerial control in the German factory was minor; in England, on the other hand, they reached the point where there was serious breakdown of managerial control over pay and work. (ibid.: 79)

At the same time, though, workers in the British plant felt unhappy about the lack of effective management, particularly about management failure to ensure a smooth flow of production (ibid.: 85). Maitland does not blame workers for the breakdown of control but attributes it explicitly to a weak and inert management (ibid.: 13–15).

In the area of marketing, according to Horovitz, the degree of formalism in control differs only slightly between the three societies and control is generally seen to be less tight than in production. Horovitz's general conclusion is that in marketing British management exerts the tightest and German the loosest grasp. This result may be partly affected by the fact that many marketing activities are carried out by central staff in Germany but not in Britain and France. This finding is completely at odds with the results of other studies which have measured the differential performance in the area of marketing in the three societies.

Several studies (e.g. NEDO, 1981: 3, 6; Bessant and Grunt, 1985) emphasize the much greater familiarity by German than British enterprises with what is happening in technically demanding markets and that the West Germans are considerably ahead of the British in 'thinking across borders' and understanding European markets. British firms, in contrast, are still seen as being insular in relation to Europe. Telesis (1986: 48) negatively contrasts French international marketing with German practice. Except for top management in multinationals, French managers do not know international markets outside Europe as well as German ones and have insufficient knowledge of international distribution networks. These differences in awareness again reflect an inadequate utilization of information and are bound to have a negative effect on planning in the area of marketing.

A comparative study of performance in the areas of marketing and buying by firms of various European countries, based on managers' evaluation of their clients' or suppliers' marketing and buying behaviour (Turnbull and Cunningham, 1981), establishes that the British are rated the poorest marketers on a whole range of criteria. This poor performance is not solely the result of loose control but also strongly related to a low level of technical competence. But such identified shortcomings as lack of analysis of, and adaptation to, customer needs, slow and unreliable delivery and poor after-sales service indicate that inadequate management control – insufficient collection and evaluation of information and too few checks of subordinates' activity, lack of coordination between departments – also plays an important role. This is borne out by a recent British study (New and Myers, 1986: 17f) which found that poor delivery performance – 25 per cent of plants delivered more orders late than on time, and 50 per cent delivered more than one in four orders late – was linked to the absence of a formal system for monitoring delivery performance. Studies of German plants, in contrast, emphasize the high degree of *Termintreue* (commitment to on-time delivery) (Naujoks and Kayser, 1983: 70; Lawrence, 1984: 93). Turnbull and

Cunningham (1981: 28) also establish that Germany gets a consistently high rating from buyers whereas France falls again between the two, but being nearer to Britain than Germany. While French marketing staff receives a higher rating than the British on technical competence, they score as low as the British on commercial competence. A lack of integration between marketing and production departments is also said to be a shortcoming hampering French marketing success (Telesis, 1986: 136).

It may be obected that this picture of lax management control and lack of effectiveness of the manufacturing function does not take account of improvements achieved in British manufacturing during the 1980s. In answer to this objection one may cite the findings of a study by New and Myers (1986) of 240 British manufacturing plants in various sectors and size categories, oriented towards export, which replicated a comparable 1975 study. New and Myers found that, despite some improvement in overall lead times[2], throughput efficiency[3] had not substantially improved during the last ten years (ibid.: 14–15). The same dismal results emerged from their survey of delivery performance and utilization of new technology (ibid.: 17, 18, 24f). Their repeat study led them to the following overall conclusion:

> The regrettable, but overwhelming conclusion to be drawn from the 1985 survey must be that very little has happened in manufacturing operations in the UK over the last ten years. This is particularly true in the key areas of 'competitive edge' ... delivery, reliability, lead times and the use of new technology (ibid.: 43).

The authors' comparison of UK-owned with foreign-owned companies showed the former to perform persistently worse on delivery times and thus underlines the importance of *management* rather than labour contribution to overall performance.

REWARD STRUCTURE

Related to different national perceptions of managerial control are different attitudes towards, and utilization of, rewards to maintain the motivation of subordinates. A consideration of reward practices needs to take into account a variety of aspects: besides a focus on the kinds of rewards given and their magnitudes it is also important to consider the manner in which they are dispensed, e.g. whether they are distributed in an egalitarian/discriminatory way or whether they are used selectively or in a general way. Rewards can be of both an extrinsic kind, such as financial rewards beyond the basic salary and promotion chances or high status, and of a more intrinsic and intangible nature, such as the gaining of work satisfaction or the enjoyment of participation in decision-making. The latter kind of reward is generally considered to be more frequently deployed at the top of the organizational hierarchy whereas direct financial inducement to performance is said to be the most prominent means employed on the shopfloor. The actual picture on reward systems in the three societies is considerably more complex, both at management and at works level.

At management level we need to distinguish between attitudes to rewards and the level and kind of rewards *actually* received. In both German and French business organizations intrinsic rewards appear to be of considerable significance for managers whereas in British enterprises extrinsic rewards receive greater stress. Thus Budde et al. (1982: 17) establish that British top managers are inclined to see job satisfaction in extrinsic terms, valuing high salaries, good promotion prospects and high job prestige whereas their German counterparts put great value on intrinsic satisfactions. Dyas and Thanheiser (1976: 126, 256) comment that both French and German top management see a strong linkage between good managerial performance and variable individualized material rewards as morally distasteful. French top managers consider it to be against 'the French philosophy' to use material incentives to incite initiative and economic performance.

An examination of actual rewards received needs to distinguish between monetary and non-monetary rewards, i.e. perks. The former have to be subdivided into basic salary received and performance-related bonus payments. An analysis of rewards in these terms suggests the interpretation that the greater dominance of extrinsic orientations among British managers may be due to the fact that, by international standards, they are poorly rewarded and thus need to worry more about levels of income whereas the French and German disdain for extrinsic and variable rewards is not reflected in the actual reward system. Two recent comparative analyses of top management pay[4] come up with slightly different results but roughly the same rank ordering. Towers Perrin's analysis of the pay of chief executives in January 1987 found that, although total pay was higher in Germany than in France, pay in terms of purchasing power was highest in France. The Kienbaum 1986 survey, in contrast, found both net income and income in terms of purchasing power to be slightly higher for French than for German managers. Britain came a poor third in both respects although, since the mid 1980s, British firms have made a strong effort to raise managerial salaries/bonuses, in order to reduce the gap in relation to firms in other

advanced countries (*The Economist*, 8–14 October 1988: 48). In all
three societies managerial income is related to performance of the
enterprise, i.e. profits, and part of the income comes in variable bonus
payments. The proportion of bonus payments in recognition of performance is relatively high in Germany and low in France and Britain. Such
profit-related bonus payments, according to the Kienbaum survey, were
received by 70 per cent of German top managers and amounted to about
25 per cent of total income. Most of the remaining top managers were
entitled to bonus payments, but their firms had not achieved the
necessary economic success (*Manager Magazin*, 10/1986: 351). There is
no indication in the literature whether the lower proportion of bonus
payments received by French managements reflects performance or
whether it is the result of policy decisions. In Britain, according to
Edward's survey of general managers in large firms, just over 50 per
cent of managers receive bonus payments or a share in profits but these
rarely depend on the performance of managers' own firm and they only
gave a mean addition of 13 per cent to salaries (Edwards, 1987: 49–50).
When non-cash benefits and stock options are included, British managers considerably improve their international ranking.

Rewards act not only as incentives but they also symbolize divisions
between different hierarchical levels and reinforce social distance. The
pay structure is said to be most egalitarian in Britain, i.e. distances
between income categories are least pronounced, and least egalitarian
in France whereas Germany occupies a middle position between the
two, but is closer to Britain than France.[5] According to 1970s data,
supplied by Saunders and Marsden (1981: 138–9), average monthly
earnings (excluding non-regular bonuses) of male French top managers
were 328.7 per cent of the average income of all workers in industry,
and the comparable figures for Britain and Germany were 248.1 and
206.5 per cent respectively.[6] The corresponding proportions for executives were 230.7 per cent, 156.7 and 156.8 per cent respectively. These
data thus bear out the French–British contrast but are ambiguous on the
fact whether the pay structure is most egalitarian in Britain or Germany
(ibid.: 207).

But differences in cash income between management and works are
not necessarily the most divisive as they are not visible and often not
known by workers (see Gallie, 1983: 10). Differences in perks/
provisions, in contrast, may serve to underline status differences and
social distance more starkly. Differences in this respect between Britain
and Germany have been commented upon. Lawrence (1982: 25f)
reports fringe benefits (of German personnel managers) to be extensive
but claims that, in contrast to the British situation, they accrue to *all*

employees and not just to managerial staff. A similar point is made by Millar (1974). Dore (1973: 255f), too, emphasizes that in Britain a differential distribution of perks/provisions, such as separate dining-rooms, toilets and differential holiday and fringe benefits arrangements, emphasize the class divisions between managerial staff and works. Significantly, Britain's most successful companies, as defined by Goldsmith and Clutterbuck (1984), had adopted a policy of extending the receipt of fringe benefits and, sometimes even share options, right down to the shopfloor (ibid.: 64).

Different reward systems are operated at the lower levels of the hierarchy. French enterprises maintain the highest differentials between manual skill categories (Saunders and Marsden, 1981: 137). It is also common to reward loyalty and obedience in individualized ways through the payment of merit bonuses and promotion into supervisory positions. The system for awarding bonuses is very opaque and its operation very dependent on management discretion (Gallie, 1978). But generally, up to the 1980s, the French system has been one which rewards seniority rather than individual merit. By the middle 1980s, however, the reward system had become more individualized (Schwab, 1987).

In Germany differential rewards are also used as incentives to good performance but, in contrast to the situation in France, a meritocratic system prevails. Pay is closely linked to the level of skill exercised and to experience within a skill category. Not only are there moderate differentials between the three main skill categories but also within them (NEDO, 1981: 4). In addition, there are effort bonuses (*Leistungszulage*) for good performance. These are paid, on the recommendation of foremen, to around 10 per cent of the workforce (Lawrence, 1982: 23). Although this latter practice can be misused for purposes of social control, German skilled workers, having access to an external occupational labour market, are not as easily manipulated as their more dependent French colleagues. The rating system in Germany is very transparent. Works councils participate in working out the system, and unions have their own REFA (Association for Work Study) expert to help them determine such a system.

In Britain the reward structure is very egalitarian, and a policy of selectively rewarding good performance is eschewed. Differentials between skill categories are very small, and differentials within such categories are uncommon. This pattern, which is due to pressure from the numerically strong unions of the semi-skilled, is regretted by many employers (NEDO, 1981: 4), as well as being fiercely resented by skilled craftsmen (e.g. Harris, 1987). From the mid 1980s onwards, however,

British firms, too, have begun to introduce merit pay (ACAS 1988: 23). In sum, the reward system is most consistently performance-oriented in Germany, from top management levels down to the shopfloor. The largely meritocratic nature of the reward system and the evenly graduated income hierarchy, together with the absence of perks distributed according to status criteria, is perceived as equitous by subordinates and is less likely to incite conflict. The French system, in contrast, is more starkly unequal as well as being less meritocratic, and it leaves more scope for management discretion and, hence, manipulation. The British system applies different criteria at the top and the bottom of the reward hierarchy although it is not very performance-oriented at either level. It is relatively egalitarian in terms of wage/salary income but cancels out the positive effect of this by its adherence to outmoded status differentials.

STRATEGIES OF CONTROL

To summarize and conclude the examination of management control in the British, French and German business organization, it is useful to analyse the data presented in this chapter in terms of the four strategies of control in organizations elaborated by Child (1984: 159) and outlined in Table 5.1.

Some of the elements of the four control strategies in Table 5.1 need further explication. The elements of 'bureaucratic control' are based on the ideas of scientific management with its three 'S's: specialization leading to simplification and enabling standardization. (For further details on scientific management see Chapter 6.) The financial controls utilized in this strategy are budgetary control and control of variance from standard costs. Budgetary control involves the formulation of budgets for a specified long-term period and the frequent monitoring through budget reports of income and expenditure for shorter periods in relation to the overall budget. A standard cost-variance control system, in the words of Child (1984: 161), involves a process of determining what costs should be under specified operation systems, using these costs as standards of performance and evaluating actual performance in relation to these standards. The strategy of 'output control' specifies output standards and targets in measurable, commonly agreed terms, for various sub-units of the enterprise and relates rewards to the measured achievement of outputs. In accounting terms, this approach assigns financial responsibility to specified organizational sub-units. This can occur by designating investment, profit or cost centres. This control strategy facilitates delegation of operational decision-making and

Table 5.1   Four strategies of control in organizations

Each strategy will utilize one or more of the features listed[a]

1. *Personal centralized control*
   1.1   centralized decision-taking
   1.2   direct supervision
   1.3   personal leadership: founded upon ownership or charisma, or technical expertise
   1.4   reward and punishment reinforce conformity to personal authority

2. *Bureaucratic control*
   2.1   breaking down of tasks into easily definable elements
   2.2   formally specified methods, procedures and rules applied to the conduct of tasks
   2.3   budgetary and standard cost-variance accounting controls
   2.4   technology designed to limit variation in conduct of tasks with respect to pace, sequence and possibly physical methods[b]
   2.5   routine decision-taking delegated within prescribed limits
   2.6   reward and punishment systems reinforce conformity to procedures and rules

3. *Output control*
   3.1   jobs and units designed to be responsible for complete outputs
   3.2   specification of output standards and targets
   3.3   use of 'responsibility accounting' systems
   3.4   delegation of decisions on operational matters: semi-autonomy
   3.5   reward and punishment linked to attainment of output targets

4. *Cultural control*
   4.1   development of strong identification with management goals
   4.2   semi-autonomous working: few formal controls
   4.3   strong emphasis on selection, training and development of personnel
   4.4   rewards oriented towards security of tenure and career progression

---

Notes
a. The types of employee who are recruited can be varied to suit employment under each of these control strategies, within the constraints of cost and supply imposed by labour market conditions.
b. Some authorities, such as Richard Edwards (1979), distinguish this as a separate control strategy.
Source: Child (1984: 159).

de-emphasizes bureaucratic or personal control in favour of semi-autonomy *vis-à-vis* higher levels. (For greater detail see Child, 1984: 161–2.)

In French business organizations management control was found to have the following characteristics: control is highly centralized at group level where a relatively large central staff has taken over most of the planning and control functions for the individual units. In many cases the chief executive tries to retain control in his own hands and delegation is minimal. Planning is operations-oriented and tends to be quantitative. But chief executives have little faith in long-term planning while short-term planning appears to be more developed. Top management views on control are inconsistent: on the one hand, chief executives dismiss the cybernetic view of control and believe that it is impossible to prevent or correct subordinates' errors, but, on the other hand, they have adopted all the control procedures designed to achieve a maximum degree of control, albeit not always in a very systematic way. Control is said to be exercised most intensively in production but finance comes a close second. Information to monitor performance is extensively analysed but again consistency and rigour is often lacking. As concerns production control, Horovitz's findings clash with those of other more behaviourally-oriented studies. Whereas Horovitz finds formalism in production control relatively low – particularly as far as specificity of performance criteria, closeness of supervision and links with rewards are concerned – other studies have rated formalism as particularly high and have pointed to the high degree of rule application and the closeness of supervision. These differing results may partly be due to differences in measurement and may again reflect the inconsistency between French management attitudes and actual behaviour. Lastly, the French are considered to have a reasonably tight grasp both in the control of production and of marketing, occupying a middle position between Germany and Britain.

The most notable feature of the French managerial control strategy seems to be the marked inconsistency between different aspects of control and between attitudes and behaviour. This may be due to the fact that *two* strategies of control, which are difficult to harmonize, are applied in combination – personal centralized control and bureaucratic control. Strong elements of personal control are indicated by the efforts of chief executives to exert personal leadership and keep all the threads in their own hands. Conformity to personal authority is sought through the utilization of reward and punishment – determined according to managerial discretion at the lower levels of the organization but not among managers. Top management seeks to counteract the lack of effectiveness of this strategy in large, complex organizations by supplementing it with elements of bureaucratic control. The development of a system of formal rules and procedures is particularly marked but other aspects connected with Taylorist practice are also well developed. Aspects 2.5 and 2.6, delegation of routine decision-taking and a systematized procedure to apply sanctions, however, are superseded by the personalized and highly centralized style of management control.

The German pattern of management control is characterized by a high degree of centralization of both planning and control at group level, executed by a large central staff. Marked centralization of control at headquarters is combined with a policy of 'responsible autonomy' at the lowest, shopfloor level. Both long-and short-term planning are well developed and are characterized by their detailed and systematic nature and their strong emphasis on operations and quantification. The nature of management control is entirely consistent with that of planning. Designation of cost centres, coupled with the precise specification and monitoring of output standards and targets, is aided by a highly developed information system at all levels. This secures management a tight overall grip and particularly in production. On the shopfloor success or failure in the attainment of output targets is rewarded according to clear and mutually agreed rules. In addition, commitment to target attainment is fostered by a relatively strong identification among shopfloor workers with management goals and a strong emphasis on personnel training and development. The latter, inculcating a task orientation, strengthens the former but identification is also fostered by the ideology of a works community (see the discussion in Chapter 2). The German pattern of management control, like the French, is also characterized by a combination of two control strategies – output control (in the weak form of cost centres) and elements of cultural control. In contrast to French practice, however, these two strategies reinforce rather than contradict each other, in as far as the establishment of cost centres at shopfloor level presupposes a high degree of operator competence as well as the existence of trust in management's intentions to honour the equation between rewards and performance. These two congruent strategies thus generate the high degree of consistency and effectiveness, widely associated with German management control. Elements of bureaucratic control are, of course, also utilized – particularly in the larger enterprises and, if given a strong emphasis, come to conflict with the aims of cultural control. This is now widely recognized and there is mounting evidence – examined in Chapter 7 – that bureaucratic control is going to be de-emphasized in future.

In Britain the strategy of bureaucratic control dominates and shapes the pattern of management planning and control. Financial planning and control is clearly dominant and concentrated at group level. Otherwise control is decentralized. The view of control by top management as merely a guiding or steering instrument or, at best, as an early-warning device, is consistently reflected in control practice. Close monitoring of performance, particularly in operations, is not attempted, and the control procedures adopted make for a generally loose management grip. The low degree of conformity to procedures and rules achieved on the shopfloor is further exacerbated by the de-emphasis of a differential reward system, due to union pressure. A system of differential rewards for good performance is eschewed in favour of an egalitarian reward structure, both in terms of basic pay and bonus payments. Although there are elements of output control in as far as subsidiaries are usually treated as profit centres, this strategy is not extended to lower organizational units on the shopfloor where control problems are particularly acute.

This chapter has viewed control largely from the management point of view and has regarded it as an activity designed to ensure that performance is according to plan. It has reviewed the different control practices in Britain, Germany and France and has assessed them in terms of organizational effectiveness. In the following chapter the focus will shift to an analysis of control as perceived by subordinates and will put greater emphasis on the conflict which may be engendered by the assertion of management control.

NOTES

1. For assessments of comparative performance see NEDO (1981); Prais (1981); Northcott et al. (1985); Maitland (1983); Dubois (1981).
2. Total lead time is defined as the time-lag between initiation of an order and completion of that order.
3. Throughput efficiency is the proportion of the total lead-time which is usefully employed in transforming material given the technological constraints of set-up requirements. It is a direct measure of how effectively lead time is used in the production process (New and Myers, 1986: VI).
4. Towers Perrin (1987), quoted in *The Economist*, 6 June 1987; and Kienbaum Vergütungsberatung, Gummersbach (1986), quoted in *Manager Magazin* 10, 1986: 348f.
5. Herz (1983: 104); Gallie (1983: 10) on a British–French comparison.
6. The French and German 'Higher Management' category excludes managers with pay above a certain ceiling so that the figures are not strictly comparable.

6 Job Design and Work Organization

This chapter takes up and develops the theme, first introduced in Chapter 2, of how jobs are designed and work is structured in the three European business organizations. In the first part a section on basic concepts and issues in this area is followed by a short overview of two major approaches to work organization – Scientific Management or Taylorism and the strategy of 'responsible autonomy'. In the second part of this chapter an attempt is made to show the differential impact of Taylorism on industrial practice in Britain, Germany and France and to point to the various factors which determined the three national patterns of work organization. The final section of Chapter 6 deals with the reaction to Taylorism and examines the work reform movement of the 1970s in the three European societies. Chapter 7 goes on to examine the more fundamental changes in production organization which have emerged during the 1980s and combine new forms of work organization with a new technology and market strategy. This latest stage of development was first highlighted in the influential books by Sabel (1982) and Piore and Sabel (1984). They call this new production concept 'flexible specialization' and see it as an alternative to Taylorist work organization which could fundamentally alter future industrial, and hence social development. Chapter 7, using evidence from the three societies, will attempt to evaluate their claims.

JOB DESIGN AND WORK ORGANIZATION: SOME CONCEPTS AND ISSUES

The concept 'job design' indicates the idea that jobs are to be subjected to a conscious and systematic activity of ordering according to a preconceived pattern or plan. Such an approach to jobs originated only with the onset of industrialization. Up to that time the structure of jobs had evolved naturally or was guided by tradition. With the evolvement of the factory system, organized along capitalist principles, the large concentration of people working together led to a new attitude towards labour. It became regarded as a very valuable resource which should be used in the most effective manner. Hence it was resolved that both individual jobs and the relationships between them ought to be designed in a systematic way.

Job design is guided by an underlying notion of what goals are to be achieved by a given design. The definition of these goals is influenced by an estimation of the interests of the two parties involved in the employment relationship – those of the employed who supply the labour power and those of the employers who have bought the right to utilize it. Whereas the interests of employers are fairly straightforward – the most effective utilization of labour at the lowest possible cost, labour hopes to gain not only a sufficient level of material reward but also working arrangements which give some intrinsic satisfaction and do not damage physical or emotional health. Job designers are, therefore, confronted with two formidable problems: first, to establish what the needs are which men try to realize in work and how best to satisfy them; and second – the more formidable problem – how to reconcile as far as possible the very different interests of the two sides in the employment relationship.

It has long been clear that such a reconciliation of interests can be in the economic interest of employers in as far as the effectiveness of work is greatly influenced by the degree of satisfaction workers derive from it. Nevertheless, the emphasis has long concentrated one-sidedly on productive efficiency at the cost of workers' need for fulfilment. In more recent decades, however, the perspective has widened and has increasingly stressed the humanitarian concern that work should also provide workers with satisfaction. It is thus evident that both the theory and practice of work organization is much influenced by the social and economic environment in which it is carried out and that it cannot be a purely rational scientific activity. It is also clear that work organization can be adjusted to this changing environment and that we can expect some variation in job design between societies.

The above observations are expressed in the following definition of job design, reiterated by Louis E. Davis (1979: 30), one of the pioneers in this area, from work done together with Canter in the middle 1950s: 'the organization (or structuring) of a job to satisfy the technical-organizational requirements of the work to be accomplished and the human requirements of the person performing the work.' The idea of organizing or structuring implies that a job consists of a number of elements which can be ordered in different ways. These elements are assigned work tasks. Job design for Davis and Canter accordingly consists of the following three activities:

1.   specifying the content of individual tasks;

2. specifying the method of performing each task including the machinery and tools used and any special techniques;
3. combining individual tasks into specific jobs (ibid.).

Both the specification of task content and, more so, the combination of tasks into jobs can vary along two basic dimensions: specialization and discretion. The degree of specialization can vary from the execution of one detailed simple operation, requiring only one or two body movements, such as the fitting of a part on an assembly line, to the completion of a whole product or process from the beginning to the end. The degree of discretion, afforded in the execution of tasks, is defined by the extent to which the worker can make his/her own decisions about how to execute the task(s) or, conversely, the degree to which task performance is prescribed/controlled by an outside agent. The two dimensions are closely related in as far as simple detail work requires no discretion whereas a job consisting of several tasks does afford at least some. But the degree of discretion afforded also depends on whether the tasks constituting a given job are situated horizontally, i.e. they all have the same degree of complexity, or vertically, i.e. they differ in degree of complexity and include tasks concerned with both the planning/conception *and* the execution of operations.

The above definition of job design also indicates that jobs are not performed in a vacuum but within certain organizational and technical contexts which, although they do not determine jobs, certainly need to be taken into consideration by the designer. There has developed a much greater awareness of the fact that individual jobs are situated in given social and technical contexts, and that they not only closely relate with other jobs but a whole number of organizational and technical variables. Consequently, it has been urged to move away from the design of individual jobs and concentrate instead on work organization, i.e. on how various jobs relate to each other and how they are influenced and influence various contingent factors. The study of work organization is thus a much more complex matter than the preoccupation with job design, and in practice this advice of a more holistic approach is often not heeded. But, as numerous research findings document, job design or redesign will fail unless such a broader view is adopted.

Particularly central to the activity of job redesign must be the question of the degree and nature of the skill possessed by the job-holder and whether there is a reasonable fit between the skill possessed and that required by the job. Skill here is understood as a body of technical knowledge and practical competences relevant to the performance of a given job. Such skill can be fairly narrowly defined and clearly bounded, or it can be of a broad and flexible nature. In the latter case knowledge and capabilities can be applied to a range of different and overlapping tasks. In this case we speak of polyvalency, a concept which has become central to the discussion of the more recent changes in work organization. Polyvalency as a dimension of skill is a personal attribute of the job-holder and his/her status. Polyvalency as a dimension of skill can be applied both horizontally – in direct and indirect production tasks, and vertically, in production and technical and/or supervisory tasks. This kind of polyvalency has to be distinguished from polyvalency as an aspect of work organization which consists of the worker executing more than one task or function. In this case, polyvalency does not define the worker's status.

The design of manual work will have strong repercussions on the nature of managerial work, particularly on the control function which forms a central part of the managerial role. The various theories of job design and work organization which have historically guided practice in this area thus implicitly or explicitly have been based on notions about how managerial control is best accomplished. At the same time, however, such theories are also guided by assumptions about what motivates workers to perform to a desired standard and by the necessity to achieve a degree of congruence between managerial goals and workers' aspirations. There is no space here to outline the many theories and ideas which have informed the debate on, and practice of, work organization during this century. Instead, a summary of the theory which has been influential during most of this century will be followed by a brief outline of an alternative conception which has come into prominence during recent decades.

SCIENTIFIC MANAGEMENT OR TAYLORISM

The first systematic steps in the area of job design were already undertaken at the turn of the century by an engineer (and a former worker), called Frederick Taylor. As Taylor's ideas, referred to as Scientific Management[1] or Taylorism, have remained highly influential up to the present day – albeit often in vulgarized or adapted form – they merit closer examination. Taylor started from the observation that, although management concerned themselves greatly with the capacity and efficiency of their machines, they deployed labour, an equally costly resource, according to 'rules of thumb'. He saw himself as providing a scientific theory which would eliminate a wastage of resources and permit management to utilize labour in the most efficient and effective possible way. To this end he showed, first, how to make work methods more efficient and, second, suggested how management could motivate workers to work harder.

Taylor took up the Babbage principle that efficiency, and hence productivity, increases with the division of labour. He divided jobs into their smallest constituent elements and worked out precisely what kinds of body movements were required by able workmen to execute individual tasks in the shortest possible time without increasing the intensity of labour. Similar tests were carried out to determine the most suitable equipment for each physical action and how the environment should be laid out to contribute to efficient and effective performance. This aspect of Taylor's system can be referred to as the rationalization of the technical preconditions of work. Taylor's advocacy (though not invention) of the principle of maximum decomposition of work tasks implied the minimization of skill requirements – deskilling – in the resulting manual tasks and introduced two new kinds of division of labour. The first, and most insidious, is the separation of mental labour (or conception, planning of labour) from manual labour (or execution, doing); the second is the divorce of direct from indirect labour, i.e. the production tasks from those of setting up, preparation and maintenance.

Although Taylor's 'theory', as outlined so far, regarded manual workers in the same way as machines, he realized that the desired effect would only be attained if workers could be encouraged to cooperate in the execution of his scheme. He suggested that this problem could be solved if management used the following two 'motivators'. First, the workman has to be given precise standards as to what amount of labour is expected of him in a given timespan so that he can judge his progress and achieve satisfaction in the attainment of his target. But Taylor believed in the natural laziness of workers and, therefore, recommended close supervision throughout the work. Control of work is, of course, made easier by the fact that tasks are simple and contain no indeterminate 'mental labour' requirements. Secondly, Taylor postulated that individuals would be willing to work in this way if their pay was made to rise with the amount of effort they invested.

Taylor thus propagated a view of human nature which, with its exclusive emphasis on extrinsic rewards and its implied high degree of toleration of monotonous and meaningless activity, was extremely narrow and confining. Henry Ford's adaptation of Taylor's ideas to the operation of specialized machinery[2] further intensified both the division of labour and its intensity which became dictated by the machine. A quotation from Ford (1922: 168), clearly illustrates the degraded and machine-like nature of the resulting work:

> The lightest jobs were again classified to discover how many of them required the use of full faculties, and we found that 670 could be filled by legless men, 2,637 by one-legged men, two by armless men, 715 by one-armed men, and ten by blind men. Therefore, out of 7,882 kinds of job... 4,034 did not require full physical capacity. (quoted by Littler and Salaman, 1984: 108)

The subsequent world-wide diffusion of Taylorism has not always entailed the adoption of all its elements and frequently involved a merging with elements of other management philosophies and/or techniques of work organization to suit specific national traditions or economic conditions. This circumstance has given rise to disputes among scholars about what can or cannot legitimately be described as Taylorist managerial practices. (For a discussion of this problem see the work of Littler, 1982.) To aid this process of identification of managerial practice it is, therefore, wise to adopt a minimum definition. The following criteria are widely accepted as constituting such a working definition: a high degree of division of labour; a low degree of worker discretion; close task control; and 'a minimum interaction' employment relationship based only on the cash nexus. Despite a lot of worker resistance to the implementation of Scientific Management and even considerable hostility towards it by managers, Taylorism, as defined above, has nevertheless won a widespread and enduring acceptance among management.

There is no doubt that Tayloristic forms of work organization have gained management huge increases in productivity, achieved both directly and indirectly through enhanced control over the labour process. The various advantages accruing to management from a high degree of specialization and a low level of discretion in work organization have been usefully summarized in tabular form by Child (1984: 30, Table 2.1:).

But Taylorism is much more than a mere set of techniques to increase the efficiency of labour. Marxist analyses of Scientific Management, such as the influential work of Braverman (1974), see it as fundamental to the development of monopoly capitalism. Braverman focuses on the control strategy which enabled management to increase capital accumulation by stepping up worker output. Taylorism, says Braverman, enabled management to assume direct control over the labour process and, at the same time, led to the degradation of shopfloor work.

Braverman particularly underlines the point that the separation within work of the tasks of conception from those of execution and their

Table 6.1   Advantages to the employer claimed to arise from greater specialization and reduced discretion in jobs at the operative level

1. *Advantages ascribed primarily to greater specialization*
    1.1 increase in the workers' dexterity
    1.2 saving of time lost in switching from one task to another
    1.3 reduction of time lost when jigs and tools have to be changed
    1.4 ability to hire lower skilled labour which is cheaper and more readily replaced
    1.5 reduction in training time and the attendant wastage of materials
    1.6 development of specialized machinery is encouraged
    1.7 facilitation of the substitution of machine for manual pacing and guidance, and eventually the mechanization or automation of manual operations
    1.8 eases the application of 'scientific' method study based on measurement instead of the workers' 'rule of thumb'

2. *Advantages ascribed primarily to reduced discretion*
    2.1 permits management rather than workers to establish methods of work
    2.2 permits management rather than workers to establish standards of performance
    2.3 reduces loss of time involved in consultation and discussions with workers
    2.4 is consistent with hiring of less trained and cheaper labour

transfer to management robbed labour of any remaining control over the labour process. He spells out vividly the effects of Scientific Management on the nature of work: it has become fragmented, monotonous, meaningless detail work, robbing the worker of the opportunity to apply skill or exercise discretion. It is closely monitored and controlled by management and, lastly, labour has become cheapened and easy to substitute.

For Braverman, as Wood and Kelly (1982: 76) point out, management under capitalism has reached its purest expression in Taylorism. Hence any post-Taylorist developments in management are either viewed by Braverman as complementary to Taylorism or are dismissed as inconsequential. Braverman implicitly denies that an alternative strategy of work organization could ever develop under capitalism. Subsequent critiques of Braverman have challenged the view that there is a coherent and persistent management strategy and that management practice is only or primarily aimed at increasing the direct control over the labour process. More empirically-based studies have shown that the goal of capital accumulation can be pursued by other means or that control over labour can be achieved by a variety of strategies, such as by bureaucratic or ideological control.

THE STRATEGY OF 'RESPONSIBLE AUTONOMY'

One such alternative management strategy to organize and control labour, referred to as 'responsible autonomy', has been elaborated by A. Friedman (1977). Friedman's starting point is the Marxist insight that when an employer buys labour power he acquires something which is highly variable in its possibilities and can be moulded by management to suit its particular purpose. The strategy of 'responsible autonomy' 'tries to harness the adaptability of labour power by giving workers leeway and encouraging them to adapt to the changing requirements of the firm'. To induce workers to behave in this way and to even display loyalty towards their employing organization, managers give workers status, authority and responsibility (ibid.: 84).

The adoption of this management strategy, argues Friedman, requires not only the construction of an elaborate ideological apparatus (ibid.: 101) but also many drastic organizational changes, such as, for example, a reduction of supervisory labour and the introduction of employment security. Hence this strategy cannot be adopted or abandoned at will. Friedman nevertheless implies that it is entirely within the choice of management to encourage 'responsible autonomy' and that management usually does this in response to worker unrest or conflict. We shall argue in the following chapter that all these assumptions greatly over-simplify matters. These weaknesses in Friedman's argument are due to the fact that he neglects to consider that a successful implementation of the 'responsible autonomy' strategy depends on the availability of workers who have been systematically prepared to operate in a responsible and autonomous fashion. In short, he neglects the crucial variable of skill and the various attitudinal qualities, acquired through systematic vocational training.

TAYLORISM IN BRITAIN, GERMANY AND FRANCE

The description earlier in this chapter of the philosophy and practice of Scientific Management indicated that, because it brought tremendous advantages to management, it became a strong influence on management practice which has retained its hold right up to the present day. Taylorism or Fordism spread from the USA all over the industrialized and industrializing world and was widely accepted – albeit often in a partial or altered form – by European management from the 1930s onwards.[3] Diffusion of Taylorism was aided by the internationalization of technology – which was usually accompanied by American management techniques, and by the spread of multinational companies. Important in the widespread acceptance of Taylorism were the facts that, during the first half of the twentieth century, and particularly from the 1930s onwards, there occurred the emergence of a world economy and, for the more advanced industrial countries, of vast mass markets for industrial goods. The principles of Taylorism are, of course, particularly adapted to the production of large quantities of standardized and relatively cheap goods by special-purpose machinery. This was first spectacularly demonstrated by Henry Ford in the first decades of this century with his mass production of Model-T cars, based on assembly-line technology and the labour of semi-skilled operatives. A few decades later, European industrialists such as the Michelin brothers strove to emulate him, and gradually Taylorism, or at least Taylorist techniques, became an accepted practice in all three societies. But Scientific Management has never penetrated the three European societies to the same extent and today still shows a correspondingly different hold on their production organization. It had to interact with, and adapt to, pre-existing national economic strategies, managerial culture, industrial relations systems and, above all, with the extant qualification structure of the labour force and expectations of both managers and workers resulting from it. A Taylorist strategy was always operated, to a greater or lesser extent, side by side with a strategy of 'responsible autonomy', as outlined on p.144. To document this differential mix of Taylorist and alternative strategies over time would require a lengthy monograph. This chapter can do no more than sketch an outline of the initial reception of Taylorism in the three societies and then concentrate the discussion on the situation in the 1960s and early 1970s, before the new forms of work organization began to emerge.

In *France*, the ground was well prepared for Taylorism as an intellectual system or a general philosophy. Both the influence of Saint-Simonian technological utopianism and the existence of a technically-minded bourgeois élite ensured that Taylor's ideas were accepted very enthusiastically at an early period. But their appeal was on a theoretical level rather than as a set of techniques to be applied in production. As the French technical élite was influential in government administration which was, in any case, suffused with a centralist and rationalist orientation, the 'rational administration' element of Taylor's thought was to prove influential in this sphere. As Merkle (1980: 148) puts it: 'the French ... siezed on Taylorism ... as a revolutionary system of technical organization with broad implications, not only for production, but for society as well.'

With few exceptions, however, Taylorist ideas and practice were met with hostility by both the French *patronat* and the working class. Employers' rejection was prompted both by economic and by (power) political interests. During the early decades of the century the French economy still consisted to an overwhelming degree of small, owner-managed firms. These produced for small quality and luxury goods markets in which the techniques of mass production had no place. French employers managed their enterprises in a highly autocratic style, basing their authority on their presumed charismatic gifts. An introduction of Taylorist methods would have meant the entry into these enterprises of an intermediate stratum of technical specialists whose appeal to knowledge as a basis of authority would have undermined owners' 'divine rights' to rule.

Owners' opposition to Taylorist practices was matched by the hostility with which the organized working class rejected them. Not only did workers resent deskilling and the negative effects of speed-ups on health and strength, they also feared that the increase in productivity this achieved would result in a permanent increase in unemployment in an economy with both limited markets and a large labour supply. The few attempts before World War I to introduce Taylorist practice into factories were met with strike action and generally attracted unfavourable publicity. The First World War, requiring mass production of armaments and bringing increasing contacts with American industrial technique, undermined the traditionalist attitudes on the part of employers to some extent. The substitution of semi-skilled workers for the skilled workers, recruited into the armed forces, also created a more favourable climate for the introduction of Taylorism.

Greater acceptance after the war was also aided by the fact that the state accepted responsibility for a more equal redistribution of the increased surplus created by Taylorist methods by instituting socialistic welfare reforms. Taylorism's acceptance by employers was also aided by its eventual integration with native management theory created at that time by Fayol. Fayolism was more concerned with the administrative problems of executive leadership at the top of the business organization and, possessing greater attraction for traditional owner-managers, was seen as complementary to Taylorist teaching which appealed to the lower, technical elements.

The French school of Scientific Management which arose after 1925 gave more emphasis to Fayol's than to Taylor's ideas. It allowed the *patron* to continue in his traditional role of top manager and also did not undermine the independence of the French working class. The result, according to Merkle (1980: 166–7), was that Scientific Management penetrated many French firms in form, but not in substance. This state of affairs lasted right until the early 1960s. After that, the growing concentration of French industry into large units and the increasing production for mass markets, together with the substitution of traditionalist owners by technocratic managers, provided a much broader scope for the introduction of Scientific Management.

In *Germany*, too, Taylor's idea found an early intellectual resonance, albeit for different reasons. But again, only certain elements of Taylor's system, such as his notion that organizations are amenable to scientific study, his emphasis on efficiency, and also his idea of class collaboration instead of class conflict, were taken up (Maier, 1970). They were seen to have an 'elective affinity' with pre-existing German cultural concerns and political interests. Rather than following Taylor's interest in industrial application, his ideas were seen as a general guide to organizational design and provided impulses for the reorganization of whole sectors of industry. In 1924, these developments culminated in a national rationalization movement and rationalization plan. All this does not mean that Taylorism was ignored by industrial engineers. On the contrary, they played an important role in propagating it. Unfortunately, we get no indication from Merkle's (1980) work to what extent Taylorism, as a method of organizing industrial labour, gained acceptance on German shopfloors. The survival of a strong craft tradition leads one to believe that, at this level, Taylorism remained relatively weakly diffused.

This receptivity to elements of Taylorism in France and Germany – because it harmonized with existing cultural traditions and social interests – was almost completely absent in Britain at the beginning of the century. The British did not believe in general managerial plans but preferred more individualized solutions to industrial problems. The gentlemanly ideal of leadership and the absence of a technical élite also meant that there were no social groups which could have acted as carriers of Taylorist philosophy. Also the more progressive British management thinkers, influenced by Quakerism, who were prone to stress owners' obligations as much as their rights, explicitly rejected Taylorite individualism and emphasized a more communal approach to industrial organization (Fox, 1974: 197). Lastly, the existence of a powerful and militant labour movement, hostile to Taylorist practice, evoked a concern in management to minimize action which would exacerbate existing conflict.

As in France, however, the war provided an opening for Taylorist practice. But the more general introduction of Taylorist techniques came only in the 1930s when declining British competitiveness could no longer be ignored. It came, however, in a softened form which combined British welfare management – with an emphasis on worker health and psychology – with Taylorist production organization. (For more detail of the British variant of Taylorism, see the work of Littler, 1982.) The introduction of this modified version of Taylorism coincided with a period of economic depression which rendered worker opposition less effective. Where Taylorist methods were introduced the emphasis was characteristically more on the cost-cutting side of Taylorism rather than on its output maximization side. Many industries, however, where craftworkers still predominated, were only minimally touched by the new managerial practice.

In the more recent past – the 1960s and early 1970s – German industry has stood out as being the least penetrated, though by no means unaffected, by Taylorist strategy whereas British and, more so, French employers have been more receptive to Taylorist techniques. The following brief examination of the three national patterns of work organization during this period will utilize Littler's (1982) comparative schema and analyse employer strategies in terms of three dimensions: division of labour/degree of discretion; structure of control; and employment relationship. This analysis, summarized in Table 6.2, makes it possible to characterize national patterns in ideal-typical form and place them on a continuum from the strategy of 'responsible autonomy' at one end of the pole to that of full Taylorism at the other. At the same time, this exercise will identify the circumstances which have shaped national employer strategies along each of the three dimensions. Particular emphasis will be given to the process of vocational training for all categories of labour and the resulting skill profile of the workforce, the labour market structure, and the ensuing authority and power relations within the enterprise. The influence of this syndrome of factors on employer strategies is eloquently expressed in the following quotation from Maurice et al. (1986a: 67):

> Although dividing up a production process and defining work stations may seem to be purely technical acts, they are in fact choices based on socially defined criteria. They are not merely contingent but also true decisions, based on assumptions about the worker's psychology, capabilities, interests, and reasons for working.

Other relevant circumstances are the system of industrial relations, the markets catered for, and the composition of the manufacturing sector both in terms of industries and of size of firms. These factors are at least partially independent from the training syndrome. Other factors which might have been important, such as degree of economic/technological development, have not differed enough between the three societies in recent decades to be of significance.

Table 6.2 Capitalist employer strategies on work organization up to the early 1980s

Responsible autonomy			Taylorism
	Germany	*Britain*	*France*
Division of labour	Large proportion of highly skilled	Deskilled (pockets of high skill in craft sector)	Deskilled
	Low formalization of both horizontal and vertical boundaries	High formalization of both horizontal and vertical boundaries	High formalization only of vertical boundaries
	High level of discretion	Low level of discretion	Low level of discretion
Structure of control	Predominantly ideological control	Weak task control	Strong task control/remnants of ideological control
Employment relationship	High degree of employment security for the core labour force	Complete substitutibility of workers	High degree of employment security for the core labour force

Adapted from Littler (1982: 193, Table 12.2).

As pointed out above, in *Germany* the craft paradigm and the managerial strategy of 'responsible autonomy' remained most central to the national economy. The first factor predisposing German management towards a strategy of 'responsible autonomy' in work organization is the skill profile of the manual working class. This has already been discussed in Chapter 3. Here it suffices to underline the main points as they are relevant to the 'work organization' debate. All through the postwar period, there has been in German industry a predominance of skilled workers with high, formally labelled and certified qualifications. This proportion has stayed almost constant up to the late 1970s (Mooser, 1984). Although there is not always a correlation between official skill labels and actual skill exercised, in Germany this correspondence is widely held to be close. The expansion of mass production industries has to a large extent drawn on un- and semi-skilled immigrant (*Gastarbeiter*) and female labour but also on skilled workers from economically declining sectors and the artisan *Handwerk* sector. The nature of the skills imparted to skilled workers is best summed up by the concept of polyvalency, i.e. knowledge and capabilities in two or more areas, acquired through systematic rotation during training. Polyvalency of skill permits a broad and flexible utilization of labour across boundaries between production and technical work. Polyvalency has not, as in the case of British craftsmen, been undermined by the erection of highly formalized boundaries between skills. Polyvalency of the German type also furthers cooperation within work groups across hierarchical divisions and thus provides a natural foundation for the institution of semi-autonomous work groups, to be discussed in more detail in later sections.

German semi-skilled workers' training, although less broad and deep, is nevertheless also systematically oriented towards polyvalency. (Their level of skill, according to Maurice et al. (1986a: 72), is as high as that of French so called 'skilled' workers in categories OP_1 and OP_2.) This is illustrated by a case study of a German petrochemical plant where 90 per cent of semi-skilled workers were capable of executing any job in the plant, according to the plant manager (Maurice et al., 1986.: 69).

This existence of a large pool of skilled, polyvalent workers has predisposed employers to implement the strategy of 'responsible autonomy'. (The concept used here is adapted from Friedman, 1979.) It refers to a strategy which allows workers a reasonable scope in utilizing their skills and trusting them to use them responsible, i.e. in the interest of their employing organization. This strategy implies a structure of control which minimizes task control and instead exerts ideological control. The control structure utilizes an ideology, inculcated during the training process. Contrary to Friedman, however, the inculcation of the tenets of this ideology does not require a complex ideological apparatus but occurs almost imperceptibly as a by-product of the technical training process. The ideology is based on the idea of a professional community in which superiors are respected as 'experts' rather than as punitive supervisors or controllers, and a common task orientation dwells on unity of purpose and de-emphasizes hierarchical divisions. Reduced task control in German industry is indicated by the facts that the authority over the organization and monitoring of work in progress is vested in the chargehand and that the foreman is regarded more as a technical expert than as a punitive supervisor. This ideology is also expressed in, and reinforced by, the system of industrial relations which is characterised by a cooperative style (For details, see Chapters 8–9.) Lastly, the foregoing makes clear that, contrary to Friedman, the implementation of the strategy of responsible autonomy constitutes not merely a management reaction to worker unrest but has been a much more enduring feature of German management control deeply embedded into the general institutional framework.

This well-established pattern of work organization has led undertakings to pursue certain development and market strategies. First, it has had the consequence that small and medium-sized firms in the 'artisan' sector have been kept alive and thriving. In the 1970s around 25 per cent of the total number of firms were still in the *Handwerk* sector, and 20 per cent of the employed worked in it. (For a discussion of the skill profile of the labour force in the *Handwerk* sector, see Mendius and Sengenberger, 1987.) It has meant, for example, that German food and drinks production, which in Britain occurs largely by standardized mass production methods in large plants, is still predominantly accomplished by craft methods in the artisan sector. As this sector also undertakes a disproportionate amount of the training of apprentices, it further reinforces employer strategies.

Secondly, the large pool of skilled manpower at all levels of the hierarchy has promoted the development of industries, requiring a large input of high-skill labour, such as the machine-tool industry, as well as orienting production within the various sectors to the high-quality end of the market where precision, reliability and good after sales service are more important than low price. Obvious examples are again the machine-tool industry and, within mass-production sectors, most of the car makers (BMW, Mercedes, Audi). Conversely, production activities requiring a less skilled labour force, such as textiles, have been relocated to 'low-wage' countries in Germany, but not in Britain or France. These economic developments, in turn, react back on training policies and labour utilization, setting up a virtuous circle.

The employment relationship which has evolved under the influence of legislation on the rights and obligations of workers within the enterprise during the postwar period (for details see Chapters 8–9) has given workers high *de facto* employment security. Skilled workers, in addition, have enjoyed the security of having access to the external labour market instead of being bound to the changeable fortunes of one employing organization. This has prevented a casualization of the labour force which has also been impeded by the centralized processes of wage determination and, hence, has led to a relatively weak development of economic dualism. Although growing unemployment began to threaten this security from 1973 onwards, it did so very selectively. The victims of unemployment were predominantly the unskilled who have been uninfluential in the presentation of worker grievances both on works councils and in the unions. Thus their growing insecurity did not significantly alter the cooperative enterprise culture. Lastly, the employment relationship in the sizeable German sector of small to medium-sized firms was often still characterized by paternalism (see Chapter 4).

It would, of course, be wrong to claim that the strategy of 'responsible autonomy' has been adopted by all German employers or has been extended to all employees within given enterprises. From the 1960s onwards, Germany too began to imitate the American pattern of mass production of standardized goods, and the Taylorist model of production organization became more prominent. The rapid expansion of industry during that period led to a shortage of skilled workers. Many industries, at that time, were forced to operate with large pools of semi-skilled labour and thus opted for a form of work organization which departed from the 'craft' type. This was particularly true of industries such as cars, metal, and chemicals manufacture. According to Sengenberger (1984b: 35), formerly skilled jobs were divided into semi-skilled ones, and a tendency towards polarization of the skill structure developed. This was first drawn to the attention of sociologists by the work of Kern and Schumann in 1970. Thus, in the early 1970s, in Germany too, the contours of production began to blur through the superimposition of the American 'mass production–mass consumption' model on the 'custom-production for export' model (Piore and Sabel, 1984: 150). But, unlike in France and Britain, the elements of the latter model never became completely destroyed and still managed to retain an important place both in production activity and in cultural/educational discourse.

But even in the mass-production industries semi-skilled workers were still being trained to become polyvalent and hence full-blown Taylorism was still eschewed. Within the 'continuous process' industries, for example, which in Britain and France have operated largely with specialized semi-skilled workers, German workers were still being trained in, and permitted to exercise, some traditional manual skills which become particularly important at breakdown points. (This example is taken from Maurice et al., 1986a: 70, who also supply other examples of non-Taylorist labour deployment within mass production firms.)

In one sense, at least, there has been a stronger predisposition in the German than the British manufacturing organization to adopt a Taylorist strategy. The high proportion of scientists and, more so, engineers at all levels of management has fostered the development of a technocratic ethos which might have induced management to favour ostensibly 'scientific' solutions to the problem of worker control. But this has been counteracted by the fact that the 'craft' origins of a significant proportion of management, who had themselves undergone an apprenticeship, had made them internalize the ideology of a professional community.

French employer strategies during the period under consideration have been the polar opposite of German ones. In France, the reservoir of skilled labour was much lower. Apprenticeship-type training did not extend beyond a very narrow artisan sector. The rapid expanison of French industry and its transformation, under state guidance, to a modern corporate type (smaller firms were merged into larger ones) between 1959 and 1970 brought additional changes. Production for mass markets on the American model became possible and meant the subversion of any remaining craft practices. The rapid expansion of the economy within a relatively short timespan necessitated the absorption of a high proportion of new workers – former agricultural workers, women and immigrant labour – completely unfamiliar with an industrial culture and its demands in terms of competence and discipline. Even those who did receive training and were classified as 'skilled' workers (categories OP_2, OP_3 and OQ) were given only a relatively narrow, firm-specific kind of skill, and they acquired it by a quite different process from that familiar to German workers.

This process, Maurice et al. (1986a: 74) emphasize, is crucial to the formation of worker identity and, consequently, to his/her attachment to, and control by, the employing firm and its management. French employers have favoured a type of labour deployment which requires workers to adapt to predefined, and rigidly classified, jobs rather than, as in Germany, moulded jobs around existing worker skills. This system of classifying jobs rather than workers' qualification gives high priority to administration rather than to professional competence. It thus becomes incompatible with achieving polyvalency of skill. In the words of Piore and Sabel (1984: 141), 'French managerial practice is obstructive of the acquisition of craft knowledge'. Polyvalent workers, however, are not totally absent in the French system but they constitute a small, financially privileged minority. They are trained in-firm to a technically high standard to cope with the rigidities the French system of work organization fosters. Polyvalency within this system, moreover, is regarded as no more than the capacity for holding several jobs/executing several tasks and not as an attribute of worker capability and professional status. This type of polyvalency is disliked by French unions. They view the existence of highly paid polyvalent workers as undermining the egalitarian bureaucratic principle, involved in the notion of advancement according to seniority (ibid.).

This skill profile at the manual worker level has been accompanied by relatively high levels of technical skill among management and staff. Among the former, engineers have set the tone. In this context, Taylorism, with its emphasis on the separation between planning and implementation, a high degree of division of labour and close supervision of labour strongly recommended itself as a work organization and control strategy. Low levels of worker discretion and a high degree of task control are thus seen as distinguishing features of French employer strategies by many authors. (For details, see Chapters 2 and 4.)

But what has been described so far applies mainly to the 'large-firm' sector and, despite the growth in significance of the latter from the 1960s onwards, there is still a sizeable sector of small and medium-sized firms in the French economy. Thus in 1976 34.2 per cent of all manufacturing employment was still in firms with less than 200 employees (Storey, 1982: 8), and in 1984 49 per cent of French firms employed fewer than 50 workers (*The Economist*, 9 February 1985). In these firms mass-production techniques are not always viable and control is often a mixture of task and ideological control. The latter is based on a paternalist employment relationship in which redundancy is sometimes excluded even if economic pressures might suggest this tactic (Berger, 1980). But this paternalist relationship is not found in all small firms. The fact that some of the labour protection legislation does not apply in the smaller firms has meant that casualization of labour is extensive in this sector (Berger, 1980: 36f). In contrast to the situation in Germany, this sector does not fulfil the function of training large numbers of apprentices and thus does not foster the idea of a professional community.

In *Britain* Taylorist employer strategies have become more widely established than in Germany during the postwar period but they have been applied in a much more half-hearted and inconsistent form than has been the case in France. Inconsistency or ambiguity flows from two sources. The first, and by now less significant one, is the coexistence in British industry of a small 'craft' sector (both in craft and mass production) in which work is still characterized by a relatively low division of labour and high level of discretion, with a large mass-production sector, dominated by semi-skilled workers engaged in monotonous, deskilled detail work. (For examples of work in the craft sector, see accounts of work organization in the engineering industry in Wood, 1982.) The second, and more formidable inconsistency lies in employer strategy. In the mass-production industries, a high division of labour (including that between direct and indirect labour) and a fairly rigid separation of planning and implementation is accompanied by a structure of control which, while eschewing ideological control, is neither fully committed to task control nor to a strategy of 'responsible autonomy'. By international standards British workers have achieved a relatively high degree of control over the organization of the labour process (e.g. joint regulation in the areas of job definition, task allocation, manning). But this control has not been granted as part of a strategy stressing worker 'responsible autonomy' which, indeed, is quite incompatible with deskilled detail work. This control orientation on the part of British management, it was argued in Chapter 4, can be attributed to both the social origins and the relatively low level of technical training of managers which hinder the development of a task and production-orientation among them.

In Britain, due to the prominent role of unions in the training and accreditation process, the notion of skill is fundamentally different from that accepted in Germany. The granting of skilled status to craft apprentices means, at the same time, the bestowing of a job territory and the subsequent defence of that territory by the craft unions against the claims of other trades or of unskilled workers; skill thus has a developed social dimension and rests as much on exclusion practices as on highly developed technical capabilities and 'craft' knowledge. This notion of skill which attaches both to the worker and to the job has been impossible to reconcile with polyvalency of either the German or the French variety. Craft workers in production are now found in only a few industries – particularly in engineering and shipbuilding – but their proportion even in these industries has been declining all through the 1960s and 1970s. In most industries, semi-skilled workers have set the tone both in the labour process and in industrial relations. British semi-skilled workers receive only a short, narrow and firm-specific training. In contrast to their French equivalents, they have few chances to advance to 'skilled' status after reaching a degree of seniority in their employing firm. Their only chance to retain or improve their working conditions lies in collective organization. Like their 'craft' counterparts, they have been committed to the practice of demarcation, i.e. defending their job territory by refusing, for example, to move to another machine.

This combination in British employer strategies of a high division of labour with only a patchy task control is complemented by an employment relationship based on the principle of minimum interaction. This is particularly true of the 'large firm' sector which, in Britain, has far outweighed the 'small to medium-sized firm' sector all through the postwar period, both in size and in influence at the ideological level. The growing importance of firm-specific training of semi-skilled workers makes them dependent on a given employer but the latter do not necessarily give them access to the internal labour market. Up to recently, unions have been able to protect their members against the ensuing threat to employment security but this capacity of unions has greatly weakened during the 1970s and early 1980s.

Thus, to summarize, although Taylorist employer practices have been widespread during the postwar period in all three societies, their penetration has been most thoroughgoing in France and least in

Germany, while Britain has occupied a somewhat ambiguous middle position. The differences, it has been argued, are due not only to the differing numerical preponderance in the workforce of skilled workers but also to the differential processes by which skill is produced among all types of workers and the uses to which it has been put. This has, on the one side, led to differing worker identities, expectations and attachments to the employing organization and, on the other, has channelled employer goals and practices in differing directions. These differences are summarized in schematic form in Table 6.2 (see p.149).

THE REACTION AGAINST TAYLORISM I: NEW FORMS OF WORK ORGANIZATION

Although Taylorist forms of work organization and control have evoked resistance from workers from the time of their very inception, the late 1960s/early 1970s saw a new stage in the rejection of Taylorism in many advanced societies. Several strike waves and the more diffuse resistance, manifested in increased absenteeism, labour turnover, and in labour recruitment problems, made it clear to employers that Taylorism now presented them with as many control problems as it had seemed to solve in the past. Increases in both levels of education and the general standard of living, together with a tight labour market situation, made workers increasingly reluctant to put up with stultifying and mentally exhausting jobs. Their dissatisfaction became heightened during this period because the intensification of economic growth, technological advance and productivity increases threw the constraints of Taylorism into sharp relief. In France, the excessively close control by management was also singled out as a major grievance (Düll, 1984: 10).

Management reacted to this situation with suggestions for work reform, designed to alleviate the negative consequences of Taylorist practices. The following approaches to work reform have been utilized:

Job enlargement combines two or more different task elements horizontally into an 'enlarged' job. The term 'horizontal' indicates that the combined task elements are at the same (usually low) level of complexity and thus do not significantly raise the permitted degree of discretion. This combination of tasks does, however, lengthen work-cycle times and may also make close monitoring of work less easy.

Job enrichment implies a more radical rethinking of task combination in that it suggests a vertical integration of tasks. This may permit the jobholder to execute tasks concerned with aspects of the planning of, and preparation for, core tasks, or it may involve the taking over of indirect tasks, such as quality control or basic maintenance of machinery. Job enrichment strategies thus try to overcome both excessive specialization and to inject some discretion into jobs, as well as permitting a more holistic approach to work which allows the job-holder to 'see a job through' from beginning to end.

Job rotation is a variant of job enlargement which demands that job-holders rotate between tasks in succession rather than executing all the tasks continually. Tasks can be either of the same or of a differing level of complexity. Like job enlargement, job rotation gains management flexibility in that workers can cover for each other during absences but it does not necessarily increase productivity.

Semi-autonomous work-groups. The label 'semi-autonomous' suggests that the group is, to some extent, insulated from external authority and, within limits, makes its own decisions. Group work permits job enlargement or enrichment to occur in accordance with the different capabilities and preferences of individual group members as well as furthering their social and communication needs and skills. Management reaps benefits from this arrangement in terms of obtaining greater flexibility, superior collective 'problem-solving' capacity, as well as being able to rely on mutual social control of group members.

The suggestions for the reform of work organization thus promoted the following objectives: greater worker autonomy – giving workers some monitoring or control tasks; greater task variety; self-regulation of work speed and of work sequence, as well as some choice over work methods; more opportunity for cooperation between workers; and, lastly, more holistic work structures, permitting the completion of task from beginning to end.[4]

But very soon, other employers' concerns – preoccupation with changed market conditions and production requirements – began to mingle with those about organization. Management became increasingly concerned to increase the flexibility of production structures and labour deployment to cope with changed market demands (European Foundation, 1978: 22f; Delamotte, 1979: 52; Stähle, 1979: 82; Auer, Penth and Tergeist, 1983: 127). The onset of recession and the changed labour market conditions, too, tended to divert employers and the state from a concern for the effects of Taylorist structures on labour. In France the political interlude of the Socialist government (1981–86) briefly reverted attention to workers' concerns and the issues of greater industrial democracy.

The movement for the enhancement of the quality of working life assumed different forms, scope and importance in each society. These divergences were due to pre-existing economic concerns and patterns of conflict/cooperation between unions, employers and the state. The reform movement acquired the widest scope in Germany, where, under the name 'Humanization of Working Life' (*Humanisierung des Arbeitslebens*), it had already started in the late 1960s. The movement took an integrated form, encompassing three different but related goals: the creation of new forms of work organization; the humane design of jobs and of the working environment (including issues of occupational health, safety and hygiene, as well as the concern for a social cushioning from the effects of technological innovation); and the participation of employees in changes affecting them (the latter refers to a strengthening/elaboration of co-determination rights through the works council).

In France, the reform movement – under the slogan 'The Improvement of Working Conditions' (*Amélioration des Conditions de Travail* – ACT) – also assumed considerable momentum in the 1970s and, although less comprehensive than in Germany, tried to integrate the above three aspects in a similar, though less systematic, way. In Britain, attempts to improve the quality of working life remained more piecemeal and never became a reform *movement*. Also the focus remained narrowly fixed on only the first of the above three objectives – the creation of non-Taylorist forms of work organization. After the assumption of power by the Conservatives in 1979 the already modest attempts came almost to a complete standstill. This state of affairs is well summed up by Littler and Salaman (1984: 81):

> Throughout the 1970s these principles (of good job design) were the gospel of a few avant-garde consultants, and though there were isolated examples of new work systems, generally job design remained tied to traditional Taylorian principles.

The relative rarity of experimentation with new forms of work organization is also emphasized by the European Foundation Report (1978: 17f) on the British situation.

A comprehensive 'humanization of work' (HoW) programme was launched in Germany in 1974, under a Social-Democratic government. It was conceived and pursued in a corporatist manner, with employers' federations, the state, the scientific community and, after some hesitation, also the unions working together in a planned and co-ordinated way. The state[5] has played a very prominent role, acting as a source of finance and as a coordinator of the project. This prominent involvement and relatively generous financing[6] on the part of the state was only partly prompted by a concern for the conditions of labour and by a new preoccupation with a preventative approach to occupational health. It was at the same time conceived as part of the state's technology policy and of its more general industrial modernization policy (for details see Chapter 10). This latter emphasis came more to the fore after the changeover, in 1982, to a Conservative government.

In France, the reform movement was more directly an urgent response to what became perceived as a major crisis in industrial relations. First the worker revolt during the May 1968 events and then the strike waves initiated by unskilled workers of the early 1970s galvanized both the employers and the state into action. The traditional reluctance of the major unions to cooperate with employers in a joint project – for fear that it might strengthen the latter, was also typical of the ACT movement. Hence the initiative was sustained by the state and the employers' federations, as well as being actively supported by many individual, and groups of, managers (e.g. Jenkins, 1981: 7f).

Initially the state's involvement was strongly motivated both by a humanitarian concern for labour and by the attempt to use the situation to stimulate a dialogue between the two sides of industry. Both concerns are expressed in the 1973 law, the major state response, taking the initiative on a number of different fronts. This preoccupation continued to be expressed in the 1975 Sudreau Report.[7] But, as in Germany, the state's initiative was also tied into its more general policy of industrial restructuring and modernization, and in time this latter focus became stronger (Auer et al., 1983: 149). The state (through the Ministry of Labour) made available considerable sums (though less than the German state) for research, preparing for, guiding and evaluating experiments in industry with new forms of work organization.[8] In addition to these state-sponsored and supervised experiments, trying to involve both sides of industry, there were also countless projects, initiated by individual firms, acting either independently or under the umbrella of the CNPF, the national employers' federation. (For details on the latter, see Jenkins, 1981.)

In Britain, discussions on work restructuring started under the Wilson government. In 1973 a tripartite steering group was set up to study the problem. One of the initiatives of this group was the founding of the Work Research Unit (WRU) financed by the Department of Employment. Its initial brief was to do research on work restructuring and to set up and evaluate specific projects in this area, as well as generally assist both management and unions in practical ways in their efforts to reform work. Although attempts were made to tackle the problem of work restructuring in a corporatist manner, the fragmented and decentralized nature of both trade union and employer organizations, as well as the scepticism of the unions about employer intentions, prevented the development of sustained concerted action. The decentralized union power structure makes it almost impossible to integrate general economic policy with union policy on labour issues. In those cases where individual employers took the initiative in restructuring work, objectives were largely the same as in Germany and France, though slightly greater emphasis has been put on raising productivity and on improving industrial relations (European Foundation for the Improvement of Living and Working Conditions 1978: 22f). The commitment of many British unions to demarcation practices often undermined any restructuring attempt which tried to introduce greater fluidity of job boundaries (ibid.: 38–9).

The non-interventionist stance of the state also precluded the emergence of a strong initiative from this direction, and hence work restructuring never gained the wide scope nor the same momentum as it did among Britain's continental neighbours. British unions, operating in a more depressed economic environment than their continental counterparts, also became much more concerned with job security and levels of income than with the quality of working life and thus did little to keep the issues in the public eye. Consequently, the whole problematic seems to have disappeared from public agendas since the early 1980s.

If we now turn towards the content of policy and practice of the work reform movement and towards evaluations of its achievements and/or missed opportunities, both commonalities and divergencies between the three societies need to be drawn out. In all three attempts were made to overcome Taylorist rigidities by introducing the new forms of work organization. (For further details on the many restructuring exercises, consult European Foundation for the Improvement of the Quality of Working Life, 1978; ILO, 1979; Jenkins, 1981; Savall, 1981; Auer et al., 1983; Ruffier, 1984.) Generally speaking, the less radical job enlargement and job rotation loomed larger than attempts to enrich either individual jobs or series of jobs through the creation of semi-autonomous work-groups. Also the transformation of assembly-lines and the lengthening of work-cycles are widely reported as modest achievements of work restructuring in all three societies (Auer, Penth and Tergeist, 1983). French and German practice, in addition, has been distinguished by systematically tying these restructuring exercises to attempts to reduce both the physical hazards and the mental stress of work. It is in this less controversial area that the most significant gains for workers have been made. (The French 1976 Work Protection Act, for example, is credited with having achieved such gains.)

Turning to a more general evaluation of the reforms, the balance of opinion is one of disappointment. The failure of many individual restructuring exercises has been due to the fact that there has been a lack of recognition that work has to be analysed within a socio-technical system in which social and technical relations have to be redesigned together and in which change in one area excites a whole chain of adjustments in other parts of the organization. In other words, changes have been too piecemeal and not radical enough in their scope. Although countless individual restructuring exercises have been evaluated very positively by both the workers and the management involved, they have often remained isolated experiments. This lack of a broader diffusion is due to the fact that, although the experiments have solved old problems, they have often created new ones which are difficult to solve in the current economic framework. Thus, for example, the establishment of semi-autonomous work groups in a German Volkswagen plant in 1975, involving the replacement of a foreman by an elected group leader, evoked objections from both management and unions. On the one side, it was seen to disrupt the traditional enterprise hierarchy and, on the other, it was suspected that the group leader might usurp traditional union functions. This experiment was discontinued in 1978 (Auer et al., 1983: 17f). In addition, the high cost of restructuring often served as a disincentive for widening the scope of experiments (ILO, 1979: 53).

Some French and British unions, indeed, have claimed that work restructuring is no more than 'a capitalist trick' and, by the very nature of capitalism, cannot bring workers any real advantages. The less antagonistic German union federation, too, has objected that employers have often exploited changes in work organization to intensify the pace of work and have been tardy in accompanying restructuring by upgrading in terms of skill and pay (Auer et al., 1983: 17).

The French data, collected by ANACT, also allow some impression to be gained about what advantages employers have gained from restructuring. Besides some improvement in the social climate, firms mentioned an improvement in the quality of work (fewer rejects), significantly increased labour productivity, a reduction of the quantity of work in progress, and greater flexibility of the production system. On the debit side, many enterprises reported very high initial costs, but it remains unclear whether or not these were eventually offset by increased productivity (ILO, 1979: 53).

Thus, on balance, the work reform attempts up to the late 1970s/early 1980s have remained at the experimental stage and have not fundamentally changed the old Taylorist forms of work organization. But these reform attempts should not be totally dismissed either. At the very least, they undermined the hitherto widespread acceptance of the fact that Taylorist managerial practice was the *only* possible, and a wide debate about the necessity for change was initiated. This made worker activists aware of the issues involved,[9] gave workers' representative bodies some (albeit limited) new powers,[10] and, in some cases, served to equip them better to negotiate changes during the second wave of work reorganization, starting in the late 1970s. The following chapter will be devoted to an investigation of how far such a second, qualitively different stage, can be identified in the three societies under consideration and what its underlying motive forces and transformative potential, if any, are.

NOTES

1. Taylor published a book called *The Principles of Scientific Management* in 1911 which set out his ideas in this area.
2. For a good description/discussion of Fordism see Tolliday and Zeitlin (1986: 1f).
3. The process of adoption and adaption in England is analysed in detail by Littler (1982), and shorter accounts on the penetration by Taylorism of all three societies can be found in Merkle (1980).
4. Readers interested in greater detail in the attempts to reform the quality of working life in the 1970s are referred to the following: Auer, Penth and Tergeist (1983); Jenkins (1981) on France only; ILO (1979); Littler and Salaman (1984).
5. The HoW programme is carried by agencies within the Ministry of Research and Technology and the Ministry of Labour.
6. The (planned) budget for 1985 amounted to a sum of 140 million DM which was, however, still only 1.5 per cent of the whole budget of the Ministry of Technology (Auer et al., 1983: 15).
7. This introduced the idea of a compulsory social audit for firms with more than 750 employees. The latter is a kind of labour and social balance sheet which requires firms to report on all aspects of 'human resources' management and labour relations as well as stating plans and budgets for proposed improvements (Jenkins, 1981: 7).
8. This work has been undertaken by the National Agency for the Improvement of Working Conditions – ANACT (founded in 1973) and by the Fund for the Improvement of Working Conditions – FACT (1976).
9. Unions and works councils became aware that the complexity of the issues involved required that their negotiators be prepared for their tasks in special training courses (Auer et al., 1983: 17).
10. For example, the French 1973 law extended the consultation rights of the works committee and slightly widened its competences, and the German 1972 Act on the Works Constitution gave the works council new rights of information and consultation in connection with job design, working conditions and work operations. Also, in the German case, unions became, for the first time, included in the formulation of research programmes at national level.

7 New Technology and Changes in Work Organization

THE REACTION AGAINST TAYLORISM II: THE STRATEGY OF FLEXIBLE SPECIALIZATION

During the first half of the 1980s the debate on new forms of work organization took a new and more dramatic turn. Two books by Sabel (1982) and Piore and Sabel (1984) alerted British social scientists to the fact that new developments in the organization of production were under way in some advanced societies. These, Piore and Sabel claim, put into question not only Taylorist practices of work organization but present a more comprehensive new industrial strategy in which a new approach to product markets has coalesced with the emergence of more sophisticated production technology and new forms of utilizing labour power. They call this new model of industrial production organization 'flexible specialization'.

Piore and Sabel regard this new strategy as a reaction to worldwide economic changes. These have rendered problematic the old form of industrial development – mass production of standardized goods with the use of special-purpose machines and of semi-skilled labour. Such production requires large and stable markets, and during the 1970s various economic developments combined to undermine this stability. The most important of these has been a shift in the international division of labour and world trade. The emergence of industrial economies in low-wage East and South-East Asian and Latin American countries, which can produce standardized goods cheaper than the advanced industrial countries, has forced the latter to reconsider their role in the international division of labour and to look for alternative markets. The production of specialized/customized and/or high-quality goods, particularly producer goods, suggested itself as a new strategy. This applied also to home markets where the demand for standardized goods was often saturated and where the development of more sophisticated tastes required more individualized goods as well as more frequent changes in product.

This changeover to a new market strategy was facilitated – and sometimes stimulated – by the emergence, during the 1970s, of new technology. This computerized equipment can be deployed more flexibly as it makes possible the frequent conversion of machinery and its adaptation to the production of small batches and/or individual customized products at relatively low costs. It also makes possible instant adjustments of machinery to changing market demands – hence the term 'flexible specialization' to characterize the new form of production. The computer-controlled machinery not only facilitates the production of specialized goods at greater speed but also at a higher degree of precision and thus of higher-quality standards. In short, products of a craft-type can now be produced at a similar speed and price as are standardized mass goods. Further advantages flowing from the new technology are that the shorter production runs commit less capital and that its flexible nature, making the enterprise less dependent on large and stable markets, renders investment in machinery a less precarious matter. A brief review of the 'new technology' utilized during the early 1980s is given below. It is important to note that this technology is still developing at a relatively fast pace and that new types of machinery and processes are constantly evolving.

THE MOST IMPORTANT FORMS OF NEW TECHNOLOGY

Numerically Controlled Machine Tools (NC Tools)

These are the earliest forms of computerized machine tools. They became current in the early 1950s and were dominant until the mid-1970s. The operations of machine tools were determined and controlled first by an electronic plug-board and later by a simple computer. In this early form the sequence of operations which the machine was meant to perform was contained on a paper or magnetic tape. The computer was separate from the machine tool and usually not on the shopfloor at all. To change the operations of the machine-tool – previously a complex and costly task – one now simply had to change the tape.

Computer Numerically Controlled Machine Tools (CNC Tools)

These operate on much the same principles as the above but with a more advanced form of computer. They came on to the industrial scene during the mid-1970s and are superseding NC tools. The new *micro-computer* is now built into the machine tool itself and has a 'dialogue' video display unit and key board. Thus the process can be monitored and machines can be adjusted while production is under way. Alterations or refinements dictated by production conditions at a given time can be taken into consideration. The need for human intervention directly with the machine is still further reduced. The more sophisticated computer allows the production of more complex and sophisticated parts with ever greater precision.

Direct Numerical Control Tools (DNC Tools)

These are an extension of the above in that one central computer directs and controls several machines.

Flexible Manufacturing Systems (FMS)

Flexibility is achieved by combining three principal elements: a set of machinery stations; automated transfer mechanisms which move parts between machine stations and can sometimes even change tools; and a computerized steering system which controls and coordinates processes in the system and connects them with the manufacturing process in the rest of the works.

The FMS allows ghost shifts at night, i.e. production occurs without any human presence. The development of FMSs began in the US. Then the initiative passed to Japan where they exist in most developed form. FMSs entered Europe only in the 1980s. More commonly used are the simpler Flexible Manufacturing Cells which have the same high level of automation but not the aggregation of machines.

Robots

Robots are basically machines which can move one or more of their parts like mechanical arms, and this movement is computer-controlled. There exists a great variety of robotic devices from simple pick-and-place devices to sophisticated ones, programmed to carry out a complex and varied sequence of movements. Their development is still at an early stage (our pictures from science fiction of robots are far in advance of reality). More advanced robots with built-in sensitizing devices are able to handle and react to a much greater variety of objects and thus are more widely deployable. These are now being introduced into production.[1]

A third variable in the strategy of flexible specialization, it is argued by Piore and Sabel, is the new way of deploying labour power. The operation of the more complex technology and the frequent changes required are more satisfactorily accomplished by the utilization of skilled labour and the organization of work along the old 'craft' lines. The Taylorist strategy of designing high-specialization/low-discretion jobs or work roles is replaced by one seeking a high degree of overlap between specialisms and flexibility of deployment, as well as the exercise of 'craft' judgement and skill. Thus polyvalency of skill is given particular emphasis in the new form of worker deployment. 'Flexibility', in the Piore and Sabel scenario, is regarded purely as 'functional flexibility' or, to use Streeck's (1987b: 289) term, as 'custom-made work organization'. As a consequence workers are assigned more holistic work tasks, have enriched jobs and enjoy greater autonomy and responsibility. This new form of work organization is not the result of direct or indirect pressure from labour but is usually initiated by management in response to changed market requirements.

Piore and Sabel contend that this non-Taylorist way of labour utilization is the most appropriate to the strategy of flexible specialization. They point out that not all advanced societies will be guided towards adopting this new form of work organization but only societies with a surviving craft tradition, i.e. a tradition relying on skilled, all-round workers, operating in a high-trust environment, free from detailed or continuous management control. The authors identify such remnants of a craft tradition in Germany, Italy and Japan and see the new production concepts emerging mainly in these three societies. In the USA and France, in contrast, they suggest, the extinction of this tradition and the extant forms of union and state control respectively militate against the adoption of the strategy of flexible specialization (Piore and Sabel, 1984: 17f). The case of Britain is not discussed at all, but one can presume that they would have included Britain in the latter category of societies. Piore and Sabel remain unclear, however, about whether these latter societies will remain confined to the old industrial strategy of mass production of standardized goods by special purpose machinery, allied to Taylorist forms of production organization, or whether some hybrid strategies can be operated which combine features of the old and the new model of production. The main weight of their argument points in the first direction. They never consider whether societies without this craft tradition can aim for flexible specialization without radical adjustment of work organization but instead aim to achieve flexibility in a different way. An examination of recent developments in British and French business enterprises in the last part of this chapter will attempt to answer such questions and show that the Sabel and Piore thesis greatly oversimplifies the issues in their case.

A last element of the new model of industrial production, outlined by Piore and Sabel, is a new form of industrial community which achieves a balance between competition and cooperation, in order to instigate and sustain innovation. The role of unions is seen to be crucial in this respect. This element of the Piore/Sabel thesis remains the least clearly elaborated and, therefore, is liable to misinterpretation. Their argument in this part of the book is understood by this author to relate to the role which the societal system of industrial relations plays in the new industrial strategy and will be discussed in these terms.

Piore and Sabel suggest that in many enterprises, and in some cases whole societies, these various new developments have now moved beyond mere tactical experiments into a strategic model (ibid.: 195). They see the new industrial strategy, however, only as an emergent development. At the present time, it exists side by side with the old model of production organization, and it is by no means certain that the new strategy will completely oust the old one in advanced societies. Given that regulatory adjustments at the macro-economic level are made, the old model may continue to be preferred in some societies. But they nevertheless view the new developments as being so momentous as to justify speaking about the occurence of a 'Second Industrial Divide' – the title of their book. This second 'industrial divide', they conclude, will usher in changes which not only transform industrial production but economic and social life in general.

They view the strategy of flexible specialization as superior to the old strategy because, in their view, it promotes more 'human' working conditions and less hierarchical and adversarial management/labour relations. But, they caution, the degree of realization of the advantages facilitated by this strategy depends on what social and international groups are included in each system, i.e. how general it becomes in a society or in the world (ibid.: 278). Although their thesis implies far-reaching changes in capitalist production which are held to be inconceivable by Marxists in the Braverman mould, they never explicitly discuss the implications these new developments might have for the nature of modern capitalism.

The far-reaching claims by these two authors about fundamental changes in advanced industrial societies naturally sparked off a lively debate among social scientists as well as some empirical studies to test their claims. Critical debate has centred on the point of whether a more humane design of jobs and a more satisfying form of work organization is compatible with the principles of capitalist production, or whether the new mode of work organization is just a more subtle form of exploitation which allows a more comprehensive and intensive utilization of labour power. Frequently, British leftist critique of flexible specialization views it merely as a managerial plot to destroy specialized craft unions and hence union power.

Empirical research undertaken in several societies – though mostly one-country studies – permits us to comment on the above debate as well as test the more specific claims of the Sabel and Piore thesis from a comparative European perspective. In the following, we shall review the data gathered in case studies of German, British and French industrial enterprises in different industries. It will be shown how factors in the social and economic environment can either support or inhibit the move towards flexible specialization, and differences in this respect between the three societies will be underlined. Whereas the evidence on flexible specialization from the FRG is now quite rich and systematic, that on similar developments in Britain and France is, characteristically, still only fragmentary. Hence the following comparison will devote more space to the German than the British and French situation.

FLEXIBLE SPECIALIZATION IN GERMANY

An identification of the emergence of new forms of work structuring in German industry was first made by members of the ISF München[2] during the late 1970s, well before the Sabel thesis was formulated. The case for an emergent new industrial strategy in German manufacturing has been most cogently stated and most fully supported by empirical evidence in the work of Kern and Schumann (1984a and b). Their theoretical claims and empirical data are based on a follow-up study of several industries – the car, machine-tool, chemical and, to a lesser extent, food-producing and shipbuilding industries – which they first investigated in the middle 1960s. The following review of case studies relevant to the 'flexible specialization' debate will draw heavily on the work of Kern and Schumann but also consider other studies, both sympathetic to, and sceptical of, their claims. The discussion will compare and contrast the main general conclusions from the German evidence with the arguments advanced by Piore and Sabel (1984) and suggest some amendments to their thesis. In addition, this discussion will indicate how the new approach to labour deployment fits into a capitalist organization of production.

The Evidence

In the *car industry* (Kern and Schumann, 1984b: 48f), the overall trend has been the combination of a technology strategy – the energetic and fairly comprehensive introduction of flexible automation, with changes in work organization. At Volkswagen the direction of change has been towards workplace definition on the principle of task integration and a holistic conception of work, combining production tasks with the less complex maintenance operations and/or with quality control. An up-skilling of production work has been achieved. This has been manifest in the greatly increased internal training effort (ibid.: 58). Worker discre-tion has been increased in order to encourage diagnostic activity and generally autonomous action. These trends are particularly pronounced in the body shop (*Rohbau*) where the new production concept has become embodied in the job of the stationery press line monitor (*Strassenführer*) who is invested with extensive responsibility and trusted to act autonomously. It has also been discernible in components production. Here repetitive detail work has declined from 90 per cent in 1960 to 15 per cent in 1981, and the job of monitor of complex equipment (*Anlagenfahrer*) has been given a much wider competence. Similar developments have occurred in the stamping shop. In assembly (*Montage*), change has been the least but even here some work enrichment has taken place. Restructuring has been aided by the new flexible wage system in operation at VW. This makes provision for maintenance of wages levels in cases of transfer and for homogeneous wages, fixed at the highest previous level, in so-called work sub-systems in order to encourage job rotation (Brumlop and Jürgens, 1986: 80). Workers' reactions to these changes have generally been positive and have manifested themselves in responsible performance. But there have also been complaints about increased pressure. Works councils and unions in the industry have been particularly active and influential in shaping the new forms of work organization, and the job of equipment monitor (*Anlagenfahrer*) is largely the result of union pressure (Jürgens et al., 1984: 12f).

The authors' analysis of the car industry is partially supported by another team of German researchers (Jürgens et al., 1986: 259f). The latter also present additional evidence on semi-autonomous work groups (at Opel) and production teams (at Audi). But Jürgens et al. see the reorganization of work as less dramatic. They contend that produc-tion jobs have only been slightly supplemented by traditional skilled tasks and that the old division between production and 'skilled trades' departments has not been abolished (ibid.: 278). Accounts of changes in work organization at the car producers BMW, Audi and Ford (Germany), given by *Industriemagazin*, (April 1987), in contrast, fully support the Kern and Schumann thesis.

A more detailed account of changes in work organization at Audi is given by Heizmann (1984), an Audi employee in the department of Work Systems. At Audi, he claims, the move towards flexible automation in the body assembly unit was from the beginning connected with the planning of change in work organization. The solution favoured at Audi is the idea of production teams and work enrichment for group members in order to increase the availability of plant by preventive trouble recognition and quick faults elimination. Particularly notable is the attempt to enrich the residual work of the loader who is usually only charged with the monotonous function of manually inserting parts into the line. In addition to his loading functions he has assumed the more qualified tasks of line monitoring, simple maintenance and repair, and checking. The loader is given a short preparatory training and is then given 'on-the-job' training by the other team members. The philosophy of Audi that the new technology can only be adequately handled by skilled production workers is summed up by Heizmann (1984: 113) as follows:

> For effective personnel deployment in automated plants it is essential for the overall level of production personnel qualifications to be raised, even if these higher qualifications are not called for all the time.

In the *machine-tool industry* a greater concentration on the production of customized machine tools for more and more demanding customers both at home and abroad has also coincided with an increased use of new complex technology. After NC machines (in the early 1970s) came CNC machines (since 1975) and Flexible Manufacturing Systems (FMSs) (in the 1980s). Although CNC machines have, so far, been adopted only by a minority of enterprises their deployment is steadily increasing. FMSs are still fairly rare in the industry but Flexible Manufacturing Cells (FMCs), with the same high level of automation but no aggregation of machines, are more widely used. Both of the latter types of new technology are more prevalent in Germany than in Britain (Northcott et al., 1985: 31). The new market strategy and greater automation of production have been accompanied by the retention of the largely skilled work force and by the preservation of the holistic task design and the utilization of existing 'conceptual' worker skills. The skill requirement on workers has even increased, due to the greater variety and complexity of products and the greater need for a knowledge of electronics. The new type of worker in this industry, represented by the equipment monitor (*Maschinenführer*), combines a high level of practical expertise with an abstract approach. Instead of advancing step by step, as the old craftworker did, he has to anticipate and plan the whole process. Kern and Schumann (1984b: 147) report that the proportion of skilled workers in the industry has increased from 67 per cent in 1970 to 79 per cent in 1982. Semi-autonomous work-groups were also found to be emerging.

The crucial issue with CNC machines is whether and how much of the programming function is executed in the workshop/by workers. Organizational solutions can be divided into three broad categories: (a) all programming functions are carried out in a separate programming bureau; (b) programmes are made in a bureau but are tested and optimized by the workers themselves, or only the most complex programmes are made by the bureau; and (c) all functions are carried out in the workshop. Kern and Schumann found that, although the choice of strategy was influenced by the task at hand, strategies (b) and (c) combined outweighed the choice of strategy (a). This finding also receives support from other German studies in a wider range of industries (ibid.: 148) and is borne out by an English/German comparative study (Hartmann et al., 1984). These authors conclude that

> the German companies ... distinguished less than those in Britain between specialised functions and departments for production management, production engineering, work planning and work execution functions. Similarly, there was a consistently greater use of shop floor and operator programming in Germany: programming is seen as the nucleus around which the various company personnel, the managers, engineers, foreman and operators are integrated.

Other less detailed and explicit national comparisons, by d'Iribarne and Lutz (1984) and Lutz and Schultz-Wild (1983), involving FMS in the engineering industry, make similar points about a lesser division of labour in Germany between conception and execution, and between technical services and shopfloor workers. Because of the greater availability of skilled manpower, this pre-existing pattern has frequently carried over into the automation phase.

In the *chemical industry* (lg. producers) computerization has been relatively slow, but more recently full automation has been approached step by step. Although technological change has thus been less than in the other two industries considerable organizational change has occurred during the last fifteen-odd years. The model has been staff reduction through a fusion of functions, accompanied by upskilling. The new job designation of equipment monitor (*Anlagenfahrer*) is the result of the integration of the previously separate functions of process control and process regulation. More fluid job boundaries have also been created in the maintenace sector. This process of upskilling has been formally recognized by a professionalization of chemical production work. Existing workers have received training to be raised to a 'skilled worker' standard, and new workers now undergo an apprenticeship for a 'skilled chemical worker'. But, according to Kern and Schumann (1984b: 274f), production work does not require the same degree of skill and discretion as in the other two industries, and it neither utilizes all the training received nor does it fully engage the worker as a person. The situation is different, however, for maintenance workers.

Almost identical processes of task integration, upskilling and of formal professionalization of production work are described by Drexel and Nuber (1979) for both the chemical and the steel industry. In the latter, an apprenticeship for a skilled steel worker has been newly created and access to skilled status has been given to both existing semi-skilled workers in the industry and to new young workers. In the steel industry the restructuring of work and the upskilling are part of a comprehensive strategy, combining a new market approach – the selling of speciality steels, with new technical processes – mini-mills with electric arc furnaces, and a reorganization of work and professionalization of workers (Piore and Sabel, 1984: 209). In contrast to the situation in the other industries surveyed so far, the crisis situation in the industry and the consequent drastic restructuring have been an important contributory factor to the reorganization of work (Drexel, 1985: 112f). Also the restructuring of work has not encompassed all steel workers but has left some semi-skilled who, after the formalization of skilled status, have lost their promotion chances (ibid., 117).

Further evidence, supporting a move towards 'flexible specialization', comes from an article in *Industriemagazin* (April 1987), a journal for practising managers, which is devoted to the issue of work organization and automated technology across a whole range of industries. Examples include the whole repertoire of advanced technology, from CNC machines via industrial cells (*Industriezellen*), flexible manufacturing cells, robot lines to complete flexible manufacturing systems. The general conclusion, reiterated in different form throughout the article, is that investment in automated technology can only succeed if it is allied to investment in human resources and that any automation strategy has to be combined with a work organization strategy based on upskilling and increased worker autonomy.

These changes in work organization have had strong repercussions for training both at national, and, more so, at enterprise level. The old

Table 7.1   Changes in the qualification structure in production:
Germany

Degree of qualification	in %		
(highest level)	1982	1990	2000
Without initial (apprenticeship) training	38.1	31.1	24.4
With short or long (apprenticeship) initial training or equivalent	54.0	59.9	65.9
Certificate of foreman (*Meister*) or technician or equivalent	6.9	7.6	8.3
Degree from polytechnic (Fachhochschule) or university	1.0	1.2	1.5

Source: Prognos, AG, Institut f. Arbeitsmarkt-und Berufsforschung. Quoted
by *Industriemagazin*, April 1987: 174.

apprenticeship training in specialized skills is no longer considered
adequate. New broader skill profiles for engineering occupations,
worked out by the union IG Metall and the industry's employers'
association, have come on stream for apprenticeship training in 1987.
But many enterprises have anticipated this move and have initiated their
own initial 'apprenticeship' and further training for multi-skilled production and maintenance workers. Investment in both initial and further
training has greatly increased during the 1980s. Table 7.1 makes
forecasts up to the year 2000, and indicates the increasing demand for
skilled employees at all levels of production as well as the declining
employment chances of the unskilled.

Lastly, the article considers the impact of changes in work organization on organizational structure and payment systems. The greater
degree of integration between different segments of production,
brought about by flexible automation, has led to a blurring of horizontal
and vertical boundaries, such as between production and maintenance
workers, shopfloor and technical services, manual and non-manual
workers. The higher degree of worker autonomy, particularly in group-
work, has called for less supervisory staff and for changed work roles for
such staff, but moves in this direction have so far been very slow. The
reform of payment systems to give greater recognition to the new
technical and social skills rather than rewarding mainly physical effort
(piecework rates) is also being contemplated but has, so far, run up
against obstacles.

A less optimistic picture emerges, however, when one moves outside
the core industries. In the *margarine-producing plant*, investigated by
Kern and Schumann (1984b), the newly-created position of equipment

monitor presents a similar trend as in the three core industries, but the upskilling of previously semi-skilled workers has left the unskilled packing workers without any chance of promotion. An attempt to humanize their work has failed since the tasks of packing did not yield enough substance for work enrichment. Hence the workforce has become more polarized now than before. This phenomenon must be more widely applicable than Kern and Schumann imply and is, indeed, an inevitable consequence as long as work enrichment and upskilling are extended only to a minority of workers. Altmann et al. (1982), presenting data from a variety of industries which use largely semi-skilled labour, highlight another problem encountered in such contexts. Attempts to make the organization of production more flexible, by enlarging operators' task range and increasing the overall complexity of work, are not successful if they are not accompanied by the necessary training measures. Semi-skilled workers often feel overtaxed by the altered task content and perceive the new demands on them as burdensome and stressful. The new industrial strategy also had not penetrated industries in deep crisis such as shipbuilding, because the severity of the economic situation has concentrated all efforts on survival and attempts to achieve health through contraction. Lastly, Kern and Schumann point out, the current work reorganization and upskilling activities make it much harder for the unemployed to become reintegrated into work.

The evidence on industrial transformation in Germany during the late 1970s/early 1980s presented so far leaves no doubt that, at least in the core industries, changed market and technology strategies have led to the creation of more flexible production arrangements which have involved job enrichment, enlarged autonomy and upskilling for significant numbers of workers. It is more contentious, however, whether these developments amount to a new strategy or new production concepts, to use Kern and Schumann's term (1984a and b). The latter make it clear that, at the present time, only a minority of production workers in the core industries are engaged in new forms of production work and that the full development of the new production concepts will not occur until the late 1980s/early 1990s. They also suggest that labour needs to exert more influence both on management to follow the new strategy more broadly and on the state to distribute the ensuing costs and benefits more widely.

The Implications

The question, therefore, remains whether the new forms of labour utilization signal an emergent trend which will eventually become a fully-fledged industrial strategy or manufacturing policy, or whether, as some German commentators suggest (e.g. Düll, 1985), they constitute merely island solutions which will remain confined to small sections of production and leave the overall Taylorist pattern intact. My own view is that, in the German industrial context, there exists a number of distinctive features which make the Kern and Schumann scenario at least very likely, if not inevitable. Some of these features which support a move towards a broader application of the policy of flexible specialization and which were not recognized or underemphasized by Piore and Sabel (1984) will be outlined in the following section.

First, analysis of industrial change in the 1980s requires that a stronger emphasis be put on the key role the new technology plays in the process of change. Kern and Schumann (1984b) and Jürgens et al, (1986: 273) make it clear that the new technology is an indispensable factor in realizing the new market concept and in facilitating and, sometimes, stimulating changes in work organization. But this emphasis on new technology is not to be interpreted as the adoption of a stance of technological determinism. Kern and Schumann underline that the new technology can be exploited the more broadly the stronger the policy of labour utilization has created the preconditions for such an exploitation. The computer-controlled technology has made the enterprise more transparent and hence more amenable to organizational integration. The new flexibility in worker deployment is mainly desired because the complexity and high degree of integration of technology makes machine down-time more disruptive and costly, and upskilling is practised because it is believed that the new technology can only be fully exploited with a skilled, autonomous workforce (*Industriemagazin*, April 1987). In each of the four industries where significant moves away from Taylorist work organization had occurred, these had been preceded by the introduction of new technological processes. The most highly automated industry – the auto industry – has also been the most innovative one in terms of work organization.

For German management, maximum technical sophistication appears to be a central weapon in all the core industries surveyed. This technology-led competitive strategy presupposes the availability of both a high level of managerial technical competence and of investment resources. Thus, whereas Piore and Sabel (1984) stressed only the availability of worker skill as a precondition for achieving flexible specialization, the German evidence also highlights the critical importance of managerial competence.

Secondly, German sources stress the situation on the labour market as an equally important intervening variable. The unemployment of even skilled workers guarantees an ample supply of skilled labour. This is further increased by the fact that, to alleviate youth unemployment, employers have yielded to union pressure and have trained apprentices in excess to their own immediate needs. This makes non-Taylorist work organization a feasible goal and renders the conversion process suggested by the new strategy relatively painless. In part, skilled labour is substituted for semi-skilled labour because the new market strategy and production technology require it, and in part production tasks are made more complex and demanding in order to make them attractive to the growing number of skilled workers now employed in production. One example of the latter is the new position of equipment monitor (*Anlagenfahrer*) in the car industry (Kern and Schumann, 1984b: 92). Another cruical factor is the *nature* of the skill possessed by the available labour force. Polyvalency is a characteristic of both German skilled and, to a lesser extent, qualified semi-skilled workers (*qualifizierte Angelernte*).

German sources see flexible deployment of labour only in functional terms. The pursuit of numerical flexibility, i.e. the adjustment of labour inputs to meet fluctuation in output, receives no mention. Such adjustment of labour inputs can be confined to the core labour force and the internal labour market and mainly takes the form of overtime/short-time working. Alternatively, external numerical flexibility is achieved by making adjustments to a peripheral labour force by means of part-time and/or temporary working. Whereas internal numerical flexibility can usefully complement functional flexibility and does in no way undermine it, external flexibility is incompatible with it and represents an alternative form of labour deployment. The lack of attention to numerical flexibility is probably due to the fact that external numerical flexibility has not been very prominent in German industry during the early 1980s. Generally speaking, German employment legislation has made it difficult for employers to solve the problem of fluctuating demand by a casualization of the labour force. The high degree of *de facto* employment security and the strong involvement of works councils in manpower regulation have compelled employers to engage in more careful and long-term manpower planning and to deploy the core labour force flexibly in both functional and numerical terms (Streeck, 1987). But more recent developments suggest that German employers, too, are seeking greater numerical and wages flexibility. Although attempts to attain this have remained infrequent during the early 1980s they have become a more pervasive trend during the late 1980s (see Chapter 11).

Thirdly, as is emphasized by Streeck (1987b), the nature of the

German industrial relations system facilitates the implementation of the new strategy. Arguing from a comparative theoretical perspective, he concludes persuasively that industrial relations must be perceived as a critical parameter of economic adaptation. Whether employers opt for the new flexible form of labour deployment or retain a high-tech version of the old Taylorist practice will depend to some extent on the system of industrial relations in which they have to operate. The three distinctive features characterizing the German situation are:

(a) The rigidity of the employment relation, i.e. the lack of employer freedom in hiring and firing, imposed by the Works Constitution Act, is largely counteracted by the fact that unions and works councils support a flexible deployment in qualitative terms. Consequently, the move to greater functional flexibility in labour deployment is not regarded as a threat to union power as unions are neither organized along craft lines nor do they support demarcation between crafts.

(b) The works council, rather than the union, is the representative body, competent to negotiate technical rationalization, and works councils, tending to identify with the enterprise, support technological innovation as a competitive measure. Works councils tend to be dominated by skilled workers who, having less to fear from technological change, are more likely to accept it. They see their main role as negotiating the way in which the transition is managed, and they concentrate on achieving gains for the remaining workers in terms of increased training and skill levels (Kern and Schumann, 1984a: 155).

(c) The predominantly cooperative nature of industrial relations makes it likely that the greater worker responsibility for a continuous flow of production, implied by the new production concepts, is not misused.

The preceding observations have indicated that several features of the German industrial system act to support the move towards a broader adoption of policies, summarized by the concept of 'flexible specialization'. But critical reaction to the Piore and Sabel (1984) thesis has not only focused on the issue of whether recent industrial changes in advanced capitalist societies are of a strategic nature and signal a paradigm change but also on the question of how 'new' this strategy is. The Piore and Sabel account of flexible specialization, which stresses the 'craft' nature of both production organization and of workers and underemphasizes the role of the new technology, has given rise to the claim that recent developments constitute a return to older patterns of production organization (e.g. Littek et al., 1986). Although it is certainly true that an old German tradition of labour utilization is coming more strongly to the fore, empirical studies of recent industrial change leave us in no doubt that there is, at the same time, a new type of production organization emerging.

With the exception of the engineering plants, all the cases studied are in former mass-production industries. Their new market and production concepts neither signal a return to small-scale, customized production nor a heavy reliance on manual skill. Instead they have adopted a more differentiated product range by making alterations/refinements to a number of basic types, each produced in medium-sized to large batches. The emphasis may also be on high quality and/or on frequent product change, and the utilization of advanced technology is essential to the new production concept. Thus the new model of production constitutes a blending of specialist into mass production or, in the words of Sorge and Streeck (1987: 15a–16), diversified quality production. Conversely, the new technology has enabled former craft producers to move towards the production of larger batches, without sacrificing individuality and/or high quality. Consequently, Sorge and Streeck conclude, the boundaries between the former craft and mass production sectors are becoming eroded.

Kern and Schumann also make it much clearer than do Piore and Sabel (1984) that the type of worker at the centre of the new production concepts is *not* identical to the craft worker of old. The rediscovery of the 'professional' production worker (*Berufsarbeiter für die industrielle Produktion*) does only partially signal the return to craft work. This worker – who is largely male, German and young – has to achieve a lengthy systematic training. But this training transmits a broader, more basic knowledge and competencies and the ability to build on these, rather than the specialization on one clearly defined/bounded craft. Although the new skilled production workers are similar to the old craft workers in terms of status and pay, they differ decisively in terms of their skill content and functions. The work carried out by the new production worker is full of contrasts: the work is skilled and offers chances for autonomous regulation *but* it also entails a high level of stress; it is open to the exercise of worker initiative *but* it is also highly condensed (*verdichtet*). This clarification of the type of work/workers created by the new production concepts is particularly important as it dispels some of the false romanticism about a return to the old 'craft idyll', implied by Piore and Sabel.

A last important issue to be settled is whether the emergence of a paradigm change is compatible with the capitalist organization of production and, if so, how it fits into Marxist theorization of the labour process. Kern and Schumann point out that the new industrial strategy is an employer initiative, aimed at adjusting the production process to their changed market strategies. The reorganization of work is not a response to worker unrest or demands nor is it based on humanitarian impulses. Thus a non-Taylorist mode of worker deployment is not an end in itself but is a consequence of a different mode of capital utilization. The new automated technology demands very high rates of capital investment, and the return on that investment is more assured if it is complemented by greater investment in labour. Thus, flexible specialization is regarded as a capitalist rationalization strategy which happens to yield considerable benefits also for labour. It tries to increase industrial efficiency through, and not against, worker competence (*Handlungskapazität*). Often the reorganization of work is not consciously planned but evolves, after periods of trial and error, as a consequence of other changes in production (Drexel, 1985: 108).

The new mode of labour utilization does, however, constitute a break in capitalist thinking. Labour has long been thought of as a factor disruptive of production, to be substituted as far as possible by machines and restricted and controlled as much as possible. This has been a central tenet of the Braverman thesis on the labour process in capitalist society. The new strategy, in contrast, implies that labour is a valuable resource and that worker skill and initiative are productive forces which should be fully utilized (Kern and Schumann, 1984: 149). It has been argued, for example by Düll (1985), that the new production concepts constitute an attempt to increase effort in a new direction by aiming to release subjective motivational components and that, consequently, labour has been subsumed more completely in the labour process. But to regard the new policy of labour deployment merely as a clever manipulation of labour misses an essential point. As Drexel (1985: 123) points out, the new attitude to labour deployment implies not *just* a broader utilization of existing labour power but also its greater unfolding and development. The new mode of labour utilization does not represent a one-sided gain by capital but one which has been achieved by developing worker potential to a higher degree. The worker receives a pay-off in terms of higher skill level, greater autonomy and increased satisfaction and material reward. Granted, development of worker potential remains strictly within the limits set by the capitalist enterprise, and the unfolding of the full potential of labour is prevented by the remaining contradictions between the interests of capital and labour.

German management is primarily concerned to obtain functional flexibility and is *not* motivated to achieve a downwards adjustment of terms of employment. On the contrary, in the cases examined by Kern and Schumann, upgrading of labour has regularly followed the new mode of deployment. Employers are not trying to reduce labour costs as far as individual workers are concerned. But in some industries, notably the steel industry, they have probably reduced overall labour cost by reducing the number of workers employed. In such cases, the quest for flexibility is partly a response to this decrease. An increased density and intensity of work is widely observed.

Achieving domination (*Herrschaftsabsicherung*) is no longer considered such an important goal by German management. This is the case, partly, because automatic control of production processes secures sufficient worker effort. But it is also true that workers are no longer regarded as system opponents. They are viewed as people who are willing to make compromises because their own interests are becoming more closely tied in with those of their employer (Kern and Schumann, 1984: 152). But, at the same time, management has become more dependent on the goodwill of workers to keep the new, highly complex and vulnerable productive apparatus in operation. This is not to say that management control of workers has become unimportant but merely that it no longer takes the old form. As has been pointed out by many of Braverman's critics, subsumption of labour does not necessarily occur by close task control in the labour process. But this relaxation of control over the labour process, it will later be shown, is a peculiarly German phenomenon.

To sum up this section, flexible specialization in Germany is seen to have the following characteristic features. It is, as yet, only an emergent trend. Taylorism has not been completely abandoned, but fundamental organizational innovation is very much on the agenda; technology is held to play a crucial role in the process of change, and a management committed to, and capable of instigating, far-reaching technological innovation is an integral part of the transformation process; the labour market situation has made available a sizeable pool of skilled polyvalent labour to operationalize the new strategy; the system of industrial relations facilitates relatively smooth technological change and the attainment of functional flexibility; the new 'professional' worker, although sharing some features with the craftworker of old, is not identical to him; the benefits of the new industrial strategy for workers need to be generalized by political means beyond the core industries; the strategy of flexible specialization is an integral part of capitalist rationalization but it signifies an important change in capital's attitude to labour deployment which has more positive consequences for labour than the old Taylorist concept. Kern and Schumann's claim that the new strategy is therefore to be welcomed as a progressive move which does, however, require further political development by both organized labour and the state, in my view, deserves endorsement in the German context.

FLEXIBLE SPECIALIZATION IN BRITAIN AND FRANCE?

There has been a growing awareness also among British managements that, to regain competitiveness, the adoption of a new market strategy and, allied to it, the creation of more flexible production structures have become an unavoidable necessity. The production of diverse/specialized and/or high-quality goods with the new flexible technology has become the new management credos in many industries during the 1980s (e.g. Cross, 1985; Willman, 1986; IMS, 1986). But there is still less enthusiasm among British managements than among their European competitors for developing new products or venturing into new markets, and often manufacturing practice lags very much behind avowed management goals (New and Myers, 1986). Where the strategy of 'flexible specialization' is adopted the British version differs from the German one in several ways. It is rarely conceived of as a comprehensive industrial strategy in which the use of complex new technological systems is integrated with the creation of greater skill resources and the broader deployment of skilled labour on the one side, and a new 'industrial relations' approach, evoking worker commitment and cooperation, on the other. An attempt to adopt such a comprehensive strategy in the British context meets with too many impediments. Consequently, it is usually the case that the strategy is embraced only partially and is combined with elements of the old Taylorist model of labour deployment into a hybrid type.

What then are the impediments in the British industrial context which hinder the successful realization of the new industrial strategy in a consistent form? One important constituent element of the new model is the reorganization of the productive apparatus, replacing old special purpose machinery with new automated equipment of a highly complex type. The degree of flexibility permitted by the new technology increases with the technical sophistication of the equipment and with the degree of integration of individual technical devices into a comprehensive system. Such a reorganization of production requires a management committed to technological innovation, confident to forge ahead, and competent to both acquire the right type of equipment and to put it into operation and maintain it without too much disruption of the productive process. Such energetic technological innovation requires not only the commitment of considerable financial resources but also a high level of technical expertise among management and support staff at all levels. Neither precondition typically exists in British industrial organizations.

Recent research on technological innovation in British firms has provided evidence of hesitancy and even backwardness in this area. Daniel's (1987: 33) national study found that microelectronic process and product applications in industry were significantly more advanced in foreign-owned than in British-owned establishments. The comparative survey of the use of microelectronics in British, German and French industry by Northcott et al. (1985) established that Britain cannot compete with Germany and, to a lesser degree France, as far as the more sophisticated devices and process controls are concerned (ibid.: 67). Patel and Pavitt (1987: 72f) reveal that both the rate of diffusion of four significant engineering innovations (oxygen steelmaking, continuous casting, NC machine tools and robots) is very much lower in Britain than in Germany and that British managers have a much weaker commitment to developing and commercializing new products and processes. This lagging behind must, to a large extent, be due to a lack of engineering expertise among managements but also to the lesser availability of development finance. New and Myers (1986: 24f) report that among their sample (240 plants) of large, export-oriented firms in a range of industrial sectors, only a minority had experimented with the more advanced technological devices/processes (FMSs, robotics, CAD/CAM). The majority of these firms, perceiving a low or negative pay-off from experimentation with new technology, did not intend to put a high emphasis on the use of these technologies in future. Also the production of high-performance products and rapid product design change were given relatively low priority by the managements in the sample whereas production of standard products at low cost – consistent with the old production model – is given relatively high emphasis (ibid.: 26, 32). Brady (1984: 112), in a review of case studies on the introduction of new technology, aptly sums up the situation as follows:

> many managements do not possess the necessary technical skill to assess the feasibility of investing in the new technology nor do they fully understand the implications for the organisation of work, for manpower requirements and for training needs.

The continued adherence to the old production model is also highlighted by Jones (1988), but he puts forward a different explanation for this. He attributes the insufficient exploitation of the new technology's potential for versatility to the constraining financial – institutional environment of British industry. The short-term orientation of companies' financial organization and accounting philosophies, induces managers to pursue quick financial returns from technological investment (ibid.: 455, 474). This is a persuasive argument which can explain the continuation of the old production strategy even in such high-tech sectors as the automobile and aerospace industries. It usefully supplements rather than replaces the analysis pointing to insufficient technical expertise by management.

Although the high level of unemployment in Britain makes available a large pool of labour, this labour is, on the whole, not of the right type to restructure work organization in line with the new production concepts. Due to the decline of the apprenticeship system, skilled labour has been declining in relative terms. In the engineering industry, for example, where skilled labour has traditionally been most prevalent, the number of craftsmen undergoing training has halved between 1978 and 1984 (*Skills Bulletin*, 1, 1987: 11). Moreover, the traditional skilled worker does not possess the polyvalency which ensures flexible deployment. In those cases where management is committed to operating the new technology with skilled polyvalent labour – for maintenance such labour is becoming a *sine qua non* – they have had to both invest resources in initial and further or retraining *and* to overcome union resistance to the elimination of demarcation between crafts. Many recent investigations of training practice (e.g. IMS, 1984) have shown that, on the whole, British management is unwilling to make the long-term investment of resources which a sustained programme of training and retraining requires. The IMS study (1986a: 9) of flexibility in firms found that firms tended to have no long-term manpower strategies. Technology is operationalized and maintained in such a way as to minimize reliance on highly skilled maintenance labour. Thus Scarbrough (1986) mentions that a new production facility in the body shop of Austin Rover was deliberately designed in a way to minimize skill requirements in maintaining it in operation, and Brady (1984: 28) and Cross (1985: 45) emphasize the fact that many managements contract out their highly skilled maintenance and service tasks, as well as work requiring specialist skills and knowledge. Training efforts have remained piecemeal and generally insufficient to satisfy the requirements of the new forms of work organization believed to be an indispensable part of the new industrial strategy by Piore and Sabel (1984). A survey by *Incomes Data Services* (407, 1988: 5) shows that although there are a few examples of exemplary practice, showing a genuine commitment to multi- or dual-skilling, in general companies are not prepared to offer the systematic and lengthy training required. Where further training has been provided it has mainly been extended to maintenance workers. There has been no mention in the literature of any systematic upskilling and upgrading of direct or production workers.

All this is not to say that functional flexibility is rarely sought or obtained by British management. The recent IMS study (1986a: 8) of this problem found that nine out of ten manufacturing firms in their sample had been seeking to increase functional flexibility of their workforces since 1980. The ACAS 1987 survey of employers in a variety of industries, regions and size categories of firms established that over a quarter of respondents had *succeeded* in introducing functional flexibility in the preceding three years (ACAS 1988: 19). Daniel (1987: 168f) established that management had a greater commitment to flexibility in worker deployment and that establishments using microelectronic technology were twice as likely as those not using it to have taken steps to promote it. But 34 per cent of all works managers still felt constrained in their freedom to distribute tasks between different categories of workers. A survey of employers on flexible working by *Incomes Data Services* (407, 1988) showed that, in general, progress on this front had been very moderate and slow. The study concluded that 'for the vast majority of companies flexible working consists of slow change over a number of years' and that 'flexibility as a way of life is still confined to a small group of firms' (ibid.: 1). Although some companies introduced flexible working with the adoption of new technology most tried to get acceptance for it via a lengthy negotiating process with the unions. These negotiations (offering substantial compensations to unions) have often resulted in the conclusion of enabling agreements but have mostly not been translated into actual practice. In some crucial cases even this modest achievement was not reached. National talks on flexibility between employers' organizations and unions in the engineering industry broke down after four years, and a document calling for relatively modest changes in working practices was rejected by the unions (ibid.: 1–2). Among those companies where agreements on flexible working were actually implemented the employers' commitment to providing multi- or dual-skill training has often only been honoured in a very perfunctory and inadequate way. The impediments to the realization of flexible labour deployment are such that success is often only limited or of short-term duration. Among maintenance craftsmen in the engineering and food and drinks industries, for example, the merging of mechanical and electrical skills, thought to be particularly important for the new technology, has relatively rarely been achieved, and dual-skilling even within the mechanical or electrical trades has been achieved in only a third of the cases studies by the IMS (1986a: 8).

Given the fact that the old industrial strategy and model of labour deployment have not been easy to change, it is not surprising that Taylorist practice has persisted. It is even claimed that the introduction of the new technology has sometimes extended the division of labour and intensified deskilling. The evidence to verify this claim comes mainly from studies of the operation of CNC machines and of flexible automation in the car industry. Concerning CNC machines, there is wide variation also in British industry in the way the programming function of these machines is handled. But there appears to be agreement that programming is more often than not regarded as a function, to be separated off from shopfloor activity and to be allocated to technical staff. This is partly the consequence of a traditionally more rigid division of labour between conception (technical staff) and execution (shopfloor operators) and partly of union demarcaticn practice. The more rigid division of labour was highlighted by the Anglo-German comparison, conducted by Hartmann et al. (1984). It is also indicated by other British studies, cited by Brady (1984: 18–19) who, furthermore, emphasize the 'industrial relations' dimension in this division. Scarbrough (1986: 112) reports an example from the motor industry, illustrating the hierarchical division of labour between conception and execution. In this case the more abstract electronic and programming skills associated with the computer-controlled technological system of the body-in-white shop were not included in the jobs of maintenance craftsmen but were transferred to a newly-created 'control engineering' function at managerial level. Otherwise there is insufficient empirical support for the thesis that the new technology has led to further deskilliŕg. Daniel's (1987) national survey in all industries of the effect of new technology on skill and employment conditions of workers does not support a general deskilling claim nor is such a claim upheld by Jones' (1988) survey of work organization patterns in relation to new technology. Despite considerable change in the task content of particular occupations, Jones detects only stasis in their overall organization. He identifies neither deskilling nor systematic upskilling and increased descretion (Jones 1988: 469–70, 480).

A different example of Taylorist production organization comes from the motor industry and is reported by Willman (1986). Willman's study of the firm of Austin Rover, which has experienced extensive technological innovation and organizational rationalization during the late 1970s/ early 1980s, noted the reassertion of Taylorism in a different guise. This phase in the development of the firm was above all characterized by management attempts to regain control over work allocation and organization and to institute a drive to increase efficiency. Task control, which had previously resided largely with workers themselves, became again a management prerogative. The reassertion of management control over production workers was aided by the general crisis situation and the fear among workers of job loss. The more difficult task of breaking worker control among maintenance craftworkers was accomplished through the introduction of the new technology which made the demand for flexibility appear as an objective necessity.

For Piore and Sabel (1984) greater flexibility in the deployment of labour meant always functional flexibility. Flexibility, it has since been pointed out (e.g. IMS, 1986a), can also be obtained by adjusting the quantity of labour employed in accordance with fluctuations in demand. In the British context, it has been argued, a mixed strategy is being pursued. Management seeks functional flexibility from a core labour force and numerical flexibility from a peripheral labour force. This issue is pursued in some detail in Chapter 11.

It has already been indicated that 'industrial relations' issues represent an impediment to the attainment of work restructuring in the direction of greater functional flexibility. The new forms of work organization, it was shown in the German context, require that workers act more autonomously and adopt a greater amount of responsibility for the smooth and continuous functioning of the complex productive apparatus. This exercise of responsible autonomy on the part of workers presupposes that management trusts them to use this autonomy in the interest of the enterprise. A strategy of 'responsible autonomy' assumes that management feels fairly secure and confident about the existing balance of control in the enterprise and is not constantly locked into a contest for control. It also presupposes that workers identify to a large degree with management goals and accept a part of the responsibility for the accomplishment of these goals.

In the British industrial relations context, with its long tradition of 'minimal involvement' and adversarial pursuit of sectional interests, such a climate of mutual trust and cooperation cannot easily develop. Many studies have shown that British management does not and cannot feel confident and relaxed about the existing balance of control. In many instances management has shown itself intent on exploiting labour's current weakness and change the balance of control in management's favour (IMS, 1986a). Instead of seeing the elimination of demarcation as one necessary step in the larger strategy of creating a polyvalent, flexible and more responsible labour force it often becomes a goal in its own right and degenerates into a contest of strength between management and labour. Willman's (1986: 194f) analysis of recent developments at Austin Rover suggests that management there is aware that cooperative management–labour relations need to be developed. The cultivation of worker responsibility for the attainment of production goals has become an important precondition for the efficient utilization of the new complex technology which is much more vulnerable to disruption. Although management is anxious to achieve worker cooperation the attainment of this goal is jeopardized by the pursuit of their other goal – efficiency through increased task control. Also contraction had bred confrontation and imposed change and has greatly increased employment insecurity. Although this climate was conducive to elicit worker acquiescence in imposed change, it could not succeed in gaining their active and responsible cooperation. Jones (1988: 480f) also emphasizes the predelection of British management to use the new technology to achieve centralized integration and control of the various pre-production and production processes. But he rejects the idea that managements have consciously adopted low-trust relations and instead attributes their control strategy to pressures emanating from the British cost accounting system.

At the same time, no impetus for changes in labour deployment and work restructuring is coming from the unions either. Although, at the level of union leadership, there is widespread support for technological innovation at the level of the enterprise a merely defensive stance still tends to be the rule. Given the absence of a policy providing employment security, this defensive stance is hardly surprising. Moreover, the relatively inadequate financial and organizational resources of British unions make it difficult for them to come forward with union suggestions as to how to implement the strategy of flexible specialization in accordance with the interests of labour in upskilling, upgrading and increased levels of discretion. For various reasons workers themselves do not press for work restructuring in the direction of responsible autonomy either: in many industries they are more concerned with survival than with change; they are conditioned to think in terms of extrinsic rewards; and, lastly, there exists a wariness of management motives, and any new initiative tends to be regarded with suspicion.

The foregoing argument has made it clear that, although a new market strategy and a quest for the more flexible organization of production are also a lively concern of British management, there are formidable impediments in the way of realizing a comprehensive and consistent industrial strategy. There exist difficulties about creating the necessary technological foundations. But the more formidable problems appear to be those of achieving a new approach to management–labour relations and a non-Taylorist practice of labour deployment. The example of Britain shows, contrary to the claims of Piore and Sabel (1984), that countries without a pervasive craft ethos will not necessarily remain wedded to the old model of industrial organization. Instead managements in such countries are more likely to develop a hybrid strategy, combining an only partially changed market orientation – a low-cost mass production orientation predominates over a concern with versatility – with a high-tech version of production organization along the old Taylorist lines. Although an intensification of deskilling is not common and greater functional flexibility of labour and some upskilling is practised, there is little systematic attempt to create polyvalent workers, workgroup autonomy and high trust relations. The pursuit of numerical flexibility and of the greater casualization of the labour force appears to be an equally widely adopted alternative. Although numerical flexibility can successfully cope with uncertainties in demand of a quantitive type it is doubtful whether a casualized labour force can handle other aspects of market uncertainty, such as frequent product changes or product diversification, and the demand for customized high-quality goods.

In France, too, the need to change from the old to a new model of industrial organization is widely acknowledged by managements, and considerable efforts have already been made to move towards greater technical and organizational flexibility. The widespread experimentation with new forms of work organization during the 1970s had already alerted managements to the advantages to be gained but also made them aware of the extreme rigidity of French production organization, shaped by the practices of Taylorism–Fayolism (Maurice et al., 1986b: 384).

Thus although the will to abandon the old model appears to be strong (Maurice et al., 1986b: 382) the impediments to such change are also formidable. The entrenchment of the Taylorist–Fayolist system and the high level of control it bestows on management makes it hard to overcome. It has shaped the whole division of labour and the organizational hierarchy developed around it, as well as determining the national approach to vocational training and the skilling process of shopfloor workers. Respondents in firms investigated by Maurice et al. (1986b: 384) described the strong compartmentalization in French firms in terms of 'bastilles' and 'fiefdoms'. The French use of a complex system of task classification, influencing levels of pay, makes work organization particularly rigid (Maurice et al., 1986b: 268). But the impediments to change are balanced by greater unanimity than in Britain about the necessity for change, although this necessity is strictly viewed in economic terms (Dubois, 1986: 169).

In contrast to the situation in Britain, the state has played a large part in encouraging organizational change and greater participation by labour in it. This encouragement has been purveyed by a whole range of initiatives, such as in the areas of vocational education, industrial relations legislation (see Chapters 8 and 9) and financial and moral support for activities under the umbrella of the 'Improvement of Working Conditions' movement (Piotet, 1984: 262-3). Despite the diversity of responses by the major union federations and employer groups, there appears to be a consensus about the necessity for change, even if there is no agreement about the meaning of 'flexible specialization'.[3]

The solutions adopted in order to obtain greater organizational flexibility are in some respects similar to those favoured in Britain, but in other respects possess a distinctly French flavour. Although they have managed to overcome some of the old rigidities they have not fundamentally changed the old model. The charge is still widely levelled against French management that Taylorist practices have continued (e.g. Dubois, 1986: 169; Maurice et al., 1986b: 316, 338). On the other hand, however, French supporters of industrial change do not face such a large number of impediments as are confronting British managements.

It has already been pointed out that a successful implementation of the strategy of flexible specialization requires not only a high level of skill among workers but also considerable technical and organizational capabilities on the part of management. The examination of French management education in Chapter 4 has shown that, in contrast to the situation in Britain but similar to that in Germany, a high proportion of managers – 74.3 per cent of younger managers in 1985 (NEDO 1987: 7) – were qualified engineers (most from a *grande école*) who can be expected to display an openness towards new technology in processes and products. But French engineers, according to Telesis (1986: 44-5, 300), do not usually match their technical virtuosity with organizational competence. They have not shown themselves very adept at translating complex technological solutions to the requirements of production. They often lack the organizational skills which are becoming indispensable in the highly integrated production systems, facilitated by the new technology. Their expertise is at the theoretical level and lacks the 'craft' orientation which strives to integrate a skilled team around the performance of complex tasks. Also French engineers seem to be highly concentrated in certain sectors of industry (energy, vehicles, aerospace) and in large firms [4] and thus less influential in others, such as in mechanical engineering. According to the comparative survey by North-cott et al. (1985: 3), in the early 1980s France was behind Britain and, more so, Germany in the proportion of factories using microelectronics in processes, although it was in advance of Britain in the number of CNC machines [5] and robots used (ibid.).

For a long time French managers, like their British colleagues, have been conditioned to operate with a production and market strategy, using cheap labour and competing on low price (Telesis, 1986: 22–3). Hence, a switch to flexible specialization requires a fundamental change of outlook in the field of training and deploying labour which is not easily achieved. But the extensive shake-out of older and more traditional managers during the recession and their replacement with younger more progressive ones (Maurice et al., 1986b: 384) has been favourable to the creation of new attitudes.

At the present time, however, French management cannot draw on a plentiful supply of highly skilled and polyvalent production workers. The underdevelopment of an apprenticeship training of either the British or German kind and a reliance on on-the-job training has led to the creation of narrow and inflexible skills. The French system of classifying tasks, rather than workers, according to skill level and linking this classificatory scheme to levels of pay has further contributed to the rigidity of work organization (Maurice et al., 1986b: 268).

But during the 1980s French management has become very conscious of the harmful effect of this system and has introduced a new approach to solving the problems of skill shortage and lack of flexibility on the shopfloor. The adopted solution has a distinctly French flavour in its enduring commitment to elitism and hierarchical structures. Instead of increasing the levels of skill and discretion of existing workers, they have created new occupational categories and corresponding positions. The latter have been filled by external recruitment of young people, trained to a relatively high standard by state schools and colleges of technical education. Young persons with a technical baccalauréat or even a technical diploma are recruited to positions, combining technical functions at the level of technician with those of line management, and their place is on the shopfloor rather than in the department of technical services (Freyssenet, 1984; Piotet, 1984; Maurice et al., 1986b). In this way they are bridging the traditionally deep divide between technical departments and the shopfloor. This has, of course, become particularly crucial in the use of CNC technology. The creation of this kind of 'super-worker' has been made possible by the much expanded output in recent time of people with technical qualifications (Piotet, 1984: 204f). This élitist practice of training only a selected few to high levels of competence is ascribed by Eyraud and Rychener (1986: 224) to the high costs of internal training. The French solution achieves greater functional flexibility through increased homogeneity of qualifications of the new categories of workers, the *régleurs*, and those in technical services. It does little, however, to improve the situation of ordinary production workers. On the contrary, it leaves them locked into a position where a low level of skill perpetuates the old Taylorist–Fayolist scenario (Piotet, 1984: 284; Freyssenet, 1984: 422; Eyraud and Rychener, 1986: 224). This solution is also liable to create a disruption of the established system of internal promotion by seniority and will diminish the long-term chances of production workers to improve their status. It may eventually destroy the French system of internal, job-specific training, which has been typical up to the late 1980s.

Case studies of the deployment of CNC technology in mechanical engineering (Maurice et al., 1986b), of automated production lines in the vehicles industry (Freyssenet, 1984), of firms in the cement industry (Piotet, 1984) and of the use of robots in various industries (Berry, 1988) confirm the view that Taylorist practices are still entrenched. Although these studies report a high degree of diversity *between* enterprises in technical and organizational solutions, they nevertheless detect some common patterns and trends. Some studies have found further deskilling of workers. Freyssenet (1984: 244), for example, discovered that managements in the vehicle industry preferred increased expenditure in terms of machinery and equipment rather than depending on the experience of operators. Others, like that by Maurice et al. (1986b), report a marginal enlargement in the task content of operators. Both Piotet (1984: 281) and Eyraud and Rychener (1986:223) speak of a change in the nature of operators' knowledge towards the more abstract kind, previously only possessed by technical staff. But there is widespread agreement on the fact that the division between planning and execution has remained formidable and that close task control has endured. It is also suggested that a new form of skill reduction, i.e. that of the production unit, has become significant since the late 1970s. The marked increase in subcontracting, affecting both the most menial and the most skilled tasks, such as the installation and maintenance of the complex automatic machinery, has removed chances of upskilling and upgrading from core workers (Piotet, 1984: 282–3; Maurice et al. 1986b). This practice of subcontracting highly skilled maintenance tasks, due to insufficient internal skill resources, presents a new form of the division of labour and distribution of skill. It was also found to exist in Britain but, characteristically, no mention of it was made in the literature on German industrial change.

The case studies by Maurice et al. (1986b)[6] on the use of CNC technology, constituting an attempt to replicate in the French context the comparative study by Hartmann et al. (1984), merit particular attention. It is interesting that, in contrast to the German situation, the French authors found no example of machines being used which can be continuously reprogrammed and which permit operator involvement in programming. This is also confirmed by Piotet (1984: 259) who ascribes it to a shortage of highly-skilled production workers. The situation in French mechanical engineering firms differs from that in Britain in that the programming function is carried out by a kind of lower management – the *régleurs* – in direct contact with the workshop. Operators are not entrusted with programming tasks but merely with adjustment of machinery (Eyraud and Rychener, 1986: 220).

Given the fact that the functional flexibility of French production workers has not been greatly enhanced it is not surprising that the pursuit of numerical flexibility has increased markedly during the last decade. It appears as if recourse to certain forms of it, such as the use of temporary and fixed-term work, as well as subcontracting, is becoming as prevalent as in Britain.[7] The increase in numerical flexibility is widely acknowledged to be a problem by both social scientists and policy-makers (Piotet, 1984: 260; Freyssenet, 1984: 427; Caire, 1984: 728). (For greater detail see Chapter 11.)

The organization of industrial relations in France has not constituted the same impediment to industrial change as it has in Britain. Although employer–union relations have been far from harmonious there are signs of a limited consensus, both between the three sides of industry and between different unions, that improvements in the organization of work are a matter of high priority and that the rigidities created by Taylorism/Fayolism must be overcome (Piotet, 1984: 264f, 282). The introduction of the *groupes d'expression*, attempting to increase worker participation and involvement at shopfloor level (see Chapter 9) are one notable result, although these groups have so far had only limited effects (Eyraud and Tchobanian, 1985: 247). The unions, too, mobilized by the Movement for The Improvement of Working Conditions, are now persuing more qualitative goals, such as changes in work organization, rather than wage increases (Caire, 1984). The emergence of younger groups of managers, more interested in establishing a dialogue with workers (Piotet, 1984; Telesis, 1986) has also improved relations. Lastly, the absence in France of worker control over the allocation of work tasks has not presented a barrier to the pursuit of flexibility in the maintenance sector (Dubois, 1981) and thus has not unleashed the same contest for control as we are witnessing in Britain. But, at the same time, more general employer–union relations in France are still too conflict-ridden to facilitate the emergence of the high-trust relation, required by a manufacturing policy which is consistently oriented towards flexible specialization.

A quest for flexible specialization has been characteristic of managements during the 1980s in all three societies. But the attempts to adjust the organization of production to new and changing market demands have taken different forms in the three societies, and the industrial strategies devised possess different degrees of logical consistency. These differences are summarized in Table 7.2. Whereas in Germany the new strategy is very much technology-led and inspired, in Britain the impetus has come more strongly from the relaxation of constraints previously exerted by labour market conditions and the industrial relations system. In France, the arrival on the industrial scene of a new category of trained manpower and thus of a new social actor is considered to have provided the transformative power (Maurice et al., 1986b) although relaxation in the labour market has also created opportunities for change. In Germany the implementation of the new strategy has required only the reactivation and adaptation of old patterns of industrial organization which had become diluted during the postwar expansion of mass production. In Britain and France, in contrast, the pursuit of flexible specialization requires a drastic reorientation in worker training and deployment and in the sphere of industrial relations. British managements have had to contend mainly with horizontal structural rigidities, while French reformers have found hierarchical rigidities the greatest problem. In Britain the insufficient development of management technical skill also remains a big stumbling-block, whereas in France management attitudes to labour are in need of drastic revision. In Germany labour is increasingly regarded as a valuable productive resource which is central to the new strategy. In France, in contract, it is still often viewed as a constraint on management or as a source of headache (Telesis, 1986: 300). These different pre-existing resources and problems have led managements in the three societies to adopt different strategies to obtain greater flexibility.

German employers, able to draw on a large pool of skilled, polyvalent labour and union cooperation, have sought to reinforce and extend the functional flexibility of labour. British and French managements, possessing none of these advantages, have made more limited moves in the direction of greater functional flexibility and have, at the same time, increased numerical flexibility. While British managements have attempted to gain greater functional flexibility by the destruction of old and rigid forms of craft skill their French colleagues have tried to solve the problem by inserting new skill categories in the old contexts. The

Table 7.2 Factors supporting or inhibiting the move towards flexible specialization: a comparative perspective

	Germany	Britain	France
Management	Actively committed to continuous technological innovation and competent to initiate and establish new technical systems.	Lack of confidence and, therefore, hesitancy about technological innovation and a lack of competence to handle the more complex variety.	Technologically innovative management but less successful in adapting designs to the needs of production
Labour market supply	An ample supply of all-round skilled labour which can be broadly deployed and easily retrained.	A shortage of skilled labour and an absence of flexibility in existing skilled labour.	A shortage of highly skilled and of polyvalent labour.
Training system	A well-established training system and a willingness by both management and labour to invest in further or retraining.	A haphazard and underdeveloped system and a general reluctance by management to making the long-term investment required.	Recent state intervention to increase the supply of skilled production workers and a management strategy of creating a small polyvalent worker élite.
Employment relationship	Relatively high degree of employment security and low degree of labour market segmentation.	Relatively low degree of employment security. Segmented internal labour market.	Relatively high degree of employment security for the core labour force but a notable increase in labour market segmentation.
Idustrial Relations System	A cooperative system aiding worker identification with, and joint responsibility for, the efficient and competitive organization of production. Management no longer actively concerned with achieving domination.	An adversarial system based on a 'minimum interaction' employment relationship. Incompatibility with notion of worker responsibility for production flow and product quality. Management still struggling to re-establish control.	An adversarial system with an emphasis on hierarchy and close management control. Not conducive to the development of general worker responsibility and cooperation.

ability to do so has been crucially dependent on state support, in the form of expansion of intermediate technical education. State encouragement of change in other areas, too, has been a very important factor in France, but a less prominent feature in Britain and Germany.

The German strategy has ousted Taylorist forms of work organization in the core sectors of the economy, whereas in Britain and France aspects of the Taylorist model have been retained. Thus a more consistent strategy of flexible specialization in Germany can be contrasted with a hybrid, neo-Taylorist strategy in the other two societies. Hence, the consequences for labour have been mostly positive in German industry, whereas in Britain and France the effects for labour have been more ambiguous. In both societies, the conditions of the large contingent of semi-skilled labour have not improved at all and, where they have been subject to the implementation of numerical flexibility, have even deteriorated. It is unlikely that the hybrid strategy, adopted by British and French managements, will create the conditions for a successful realization of the new market strategy. High quality and product diversity/change can only be accomplished with skilled, poly-valent and responsible labour. Germany continues to enjoy a head start in this respect over the other two European societies.

NOTES

1. For greater detail see Gill (1985); Littler and Salaman (1984); d'Iribarne and Lutz (1984), Buchanan and Huczynski (1985) Chapter 14.
2. Drexel, I. and Nuber, C. (1979), *Qualifizierung fur Industriearbeit im Umbruch*, Campus. Altmann, N., Binkelmann, P., Düll, K., Stück, H. (1982), *Grenzen neuer Arbeitsformen*, Campus.
3. A fuller exposition of a new model of industrial organization in the French context, referred to as a model combining integration and diversification (Modele I.P.), has been provided by Maurice et al. (1986b: 36b).
4. A survey of small employers, reported by Piotet (1984: 264), has, however, revealed a much greater openness among heads of small to medium-sized enterprises towards installing automatic equipment and improving worker skills.
5. Piotet (1984: 250) cites various reports which point to an increase from 2200 NC machines in 1974 to 5800 in 1980 and forecast a rise to 10,000 by 1985.
6. These authors have done detailed case studies in the early 1980s of ten enterprises of varying size in the engineering industry which had recently introduced NC technology.
7. Part-time, female labour, however, is not nearly as frequently used as in Britain (Beechey and Perkins, 1987: 40f).

8 The System of Industrial Relations

Trade unions and other bodies representing labour are founded on the realization of a fundamental conflict of interests between capital and labour. Whereas it is in the interest of capital to extract from the worker the maximum possible effort at the minimum possible level of reward, the interest of workers is the reverse. Individual owners/managers derive from their ownership/control of the means of production considerable power over workers. Individual workers, in contrast, dependent on the sale of their labour power, are powerless *vis-à-vis* capital. This imbalance of power, coupled to the conflicting interest, led workers to the realization that they had to combine and counterbalance the power of capital by the collective power of labour.

The conflict of interests between the two sides of industry manifests itself at various levels of the relationship. The ensuing contest for control can either focus on only some control issues, or it can be dedicated to abolishing the whole power relationship. It is, however, oversimplified to portray worker/employer relations only in terms of conflict. There is usually also a degree of consensus between them about the fact that the continued economic viability of the firm must be preserved, and this requires a measure of cooperation. Thus it is more apposite to see worker–employer relations characterized by a continual tension between conflict and cooperation. The balance between the two will vary between societies and also within societies over time. It is very much influenced by class relations and methods of conflict regulation. Class relations should not solely be conceived of as conflict relations between capital and labour but also as relations of social interaction at work between various groups of employees, as in the 'societal effects' approach of Maurice and Sellier (1979). Hence it is important that industrial relations are studied in the context of the whole structure of relations within a business organization and related to other aspects of it, such as the system of vocational training.

A comparative study of industrial relations and industrial democracy has to develop an awareness of differences in the way, in which class relations have been shaped historically and the manner, in which they have moulded institutional frameworks and political orientations. Such study has to distinguish between the various issues, taken up by labour in different societies, i.e. control over wages, work organization or over general corporate policy. It has to analyse the different institutional forms which have evolved to deal with different clusters of 'control' issues. Lastly, in addition to considering long-term societal determinants, one also has to take account of more short-term economic changes which may alter the balance of power between the two sides of industry in significant ways.

HISTORICAL DEVELOPMENTS OF UNION MOVEMENTS

The following brief accounts will only provide very general outlines and cannot do justice to the overriding importance of historical legacies for the contemporary organization and tenor of industrial relations.

Britain has the oldest labour movement, with recognition of unions going back to the beginning of the nineteenth century. It is central to an understanding of the present system that the British union movement evolved before collective bargaining became institutionalised and that unilateral trade union regulation of work and conditions was the predominant mode of operation for skilled unions throughout the nineteenth century (Clegg, 1983: 3). Excepting only the last fifteen-odd years, the British union movement has developed without much outside intervention in a piecemeal manner. The result is a strong union movement, legitimized by long-standing tradition and custom. It has been integrated into British society by relatively liberal and flexible political and economic élites. For most of this time, the state has left the industrial opponents to sort out their differences in their own way. Although the principle of non-interference by the state is still upheld in theory today, in practice the malfunctioning of the system of industrial relations has called forth extensive intervention. It has mainly taken the form of introducing legislation which has subjected industrial relations to greater regulation. Whereas the legislation passed under the Labour government has mainly tried to compensate for the risks arising from loss of employment, legislation under the Conservatives has started to reshape the whole framework, regulating union activity. Although the effects of the 1980s legislation are not yet fully discernible and cannot always be distinguished from those of industrial decline, a short assessment will be made in the last part of this chapter.

The idea of a conflict of interests between capital and labour has never ceased to inform union activities, and efforts to incorporate workers through organizational devices have been consistently rebuffed. This conflictual orientation, however, has largely remained confined to the level of industrial relations and has not been transformed into a more general political ideology, opposing, and vowing to overthrow, the capitalist system as a whole. The pervasiveness of this 'conflictual' stance has led to the characterization of the British mode of conducting industrial relations as 'an adversarial style'. Allied to a reformist stance has been a pragmatic willingness to achieve improvements for workers through collective bargaining and to create institutionalized channels of employer–worker communication and conflict resolution. Demands have largely, though not exclusively, focused on economic reward and conditions of work, and attempts to alter the balance of power between the two parties in any fundamental way have not been prominent. Instead, relations have been characterized by a constant contest for control at the level of the shopfloor only. There has always been a strong connection between the unions and the Labour Party (political levy), with the unions exerting a stronger influence on the party than vice versa (Crouch, 1979: 117).

In France a totally different development has prevailed. France industrialized relatively late and industrial development proceeded slowly. Small and medium-sized owner-managed firms have tended to dominate the industrial scene, and the autocratic/paternalist attitudes of their heads towards workers have fundamentally coloured industrial relations. Although a labour movement existed already in the nineteenth century, unions received formal recognition only through a labour law passed in 1919. Actual acceptance of unions as legitimate social institutions came as late as 1950 (Caire, 1984: 724). Their legal recognition as negotiating partners at the level of the industrial enterprise was conceded only in 1969 after the 1968 strikes. *De facto* recognition is still being withheld today by many employers, particularly in smaller enterprises. The union movement, reflecting the divisions within the French working class, has not managed to achieve organizational unity. Its division into several politically-oriented union federations are described by the term 'plural unionism' (Smith, 1984). Non-recognition by employers has been paralleled by union cultivation of a militantly conflictual stance towards employers, with the two biggest still adhering to the revolutionary goal of abolishing capitalist relations at the level of production and of the whole society. They refuse to enter into relations with employers which imply a recognition of the legitimacy of the capital–labour relation and which would weaken them in their maintenance of militant anti-capitalist and anti-employer stances. (These orientations are well brought out in the study by Gallie, 1978.)

Consequently, unions in France have remained weak in numerical and organizational terms and collective bargaining is poorly institutionalized. (During the 1970s, however, the number of labour's representative bodies at plant level, i.e. of union sections and works committees, grew significantly – Caire, 1984: 727.) The fundamental all-round conflict of interest is always at the forefront and characterizes employer–worker relations at all levels of collective encounter. Consequently, the state has come to assume a large role in regulating industrial relations which, in turn, has served to reinforce the stance of non-cooperation of the two industrial opponents. The role of the state is further enhanced by the fact that it is a major employer, employing 23 per cent of the economically active population in the early 1980s (Bunel and Saglio, 1984: 233).

The comprehensive Auroux reforms of industrial relations at the beginning of the 1980s were explicitly designed to alter the fundamental pattern of industrial relations and to create a system aiding the peaceful articulation and processing of worker grievances (Eyraud and Tchobanian, 1985: 241). Although it is too early to arrive at definitive conclusions about whether or not this change has been accomplished, scepticism about their ability to achieve a transformation is widespread (e.g. Kesselman, 1984: 315; Coriat, 1984: 47; Caire, 1984; Smith, 1984).

German industrial relations have not experienced the same consistent development as the other two. Although Germany also began industrialization relatively late (1850), it proceeded at a fast pace within a relatively short timespan. The result was a sizeable number of very large industrial firms and the creation of a large, relatively homogeneous working class. This led to the early creation of a union movement which, despite strong opposition from rigid conservative élites, received relatively early recognition in 1865. The result was a strong union movement, dedicated to socialist economic and political goals. During World War I this unity of purpose became undermined, and the reformist wing came to predominate, but during the time of the Weimar Republic (1918–33) the movement for industrial democracy, through the establishment of works councils, still provided radical impulses. During Hitler's regime the union movement was destroyed as an independent force. After World War II, under the influence of the Allied Powers, union organization was reconstructed in 1949, along new lines but the old German institution of the works council became resurrected and gained new strength. The union movement re-emerged as a potentially important political actor. For a short spell, the early anti-capitalist stance was resurrected and substantial concessions from capital were gained. But relatively soon, this militant conflictual orientation was abandoned. The idea that employers and workers are 'social partners' endeavouring to create a consensus gained the upper hand. Industrial relations were institutionalized to a high degree and have assumed a relatively peaceful and harmonious quality. The style of industrial relations is generally regarded as cooperative. The good record in this respect has gained unions a trusted position among diverse sections of the German population (Bunn, 1984: 194).

An emphasis on the cooperative nature of German industrial relations does not imply that unions are totally incorporated and weakened in their ability to constitute a countervailing force. Not only have they managed to achieve substantial gains for their members but they are also continuing to fight for a potentially radical goal: to change the balance of power between capital and labour in favour of the latter through 'real parity' co-determination. Just as in France, the state has traditionally assumed a prominent role in society. But, contrary to the situation in France, a smooth functioning of industrial relations between strong industrial opponents has secured a large measure of autonomy for the latter in the conduct of industrial relations. The great importance in Germany of the legal regulation of industrial relations does not make the state a dominant actor but more of a 'middleman'. Legislation is strongly influenced by the two sides of industry, and law usually embodies a compromise solution. This contrasts with the French practice where neither of the opponents has had a strong influence on legislation, and with recent British practice where influence on legislation varies according to which party is in government. Like their British counterpart, the German peak union organization, the DGB, maintains close relations with the Social Democratic Party (SDP). But it maintains greater autonomy than the TUC as it does not raise a political levy to finance the SDP and has also kept close contact with the labourist left wing of the conservative Christian Democratic Union (CDU).

UNION MEMBERSHIP AND ORGANIZATION

In 1985 around 40, 50 and 22 per cent of all employed were unionized in Germany, Britain and France, respectively (Berghahn and Karsten, 1987: 38). (The French statistics are said to be very unreliable and union density is widely believed to have fallen below this level in recent years.) The lower level of unionization in Germany, compared with Britain, is partly due to the absence of the 'closed shop' but can also be attributed to the lower degree of unionization among white-collar workers and the numerically greater weight of small owner-managed enterprises. The latter is also the case in France, but more important explanations for the discrepantly low union density refer to the fragmented and ineffectual nature of unions, as well as to the higher degree of *de facto* non-recognition of unions by French employers (Hough, 1981: 54).

Both in Britain and Germany, the overwhelming majority of the unionized belong to unions, affiliated to one central union federation – The Trades Union Council (TUC) and the Deutscher Gewerkschafts-bund (DGB), respectively. In France, in contrast, unions belong to five major and several minor competing union federations (see details on p.207). The unions organized under the TUC and DGB are unitary unions, i.e. they are not divided by adherence to political ideologies or religious creeds. French union federations, in contrast, are ideologically oriented and have experienced frequent and bitter dissension over their conflicting ideological orientations.

The outward similarity of the British and German pattern of coordi-nation by a central union organization hides several important differ-ences. Whereas in Germany central control over constituent unions is strong, the British TUC finds it difficult to enforce coordinated policies. The weak control of the TUC is partly due to the large number of disparately organized constituent unions and partly to the relatively low degree of professionalization of administration. In Germany, in con-trast, professionalization is developed, and the small number (seven-teen) and uniform nature of constituent unions makes coordination of policies and tactics easier. In France, control over member unions by federations is said to be extremely weak. Maurice and Sellier (1979: 325f) characterize French union organization and leaders as charismatic, i.e. they appeal to members' common political sentiments and emotions rather than justifying their existence by reference to bureaucratic procedures and concrete negotiating achievements. They contrast this charismatic aura with the German bureaucratic style and the specially trained, permanent officials. Whereas a strong union federation is both an effective coordinator of interests and a valued negotiating partner at the highest level, a weak federation is disqualified on both grounds.

Further major differences become apparent when one examines the basis on which individual unions recruit their members and the levels at which bargaining and industrial action occur. German unions recruit on the basis of industry, representing all types of workers (manual and non-manual) in a given industry or set of industries. This makes for a mere seventeen industrial unions which are empowered to conduct collective bargaining as well as to organize industrial action. Both fields of activity are regulated to such an extent by law that the German system is said to be characterized by juridification, i.e. dominated by law. Although autonomy of bargaining is guaranteed, the juridification of industrial relations limits both the form and the issues for negotiation. But it must be remembered that the law not only severely restricts unions' freedom of action but that it also secures, and effectively protects, workers' interest. This latter fact has become particularly notable in a German–British comparison of unions during the recession.

Restrictions are particularly developed in the field of industrial action. To be recognized as legal, a strike must comply with a host of regulations. A strike can only be called as a last resort, i.e. after all other possibilities to reach agreement have been exhausted, and after balloting has established that it enjoys the support of at least 75 per cent of the membership. Further restrictions on strike activity are given by the stipulation that a strike can aim only for an objective which can be made subject to a collective agreement (i.e. not a political objective) and which does not blatantly violate the common welfare of society. A strike during the duration of a collective agreement is also illegal. Although unions generally stay within the bounds of law their members have been known to ignore legal restrictions, e.g. the September strikes of 1969. But such independent action is much less common than in Britain or France. Employers can counter strike action with lockouts, and these have been increasingly utilized in recent years. The unions regard lockouts as unconstitutional but have, so far, not managed to get a legal ruling on this.

Collective agreements are mainly concluded at regional industry level and are binding for both sides for the period of their duration. Traditionally most agreements have been about basic wage rates (*Lohntarifvertrag*), but they can also regulate the framework for wage determination or wider social aspects of work and conditions (*Mantel-tarifvertrag*). Individual unions have a relatively strong control over their membership and can usually enforce the agreements they have entered into. Although unions are represented at plant level, they are not entitled to negotiate or organize strikes at this level. Their represen-tatives, the union stewards (*Vertrauensleute*) – one steward for 30–50 members, according to Müller-Jentsch (1986: 231) – can act only in an advisory capacity. While Müller-Jentsch describes stewards as 'the extended arm of the works council', Berghahn and Karsten (1987: 63) suggest that their independence from works councils and their influence at plant level have increased in recent years.

At plant level, the works council (*Betriebsrat*) is the most important representative organ and exclusively conducts negotiations with indi-vidual employers. (The works council is described in greater detail in Chapter 9 on industrial democracy.) The works council is elected by, and represents, all manual and lower white-collar workers (*Tarifliche*

Angestellte). It negotiates with the employer on all matters, affecting work and workplace. Although it cannot engage in collective wage bargaining one of its main functions is to implement industry-wide agreements and to transform basic wage rates into actual wages, taking heed of enterprise economic strength. In addition, the works council has legally defined rights of co-decision (*Mitbestimmung*), consultation (*Anhörung*) and information in various areas. (For details see Table 9.2.) Results of negotiation are formalized as works agreements which assume the force of law. Juridification at this level is as strong as in union–employer relations. Disagreements are resolved by conciliation (internally) or by compulsory arbitration through labour courts. The latter is very much regarded as a 'last resort' measure and occurs relatively rarely. The works council cannot call strikes, and its only sanctions against the employers are non-cooperation or legal action. The discussion in Chapter 9 makes clear that the threat of non-cooperation is widely regarded as an effective weapon, given the council's co-determination and veto rights in several crucial respects.

The works council reports to a three-monthly meeting of the works assembly and, in larger enterprises, also appoints an Economic Committee (*Wirtschaftsausschuss*) and a Youth Representation body (*Jugendvertretung*). The former receives from management information on all financial and economic developments and on their implications for manpower planning and deployment, and the latter articulates the interests of apprentices to the works council.

Thus we have in Germany a dual system of worker representation, with competences and powers clearly divided between unions and the works council. Rights and obligations of both sides are spelled out by law. At both levels the obligation to maintain industrial harmony between the socalled social partners receives more emphasis than the right to engage in industrial conflict. The consequences of such a system for industrial relations will be discussed in a later section of this chapter.

The system of industrial relations extant in Britain is in most ways the polar opposite of the German system. The legal position of British unions has been unique in Europe in that, until 1982, unions have enjoyed immunity from law, and union activities have been exempt from legal regulation. Thus, for example, unions could not be held responsible for any damage their members' actions had caused employers or the wider community. Instead, rules governing bargaining and industrial action have been established by custom and tradition and are only loosely defined. Collective agreements do not have binding validity, and there has been no obligation to refer to external bodies for conciliation or arbitration. It is noteworthy that the absence of legal regulation has, at the same time, left workers without legally guaranteed rights, such as the right to return to their job after industrial action. Major Acts during the 1970s and 1980s have begun to change the legal situation in fundamental ways. These changes will be discussed in a later section of this chapter.

British unions recruit and organize their members on a mixture of bases: craft/occupation, general worker status, industry and, more recently, white-collar status. The result is not only an extremely large number at national level – during the 1970s as many as 113 unions were affiliated to the TUC alone (Jacobs et al., 1978: 4) – but also multi-unionism in a large proportion of workplaces. Thus, in 1980 45 per cent of all establishments had more than one manual union (and many more had also several non-manual unions), and these establishments covered a majority of manual employees (Daniel and Millward, 1983: 45). 40 per cent of these multi-union establishments did, however, conduct joint negotiation of the various unions involved (ibid.: 54).

Unions are widely recognized as legitimate negotiating bodies and, despite variation in union density by industry and size of firm, union representation is normal throughout British industry (ibid.: 279). Collective bargaining in recent decades has shifted from the national or industry level to that of the plant. Decentralized bargaining and single-employer agreements now predominate, particularly in manufacturing industry. In 1979 such bargaining with manual workers occurred in two-thirds of manufacturing establishments while bargaining at company, regional or industry level was practised by the remaining third. (For further details, see Brown, 1981: 8–9.)

The movement towards plant-bargaining caused a greater incidence of industrial action at this level. Plant-level industrial action appears to be almost the norm and is often only weakly controlled by union organizations outside the establishment, let alone by union leadership. The erosion of union central authority and the resulting confusion over dispute procedure was already noted by the 1968 Donovan Commission, i.e. the Royal Commission on Trade Unions and Employers' Associations. Since then bargaining procedure has become more formalized and shop stewards, the union representatives at the workplace, have been fully recognized as legitimate bargaining partners. Industrial action can be initiated at any level and, before 1984, by any method of membership consultation. Objectives of strikes have not been defined by law and political strikes have, therefore, not been proscribed, although their incidence has not been particularly high. Employers rarely counter strike action by lockouts or other sanctions.

In Britain labour representation occurs through a single channel –

unions – at every level. At plant level, representation of work groups by shop stewards for each union has become a widely established pattern. Stewards of represented unions may combine into Joint Committees or Combine Committees to negotiate at higher levels. The facilities granted to stewards to do their union work depend on local agreements with employers. In 1980, only 5 per cent of senior stewards or convenors spent all or nearly all their work time on trade union affairs, 20 per cent had their own office, and only a minority, even in the largest establishments, had received training (Daniel and Millward, 1983: 33, 38, 43). The single channel of representation, depending on union presence and density in a plant, means that a significant proportion of workers remain unrepresented. In 1980, 25 per cent even of unionised workers were not represented by stewards (ibid.: 33).

The range of issues covered by joint regulation is wide. Although pay bargaining remains the dominant concern among clearly classifiable grievances (Daniel and Millward, 1983: 236), it must be borne in mind that pay issues often become proxies for problems which are more difficult to articulate. Other issues which have figured prominently have related to union control over the distribution of work tasks and the organization of work. Bargaining activity in Britain has always concentrated on issues close to the shopfloor and has failed to seek more influence over strategic decision-making at top enterprise or company level and over economic matters which, in the end, vitally affect shop floorworkers. This is partly a result of the difficulty of adapting the shop steward system to the postwar trend towards concentration and company, rather than plant, strategic decision-making.

Such a wider perspective could be developed by consultative committees which have assumed greater prominence in recent years. These are meant to provide a basis for an exchange of views over matters of common interest. They should not be seen as alternative channels of worker representation as their formation and composition is strongly union-influenced (Daniel and Millward, 1983: 78f). Although these are generally positively regarded, they have not developed the wider perspective which has become so important at the present time. Another, numerically significant institutional development in recent years has been the establishment of Health and Safety Committees.

The French pattern of union organization, collective bargaining and industrial action also has a very distinctive character. Union federations do not distinguish in their recruitment and organization along craft/ occupation or industry lines but policy is determined by general objectives for all workers. Workers choose their union on the basis of political, or less often, religious conviction, although some division of labour between unions along functional and skill lines has evolved. The major unions do not regard themselves as organizations engaged in interest representation but as agencies to mobilize members in a class war. The chart overleaf shows the ideological orientations, areas of recruitment and numerical strength of the five major union federations. There are no official statistics on union membership, and the figures given are based on guesstimates, derived from union pronouncements and results of elections to plant representative bodies. They refer to the late 1970s/early 1980s. Since then the picture has been changing, and the more recent developments will be reviewed in a later section of this chapter.

Smith (1984: 30), basing himself on slightly different membership figures, based on 1979 elections to works committees, (published in _Le Monde_ 25 May 1982) indicates the differing strength of the union federations in terms of proportions of union members, affiliated to them: CGT – 34.4 per cent; CFDT – 20.5 per cent; FO – 9.7 per cent; CFTC – 3.1 per cent; and CGC – 5.8 per cent.

The legal framework for regulating collective bargaining before 1982 has been characterized by great vagueness, and it has not been clear what is negotiable and what is a matter of employers' prerogative nor have the appropriate levels for bargaining been spelled out. Bargaining between unions and employers takes place at a number of different levels, depending on the issue, but both employers and unions have largely avoided plant-bargaining. Periodic government attempts to shift bargaining to the company level have remained unsuccessful. In 1981, for example, only 9.9 per cent of firms were covered by company-level agreements (Eyraud and Tchobanian, 1985: 242). Unions have opposed plant-level bargaining because their haphazard success in mobilizing grass-roots support makes them afraid of being outmanoeuvred by employers. Employers' associations see plant bargaining as a threat to unity among their members, and individual employers regard it as a limitation of their managerial freedom (ibid.: 243).

Wages are usually set at industry level in terms of minimum wages which can then be adjusted upwards according to local economic capabilities and bargaining strengths. Agreements on general social issues, such as a reduction in working time or the establishment of procedures for collective redundancies, have usually been made at national level between the main employers association and one or more of the major union federations. Many commentators say that collective bargaining still hardly exists (e.g. Hough, 1981: 43). This is partly due to the fact that union density in many firms is so low that employers can safely ignore the unions. Most agreements have been unilaterally

Major French union federations

Confédération Générale du Travail (CGT)

Maintains strong links with the Communist Party. Works for a transition to socialism by the parliamentary route but still wants to defend workers' living standards and conditions within capitalism. Aims for a redistribution of income between capital and labour and hence does not believe in austerity during economic crisis. It opposes a redistribution of income within the working class, widely defined. Denounces any kind of participation in enterprise management and is not favourably disposed towards collective bargaining (Smith, 1984: 16). Recruits mainly from skilled manual workers in the older industries and the public sector. Has around 1.5 million members (*The Economist*, 18 February 1989: 79).

Confédération Francaise Démocratique du Travail (CFDT)

Split off from the Catholic CFTC in 1964, dropped its overt Christian character and moved leftward. Tries to achieve structural reforms which undermine the logic of the capitalist enterprise. It has a syndicalist political outlook, i.e. it favours local self-management of workers (*autogestion*). It is more volatile than the CGT in its ideological orientations, and, since the late 1970s, has become more reconciled towards negotiation and the achievement of obtainable objectives (Smith, 1984: 18). Gives support to the Socialist Party. Is not favourable towards collective bargaining but has tended to adopt a more pragmatic stance than the CGT. Is particularly concerned to bridge the gulf between 'core' and 'peripheral' workers, i.e. workers in secure and unstable employment. Recruits both manual and non-manual workers and has around 500,000 members (*The Economist*, 18 February 1989: 79).

Force Ouvrière (FO)

Split off from the CGT in 1948. Is a moderate socialist union. Accepts collective bargaining and favours workers' participation. Recruits mainly white-collar workers, professional groups and government employees. Has around 1.1 million members (*The Economist*, 18 February 1989: 79).

Confédération Française des Travailleurs Chrétiens (CFTC)

Founded in 1919 in opposition to the socialist movement. Promotes cooperation between capital and labour. Is strongest among non-industrial workers but has a presence in the mining and oil industries. It claims 150,000 members (IDE Research Group, 1981: 187).

Confédération Générale des Cadres (CGC)

Founded in 1944. Recruits mainly from managerial and administrative staff. Claims a membership of 250,000.

decreed by employers (Torrington, 1978: 39). Unions, as long as they are representative, can now legally represent workers at any bargaining level but, due to their fragmented nature and their ideological aversion to bargaining, they have, in fact, remained uninfluential. The legal provision for compulsory arbitration of disputes also militates against the development of collective bargaining.

The French collective agreement is nearer to a regulation than to a contract. Although its content is stipulated by both parties it becomes binding even if only one party has signed it. Often agreements at industry or multi-industry level have been signed with unions which are not uniformly representative. The validity of an agreement is indeterminate and cannot be unilaterally renounced by one party. In practice, however, neither the unions nor the employers have felt themselves bound by agreements (Caire, 1984: 724). The state may extend the applicability of the agreement also to sectors or groups not involved in drawing it up (Piotet, 1984: 269).

Union organization is characterized by a low degree of professionalization, and control over rank-and-file members is weak. Hence strikes often develop spontaneously without authorization or guidance. Strikes are not regulated by law. The lack of strike funds makes sure that they are usually of short duration. They are often accompanied by other militant actions, such as plant occupations, pickets or demonstrations. Employers may counter strikes by lockouts, individual sanctions, firings, use of police and of strike-breaking with administrative employees (Smith, 1984: 26f).

In France, unions are only one of several representative bodies. At plant level, there exists a multiple system of representation which has developed historically in a piecemeal fashion at crisis points of capital–labour relations. In addition to union sections, there are works stewards or delegates (*délégués du personnel*), a works committee (*comité d'entreprise*) and a Health and Safety Committee. Functional differentiation between them is insufficiently clear (IDE Research Group, 1981: 190).

Works stewards were introduced by law in 1936, in firms with more than ten employees, i.e. at a time when unions were not legally represented at plant level. They are elected yearly by a secret ballot of the workforce. Their task is to take up with management both individual and collective grievances, particularly those relating to the unsatisfactory implementation of legal regulations or of clauses of collective agreements. Problems with individual job and skill classifications are also prominent issues. In extreme cases, stewards can appeal to the state's Inspector of Work.

The works committee was legally instituted in 1945 for enterprises with more than 50 employees, in order to promote a dialogue between management and workforce. Representatives on the works committee are elected by the whole workforce, and meetings of the committee are chaired by the employer. The works committee enjoys rights of consultation and information mainly on social and personnel issues, such as conditions of employment and welfare provisions. In 1982 rights were extended to cover information about major changes in a firm's overall operations and about the firm's financial position. Since 1982 works committees can be formed by groups of associated small enterprises with a total of up to 50 employees, as well as at company level where representatives from subsidiaries will be represented (Piotet, 1984: 286, footnote 28). Generally, the works committee fulfills functions similar to those of the German works council, but it is said to be much less influential than the latter (Marsden, 1982: 42). Employers favour this channel of communication above the others (Eyraud and Tchobanian, 1985: 245). In 1980 works committees existed in 80 per cent of eligible enterprises (Caire, 1984: 727).

Union sections (*sections syndicales*) have been legally entitled to form within firms with more than 50 employees only since 1969. During the 1970s their number received a 2½-fold increase (Caire, 1984: 727). Unions alone are entitled to signing agreements with employers. The union delegates, nominated by all representative unions within the plant, liaise between members and management, concerning grievances and obligations laid down in collective agreements. Unions have the right to put forward candidates for the first ballot on works stewards and delegates to the works committee.

Regulation of industrial relations has become largely the domain of the state through the use of law. Often the laws do not find the approval of either of the industrial opponents. Consequently, the legal definition of industrial relations corresponds poorly with actual practice. Although the rights of workers appear substantial on paper, in reality unilateral employer regulation is still paramount. Also the legal codification of industrial relations has remained uneven. It is pronounced in some areas, e.g. on social aspects of work, and weak in others, e.g. strike activity.

THE IMPACT OF INSTITUTIONAL FRAMEWORKS ON THE QUALITY OF INDUSTRIAL RELATIONS

Germany

The impact of institutional frameworks on the balance between conflict and cooperation is particularly clearly expressed in Germany where a change in structural arrangement after World War II brought about a significant reduction in the level of overt conflict and where economic change in the 1980s has not undermined stability. The following institutional features have been particularly significant. The shift to industrial unions means that employers are dealing with only one relatively strong union which, in turn, makes it easier to reach agreements, to make them stick, and to avoid industrial action. The formidable numerical strength of unions, paralleled by employers' organizational strength, act as a strong deterrent to the engagement in industrial action. The highly formalized character of industrial relations, leaving little room for ambiguity, further reinforces this tendency. The number of strikes is, in fact, one of the lowest in Europe. As far as the unions are concerned, representing *all* workers in a given industry favours the adoption of a solidaristic wage policy. This means that the workers in weaker firms benefit from the industrial muscle of the stronger workers, and sectional interests are not allowed to influence bargaining. This minimizes internal working-class divisions which, in turn, reinforces bargaining strength. German workers' organizational strength is also enhanced by their high level of vocational qualification which facilitates mobility in external labour markets (Sengenberger, 1984a: 23). Employers benefit from this form of bargaining in as far as it necessitates the formulation of moderate 'averaging' demands and screens out the more extreme and/or sectional claims. Bargaining becomes confined to areas where standardized, quantitative demands can be made (ibid.: 28). Rigidities created by centralized bargaining can, however, be softened or counteracted at plant level through the works council. The whole economy profits in two ways. First, such centralized bargaining need not make allowance for economically weak employers and thus helps to ease out the inefficient enterprises within an industry. Secondly, centralized bargaining makes it easier to limit wage drift and to engage in economic forecasting and hence to stabilize the economy.

The dual system of representation is generally regarded very positively. It is credited with having contributed to the smooth functioning and high degree of stability of German post-war industrial relations. It has proven its worth not only during times of economic expansion but also during the recession (Brandt, 1984: 12f). Many British as well as some German commentators, however, regard the dual system more critically. Because the works council hives off, and canalizes, many conflicts it undermines union influence at plant level and generally impairs the mobilizing power of unions. This analysis is elaborated by Marsden (1978: 11) who speaks of the 'neutralization' of the workplace and its institutions with respect to the trade unions. It allows employers to insulate different clusters of 'control issues' from each other and thus prevent the intensification of conflict to a degree where workers can be mobilized against employers. While it is certainly true that German unions are much more restricted in their choice of mobilizing issues and in their direct influence at the work place they are not as firmly excluded as a study of formal arrangements suggests. As Streeck (1984a: 27) points out, the *de jure* absence of collective union representation on the works council does not usually signify a *de facto* lack of influence. As works council delegates are overwhelmingly (over 80 per cent) union members, unions can, and do, bring a good deal of pressure to bear that their line is pursued by delegates. Streeck (ibid.) prefers to speak of mutual incorporation of the two representative bodies rather than of a dual structure.

Another feature of the German system which has promoted peaceful and stable industrial relations is, no doubt, its juridification. This has not only served to channel conflict and minimize industrial dispute but, by increasing bureaucratization, has served to isolate ordinary workers from decision-making processes in works councils and, more so, central union organizations.

Britain

What are the consequences entailed by the British structure of industrial relations? The facts of multi-unionism and of a lack of formalization of rights, obligations and procedure make for complexity and ambiguity (Brown, 1981: 61). Consequently, they generate a relatively high level of friction and even conflict, both beween employers and unions and between different unions (ibid.). The tendency to express conflict in industrial action has been enhanced by the fact that unions are strong in numerical terms, have been able to legitimate their demands by reference to tradition and custom and have been faced by relatively (in comparison with France and Germany) weak employers. The weak institutionalization of channels of conflict resolution has meant that industrial action has often been regarded as the first, rather than the last resort. The existence of multi-unionism is also said to promote sectional interests, create inter-union conflict and to divide the labour movement. But Daniel and Millward's national study found that strike action was only slightly more common in establishments with more than one union (ibid.: 224).

The pattern of plant bargaining has also become associated with a number of negative consequences. First, it contributes to the high level of industrial action (Daniel and Millward, 1983: 222). Secondly, localized pay bargaining creates undue competition between employers, without improving the relative gains of any one group of workers in the longer term[3] (Saunders and Marsden, 1981: 349). The diffuse nature of plant bargaining encourages wage drift and hence inflation and also impedes general economic planning. Although plant bargaining may be to the advantage of economically weaker firms and workers in thriving enterprises, it is not beneficial to the working class and the economy as a whole. It impedes the process of economic restructuring from ailing to thriving firms.

The process of economic restructuring and technological advance is also widely held to be impeded by managers' fear of, or uncertainty about, industrial conflict, as well as being slowed down by restrictive practices (e.g. Maitland, 1983; Bessant and Grunt, 1985). Among the latter, demarcation practices by craftsmen have been singled out as impeding the attainment of the new flexibility, required by changed market and production conditions. (See the discussion of this in Chapter 7.) Lastly, demarcation practices have come to undermine the employment security of craftsmen and the continued viability of their unions. Thus, although union opposition to technological change is relatively weak (Daniel, 1987) their actions may nevertheless indirectly hold up essential technological change.

Some commentators, however, see the low degree of formalization of rules and procedure and the strong emphasis on voluntary arbitration as positive features of the British system. It is said to give the possibility of flexible adjustment according to local conditions. Also the high degree of influence by ordinary workers over industrial issues – as contrasted with the more formal and bureaucratized pattern of delegation to elected representatives in Germany – is seen as one of the positive features of the British system. Although multi-unionism dissipates numerical strength, the single channel of representation counteracts this and makes for a strong and autonomous union movement with possibilities for grass-roots involvement. But informality is a double-edged weapon and the way it cuts depends on the conditions surrounding it. An examination of the most recent developments will show that it is less advantageous to the unions during a time of economic decline.

France

How does the institutional structure found in France affect the industrial opponents and the general economy? Although the working class is said to be highly conscious and conflict-oriented (Gallie, 1978 and 1983), plural unionism, making for inter-union conflict, dissipates labour's strength *vis-à-vis* employers. The weakness of all representative bodies obviates the articulation of militancy in plant-level bargaining where autocratic management behaviour has been able to perpetuate itself. In addition, the confinement of workers to intra-organizational labour markets further weakens their position *vis-à-vis* employers (Maurice, 1986a: 360), precludes mobility from weak to strong sectors of industry and thus impedes adjustments in a changing world economy (Marsden, 1987: 190).

The multiple structure of representation at plant level, with its blurred lines of functional differentiation, also plays into the hands of employers. They can manipulate the system and deal with whatever body appears most amenable to negotiation. Lastly, wage determination at industry-level in the form of adjustable minimum wages creates a relatively homogeneous wage structure and aids planning for economic stabilization. More generally, it is probably fair to say that, as collective bargaining is insufficiently institutionalized and the state plays a prominent role in regulating conflict, the legally defined structure of industrial relations has had comparatively little impact (Maurice and Sellier, 1979: 329).

The preceding outline of the three national systems of industrial relations and the analysis of the consequences they entail for workers, employers and the whole economy have revealed three fundamentally different patterns. The British system affords ordinary workers – as opposed to functionaries – the highest level of direct involvement and, with some reservations, effective representation. But it does not ensure the smooth functioning of the industrial relations process. Although British employers and unions are not locked into irreconcilable 'class conflict' positions and remain committed to pragmatic conflict resolution, achievements are not commensurate with efforts. The ambiguity and complexity of the system leads to a state of affairs where constant friction is endemic and the level of industrial conflict remains high. During the time of recession this system has served neither side well, and there is considerable doubt about its continued viability.

The French system of industrial relations, despite the openly hostile underlying class relations, has not generated the same high level of friction and overt conflict. This is, however, not due to the superior functioning of the system but is clearly the consequence of the weakness of the industrial opponents and the prominent role of the state which has arisen out of this deadlock situation. The result is an unstable system of industrial relations which is still exposed to the recurrence of spontaneous political eruptions of the sort encountered in 1968. The realization that the system is not functioning satisfactorily and that the rights of individual workers still receive insufficient respect has led to the comprehensive reform of industrial relations in 1981/82. The effects of this will be examined in the final section of this chapter.

The German system of industrial relations has ensured the smoothest functioning of industrial relations and has also proved to be the most stable of the three. The combination of a clearly differentiated dual system of representation with a comprehensive legalization of industrial relations has served both to keep the level of conflict low and to resolve disputes effectively when they arise. It has secured workers relatively effective, by international standards, representation on a wide spectrum of issues and has, by and large, had a positive impact on general economic development. This stability in terms of industrial relations is said to have played an important part in maintaining Germany's reputation as an exporting country, trading not only on quality but also on reliability. If it has entailed any costs, it is that the system of representation is too centralized and bureaucratized to give any sense of grass-roots participation. Also the high degree of juridification might be regarded by foreign observers as impeding employer flexibility, but generally German employers do not regard this as a very grave problem. (See the views of employers expressed in the volume edited by Lezius, 1982.)

These three patterns are reflected in the degree and nature of industrial action in the three societies. Industrial action includes not only strikes but also activities, such as go-slows, work-to-rule and overtime bans, which are said to have an equally disruptive effect on production. But as the latter forms of industrial action are not sufficiently well documented to make reasonably accurate cross-national comparisons, the following account will deal mainly with strike action. An examination of statistics on stoppages and working days lost through them during recent decades gives a clear and consistent picture of differences in this respect between the UK, France and Germany, despite the problems of making international comparisons.[4]

Table 8.1 gives both the number of stoppages and that of working days lost per striker. Table 8.2 records only working days lost per employee but brings the statistics more up to date, while Figure 8.1, showing the differential pattern in graphic form, drives home the differences in this respect between the three societies. Table 8.1 shows that during most years France has had a larger number of stoppages than Britain. But, due to the weakness of the French unions, these strikes have remained mainly localized and of short duration. Consequently, the number of striker-days per 1000 employees tends to be significantly lower. In Germany the time lost through strikes is negligible

Table 8.1   The pattern of strikes in comparative perspective

	Stoppages per 1000 employees			Striker-days per 1000 employees		
	1965–69	1970–74	1975–81	1965–69	1970–74	1975–81
Federal Republic of Germany	No information			6	49	22
United Kingdom	9.5	12.0	9.1	156	585	467
France	9.6	17.7	18.5	126*	166	178

* 1968 excluded from average.

Source: International Labour Office, *Yearbook of Labour Statistics.*

Table 8.2   Industrial disputes. Working days lost per 1000 employees, 1975–84

	1975–79[a]	1980–84	1975–84
United Kingdom	510	480	500
France	210	90	150
Germany	50	50	50

a. Annual averages for those years weighted for employment.

Source: Employment Gazette; July 1986: 267, extract from Table 1.

in comparison with the other two countries. This relative rarity of strikes is due to extensive legal restrictions but also to their costliness in terms of strike pay, due to industry-wide organization. But when strikes do occur they are, as a rule, of long duration and involve a lot of workers although about half of the workers are out due to employer lock-outs (Streeck, 1987a: 32). The United Kingdom has experienced by far the greatest disruption from strikes. One reason for this is the greater number of large firms which are significantly more strike-prone than smaller ones in all three societies (Prais, 1981a: 66f on Britain and Germany). Although the UK occupies only an intermediate position, with regard to working days lost, when compared to all OECD countries, this should not distract attention from the fact that, with the exception of Italy, it has the worst strike record as far as its main European competitors are concerned. Furthermore, its record and reputation is made worse by a high incidence of short, unrecorded strikes (Prais, 1981a: 63f) and of the other types of industrial action, mentioned above. Thus, a national study by Millward and Stevens

Figure 8.1   Industrial disputes in France, Germany, Italy and the UK

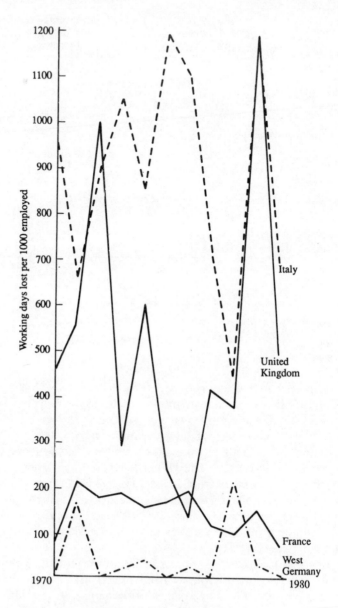

Source: Walsh K. (1982), 'An analysis of strikes in four EEC
          countries', *Industrial Relations Journal*, 13,4: 71.

(1986: 264) established that in 1984 non-strike action among all workers was as frequent as strike action and that, among manual workers only, unofficial action in 1983/84 had been as common as official action. The high incidence of unofficial action makes it, of course, more difficult for management to anticipate, and make contingency plans for it. The reverse is true for Germany. There is little evidence for Hyman's (1984: 59) claim that if, as in Germany, strike activity is made difficult, conflict will manifest itself in other forms of collective or individual protest action. Since 1984 and up to the time of writing, the number of working days lost has declined significantly in all three societies (Caire, 1984; Millward and Stevens, 1986; Streeck, 1987a).

The foregoing account has regarded the nature and scope of conflict as shaped by the institutional system but also by the balance of power between capital and labour, as it has historically evolved. In addition, however, attention has to be focused on the economic context in which industrial relations are conducted. The great changes in the economic environment during the last decade or so of all three societies and their impact on industrial relations will, therefore, be examined in the following section.

RECENT CHANGES IN INDUSTRIAL RELATIONS

In all three societies a series of interrelated changes have undermined union strength and partially transformed the institutional framework and ideological tenor of industrial relations. Economic recession and unemployment have reduced both numerical strength and political appeal of unions and have, at the same time, strengthend the hand of conservative forces in both industry and government. A further influence on industrial relations has flown from far-reaching changes in general industrial strategy and the accompanying transformations at the level of technology and work organization. Such transformations of industrial relations have been most pronounced in Britain and have had the least impact in Germany. In France, the accession to power of a socialist/communist coalition in 1981 has brought about the instigation of changes in favour of labour although the impact of recession has also been felt in France and limited the positive effects of legal changes. It is too early to judge the impact on industrial relations of the return to power of a conservative party in 1985.

France

The reform of industrial relations, initiated by the passing of the Auroux laws in 1982[5] tried to achieve 'a peaceful revolution, aimed at modernising the French system of industrial relations' (Caire, 1984: 723). The legislation is primarily a government initiative although the influence of the bigger unions, particularly of the CFDT, is clearly visible. There is less trace in the legislation, however, of any consultation with employers. The laws tried to achieve a higher degree of institutionalization of industrial relations, in order to reduce the level of conflict between employers and their workforce. But other objectives were to make worker representation more effective, to enlarge the rights of individual workers, and to restore the works community as a meaningful entity in the face of divisions, flowing from new employment practices under the recession (ibid.: 728). The attempt to afford both individual workers and their representative bodies more opportunities for participation will be discussed in Chapter 9 on Industrial Democracy, but three further objectives can be examined immediately.

The goal to achieve a greater institutionalization of industrial relations has been pursued by giving more emphasis to, and clarifying, the process of collective bargaining, as well as strengthening the unions' representative role at plant level. There is now a legal obligation that employers and union sections enter into annual bargaining at plant level over wages, hours of work and working conditions and that parties, bound by industry-wide agreement, meet at least once a year to renegotiate wages. In addition majority trade unions, i.e. those which obtained more than 50 per cent of votes at the last elections of the works committee, acquired the right to veto the entry into force of works agreements, providing for exceptions to national laws, regulations, collective agreements (Caire, 1984: 729). The effect of this particular complex of legal provision, as yet, cannot be discerned clearly. In 1984 plant-bargaining was still confined mainly to large firms in selected industries (Caire, 1984: 733). But the opposition of many employers to compulsory regulation of this sort, the increasing numerical weakness of unions, as well as the impact of recession, make it unlikely that the legislation will achieve the desired effect although a more gradual shift need not be ruled out. Gaudier (1987: 52) discerns a greater decentralization of bargaining and its closer linking to the market position of the enterprise. But this has not led to the strengthening of trade unions as managers have moved towards more direct cooperation with works committees and other, less formal, enterprise groups.

The Auroux legislation also addresses itself to the consequences of recession and tries to minimise its impact on the weaker sections of the working class. A host of new regulations, trying to protect those in part-time and temporary work as well as those hired under short-term contracts, is meant to ensure equal treatment for workers in 'core' and 'periphery' employment. Other regulations attempt to ensure that the restructuring of declining industrial sectors and enterprises gives some protection to workers affected by it.

Both the recession and the change in industrial strategy have called forth new bargaining issues and have caused a shift in emphasis towards more qualitative demands. The issues of work-sharing, working conditions, and changes in work organization towards greater flexibility and greater task integration have been high on the agenda since 1975, both for collective bargaining and for legal regulation.[6] As the latter issues appear to be a priority also of many employers (Jenkins, 1981; Caire, 1984), it seems likely that French enterprises will make some advances on this front.

Lastly, the recession and the change in political climate have had an impact on unions' numerical strength. Although no precise figures are available, it is widely suggested that both socialist unions have suffered a drastic loss in membership, particularly the CGT, and that the more moderate FO has gained new members (Piotet, 1984; Telesis, 1986: 314). These changes are due to a number of reasons: industrial decline and loss of employment has been particularly strong in the older, heavy industries and state-owned monopolies, where the CGT had enjoyed particular support; the new employers' strategy of disintegration of large, more unionized enterprises into smaller units[7] and their relocation away from 'left' strongholds or to geographically more peripheral and less politicised areas (Coriat, 1984; Erbes-Séguin, 1984); and lastly, to a loss of political appeal of the political left more generally (Howarth, 1982). Such loss of organizational strength seems to have been accompanied by loss of influence (Gaudier, 1987: 52).

Germany

German unions and the whole system of industrial relations have weathered the extensive changes of the late 1970s and 1980s, resulting from recession and industrial restructuring, relatively well. So far their numerical and organizational strength has only been marginally affected, but there are signs that, during the late 1980s, they will have to face up to a range of new organizational problems. (The following account of recent developments is based mainly on Fürstenberg, 1984; and Streeck, 1987a.)

Trade union membership, coming predominantly from workers in the core industries of the private manufacturing sector, has been remarkably little affected by recent changes. This has partly been due to the lesser severity of economic crisis in Germany and partly to union gains at the workplace, promoted by a 'quasi-closed shop' arrangement operated by works councils in the recruitment of new workers. Overall trade union density has even risen from 37.9 per cent in 1973 to 40.5 per cent in 1985 (ibid.: 20, Table V), and union funds have remained at a relatively high level (one per cent of wages before tax). The German employer organization, dominated by large firms, has so far resisted calls from smaller employers to weaken union powers, and the Conservative government has also refrained from making a major onslaught on the central features of the bargaining system.

But significant changes – some of them in the making for many years, others of more recent origin – are coming to a head and will require action, if the future stability and cooperative nature of the system of industrial relations is to be maintained. The shift in collective bargaining to more qualitative concerns, such as improvements in working conditions, work organization and more flexible working hours, has at the same time shifted the centre of gravity away from industry-level union bargaining to negotiation at workplace level by the works council. Thus works councils have become more autonomous bargaining units, and the role of unions has become more limited. Although this development is well adapted to the requirements of greater internal flexibility (see Chapter 7), it will further undermine the power of unions to mobilize their members.

Another dilemma has been presented by the changing pattern of industrial conflict. The recent tactic of the metal workers' union IG Metall to concentrate strike activity on a limited number of establishments, chosen with the aim of causing maximum cumulative disruption in other geographic areas,[8] has provoked employers to retaliatory action, supported by the Conservative government. Employers not only increased lockouts but also persuaded the government to pass the 'Section 116' legislation to prevent unions from turning the social insurance system into a 'second strike fund'. The effects of this hotly contested piece of legislation are yet to be established. A short-term effect is a deterioration in union–government relations, and a future onslaught on more central co-determination rights, which has recently been contemplated by the spokesmen for smaller firms and by politicians on the extreme right, is an obvious danger. But so far, to quote Fürstenberg (1984: 629), 'conflictual co-operation seems to stand a very good chance of remaining the dominant pattern'.

Britain

Changes in the nature of industrial relations and the degree of union strength have been most pronounced in Britain, due to the severity of industrial decline and the new legislation on, and general attitude towards, the unions by the Conservative government. These changes do, however, not reflect a dramatic shift in attitudes by British managements, and there is little evidence to support any sensational claims about extensive 'union-bashing' on their part, although more limited changes have been achieved by them (Edwards, 1987).

The effects of industrial decline on union membership and practices are well documented for the 1980–84 period by the national study of workplace relations by Millward and Stevens (1986). The drastic reduction in employment[9] was heavily concentrated in large, private manufacturing enterprises, employing predominantly male workers, in the older industrial sectors, as well as in engineering and vehicles, where 'closed-shop' arrangements had been prevalent and levels of unionization high (ibid.: 11, 57, 103). Consequently, a reduction in the number of establishments with some union members by 10 per cent, and with a 'closed-shop' by 11 per cent, as well as a decline in union density from 76 to 66 per cent (among manual workers in manufacturing) were mainly due to structural changes of this kind, rather than to management withdrawal of union recognition (ibid.: 52, 54, 102). Apart from numerical decline, the study found more evidence of continuity than radical upheaval in union practices and management responses. In the area of pay settlement, for example, managements in 1984 were still uninfluenced by such factors as recent financial performance, output trends or questions of price competitiveness. The study by Edwards (1987: 115), however, while confirming the absence of management attacks on shop steward organizations, nevertheless found a clear change on the part of management in its approach to labour. The emphasis in management–labour relations has shifted from negotiation with representative bodies to persuasion of workers as individuals that their interests are best met by cooperation. Management are now concerned to foster the involvement of labour.

Government legislation in the 1980s has been inspired by the aims of fundamentally reshaping the British system of industrial relations and of weakening union power. Although reform attempts (e.g. in 1971) in this area had always been defeated by the unions, the combined effect of economic recession, widespread popular support for curbing union power (Hyman 1984: 225) and a more resolute, free-market oriented Conservative government secured a reasonably successful implementation of a range of far-reaching legal provisions. The two Employment Acts of 1980 and 1982 attempt to restrict union rights in the areas of picketing, secondary action, closed-shop arrangements and the formulation of strike objectives. The 1982 Act also makes unions, engaging in unlawful actions, liable to pay damages to firms or individual employees, as well as laying down high fines for contempt of court, in case of failure to answer a summons. The 1984 Trade Union Act intervened in internal union organization with the aim of increasing internal democracy in decision-making on strikes and election of functionaries. It is too early to assess the full effects of this legislation and also difficult, in some cases, to determine unambiguously causation, but some general observations can nevertheless be made.

Clark (1985) usefully investigates the impact of the legislation in three areas: limitation of the right to strike; union liability in the face of employers' damages claims; and agreements to safeguard union interests. He finds that, although many provisions of the new laws have been ignored by both unions and employers or cannot be enforced, the provision of union liability for damages, arising from unlawful action, has been taken up with sufficient frequency to have had a serious effect on unions' freedom to engage in industrial action. Significantly, unions are rarely taken to court by the employer who is the primary target of their action but by firms which are indirectly affected and need not worry about the longer-term negative effect on industrial relations climate. This fact also indicates that impact should not solely be considered in terms of a direct effect on industrial relations practices but also in terms of its symbolic or 'demonstration' effect. Many studies confirm that the new legislation has had important psychological effects on management who feel assured of governmental moral support for their effort to restore greater managerial control (see, for example, the study by Kahn et al., 1983, quoted by Clark, 1985: 178).

This ideological support for greater management assertiveness against unions has led to further changes in 'industrial relations' practices in areas which are not regulated by the new laws. In a large minority of enterprises management have re-established control over the allocation and organization of work and, in particular, have succeeded in eliminating demarcation practices (Daniel, 1987: 168f; Basset, 1986: 98; IMS, 1986a: 8; Willman, 1986). Thus Daniel's (1987: 168) national survey of industrial relations and new technology found that 34 per cent of works managers felt constrained in their freedom to distribute tasks between different categories of workers whereas the Donovan Report in the late 1960s had found this proportion to be 13 per cent higher. Usually, though, management objectives are obtained by concessions on pay increases, rather than by management decree. Other developments, indicating a new industrial relations style, are outlined by Basset (1986). He emphasizes particularly a movement towards a more cooperative style by unions and also points towards an increasing number of 'single-union' agreements, as well as towards a small number of 'strike-free' agreements. The latter have, however, mainly been concluded by foreign-owned companies with a minority of British unions.[10] But the demonstration effect of such agreements, particularly of the 'single-union' type, should not be underestimated.

In conclusion, the British system of industrial relations, although by no means fundamentally reconstructed, has nevertheless been changed in several significant ways. If the factors causing change should, as seems likely, be operative for several more years to come, more drastic reorientations in 'industrial relations' style can be expected.

NOTES

1. Relatively few establishments, according to Daniel and Millward (1983: 289), even provided workers with information on their financial position.
3. In 1987 DGB unions comprised 86 per cent of all unionized, and the other 14 per cent were divided between an independent white-collar union (DAG), the Civil Servants Union, and a small Christian Union Federation (Streeck 1987a: 20).
3. Saunders and Marsden (1981: 349) comment that 'the stability of the pattern of differentials between industries shows that only a few strong and fortunate bargaining groups have been able to secure gains in relative real income for more than a short period' and that a competitive bargaining system leads to inflation.
4. For an extended analysis of the problems of comparing strike action, see Walsh (1982) and *Employment Gazette* (July 1986). Briefly, the figures for France slightly understate action because public sector strikes and political strikes are excluded and workers indirectly affected are not counted. The UK also excludes political strikes but counts indirectly affected workers, whereas Germany includes political strikes but not indirectly affected workers. The omission of indirectly affected workers could have a sizeable effect on final figures. Otherwise the UK and Germany apply the same criteria for recording strikes although the compulsory notification of strikes in Germany probably makes for a fuller record. In France, in contrast, the smallest stoppages are not excluded from the count but might nevertheless escape recording as strike statistics are collected by Labour Inspectors (*Employment Gazette*, July 1986: 268).
5. The Auroux Report was published in 1981, and its recommendations were implemented in 1982 in three Ordinances and four Acts (Caire, 1984: 728).
6. The creation of a plant-level committee for the improvement of working conditions, amalgamated with the committee for health and safety, which has been given new rights, provides further evidence of concern in this area.
7. Dubois (1984: 16) points out that the propensity of workers to go on strike decreases markedly with the reduction in unit size.
8. As unions are not obliged to give strike pay to workers who, as a consequence of the strike, are laid off in other geographical regions and can, instead, claim unemployment benefit, their new tactics achieved maximum effect without great costs.
9. Between June 1980 and June 1984 there occurred a fall in employment of 1.6 million (Millward and Stevens, 1986: 10).
10. Although only one union – the EETPU – has concluded most of the 'no-strike' agreements, in 1985 all the major British unions attempted to get a single-union, no-strike deal with Nissan (Basset, 1986: 148–9), who eventually chose the AUEW.

9   Industrial Democracy

Democracy means granting equal influence on decisions to all groups affected in their vital interests by these decisions. While democracy, however imperfectly realized, has for a considerable time been a reality for all citizens in the political system of our three societies, democracy in industry or at the workplace is still underdeveloped or non-existent. The notion of industrial democracy envisages the right of workers to exert an influence over the social, personnel and economic aspects of their own workplace and of the enterprise which employs them. It calls for their participation in decision-making. Conversely, it implies the obligation of managers to renounce their complete managerial prerogative and involve workers' representatives in decision-making processes on an equal footing. The demand for equal rights is based on the claim that owners and workers bear equal, albeit different, risks – the one of losing his capital, the other his health, security or whole livelihood. Industrial democracy thus goes further than conventional collective bargaining which is merely a process of interest representation in certain limited areas. Collective bargaining consists of an assertion of power or countervailing power within a framework negotiated by the two industrial opponents. The emphasis is on a conflict of interests, and the outcome of the contest between the two sides is determined by the momentary balance of power. But, in theory, collective bargaining can be extended so far that it comes to shade over into industrial democracy.

David Marsden (1978) reminds us that the struggle over industrial democracy is a contest over the possession of collective control. Such an approach is useful because it permits the adoption of a dynamic perspective dealing with contests for control and the resulting shifts in control between the industrial opponents. Industrial democracy can take a large variety of forms, depending on the level and scope of participation exercised and on the route by which effective workers' participation is attained. Participation at the highest level, i.e. at board level, is seen to encroach much more on managerial prerogative than participation at the level of the work group and has been more fiercely resisted by management. Where such participation rights at the highest level have been attained, as in Germany, their scope is more carefully circumscribed than where participation rights affect only the organization of the workplace although extensive rights even at this level, as is shown by the British case, can greatly constrain management decision-making.

It is useful to distinguish between two different routes towards industrial democracy: one is shaped by local initiatives of workers and trade unionists; the other is founded on supportive public policy and legal enactments (Poole, 1986: 144). The first variant is the one which has been favoured in Britain where, until recently, labour has been able to rely on a favourable climate of values and its relatively high level of organizational power. The second route has prevailed in Germany and France where state intervention has served to secure labour participation rights which it could not have attained by its own power. Whereas German labour has acquired sufficient organizational power to achieve a high degree of enforcement of its legal rights, the organizational weakness of French labour creates a greater gulf between legally guaranteed and actually enjoyed rights. Consequently, local initiatives by workers and unions, inspired by the syndicalist strand in the French socialist tradition, such as factory occupations, erupt from time to time but can only be sustained for short periods.

The development of industrial democracy in a society depends on the overall balance of power between capital and labour at the level of the enterprise and, more importantly, at the societal level as expressed in political struggle and political representation. Examples of the former are the brief ascendancy of French labour after the events of May 1968 or the temporary ideological weakness of German capital in the immediate postwar period. The importance of political representation has been expressed by the fact that labour has usually achieved significant gains during the assumption of government power by social democratic or socialist parties. In addition, management attitudes are influenced by the degree of acceptance on the part of labour of the notion that participation in decision-making entails a sharing of responsibility for company performance. Different societal patterns in this respect lead us to expect marked national differences in management attitudes to industrial democracy.

The right of worker control in certain areas can be granted with varying degrees of formality, ranging from law to custom, and it may be more or less clearly vested in certain representative bodies. Alternatively, the right of control in certain areas may become the object of constant contest between workers and management. In this chapter we shall mainly be concerned with the institutionalized systems (including also the lowly formalized British system of industrial democracy), whereas the contest for control over the labour process is the topic of Chapters 6 and 7. Formal institutions of industrial democracy are most fully developed in Germany, and only weakly in France and Britain. For this reason, and also because the German model has been advanced as a possible model for all EEC countries, the bulk of this chapter will be devoted to it. But a short discussion of French and British patterns will also be given. The chapter concludes with a comparative survey of the three national patterns.

INDUSTRIAL DEMOCRACY IN GERMANY

Industrial democracy in Germany is embodied in the concept of *Mitbestimmung* – co-determination or co-decision by workers on a number of issues concerning their vital interests. Co-determination can be exercised at two different levels: (a) at the level of the workplace through the institution of the works council; and (b) at the level of the enterprise through worker representation on the supervisory board and, to a much lesser extent, on the management board. Co-determination at company level exists in three different versions which will each be discussed below. Of the two forms of co-determination, that at the level of the workplace has been more influential than that at board level, and since the legislation of the 1970s it has become difficult in practice to maintain a distinction between the two (Streeck, 1984c: 404). (Works councillors are very often also employee representatives on the supervisory board.) An outline of the formal properties of co-determination bodies and procedures will be followed, in the second part of this chapter, by an attempt to assess their *actual* impact on decision-making as well as examine their evaluation by both workers and employers.

Co-determination at Board Level

The most radical version of the existing three forms of enterprise co-determination was instituted in 1951 in the coal and steel industries of the German economy – the *Montan* sector. Its major features are indicated on the left-hand side of Figure 9.1. As workers' and shareholders' representatives are represented on the company supervisory board in equal proportions – the chairman cannot be elected against union opposition – and with equal voting rights, this form of co-determination gives workers real parity of representation. Workers' representatives are partly elected by the workforce and partly nominated by the relevant central union organization and, in the latter case, can come from outside the enterprise. The functions and powers exercised by the supervisory board have already been outlined in Chapter 2, and we need only underline those with a particularly heavy influence on employee welfare. Any decision on major business changes, such as expansion, major cutbacks, relocation of production, appointment or dismissal of members of the executive, is made by a majority vote of members of the supervisory board. In theory this form of co-determination gives the employed a genuine chance to participate in the determination of major company goals or, at least, to block policies which are perceived to be against their interests. It also affords some direct influence on the executive or management board, through the person of the Labour Director, who cannot be appointed against the opposition of a majority of the workers' representatives. The existence of this Labour Director, argues Streeck (1984c: 410), has elevated the function of 'human resources' planning and development to the level of the management board. Montan co-determination affects only a small and dwindling proportion of the working population (see Table 9.1) which, for various reasons, has steadily declined during the life-time of the Act. This version is favoured by the union federation and is still seen as the model to be extended to all large enterprises. It is vehemently opposed by the employers who regard real parity in formal decision-making about company goals as an unacceptable incursion into the area of managerial control.

Co-determination, according to the 1952/72 Works Constitution Act, is practised in smaller joint-stock companies with between 500 and 2000 employees. As shown in the middle of figure 9.1, it gives workers' representatives only a third of the seats on the supervisory board – hence the German term *Drittelparität* – and no influence on the executive board. Moreover, union involvement has been reduced to a mere advisory role. This form of co-determination gives some influence on the board but no power of co-decision. It affects only a minority of the working population (see Table 9.1) and is favoured by employers but not by the unions.

The third variant of co-determination at company level – introduced by the 1976 Act in relation to large joint-stock companies (2000+ employees) – affects a much larger proportion of the employed (see Table 9.1). It gives employees equal representation on the supervisory board, referred to as numerical parity. Several devices, however, prevent it from becoming real parity. One of the employees' representatives has to be of managerial status (*Leitender Angestellter*) and can be expected to vote with shareholders' representatives. The chairman, who has a casting vote, is not neutral but is normally a shareholders' representative who is elected by a two-thirds majority of the supervisory board. Any contentious issues can thus still be decided in favour of

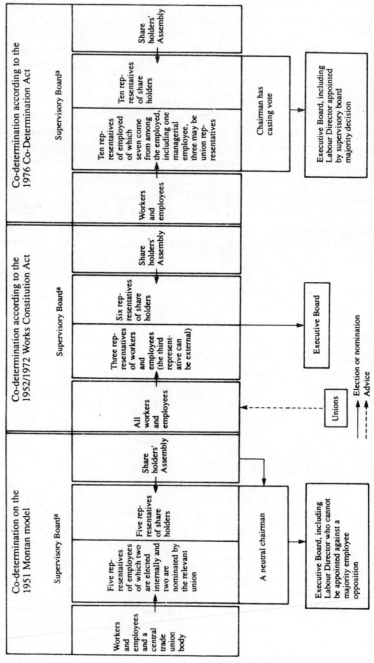

Figure 9.1 Three models of company co-determination in Germany

Co-determination on the 1951 Montan model

Supervisory Board[a]

| Workers and employees and a central trade union body | Five representatives of employees of which two are elected internally and two are nominated by the relevant union | Five representatives of share holders | Share holders' Assembly |

A neutral chairman

Executive Board, including Labour Director who cannot be appointed against a majority employee opposition

Co-determination according to the 1952/1972 Works Constitution Act

Supervisory Board[a]

| All workers and employees | Three representatives of workers and employees (the third representative can be external) | Six representatives of share holders | Share holders' Assembly |

Executive Board

Co-determination according to the 1976 Co-Determination Act

Supervisory Board[a]

| Workers and employees | Ten representatives of employed of which seven come from among the employed, including one managerial employee, three are union representatives | Ten representatives of share holders | Share holders' Assembly |

Chairman has casting vote

Executive Board, including Labour Director appointed by supervisory board majority decision

Unions

→ Election or nomination
----▶ Advice

a. The size of the board varies in accordance with the size of the company but the proportional representation of the two sides, indicated on this page, remains constant.

228

Table 9.1 Forms of co-determination in Germany and their areas of jurisdiction (late 1970s)[a]

Montanmitbestimmung since 1951	Covered 0.6m or 2.6 per cent of employed	Companies with more than 1000 employed in the mining and steel industry (Montan sector)
Drittelbeteiligung since 1952	Covered 1m or 4.3 per cent of employed	In smaller companies (AG and GmbH) with between 500 and 1999 employed
Co-determination according to the 1976 Act	Covered 4.5m or 19.6 per cent of employed	In large corporations outside the Montan sector with more than 2000 employed
No Co-determination	Existed for 3.2m or 13.9 per cent of employed	Small firms with less than five employed
Innerbetriebliche Mitbestimmung Co-determination at workplace level on selected issues according to the Works Constitution Act of 1952/72	Covered 10.1m or 43.9 per cent of employed	Covers all private workplaces[b] with more than five employed, including those already listed above

a. Based on data in Streeck (1984c: 404).
b. Workplaces in the public sector have equivalent organizations, called *Personalrat*, for 3.4 million employed or 14.8 per cent of the workforce.

shareholders. Workers have also lost influence on the executive board as the appointment of the Labour Director is no longer dependent on the consent of workers' representatives. Although the DGB is not satisfied with this version of co-determination, the employers find it too radical and tried (but failed) to get it abolished through the law courts on the grounds that it violates property rights and is therefore unconstitutional.

Co-determination at Workplace Level

The last form of co-determination is that practised at works level through the works council – *Innerbetriebliche Mitbestimmung*. Since the revision of the 1952 Act in 1972, workers are not only represented in works councils at plant level but also at company level (*Gesamtbetriebsrat*). This covers by far the largest proportion of those employed – all those covered by enterprise co-determination and an additional 10.1 million or

Table 9.2 The most important participation rights of the works council (Works Constitution Act 1972)

Kind of right	Social Concerns	Personnel Issues	Economic Matters
Co-determination rights (can be enforced)	Beginning and end of daily working time. Planning of holidays. Design of payment system. Piecework and premium rates. Humane organization of work in accordance with established scientific knowledge.	Staff file. Selection Criteria. In-firm training.	Social Plan
Veto rights		Recruitment. Redeployment. Assignment to wage group. Dismissal.	
Consultation and Information rights	Labour protection. Accident prevention.	Personnel planning. Right to be heard before dismissal.	Information about major business plans or changes in the firm. Consultation about: building or extending plant and changing/ introducing equipment; changes in work processes or places. Economic Committee.

Source: Translated from Müller-Jentsch (1986), *Soziologie der Industriellen Beziehungen*: 223.

43.9 per cent of those employed in private enterprises during the late 1970s. The various kinds of participation rights and their areas of application are shown in detail in Table 9.2. Briefly, co-decision and veto rights by workers' representatives on the works council exist on social questions; on questions of manpower utilization, such as short-time or overtime work; and on some questions of personnel – such as hiring, dismissal, redeployment and training. In a number of other areas, workers' representatives have only consultation or information rights. (For further details on the functioning of the works council, see Chapter 8.) This version of co-determination gives workers limited control in some areas affecting their workplace and practice and their conditions of employment. If fully utilized these rights give considerable scope for influence over the day-to-day management of the firm (see Streeck, 1984a and c).

An Evaluation of Co-determination

Assessments of the German version of industrial democracy vary tremendously due to a number of reasons: commentators with different political outlooks are given to different evaluations of institutionalized worker participation in decision-making; evaluations can be made either from the workers' or the employers' point of view, and they can focus on either enterprise or workplace co-determination; writers do not always distinguish between the formally granted and the actually enjoyed degree of participation; and lastly, there is great actual variation in the balance of control between enterprises, depending on various contextual factors. In the following, a number of recent empirical studies will be consulted to attempt to clear up some of the confusion although ambiguities of interpretation cannot be completely resolved.

The first point to note is that, of the two levels of participation, only participation through the works council is seen to impinge clearly on workers' daily life, and only this form of co-determination has a high degree of saliency for workers in general. Knowledge of, and interest in, co-determination at the company level is confined to worker activists and highly skilled workers (Diefenbacher et al., 1984: 127–8). Evidence on the functioning of enterprise co-determination and on its effects on the balance of power between capital and labour relates mainly to the real parity type (1951). It comes chiefly from the report of a government-appointed independent committee of enquiry, headed by Prof. K. Biedenkopf, later to become Secretary General of the conservative CDU. The findings of the Biedenkopf Report, published in 1970, will be briefly reviewed below. (For an extended discussion of the effects of company-level co-determination from the management point of view, see Säcker, 1981: 335f.) Co-determination at works level has been more widely researched and, more importantly, affects the highest proportion of workers. Consequently more attention in the following will be focused on this form.

Co-determination at the Enterprise Level

It was established relatively early on that the Montan version of co-determination had little *direct* impact on the everyday experience of workers on their jobs. It did, however, have some indirect positive consequences in as far as it increased union density and influence in these sectors as well as reinforcing the influence of works councillors who tended to be the same people as the labour representatives on the supervisory board (Streeck, 1984c: 395-7). The Biedenkopf Report, investigating the economic and social consequences of parity co-determination, established that, for management, the positive consequences largely outweighed the negative ones (Mitbestimmungskommission (MBK), 1970: 61f). Board decisions were being made in a spirit of cooperation, and economic effectiveness was not impaired. But the decision-making process became more protracted and workers' representatives' pursuit of employment stability greatly increased short-term costs. Labour gained in as far as appointment of top management now favoured candidates who, in addition to being of high professional calibre, also inclined towards a participative style; social and employment issues became prominent in board discussion, and manpower planning and employment stability became greatly enhanced. Management and labour jointly gained against capital because Montan enterprises tended to favour reinvestment of profits rather than increased dividends (ibid.; Streeck, 1984c: 394f). In view of these relatively positive overall conclusions it becomes difficult to understand why employers, through the BDA, put up such vehement opposition to the extension of parity co-determination to large enterprises outside the Montan sector.

Co-determination at Workplace Level

This type of co-determination appears to be regarded most positively by workers, unions and management, and the effectiveness and range of influence of works councils appears to be significantly enhanced by the 1972 revision of the Works Constitution Act.

A study by the IDE (Industrial Democracy in Europe) Research Group (reported in Wilpert and Rayley, 1983), which looked at ten German enterprises of varying sizes in different sectors, found a surprisingly large disjuncture between formally granted and actually enjoyed participation rights. It also underlined the fact that, although formal and actual rights of German workers' representatives are among the highest in Europe, formal and actual management control is also among the most highly developed (see Tables 9.4 and 9.5). The latter fact may go some way towards explaining the former. Faced with a strong and control-oriented management and forced to prove themselves *vis-à-vis* their electors by concrete achievements, works councillors may decide to pursue only those issues on which they are confident to get concessions. The degree of disjuncture between legal norm and actual control also varies according to issue. For example, works councils have a right to veto employers' decisions on the issues of time study/work measurement and of working time (overtime and short-time working). Whereas this right was taken up (conceded by employers) in only 16 per cent of cases on the first issue, it was asserted (conceded) in 50 per cent of cases on the second issue. Similarly, although works councils have a veto right concerning such different personnel measures as dismissal, redeployment, and further training the right was taken up by 60 per cent, 13 per cent and 21 per cent of works councils respectively (ibid.: 51f). There is no obvious reason why employers should concede these rights so variably. Hence the conclusion that different rights have a different degree of saliency for workers and are thus more likely to be pursued by works councils, must be considered a likely explanation of variability. Such a conclusion receives support from another finding of this study, namely that workers' desire to participate decreases the more remote the decision-area appears to be from immediate interests (ibid.: 55). Other studies, too, find that works council influence varies considerably according to issue. It is only slight where general policy-making is concerned (e.g. investment) (Paul and Scholl, 1981, quoted in Weber, 1982) but more significant in the area of personnel policy (ibid). It must also be noted that many managers in large firms concede more rights and consult on a broader range of issues than they are obliged to do by law (Mauritz, 1982: 80; Streeck, 1984c: 406), and that, in addition, they provide facilities for the works council in excess of what is legally required (ibid).

The great variation between enterprises in the type of participation actually enjoyed has been documented by Kotthoff's (1981) study of 491 enterprises of varying size, form of ownership and industrial speciality. He finds that a successful implementation of the legal norms depends decisively on whether management is ready to permit worker influence on decision-making. This, in turn, is determined by the balance of power within a given enterprise. The regulations of the Works Constitution Act afford the opportunity to change this balance but they are insufficient by themselves to initiate such a change. Kotthoff establishes that the most important variable explaining inter-firm differences are size and form of ownership. Co-determination functions best, though by no means well, in large joint-stock companies. It has remained a legal fiction in many small to medium-sized (70–600 employees), family-owned and managed enterprises (ibid.: 26f). Although the works council exists in these enterprises it is, according to Kotthoff, at best ignored and, at worst, completely isolated by an aggressively authoritarian owner/manager.[2]

The data reported so far are consonant with the general conclusion of Wilpert and Rayley (1983: 5) that co-determination should not be regarded as a 'democratic leap ahead' but rather as 'a lame step' in this direction. Further light is thrown on the limitations of participation through the works council by the seven case studies of successful organizational change conducted by Weltz (1978). Weltz makes it clear that works councils do not see their role in formulating and pushing through a long-term policy which would further workers' interests at the expense of those of management. They are reactive rather than active and are primarily concerned with warding off events damaging to workers or securing compensation for such events, if they cannot be avoided (ibid.: 74). Kotthoff's (1981) study even finds most works councils seriously lacking in their function as 'protectors'. He declares active opposition to management decisions to be the exception rather than the rule. What Kotthoff fails to consider, however, is that co-determination at enterprise level has led to a degree of cooperation where pre-emptive negotiation leads management to eschew the adoption of policies which violate worker interests in a serious way. The incorporation of worker interests in management decision-making has become particularly pronounced in their strategy of labour utilization. Labour in Germany, suggests Streeck (1984c), has become a fixed factor of production, and management long-term manpower planning has become an inseparable part of the initiation of economic change.

Other data, both from the above and other studies, suggest a more positive evaluation of the works council. German workers themselves regard co-determination highly positively. Thus of the workers in the car industry, studied by Diefenbacher et al. (1984: 138), a large majority thought the works council to be a 'real medium of influence' (*Machtfaktor*). Although workers know that co-determination has not *fundamentally* changed the balance of power between themselves and management they nevertheless think it has secured workers real advantages. Thus 31 per cent believed it had secured more pleasant working conditions, 28.4 per cent connected it with higher wages, and 27 per cent with secure employment (Diefenbacher et al., 1984: 127, Table 32). In the survey conducted by the IDE Research Group, 86 per cent of workers gave a spontaneous positive response when they were asked to fill a blank page with their views on the works council (Wilpert and Rayley, 1983: 71). Both the study by Weltz (1978) and the case study of Volkswagen at Wolfsburg (Streeck, 1984a) make it clear that, although management clearly retains the upper hand, they continuously have to take the works council into consideration in their policy-making, and they have to work at maintaining its cooperation. An uncooperative and well-organized works council can do much to hinder the smooth running of an enterprise. Skilful workers' representatives can use the strong legal rights in some areas, e.g. their veto right on the issue of overtime, to secure concessions in other areas, e.g. reorganization damaging to the vital interests of workers (Weltz, 1978: 112f; Streeck, 1984a: 65f). Kern and Schumann (1984b), reporting on both large and medium-sized companies, found a high degree of active participation in management decision-making by works councils, and Streeck shows that an exceptionally strong works council can even influence strategic policy in decisive ways (ibid.: 68f).

Works councillors, and particularly the leading officers, tend to become very influential members of the business enterprise. They are usually experienced, skilled workers who are often re-elected numerous times. Frequently, they are also delegates to the company supervisory board and the company-level works council (*Gesamtbetriebsrat*). Consequently they gather considerable experience in negotiating with management and acquire cumulative power.[3] Worker representatives enjoy quasi-management status in so far as they execute similar functions, are given comparable support facilities (offices, secretaries, company cars, etc.) and have considerable influence at all levels. Their formal and informal contact with management is constant and close and goes far beyond the mere 'crisis' meetings usually associated with encounters between management and worker representatives.

Co-determination through the works council is not only supported by the overwhelming majority of German workers but also by a majority of employers, except in the smallest firms. According to a 1981 survey of 130 small to medium-sized firms, reported by Mauritz (1982: 80) (an owner-entrepreneur), 95 per cent of these appreciated the institution of the works council. Employers understand that works councils not only gain workers some control over the conditions of work but also make them assume considerable responsibilities. The high degree of professionalization of works councillors means that management can depend on them to execute certain management functions as well as enforce the agreements they have entered into among the workforce. Works councils do not merely oppose management's plans but can often be relied upon to put forward viable alternatives (e.g. Streeck, 1984a). The continuous discussion of issues by management and works councillors avoids ambiguities and reduces conflict. Working daily in close contact with management, works council functionaries come to identify with the enterprise and endeavour to integrate their concern with the interests of the workforce with their own preoccupation with the economic success of the enterprise.

Co-determination through the works council also carries considerable disadvantages for employers. They complain about the increasing bureaucratization and legalization of personnel work, the cost in terms of specialised legal and other staff to deal with it,[4] and the impairment of organizational flexibility through a much more drawn-out decision-making process (Ludz, 1982: 36; Tatarko, 1982: 47f; Dräger, 1982: 86, in Lezius (ed.), 1982). Above all, it is feared that innovation and rationalization which are job-destructive will become more difficult to implement and that safeguarding jobs will become the dominant company objective (Säcker, 1981: 335). Employers weigh up the costs and benefits of co-determination according to the Works Constitution Act

Table 9.3   Costs and benefits of the Works Constitution Act 1972

Costs	Benefits
(a) *Monetary*	(a) *Organizational*
Works Council Wages, salaries and expenses for works council members freed from work.	Adaption on the part of management to the value orientations dominant in society.
Working time of other members and representatives in sessions of the works council, committees and consultations.	Channelling and reduction of conflicts.
Secretarial, room and travel money in support of works council activities.	Gain realistic information about the needs of the labour force. Cohesion and identification with the firm on the part of the employed.
Costs of works council elections.	
Labour Forces Time granted for consultation with works council and for works assemblies.	Positive effects on work attitudes and behaviour.
Management Time granted for talking and consulting with works council.	
Additional training costs to deal with works council problems.	
(b) *Organizational* Potential threat to managerial freedom of action resulting in inability to adapt flexibly to changing conditions.	(b) *Monetary* Saving of costs which would have been entailed in far-reaching conflict.

Source: Weber (1982: 73), author's translation.

1972 and, according to the Lezius (1982) volume, conclude that the benefits clearly outweigh the costs. Table 9.3, drawn up by a German specialist in this field, shows how costs and benefits are perceived.

Co-determination at the workplace also eases the introduction and management of change. The 1972 revision of the Works Constitution Act contains very clear guidelines about how major organizational change is to be handled and defines both the rights of the works council and the obligations of employers in this respect. Early and complete information of the contemplated changes and their anticipated effects allows the establishment of plans designed to soften the negative consequences as far as possible or to work out schemes of compensation where negative consequences are unavoidable. (For details of regulations see Jacobs et al., 1978: 50–1; for the actual handling of change see Weltz (1978: 18f). It becomes clear both from the latter study and from a British–German study by Bessant and Grunt (1985: 80f) that such extensive institutionalization of procedure has had very positive effects for both workers and employers. Ambiguity, uncertainty and fear are greatly reduced, and conflicts of interest are approached in a constructive manner. Although management becomes restricted in their freedom of action, they gain in terms of predictability and the relatively smooth absorption of change. In Britain, in contrast, the absence of such formal guidelines for the management of change results in delay, rumour and fear, which can only serve to reinforce the adversary style of industrial relations. In this climate the prospect of change becomes a nightmare for both sides of industry. Jacobs et al. (1978: 133) have, therefore, come to the conclusion that the low level of formalization of the British system of industrial relations – which is seen by many as giving British management flexibility – does in fact have the opposite effect as far as adaptation to change is concerned. Conversely, the extensive legalization of the German system of industrial relations is often seen as constricting management flexibility unduly. The evidence provided by Weltz (1978) and Sengenberger (1984a) and the evaluation of the German system by practising managers in Lezius (1982) show clearly that it is not perceived in this way by many German managers.

The relatively high degree of management support for the idea of the works council will, no doubt, alert the suspicion of critics. The works council, it is often suggested by British critics, gives workers only a very limited degree of control but considerably increases the integration of workers' organizations into the company. Their conflict orientations become stifled and they become completely incorporated. It is true that the cooperative style is far more developed in Germany than in the other two societies and that a considerable degree of worker identification with the enterprise prevails. In many of the smaller, owner-managed enterprises worker representative bodies do, indeed, become totally integrated and come to see the enterprise as their own. But it would be wrong to conclude, therefore, that the perception of a fundamental conflict of interests between workers and employers has completely been lost in German enterprises. Although patterns between firms vary, it is probably accurate to say that, in the majority of cases, *both* sides work hard to avoid open confrontation and are continually engaged, in the words of Weltz (1978: 130), 'in a tightrope walk between confrontation and co-operation'. Weltz (1978: 116) points out that the real pressure on works council delegates to become incorporated is counteracted by two facts:

(a) Representatives have to secure successes to legitimate themselves *vis-à-vis* the workers they represent.
(b) A works council which fails to exert influence on management is not useful to management either. A weak works council may not pose any threatening demands, but its lack of influence with the workforce devalues its offer of cooperation.

Thus independence and confrontation are as necessary as cooperation if the relation between works council and management is to be mutually beneficial. Hence the description of co-determination by Streeck (1984c: 416) as 'a mutual incorporation of capital and labour' is a very apt one.

Co-determination, it is argued, has changed the structure and peformance of German management in important ways. First, it has upgraded manpower management both in terms of its formal organizational status – it is now represented at both supervisory and management board level, and its methods and instruments. It has become more anticipatory instead of being merely reactive and more influential *vis-à-vis* other management functions. Secondly, co-determination, by forcing management to communicate more freely and effectively, has led to more objective, cooperative and equitable enterprise administration (Streeck, 1984c: 412). It has thus significantly contributed towards the historic change in management style, detailed in Chapter 4.

Co-determination has been regarded with suspicion, if not contempt, by some British and French unionists, and it is claimed that works councils serve to undermine unions. Although there is some evidence to show that this fear is justified, unions can also be seen to derive considerable benefits from co-determination. There is no doubt that German unions have little direct influence at the workplace and that work councils have bred enterprise-egoism which may impede solidaristic action on the larger regional or national stage. On the other hand, however, co-determination has provided unions with a 'Trojan horse' within enterprises. Most works councils are dominated by union members and thus have become a major source of support and information for unions at the workplace (Streeck, 1984c: 405). Müller-Jentsch (1986: 228) sees unions and works councils as having separate spheres of influence but forming a coalition, expressing their *mutual* dependence. As works councils have rights in the area of enterprise recruitment they have tended to favour union members and have thus served to increase union density since the early 1970s (Streeck, 1984c: 406).

In conclusion, an overall evaluation of the system of industrial democracy in Germany can agree with Streeck's claim (1984c: 411) that, although co-determination has not given rise to a new economic order, 'it has had a deep and lasting impact on the German political economy and has significantly changed the relations between capital and labour in German society' (ibid.). It can be said that in a significant proportion of enterprises the influence of workers' representatives has been considerably extended into areas normally reserved for managerial prerogative. The claim that the works council has led to a strengthening of the position of labour in the enterprise also receives strong support from Berghahn and Karsten (1987: 115). Thus, overall, it would be too simple to discount German forms of industrial democracy on the basis that they give responsibility without giving control. At the same time, though, it is clear that any shift in control towards labour has been moderate and that the overall imbalance of power between labour and capital remains. Lastly, the German participation structure, with its emphasis on delegated and centralized worker control is widely perceived to give too little influence to ordinary workers and to cause disaffection and lack of involvement at the very base of the enterprise (Weber, 1982: 71; Dräger, 1982: 90; Wilpert and Rayley, 1983). In this respect it contrasts negatively with the British form of workplace participation which takes industrial democracy to the very base of the enterprise. The lack of democracy at the lowest level has become a cause of concern for the DGB which now favours greater decentralization of participation (Müller-Jentsch, 1986: 210).

INDUSTRIAL DEMOCRACY IN FRANCE

In France, both formal structures for, and the actual degree of, industrial democracy have traditionally been weakly developed. Although the Auroux reforms, pushed through by the Socialist government in

1982, strengthened workers' formal participation rights in several significant respects, actual participation so far has remained unimpressive by European standards (Grünberg, 1986: 510; Telesis, 1986: 173). There exists no parity co-determination at company level in any economic sector. In private limited liability companies only two members of the works committee attend the supervisory board in an advisory capacity. In the nationalized industries there exists a tripartite board, with both government and worker representatives having a third of the seats and exercising the same rights as other directors. Participation at plant level through the works committee (*Comité d'Entreprise*) is also limited. This is due to the fact that the law grants workers' representatives only few co-decision rights (mainly on social issues) and that rights to consultation and information are frequently ignored by management or interpreted in a one-sided way. Workers feel that the consultation process is a sham and that management is concerned to keep workers' participation to a minimum. This is well illustrated by Gallie's study of French oil refineries (Gallie, 1978: 126, 152–7). He concludes that 'management remained sovereign within the plant and the control exercised by the works committee was slight' (ibid.: 157).

The Auroux laws not only extended the introduction of the works committee to a wider band of firms but also strengthened information and consultation rights. The requirement to inform works committees of impending major changes in the enterprise is considered an important improvement. A potentially greater impact on industrial democracy at the workplace is expected from a second and more innovative provision of the Law Auroux, namely the right of expression for groups of shopfloor workers. This provision envisages that employers and unions in firms with more than 200 employed reach an agreement to organize employees from the same trade or workshop into groups to enable them to express their views on the content, organization and conditions of their work, without any intervention from the unions or from management (Eyraud and Tchobanian, 1985: 247).

In contrast to previous arrangements on worker representation the *groupes d'expression* give workers *direct* representation on matters close to their interests. As such, they constitute a break in established French 'industrial relations' practice. The idea for the groups arose out of experiments during the 'Improvement of Working Conditions' campaign of the 1970s (see Chapter 6). Greater involvement of workers in the organization of their work is seen by management to reduce the rigidity of French social organization within firms, and it is hoped that it will increase both industrial democracy and organizational efficiency. In as far as these expression groups secure workers greater participation, they necessarily challenge both established authority relationships and the monopoly of unions in the field of worker representation. It remains to be seen whether these tensions can be resolved to the satisfaction of all parties involved. In June 1984, 3674 agreements to set up expression groups had been reached (ibid.: 252). But both Eyraud and Tchobanian (1985) and Dubois (1986) express a degree of scepticism about a breakthrough in French management–worker relations and feel that it is premature to evaluate the impact of this latest experiment.

This relative underdevelopment of industrial democracy in France is due to the fact that neither employers nor the bigger unions favour it. Consequently, any government action to promote it as, for example, in nationalized industries or through the Sudreau Report on the Reform of the Enterprise in 1975, has been doomed to failure. Whether the latest government intervention, the Auroux reforms, will substantially change this state of affairs, remains doubtful, especially since the return of a conservative government and a general deterioration of the economic situation. Management violently objects to the imposition by the state of structures to promote greater worker participation, and the hierarchical pattern has been entrenched for too long a time to be easily changed by legal means (Telesis, 1986: 173). The opposition of the unions to the institutionalization of industrial democracy is based on the conviction that it integrates unions into the capitalist system and thus weakens working-class opposition without giving a significant level of control. More militant forms of gaining control, which do not jeopardize union autonomy, are favoured but, due to the weakness of the unions, cannot be realized. The price workers pay for their ideological intransigence is high. They have no control over any of the conditions governing their immediate work situation or the mode of payment, let alone control over the economic goals of management. They remain very dependent on a less than benevolent management.

INDUSTRIAL DEMOCRACY IN BRITAIN

In Britain the shop steward movement has secured workers extensive participation rights at the level of the workplace, but efforts during the 1960s and 1970s to create more formal arrangements for the exercise of industrial democracy at board level have failed. There exist no institutionalized systems of industrial democracy at company level in the private or public sector. British unions have been interested only in participation schemes which are clearly integrated into the established union structure and envisage parity representation, whereas managements have been strongly opposed to any such extension of union influence. Limited experiments with German-style co-determination took place in the public sector, i.e. in the steel industry (1960s) and the Post Office (1970s) but, for various reasons, did not prove viable in the long run. (For details see Brannen, 1983; and Poole, 1986.) The appointment in the mid-1970s by a Labour government of the Bullock Committee of Inquiry to report on the most appropriate means of introducing industrial democracy constituted an important effort to achieve a more general adoption of a scheme of co-determination. The Committee's 1977 Report, split in its conclusions, indicated the unbridgeable divide between management and labour in this area. Neither the recommendations of the Majority Report, representing the union view, nor those of the Minority Report (the employers' view) were implemented. While British employers accepted the weakest of the three German models, the unions wanted real parity. But they were also not agreed amongst themselves about whether co-determination on the German model would be desirable in the British context. British unions tend to favour an extension of collective bargaining at plant level as more appropriate for British industry.

At the present time the idea of worker directors is no longer at the forefront of discussion. Recent research by Edwards (1987: 140f) established that British managers are both resolutely against any participation at board level and also do not favour greater participation by shop stewards at lower level. Although the unions and the Labour Party still favour a strengthening of industrial democracy, the recently devised Labour Party policy document on industrial relations no longer promotes the idea of workers' directors but argues for co-determination through a works council on the German model, i.e. representation abandoning the union-only channel (*Guardian*, 15 March 1988).

A British–German comparative study of technological change (Bessant and Grunt, 1985: 285) found that the shop stewards' committees often function in similar ways to the German works council but that, because management neglects to initiate early dissemination of information and consultation, they are unable to elicit the same involvement in the problems of change as achieved in Germany. Even if management moved to involvement in decision-making on a wider range of issues, local shop stewards' committees would not have the organizational resources and capacities to respond effectively to such a challenge, nor would they be likely to receive much support in this respect from external union bodies (Lane, 1987: 20–1).

The British institution of joint consultative committees, which have grown in number since 1975 (Daniel and Millward, 1983: 278), can be regarded as the nearest equivalent to the German system of co-determination at the level of the workplace. As the name indicates, they are only devoted to consultation and the dissemination of information (rarely on the financial position of the firm), and they give workers no co-decision or veto rights. Also their formation occurs on a voluntary basis and only a minority of British workplaces – 37 per cent in the early 1980s – had established one. These committees were nevertheless widely regarded by both management and employees as being a useful forum of discussion (Daniel and Millward, 1983: 278–89), and their positive impact on management–worker communication should not be underestimated.

The weak development of such formal institutions of worker participation in the British context does not mean, however, that workers and their representatives have no control over the conditions affecting their workplace, work process and remuneration. Many studies show that British workers in general, and craftworkers in particular, enjoy considerable control over various aspects of their immediate work environment. Informal understandings between workers and management, established by long-standing custom, grant workers a whole range of rights which, in some respects, surpass those enjoyed by German workers. In contrast to the situation in Germany, control is often exerted by rank-and-file workers through the work group rather than by remote delegates or formal bodies. Earlier chapters have already referred to the control over the allocation of work tasks, pace of work and recruitment of apprentices, exerted by craftworkers. More generally, British workers are usually granted some control over the process of pay determination, grading, piece-rates, and the organization and deployment of labour (Gallie, 1978; Maitland, 1983). But British workers' representatives have rarely sought, and have not been given, any participation rights as far as major economic change of their firm is concerned. The lack of such rights, together with the absence of any legal safeguards for their participation rights at lower levels, leaves British workers very exposed at the present time. Experience during the years of recession has shown that customary agreements or rights are much more vulnerable to unilateral management withdrawal than are those guaranteed by law. Although British workers have long enjoyed a favourable position in the contest for control in the industrial enterprise, in recent years the balance has begun to shift decisively in favour of management, (e.g. Edwards, 1987: 115).

PARTICIPATION IN COMPARATIVE PERSPECTIVE

These differing national patterns of worker participation have also been confirmed, with some exceptions, by the comparative study of

Table 9.4 Normatively prescribed participation for groups at different hierarchical levels within the industrial enterprise in the UK, Germany and France[a]

	Workers	Charge-hands	Middle management	Top management	Levels[b] above top management	Workers representative bodies	External groups[c]
UK	1.51	1.49	1.46	2.08	1.55	1.82	1.20
Germany	2.25	2.16	2.13	5.43	1.63	3.95	1.18
France	1.79	1.80	1.83	2.90	4.63	3.10	1.38

a. Assessment based on responses by key informants within the enterprise, rating formal participation (prescribed by law, informal agreement or contract) on a scale of 1 (lowest degree of participation) to 6 (highest degree of participation).
b. Various supervisory boards.
c. e.g. banks.

Source: Wilpert and Rayley (1983: 43, [part of table 4.1]). Author's translation.

participation structures carried out by the 'Industrial Democracy in Europe' Research Group. This study considers not only manual workers' control but focusses on groups at all levels of the enterprise hierarchy. The following summary of some of their results is based on Wilpert and Rayley (1983). Table 9.4 shows that *formal* participation structures vary significantly between the three societies. In France, we find a pattern of monolithic control characterized by relatively low participation values for all groups, except top management and the level above top management. In Britain, in contrast, there exists a pattern of low control levels, with low participation values for all groups. In Britain, participation in decision-making is thus hardly prestructured in a formal manner. In Germany the enterprise is characterized by a pattern of bipolar formal control: there is a very high control peak for top management and another, lower control peak for workers' representative bodies. The latter was found to be the highest degree of formally guaranteed participation of all European capitalist societies, although it is balanced by the highest level of control for top management as well (Wilpert and Rayley, 1983: 44). More detailed data (ibid.: 45) show that worker influence in all three societies is the highest where short- and medium-term decisions are concerned and decreases sharply for long-term decisions.

Table 9.5 presents findings on actual influence enjoyed by groups at different hierarchical levels and distinguishes also between influence indirectly asserted through representative bodies and direct worker participation. It suggests the following interpretations:

Table 9.5 Actual influence on various areas of decision-making by groups at different hierarchical levels within the industrial enterprise in France, Germany and Great Britain[a]

	Workers	Charge-hands	Middle management	Top management	Levels[b] above top management	Workers representative bodies	External groups[c]
France	2.1	2.9	3.0	4.7	3.0	2.1	1.5
Germany	1.9	2.3	3.0	4.4	1.6	2.6	1.2
Great Britain[d]	2.0	2.4	3.2	3.9	2.8	2.2	1.5

a. Assessment is based on responses of key informants within the enterprise, rating actual influence in a number of concrete control areas on a scale from between 1 (no influence), via 2 (little influence), 3 (average influence), 4 (much influence), to 5 (very high influence).
b. Board level.
c. e.g. banks.
d. The inconsistency in terms (Great Britain rather than UK, as in Table 9.4) is in the original.

Source: Wilpert and Rayley (1983: 43, [part of table 4.1]). Author's translation.

(a)   In all three societies influence increases significantly the higher the position in the hierarchy and is fairly low at the bottom levels.

(b)   The patterns of participation identified from the data in Table 9.4 remain, although the second peak in the German bipolar system is now less pronounced. *Actual* participation by labour's representatives is not as high as that formally granted. The level of influence of the workers' representatives remains, however, the second highest among European capitalist societies, after Sweden.

(c)   In Britain and France the degree of actual influence of workers differs only slightly, or not at all, from that of their formal representatives. In Germany workers' direct influence falls well below that of their representatives on the works council. This illustrates again the difference between the decentralized direct worker participation (Britain) and the centralized/delegated influence (Germany).

(d)   Internal hierarchization, measured by difference in influence between workers and top management, is strongest in France, also quite strong in Germany, but fairly weak in Britain where management is seen to have a relatively low level of influence.[5]

(e)   French workers are presented as having a higher level of *actual* influence than German and British ones. This is the only result which does not accord with the impressions conveyed by other studies, which, fairly unanimously, ascribe to French workers a very low level of actual influence on decision-making.

If we compare the ranking indicated by the data in Table 9.4 with that suggested by data in Table 9.5 (absolute figures are not comparable as different scales were employed) we find:

(a)   that German workers come highest in terms of formal rights but lowest in terms of actual direct influence;
(b)   that British worker representative bodies, although judged well below French equivalents in terms of formal participation rights, have overtaken them in terms of actual influence.

A last interesting finding from the IDE comparative study is that in all three societies the *desire* to participate in decision-making rises with position in the hierarchy. This desire to participate is most fully developed in Germany at all levels below top management, and least in Britain. At the level of the ordinary worker it is identical in Germany and France but at the next two levels German employees express a slightly higher desire to participate than French ones. Similar differences emerge when workers are questioned on their degree of interest in the idea of co-determination. To measure interest a scale from 1 (highest degree of interest) to 12 (lowest degree of interest) was used. German workers display an average of 2 1/2, French 4 and British workers only 6 1/2 (Wilpert and Rayley, 1983: 64). The degree of interest seems to be determined by the degree of effectiveness ascribed to co-determination by the three national groups, the score in this respect being 2, 4 and 6 respectively (ibid.: 66). As far as the French responses are concerned, the desire to participate through formal channels is more developed among the workers than the very negative attitudes on this issue of the larger French unions suggest.

What then, can we conclude about the state of industrial democracy in Europe? Industrial democracy, in the sense of workers' participation in decision-making, has been achieved in some areas where workers' immediate interest is at stake. The overall shift of control from management to workers, however, has only been slight. Above all, management have preserved their monopoly over decision-making on the general goals of the enterprise but have conceded limited control in areas concerning the most immediate interests of workers. Even where the legal provisions for industrial democracy are extensive, actual participation has remained modest. The fundamental imbalance in power resources between the two sides of industry means that workers do not enter the decision-making process as equal partners. Their lesser degree of knowledge and expertise and, even more so, their dependent status keeps them at a disadvantage *vis-à-vis* management. But, on the other hand, the existence of works councils and of the potential of organized worker opposition has nevertheless had a significant indirect effect on management–worker relations. Management in Germany, it is suggested by Streeck (1984c), has come to formulate policy in a way which, in order to pre-empt opposition, gives much greater consideration to worker interest. Management thinking has become more geared towards studying the long-term consequences of any economic decision for worker interests.

Both the degree and the form of participation achieved varies markedly between our three societies. Managerial prerogative has been reduced more strongly in Britain and Germany than in France. In some respects, British workers have achieved as high a level of influence over decision-making as German workers, or perhaps even a higher one, even though they have few formal rights in this area. This is true particularly for issues relating to the organization of work and pay. Representation at company rather than plant level and, particularly, at board level, which has become more imperative with the growth of large, diversified and internationally-oriented companies, is, however, poorly developed in Britain and also in France. Also the lack of institutionalization of industrial democracy in Britain has entailed the cost of a much higher degree of disruption of industrial production, and it has also turned out to serve British workers less well in a declining economy than it has in the past.

For management, the granting of limited amounts of industrial democracy has entailed some material and organizational costs, but these have largely been outweighed by the benefits. Notwithstanding this positive balance, there is great reluctance among top managements in all three societies to extend industrial democracy beyond the modest beginnings made so far. One reason for this reluctance, suggests Streeck (1984c: 418), is the fact that a strong works council has to be involved in many areas of managerial decision-making and thus reduces managerial prerogative and authority. Although there was a strong general interest in participation during the 1970s this has receded into the background during the recession. Both workers and management are preoccupied with problems they perceive to be of more immediate concern. It may also be argued that the growing need for flexibility during the 1980s (see Chapter 7) has increased the organizational cost of democratic decision-making for management. On the other hand, however, the successful realization of the new industrial strategy of flexible specialization (see Chapter 7) presupposes greater worker involvement, generated by increased participation at the level of the work group. Whether or not the French *groupes d'expression* and the increased clamour for direct worker representation in Germany constitute a modest beginning of a new trend in the development of industrial democracy remains to be seen.

NOTES

1. Co-decision rights exist, for example, on the introduction and use of technical devices, designed to monitor the behaviour or performance of employees.
2. Müller-Jentsch (1986: 227) points out, however, that as Kotthoff's study was conducted in Baden-Würtemberg, which has a disproportionate share of middle-sized enterprises, it is not representative of the national picture.
3. For example, information on a major change in company development, such as reduction of capacity, gained as a representative on the supervisory board, can be put to use to exert pressure against negative employment consequences on the works council.
4. The costs of staging elections in large firms for the plant- and company-level works council *and* supervisory board representation have become prohibitive since the revision of the Works Constitution Act (1972) and the taking effect of the Co-Determination Act 1976 (Streeck, 1984c).
5. A repeat of the IDE study in the middle 1980s might come up with substantially different results for Britain.

10 Business and the State: Industrial Policy

The relationship between business and the state has become a much discussed political issue in recent years which has been approached from different angles by different political constituencies. One debate has centred on the question of how much state intervention is compatible with the efficient development of business and whether state intervention during the postwar period has been too excessive and has interfered with the efficient operation of the market. But even among the most vocal 'free market' advocates, such as the Thatcher government, state intervention has in practice continued. Indeed, it is safe to say that the fundamental changes in the international division of labour and the development, in the advanced industrial nations, of high-tech industries cannot be managed without substantial state intervention and aid. Among those economists, business leaders and politicians who remain ideologically committed to some degree of state intervention in business, the debate has focused on what form such intervention should take and in which areas it is most important to provide guidance or direction.

Another constituency, taking state intervention in business for granted, is more concerned to show that the business enterprise is not a homogenous entity but consists of different interests which confront the state with conflicting demands. It has already been pointed out in Chapter 7 that there is an inherent conflict of interest between capital and labour. The state, it is further argued, is not a neutral arbiter standing above society and its class conflicts. Although it has a limited degree of autonomy, the state has to ensure the survival of capital and the capitalist system. During the postwar period many states have gone a considerable way to satisfy the demands of labour, but their policy-making has always been constrained by the need to maintain business confidence in order to ensure long-term economic prosperity.

Whereas capital's interest is business growth and profitability labour is concerned to secure rising wages, extensive welfare benefits, humane working conditions and, above all, full employment. During the period of economic growth, up to the early 1970s, these conflicting interests could both be satisfied, to a degree, at the same time. Consequently, class collaboration was generally achieved, and consent between management and labour was usually more prominent than conflict. In this economic context, state economic policy-making was not often confronted with irreconcilable demands and the dilemma of how to distribute scarce resources. Since then, however, it has become increasingly difficult for the state to respond effectively to the demands from both sides of industry.

At the same time, state action to maintain economic competitiveness often necessitates the pursuit of policies which may be detrimental to the growth or survival of individual enterprises or even whole industries. Thus, state economic policy-making is influenced by a variety of considerations and cross-pressures. But it would be wrong to view the state as simply reacting to pressure from various groups. On occasions, the state displays a marked capacity to resist societal pressures. To illustrate the role of the state in economic policy-making and implementation and to show the effects of this activity on both sides of industry, two broad areas of policy-making will be examined: industrial policy, and employment policy (Chapter 11). Although industrial policy is primarily state intervention on behalf of capital, it also has tremendous effects for labour. Employment policy, in contrast, is first and foremost oriented towards labour but has obvious repercussions for capital. Furthermore, employment policy is greatly affected by industrial policy and, in as far as it has an influence on industrial competitiveness, can also contribute towards industrial policy.

It will become evident that, although the same broad problems in these two policy areas have had to be confronted in all three European societies, they have often been approached in a fundamentally different manner, yielding different outcomes. The variety in the degree and manner of state intervention in these three capitalist societies – which have had important consequences for industrial competitiveness – has been lucidly explained by Hall (1986) from an institutional theoretical perspective. The basic features of this perspective have already been outlined in Chapter 1, and here we need only examine the specific institutional complexes which, according to Hall (1986: 232f), shape the formulation and implementation of state economic policy. The following three institutional entities are particularly influential: the organization of labour (numerical strength and organizational capacity of organized labour); the organization of capital (particularly the relationship between financial and industrial capital), and the organization of the state itself (the organization of, and the relationship between, the different parts of the state apparatus, i.e. executive, legislative and judiciary).

In addition, two further institutional entities can shape economic policy-making. The first, the position of the nation in the international system, has been particularly influential in the British case, because Britain has for a long time been an economically very open and internationally-oriented nation. But this institutional variable has become increasingly important also for the other two societies as they have become more integrated into international political and economic systems. The growing internationalization of markets, the accelerated diffusion of new technologies and the complex interaction of monetary arrangements have both increased the range of industrial problems confronting national governments and have made them more difficult to solve on a national level (Lorino, 1985). In addition, the nations belonging to the European Economic Community (EEC) have to reckon with the increasingly more interventionist stance adopted by the European Community, exemplified by its attempt to reorganize the steel industry at Community level (Adams and Stoffaës, 1986). The second entity, the political system (i.e. the electoral practices and the network of political parties which dominate the electoral arena) seems to be the least important and comes into play only intermittently in the three European societies.

Hall emphasizes the persistence of institutional features over time and hence of their impact on state economic policy. While Hall is generally correct in stressing the high degree of historical continuity of societal institutions, this static perspective cannot fully do justice to developments in the most recent past. The general weakening of labour during the recession, particularly in Britain, has begun to affect its internal organization and hence its relationship with both capital and the state. Thus a more dynamic orientation needs to be inserted into Hall's theoretical approach, emphasizing not only continuity but also changes in the capital–labour relationship and in the stance towards each of them on the part of the state.

INDUSTRIAL POLICY

Industrial policy is a wideranging field and the variety of measures encompassed by it can only be caught by a very loose definition. Industrial policy can be said to be any form of state intervention in the development of the industrial structure which is designed to promote industrial efficiency and growth. More particularly, industrial policy is designed to enhance a country's competitive ability on world markets. Although ideally state intervention should effect an adaptation of industrial structure, in practice it has often served to preserve the old structure and to prevent decline, and state action has not necessarily increased efficiency and growth in the long run. I am referring, of course, to industrial bail-outs which have figured prominently in recent years in all three societies.

Competitive ability depends on the complex arrangement of, and interaction between, many factors, and it is pursued by using a wide range of administrative mechanisms and policy instruments. The latter include various forms of state aid, a research and development (R & D) strategy, public procurement, a competition policy, nationalization of key enterprises, and a variety of forecasting and planning mechanisms. An analysis of state aid, the most important instrument, has to address the following questions:

How much subsidy has been given?
Who have been the chief recipients of subsidy?
What conditions, if any, have been attached to various forms of aid?

The following systematic comparison of industrial policy in France, Britain and Germany will focus on three main areas:

1. the impact of the institutional framework on policy-making;
2. the process of policy-making and implementation: goals, mechanisms and instruments;
3. the effects of industrial policy.

The Impact of the Institutional Framework on Policy-making

In *France* there exists a long political tradition of a strong, centralized and active state, dominating society. Although this tradition of state intervention in the economy is traced back as far as Colbert it became particularly developed only during the postwar period when an elaborate system of state planning of the economy evolved. The willingness and ability of the French state to intervene in the development of industry crucially depends on several features of the organization of capital and of the state itself.

The first is the extensive control by the state bureaucracy over the financial system. The French financial system is very complex both in its institutional make-up and in its working. It is a credit-based system with administered pricing. This means that most external financing of private companies is arranged through borrowing from financial institutions rather than through the sale of securities. The market for loans is regulated by government intervention. The financial system is designed to accord the state extensive influence over the allocation of funds to industry, by both direct and indirect forms of control.

Syzman (1983: 112f) describes the institutional system in terms of concentric circles around a central core. At the core are government institutions, particularly the Ministry of Finance, which controls most government funds and the broad outlines of economic policy. At the centre of this ministry is the extremely powerful Trésor, 'the economic apex of a centralized state' (ibid.: 114). It is responsible for fiscal and monetary policy, as well as determining investment policy and loan distribution. The Trésor both allocates funds from the state budget directly and influences the flow of loans from financial institutions. Other, but less important institutions at the core are the Ministry of Industry and the Bank of France. In the adjoining circle are situated para-public financial institutions, such as the Crédit National, which supply long-term credit directly to industry as well as cooperate with the state in such matters as financial policy-making, loan administration and loan guarantee. Taken together, the para-public financial institutions lend about one third of all credit extended in the French system (ibid.: 125). Although they are formally independent, government influence over them is considerable. These financial institutions raise their funds by borrowing from deposit-taking banking institutions. In the outer circle are the banks which function as private companies but are nevertheless strongly influenced by Trésor activities. French banks are divided into investment or lending banks and deposit banks. The latter are not very important in making funds available to industry but the former have risen in importance during the postwar period. (The two most important *banques d'affaires* – Paribas and Suez – were nationalized by the Socialist government in 1981 but have again been privatized by the subsequent conservative government.) Not only have lending banks become the foundation for medium-term lending to industry but they also hold substantial equity positions in it. The state is able to exert its influence in the banking sector through a set of subsidized and otherwise privileged credits which form a substantial portion of all loans. The government has inserted itself between the saver and industrial borrower by deciding which loans are eligible for special terms (Syzman, 1983: 125).

It is thus the case that the remarkable degree of direct and indirect influence over the financial system, exerted by the French state, flows from two sources: first, it flows from the state's direct influence over the funds of governmental or para-public institutions; and, second, it is derived from the state's ability to determine the attractiveness of loans from various financial institutions. Therefore the high degree of state control over the allocation of funds to industry is not merely derived from institutional ties between the Trésor and non-governmental agencies but also from the way the Trésor administers the markets for finance through determination of price-setting and of the volume for lending.

But both Syzman (1983: 131) and Cawson et al. (1987: 33) caution against too strong an emphasis on the purposive control that bureaucrats exercise over the disposal of funds. This capacity for concerted action is often undermined by complex political rivalries and the rigid routines which are seen as being characteristic of French bureaucracies and often lead to their paralysis. Because of this complex mix of paralysis and purposive action, Cawson et al. (1987: 13) argue, one cannot speak of a *single* government-industry relationship in France. Syzman (1983), in addition, points out that governmental influence over the allocation of loans only bestows control over those parts of the large-firm sector where family control is no longer maintained. Smaller and family-controlled firms stay aloof from the financial system.

An effective industrial policy depends not only on control over capital resources but also on the availability of skilled functionaries to administer it. The task of devising and implementing industrial policy has been ably handled by the élite *grands corps* of specialized and senior civil servants, distinguished by a high level of technical competence, a technocratic ethos, and an exceptionally strong degree of élite social cohesion. Social cohesion and frequent social intermixing of government officials and bureaucrats is complemented by an easy interchange of élites between state institutions and financial and industrial bureaucracies – the system of *pantoufflage* – and thus aids cooperation between civil servants, politicians, financiers and top industrialists.

Consequently, state intervention in the direction of the economy is widely taken for granted, regardless of the political ideology of the government of the day (Green, 1983: 162). The successful modernization of the French economy during the 1950s and 1960s and the dramatic increase in the standard of living has been widely attributed to state direction of the restructuring process and has thus served to further increase the legitimacy of state industrial policy. Consequently, the state is not confronted by strong opposition to industrial policy. This high degree of legitimacy of state intervention in industry should, however, not be interpreted as meaning that the latter is always effective (Cawson et al., 1987: 29).

The weak position of the unions in France has meant that unions have always been excluded from the policy-making community. The socialist government, in the early years, privileged the interests of labour over those of capital and introduced extensive social legislation which had a direct and indirect influence on industrial policy. But even the socialist government did not invite the unions to become active participants in the policy-making community (Hayward, 1986: 36). The exclusion, in France, of labour from industrial policy-making has not had the detrimental effects one might have expected because the capacity of unions to undermine policy implementation from the outside has been severely limited by their fragmented and disorganized state.

All these factors combined have meant the development of a vigorous industrial policy in France, particularly in the earlier postwar decades. More recently, the growing integration of the French economy into the world economy and the increasing economic instability at the world level have made the task of French planners and administrators of industrial policy much more difficult. Planning now occurs on a much reduced scale, and policy appears to be less far-sighted and consistent (e.g. Green, 1983: 163). There is now much less unanimity about the fact of whether policy has been successful in recent years, and voices against state intervention are raised more frequently (e.g. contributors to Adams and Stoffaës, 1986). But, generally speaking, there is still considerable social and political support for an active industrial policy, and activity in this area continues to be vigorously pursued.

The persistence of Conservative parties in government up to 1981 has meant that there has been continuity in the overall direction of industrial policy, although the details have varied considerably between periods. The short sojourn of a socialist government initially under-mined this continuity, but since 1983 policy has been back on the old course. One last feature which distinguishes French from British or German industrial policy and has given it a special impetus is its close connection of economic goals with political aspirations for national grandeur, independence and international status. Thus massive state aid to industries in the nuclear, aerospace and military equipment sectors has to be seen entirely in this light.

In *Britain*, in contrast, ideological and institutional factors impeding effective industrial policy-making are more developed than those pro-moting it. A lengthy development of industry in the context of indi-vidualism and restricted state involvement has bred a deep political and economic liberalism and a commitment to *laisser-faire* capitalism. This militates against the adoption of either the state-regulated model of France or the more corporatist model of Germany. Strong reservations about state intervention characterize not only the two sides of industry but also the state agencies themselves. As Wilks (1983: 138) points out, 'the idea that the state is "above" society with a national purpose and unique competence is anathema to British policy-makers.' This philosophical stance on the part of the British state functionaries does, however, not mean that the state has refrained from intervention in recent decades. On the contrary, as Peacock (1980) makes clear, such intervention has been extensive during the late 1960s and 1970s and has been incompatible with a *laisser-faire* stance. But the unsystematic nature of this intervention, prompted more by pragmatism and political opportunism than by philosophical considerations (ibid.: 55), may give the impression that an industrial policy does not exist.

There have been some ideological differences on industrial policy between the two main parties and also between different governments of the same party. Thus Labour governments have periodically attempted to take a more interventionist line. But these attempts have always been short-lived and have not succeeded in altering the overall pattern. At the practical level, economic philosophy has not been influential because the severity of short-term economic problems from the 1960s onwards and the ensuing political pressures have usually led to a dominance of circumstances over ideology (Peacock, 1980: 56).

Since 1979 the policy of the Thatcher government has added renewed stress to a stance of state disengagement from industry, due to its strong affirmation of a 'free market' ideology. A recent *bon mot* by Nigel Lawson, the Chancellor of the Exchequer, that 'the business of government is not the government of business' aptly sums up this ideological position (*Observer*, 25 October 1987). While the necessity to have an interventionist industrial policy is thus denied at the ideological level, in practice there has occurred only a change in degree rather than in kind. Although certain programmes have been drastically cut, for example, regional aid, others have been maintained, and overall government spending in this area has remained similar. In certain areas, such as industrial relations, an interventionist stance has become more, rather than less, pronounced. Intervention in the labour market in order to increase industrial efficiency and competitiveness has certainly been pursued more fervently in Britain than in the other two societies.

An unsystematic industrial policy is not only conditioned by ideological orientation and economic circumstances but is also strongly shaped by the institutional framework of British society. An important factor, inhibiting the development of a strong industrial policy, has been the relationship between financial and industrial capital and the role of the state in structuring this relationship. Due to Britain's historical role of an imperial nation, financial capital developed a distinctly international orientation, and Britain remained the international banking centre even after the dissolution of the empire. Hence the interest of financial capital in a highly valued currency diverged from that of industrial capital, and the state regularly intervened to support the former to the detriment of the latter. Industrial firms, being unable to rely for capital on the banking sector, have raised capital by issuing equity. Thus the securities markets and investing institutions are at the heart of the British financial system, and they are much more important than in either France or Germany. Although securities' markets are now increasingly dominated by pension funds, insurance companies and unit trusts, the latter have not used their growing influence to gain greater control over industry. According to Syzman (1983: 191), they do not have the expertise or inclination to become industrial councillors.

At the present time banks are not substantial investors in corporate equity. Although borrowing from banks has now become more common, credits have remained largely short-term, and bank involvement in, and control over, the internal affairs of industry has remained underdeveloped. Thus, in the highly important area of capital investment, neither the state nor the banks have been important agents of support and control, and consequently strong impulses for industrial restructuring could not issue from either quarter. Moreover, by favouring financial capital in its monetary policy, state action has actively hindered business growth and export achievement.

Another important institutional feature militating against an active British industrial policy has been the internal organization of the state and the social characteristics of state administrators. Until the late 1960s there was no ministry competent to oversee the overall development of industry. Responsibility to control public expenditure, and hence industrial policy, fell exclusively to the Treasury which was not geared to this task. Administrators had neither a knowledge nor an interest in industrial affairs (Wilson, 1985: 69), and informal communication networks with industrialists and bankers were poorly developed. Even at the present time, when various agencies to handle industrial policy have evolved, the Treasury still maintains its dominant position (Hall, 1986: 249).

The strong position, until recently, of the British union movement and its considerable influence over Labour Party policy has inevitably constrained Labour governments in undertaking radical industrial restructuring exercises with negative employment implications. Generally speaking, British governments have favoured a highly consensual approach to the implementation of economic policy. Both the TUC and the CBI have been regularly consulted, and policy measures have rarely been enforced against their will. 'The organizational features of Britain's unions and employer associations,' concludes Hall (1986: 61), 'rendered them more effective as veto groups than as positive contributors to an active industrial policy.' More recently, the Thatcher government has abandoned this consensual tradition. Detached from, and even hostile to, the unions, the government has simply bypassed them in economic policy-making. Although more sympathetic to business, the government has also not hesitated to enforce policies damaging to industry.

A last factor to influence industrial policy has been the two-party system and the frequent change of government party. This has served to further strengthen the inconsistent and *ad hoc* nature of industrial policy. The competitive nature of the British electoral system has also meant vulnerability to political pressure from regional interest groups and a tendency to conduct a regional development policy, following political rather than economic criteria of rationality (Wilson, 1985: 72).

The result of these various institutional influences has been a relatively late development of industrial policy which, moreover, has been reactive rather than proactive, hesitant and piecemeal. Economic decline and industrial crisis, while not created by this industrial policy, were nevertheless allowed to develop relatively unchecked.

Development of industrial policy in *Germany* has conformed much more consistently than in Britain to an ideology of economic liberalism, and it can only be described as a polar opposite to French philosophy and practice in this field. Although German industrialism arose under state direction and has experienced extensive state intervention during the National-Socialist period, postwar German industrial development has been marked by a more or less faithful adherence to the liberal ideology and practice of *Soziale Marktwirtschaft* (social market economy). This emphasizes the free play of the market and stipulates a minimum of state intervention. Thus the participation of the state in formulating and implementing industrial policy has been relatively low-key, particularly in the earlier post-war decades. The state has defined its role in economic policy-making as merely providing an adequate economic framework within which private enterprise could regulate its own affairs. Intervention at the level of the individual firm, which has been common in both France and Britain, has been eschewed in Germany.

This relatively marginal role of the state has, however, not impeded the development of economic adaptation and competitiveness. The economy functions efficiently without extensive state intervention because, according to Esser and Fach (1983: 103), it has a favourable industrial structure (both highly specialized and coherent) and a relatively high degree of self-regulation by the business community. Several commentators point towards the effective self-organization of the business community by well-organized and disciplined central employers' organizations which represent the interests of their members as quasi-political bodies (Syzman, 1983; Wilks and Wright, 1987). Most importantly, the relatively restrained role of the German state in industry is due to the fact that the banking system is well attuned to the needs and problems of industry and that banks have assumed a very active part in industrial restructuring.

The German financial system, like the French, is a credit-based system of corporate finance. In contrast to the French situation, however, the state does not intervene in the process of credit allocation but the latter occurs on a market principle by freely moving prices (Syzman, 1983: 260), and the system is dominated by a few major banks. The high degree of integration of the banking system into industry – banks are both substantial lenders and shareholders in the larger German firms – has given banks an active interest to promote the well-being of individual firms and even of whole industries. The self-interest of banks, their ability to cooperate with each other, and their cultivation of a high degree of industrial expertise has enabled them to play the early-warning, coordinating and planning role taken on by the state in France. The state merely lends political support as well as carrying the social costs arising from industrial adjustment.

It is not only ideology but also features of internal state organization which have held back the state from playing a fuller role in industrial policy. The decentralization of state power, implied by the German federal system, means that a lot of tax revenue is administered by the local states and authorities (*Länder* and *Gemeinden*). Thus a centralized administration of state subsidies – a mainstay of industrial policy – would be an impossibility. A further constraint on state financial policy is the marked *de facto* division of power in the determination of macroeconomic policy between the state and the federal bank which has traditionally exercised a restraining influence on public expenditure.

The relatively strong position of the highly centralized German union movement – particularly in those industries where parity co-determination prevails – as well as its generally cooperative stance has meant that labour has generally been included in the industrial policy-making community (Esser and Fach, 1983). Whether this position will be maintained in the face of a general weakening of union influence remains to be seen.

Another distinctive feature of the German situation is that the electoral system has, from 1967, often led to the formation of coalition governments, and the two main parties are, in any case, not as polarized as their British or French equivalents. Hence a more stable economic consensus has developed which has ensured a greater degree of continuity in economic policy than in the other two European countries.

Thus, to sum up the impact of the German institutional framework, German industry has achieved growth and efficiency without strong state intervention and has instead relied on the big banks to undertake a high degree of self-regulation. The onset of economic crisis and of severe industrial adjustment problems in more recent years have begun to involve the state more prominently in industrial policy. But the persistent leading role of the banks justifies the claim that, in Germany, industrial policy does not depend on state intervention.

The Process of Policy-making and Implementation: Policy Goals, Mechanisms and Instruments

As industrial policy has been most systematically developed in France and has, by now, a long history, policy goals have been most clearly defined in France, and distinctive policy mechanisms and instruments are most easy to discern. In Germany and Britain, in contrast, the later evolvement and the less deliberate nature of industrial policy make identification of persistent patterns a harder undertaking.

In France, two main goals of industrial policy can be identified. The first has been to create sufficient market power for selected industries to enable them to compete effectively on world markets. The achievement of this goal required not only the merging of enterprises into giant units but also the investment of large amounts of capital. As private venture capital of this magnitude cannot be found in France the state had to step in with massive support (Balassa, 1986: 103). The second goal has been to enable France to achieve national independence (Adams and Stoffaës, 1986: 6). The achievement of this goal, demanding support for industries deemed to be vital for national preservation, such as the nuclear, aerospace, energy and telecommunications industries, has also largely determined the selection, concerning the first goal. Thus, from the early 1960s onwards, French policy has involved the systematic development of high-tech industries.[1] Whereas intially these had usually a military application, more recently industries with a wider application, such as the computer, robotics and electronics industries, have also received support. But other industrial sectors have not been neglected. Major development programmes were undertaken in the steel, textiles, leather goods and footwear industries. During the last decade or so, development plans have often turned into expensive rescue operations, as for example, in the steel, textiles and machine-tools industries.

The method of implementing the various development plans has greatly varied over time. It has ranged from the selection of one or two giant 'national champions' in each industry who dominate the entire market, via a direction of such champions to cater only for certain market niches (*politique des créneaux*), to a *politique des filières* which dispenses financial support to entire vertical streams of production (Aujac, 1986), but, at the same time, has returned to the idea of national champions (Stoffaës, 1985). All through the postwar period a few giant enterprises have received the lion's share of state funds on the assumption that economic success would filter down to the PMEs in each sector through subcontracting.

Until recently, policy was devised and implemented in a highly centralized manner, involving mainly the various relevant ministries. To overcome the inconsistencies which had developed out of the participation of many ministries, a whole number of inter-ministerial committees was created during the 1970s. Each consists of very high-ranking officials and business leaders and addresses itself to a particular problem area, such as bail-outs, regional development, development of high-tech industries, etc. This concentration of high-powered administrators and of financial support usually guarantees swift action and often considerably success. More recently, this excessive degree of concentration has come under attack, and the Mitterrand government has introduced some devolution of funds and decision-making power to the regions.

The policy instruments favoured by French administrators have, with some exceptions, been remarkably constant over the years. Direct and indirect subsidies have played a very prominent role. But these have been dispensed fairly selectively with clear targets in mind and with a string of conditions attached. State funding bodies have shown themselves well able to enforce the conditions attached to financial aid. Subsidies have been systematically used, for example, to promote the export capacity of large firms. Allied to an effective industrial diplomacy, export subsidies have been very successful in gaining French firms relative advantages on a world market. The French state has always attached a very high priority to the support of R & D. Up to 1969, France occupied third place in the world in terms of R & D spending as a proportion of GNP. During the 1970s this proportion declined from 2.1 per cent to 1.8 per cent and France slipped to fifth place, but the Ninth Plan has made it one of its priorities to raise this proportion again. One consequence of generous state promotion of R & D has been the extremely low proportion of privately financed R & D, in strong contrast to the situation in Germany (Bellon, 1985: 149; Lorino, 1985: 161). Another very prominent instrument has been government procurement, systematically favouring French products over foreign ones. This procurement policy has been particularly developed as far as products with military application are concerned, and it is argued that the success of firms in these sectors has largely been guaranteed by state procurement (Soulage, 1986: 160; Stoffaës, 1986: 40).

One of the most important instruments up to the seventies has been indicative planning of industrial development but this has lately become less important. (For details on planning see Adams and Stoffaës, 1986; Hall, 1986). Another distinctively French instrument which has assumed very large prominence since 1982 is a policy of nationalizing the largest enterprises[2] in all the strategic industries, and also in banking. One of the purposes of nationalization has been to increase the scope of the state for restructuring and developing these industries and to achieve even better access to the financial means to effect this transformation. On the one hand, it has enabled the state to continue massive investment during a period of world recession. On the other hand, however, restructuring may even have been impeded by nationalization because industrial contraction – and its negative employment consequences – became a highly sensitive political issue and not just an economic measure (Hall, 1986: 205). The Conservative government, elected in 1986, has pledged itself to a reprivatization of some of the firms[3]. A policy instrument notable for its absence in the French repertoire has been a competition policy. Despite the existence of laws against the formation of monopolies, actual policy has favoured their development.

The relatively late emergence of *British* industrial policy and its inconsistent nature make it difficult to specify overall goals and objectives. British industrial policy-makers have been confronted with much graver problems than their French or German counterparts, as industrial decline from the 1960s onwards assumed more alarming proportions. British policy has, therefore, above all been concerned to reverse the process of deindustrialization and to implement measures designed to halt industrial decline (Peacock, 1980: 40f). Consequently, policy has dictated a series of *ad hoc* emergency interventions, and there has been insufficient systematic intervention in private business actively to shape the overall structure or to foster the development of particular branches of industry. Britain has been more inclined than France and Germany to give aid to 'lame ducks' and has focused less on profitable firms in sectors, targeted for long-term growth (Hall, 1986: 54). In Britain, industrial policy is not justified in the same nationalistic terms as in France. But practice, nevertheless, has involved support for firms, deemed to be vital for national independence, for example, ICL, or national prestige, for example Austin Rover. Industries devoted to the production of sophisticated military equipment have also been important in Britain.

The lack of a systematic policy reflects, and is reflected in, the absence of a consistent administrative framework to devise and implement policy (Wilks, 1983: 130). There have been a great number of different institutional actors, and individual institutions have been frequently reorganized. Thus, during the 1960s there were created in quick succession the National Economic Development Council (NEDC), the Department of Economic Affairs, the Industrial Reorganisation Corporation (IRC) and the Ministry of Technology. Although the IRC facilitated some useful mergers, such as the creation of ICL and British Leyland, and the Ministry of Technology strove to encourage technological modernization, neither organization enjoyed a long enough life to become really influential. Only the NEDC has survived, albeit in a much attenuated form. More recently, the main institutions involved in industrial adaptation/rescue have been the National Enterprise Board and the Department of Trade and Industry. The former, in turn, has been merged with the National Research Development Corporation to form the British Technology Group. The Treasury has, of course, remained important as a source of finance.

Institutional instability has fostered lack of continuity in policy and low morale among those responsible for it. Whereas in France the plurality of actors has always been coordinated by the *Trésor* as well as by inter-ministerial committees, in Britain a clear institutional base for industrial policy has never evolved. The Treasury, oriented more strongly to the interests of financial capital, has tended to put a break on, rather than promote restructuring measures. These weaknesses in the organization of state agencies have not been compensated for by self-help organizations in the business sector. The tendency of British firms to emphasize their autonomy and to discount collective forms of action, as well as staying aloof from the state has been aptly summed up by Wilks (1983: 136) as 'institutional isolation'.

A weakly articulated policy implies the absence of a consistent set of policy instruments. Although state aid to industry in Britain has been of similar magnitude as that given in France, it has been handled in a very different way (Hall, 1986: 52). Subsidies have been applied less selectively than in France and less systematically than in Germany. Until 1979, a comparatively large proportion of funds went into regional aid. They were thus very widely spread rather than being targeted on selected industries. Most importantly, subsidies have been dispensed without sustained efforts to enforce any conditions attached to them.

Consequently, the restructuring effect has often been minimal. This rather lax subvention policy has, however, changed more recently. The Thatcher government has greatly reduced subsidies to manufacturing industry (Duchêne and Shepherd 1987: 28) and has been more inclined to support already successful firms and high-tech industries (Hall, 1986: 110). Where government funds have been devoted to rescue operations as, for example, at British Leyland or British Steel, they have been tied to drastic restructuring demands. As in France, funds have been channelled primarily towards the preservation and consolidation of large firms. Since the early 1980s, however, greater attention has been paid to the needs of the 'small firm' sector.

All through the postwar period, government aid has also been devoted to the development of industry-related research and development (R & D). But research has been financed in an *ad hoc* manner by different ministries instead of being regulated by an overall plan, administered by a specialized ministry with a cumulative experience in this field as, for example, the German Ministry of Research and Technology. (Such a ministry existed for a short time under the Labour government in the mid-1960s.) Government policy in the field of R & D, in contrast to overall subvention policy, has been unduly selective (e.g. Hall, 1986; Freeman, 1978). Subvention has been concentrated on a few high-technology industries – the aircraft, aerospace and nuclear industries – which, because they are competing with more powerful American industries, have never been able to provide appropriate returns on this investment (ibid.). During the 1980s, government funding of R & D activity has remained a relatively strong priority as manifested by only a slightly decreased level of subvention (Hall, 1986: 173). Government funds have been spread more widely and have been channelled also into the areas of microelectronics, information technology and fibre optics (ibid.: 113). In contrast to the situation in France, British governments since 1979 have chosen not to compensate for the low level of industry–financed R & D. Consequently, Britain is badly lagging behind in overall R & D expenditure in comparison with both France and Germany and most other advanced industrial countries (Patel and Pavitt, 1987). Britain is the only Western nation with an absolute decline in R & D expenditure in manufacturing industry, paid for by industry and government (Coombs et al., 1987: 232). Since 1986, and especially following the publication of the House of Lords Select Committee on Science and Technology Report in 1987, there has been a renewed flurry of government policy initiatives both to stimulate and rationalize R & D activity, and a new interdepartmental ministerial committee has been formed to coordinate R & D policy. But the criticisms that neither the government nor industry spend enough on R & D activity have not been allayed (Christie, 1988).

The British state's overall economic philosophy of *laisser-faire* indicates that a system of economic planning on the French model would not fit well into British industrial policy. Nevertheless, the comparative economic failure of British industry led governments during the 1960s to experiment with indicative planning. Economic planning was pioneered in a modest way by a Conservative government in 1962, when the NEDC was created, and was developed more ambitiously in 1964 by a Labour government. Despite extensive institutional restructuring, this attempt was short-lived. The strategic objective of economic growth was abandoned in the face of pressure from the financial sector for the defence of a strong pound. Since then an interest in planning has been jettisoned and, during the 1980s, a partial withdrawal from even more modest forms of detailed intervention has been notable (Wilson, 1986: 69f).

As in France, nationalization of firms in key industries has played a prominent part in the postwar British state approach to industry, particularly of Labour governments. In Britain, according to the 1976 McIntosh Report on Nationalized Industries,

relations between government and nationalised industries [have been] characterised by ... a confusion of roles [and by] the absence of a systematic framework for reaching agreement on long-term objectives and strategy ... (quoted in Grant, 1987: 61)

From the beginning, political objectives have been more important than economic ones. But the prime goals of running key industries in the public interest and to the greater advantages of those employed in them have never been realized and were eventually completely abandoned (ibid.: 63f). The nationalization of a number of industries (e.g. coal, steel, energy, telecommunications) has never been connected with the same investment and restructuring effort as in France, and the lack of nationalization in the banking sector did, in any case, not provide the required control over investment capital. Since 1979, this policy of public control over industry has been replaced by a policy of privatization. In future, greater industrial competitiveness is to be achieved not by state intervention but by state withdrawal from business. Hall (1986: 110) predicted that by 1988 the share of state industries in total national production would had fall from its 1979 level of 10.5 per cent to 6.5 per cent. It is too early to judge the effects of this policy reversal.

The two notable features about industrial policy and adaptation in *Germany* are the subsidiary role of government in this process and the strong reliance on self-organization of the capitalist business community. The high degree of self-regulation has been facilitated by the institutional framework outlined above: the cooperative stance of the unions, the extensive coordination of business enterprises by the trade organizations, and the high degree of interpenetration of banking and industry on the one side and of individual large business enterprises, on the other.[4] The banks do not only provide private mechanisms for the direction of investment but also serve to coordinate and implement restructuring decisions.

The prominent role of the banks does not, however, imply that the German state stands completely aloof from industry. On the contrary, during the 1970s the state has embarked on 'anticipatory planning of social change' (Esser and Fach, 1983: 103) and has worked out a systematic general policy framework which guides the more detailed activities of the business community. The state provides economic information services to guide private investment (the annual plan), an R & D policy, and extensive support for vocational education and training. Also the growing scale of the restructuring and financing problem in some industrial sectors has made it necessary in recent years to increase state involvement. The policy community at the national level is formed by the federal government (the Ministries of Economics, Finance and of Research and Technology), the Federal Bank, the Federation of German Industry (BDI), the Council of Economic Advisors (*Sachverständigenrat*), economic research institutes, and the big banks. It is also worth noting that similar, though less high-powered, policy communities are active at the lower political level of the *Länder* and *Gemeinden* (local authorities).

The overall goal of industrial policy has been to modernize the economy and to adapt the industrial structure to the changed conditions of international competition. Industrial policy is strongly geared towards the maintenance and perfection of export capacity and general economic policy has consistently been oriented towards this goal. Adaptation has been conceived in an offensive manner, designed to safeguard established markets and to gain entry into new ones (Esser and Fach, 1983: 108). This was to be achieved by a sectoral policy, managing the contraction of 'old' industries such as coal, mineral oil production, shipbuilding and promoting new 'knowledge-intensive' industries such as nuclear energy, aerospace, computers and electronics. Sectoral policy is complemented by a technology policy, encouraging constant technological innovation of both processes and products, in order to gain a competitive advantage on international markets.

Although Germany, too, has had several spectacular cases of

individual firm rescues, such as those of the giants AEG and Krupp, mostly restructuring efforts have concentrated on whole sectors. The French approach of creating national champions is held in low regard (Horn, 1982: 61). Industrial adjustment of whole industries, initiating contraction, relocation of unprofitable production to low-wage countries, merger, rationalization and/or a reorientation of production, market and training strategies, has been initiated by informally organized 'modernization cartels'. These have consisted of representatives of the state (federal and/or *Länder*), the banks, the business community and, in many cases, the unions. The banks have taken the most active part both at the planning and the implementation stage, and the state has played mainly a facilitating role as well as part-financing major restructuring of crisis industries. Compared with the other two societies, the German state has invested a relatively small amount of financial aid into the restructuring of crisis industries, as, for example, steel (Hall, 1986: 240).

Among instruments of industrial policy, financial aid in terms of government grants, tax allowances and bank loans figures prominently. Subsidies are more often channelled to thriving than ailing industries and they are dispensed with a comprehensive set of conditions for adjustment attached. The government's annual subsidy report for 1978, for example, stated that 34.5 per cent of aid had gone to maintenance (safeguarding jobs and income), 56.1 per cent to adjustment (encouraging adaptation of an industry) and 9.4 per cent to encouraging growth potential and innovation (Esser and Fach, 1983: 122). The involvement of the banks acts as a strong driving force to investment which will yield a good financial return in the long run. The banks also have much greater freedom of action in restructuring exercises, as they are not subject to the same political pressures from labour or regional interest as is the state (Hall, 1986: 240). But, as the example of repeated business failure in the case of AEG has shown, even the banks sometimes back losers (Esser and Fach, 1983: 118f).

Since the early 1970s, the government has developed its R & D policy, which is administered by the Ministry of Research and Technology. Financial support for R & D has concentrated mainly on large firms and on such high-tech, export industries as microelectronics, telecommunications, computers and energy technologies. Whereas the state has given consistent support to modernization drives in a whole industry, the banks have concentrated on particular promising firms, such as Nixdorf in the computer industry. In Germany, in contrast to the situation in France and Britain, private firms themselves have invested heavily in R & D. Thus the chemical giant Hoechst spends more on R &

D than the whole French chemicals sector taken together (Bellon, 1985: 149).

Another instrument which has been more prominent in Germany than in Britain and France has been a consistent labour market policy, fostering occupational and geographical mobility of the labour force, in order to keep pace with industrial adaptation and technological innovation. The government, through the Federal Employment Bureau (*Bundesanstalt für Arbeit*), expends considerable resources on providing the framework for, and encouraging, initial, further and retraining to a high standard.

Other instruments of industrial policy which were found to be important in France, such as state procurement, selective export subsidies and nationalization,[5] do not figure strongly in the German context. On the contrary, such intervention is held to be incompatible with a commitment to the maintenance of market competition – one of the main constituent elements of the philosophy of the 'Social Market Economy' (Peacock, 1980: 40f). During the 1970s, a more active competition policy has been pursued in order to revive the important German small firm sector (Horn, 1982: 24). R & D support is now also made available to this sector (ibid.: 35).

Economic planning, starting with the foundation in 1963 of the Council of Economic Advisers (*Sachverständigenrat*), has gradually become more important but has always confined itself to providing merely a general framework for economic policy. Every year the government publishes a report, responding to the Council's annual analysis of the state of the economy and providing an exposition of the goals of governmental economic policy for the current year. The 1967 law for the Promotion of Economic Stability and Growth further extended the possibility for state regulation of economic and industrial development and consolidated the system of economic reporting. A five-year financial plan helps private enterprise to orient their own capacity planning accordingly (Claessens et al., 1981: 285), and the biannual Report on Subsidies provides a good record of government intervention (Peacock, 1980: 39).

The Effects of Industrial Policy

To assess the success or failure of industrial policy measures is a very complex matter as competitive industrial advantage is usually the result of multiple causes, some of which lie outside the scope of national government intervention. Consequently, assessments are usually somewhat impressionistic, and often they simply equate competitive achievement with the success of industrial policy, without demonstrating a process of causation. Bearing this proviso in mind, some very general evaluations can nevertheless be attempted.

There is a high degree of unanimity that, in the *French* case, industrial policy was responsible for the modernization of French industry and for the exceptionally high rate of economic growth during the early postwar decades. During that time French industrial policy achieved both its goal of greater industrial competitiveness and that of greater national independence, and it became a model other societies have studied with interest. But more recently, assessments of the effectiveness of industrial policy have become more sceptical and some aspects have been evaluated more critically. This re-evaluation of policy, evident in more recent writing on the topic (Zukin, 1985; Adams and Stoffaës, 1986), is a direct reflection of the growing industrial problems experienced from the 1970s onwards. This deterioration is exemplified by the declining export performance of industry and the increasing import penetration of the French market since 1974 (Lorino, 1985: 155).

But positive effects of industrial policy in certain areas are still being identified. Sustained increases in industry's rate of investment have been achieved. In several industries, export performance has been improved and France can still be ranked among world leaders (Balassa, 1986; Stoffaës, 1986). But, it is pointed out (ibid.: 44), competitiveness on international markets has only been achieved in those industries where government discriminatory procurement has been a prominent factor in effecting industrial growth, as, for example, in the nuclear and aerospace industries. In those industries where market forces are stronger, e.g. in electric/electronic consumer goods, French industry finds it much harder to compete (Telesis, 1986; Zysman, in Adams and Stoffaës, 1986: 105). As markets are tending to become less stable, particularly those for goods with a high-tech component, government intervention is going to become less effective in the future.

Doubts are also being expressed about the state's handling of crisis industries, such as steel, where inefficient overmanning has been artificially prolonged (Perrin-Pelletier, 1986: 73). Complaints are also more frequently raised about the heavy degree of economic regulation and about the centralization of industrial policy. Several commentators (e.g. Bellon, 1985; Perrin-Pelletier, 1986) express a worry that the French style of state intervention may stifle the creativity of corporate managers. Thus, in general, pleas are made for a less dirigiste policy but the continued necessity for active state intervention in industry is rarely doubted.

There is also widespread agreement that the stance of the *British* state to refrain from systematic active intervention in industry has done little to encourage self-help and that the decline of British industry has not been halted (Hall, 1986). There is today hardly an industry in which the British can claim to be market leaders. The industrial strategy of the Thatcher government to let the market reorganize industry has only had very limited success. Fiscal and monetary policy has had the effect of weeding out the weak in British industry and, by creating massive unemployment, to restore competition in the labour market. The remaining industrial sector has thus become significantly more efficient. But to become competitive in world markets British industry needs a massive investment programme, sustained promotion of technological innovation and a greatly increased effort to train skilled manpower. Systematic government action to achieve those objectives, although stepped up since 1979, has so far been insufficient.

German industrial policy, with its mixture of state guidance and more detailed private enterprise initiatives, is judged by its generally positive results. German industry has greatly expanded its exporting activity during the post-war decades, and German firms are among world leaders in a whole number of industries, such as transportation equipment, chemicals/pharmaceuticals, metallurgy/materials and mechanical equipment (Stoffaës, 1986: 45). The active role of the banks has avoided the institutional isolation characterizing British industry, whereas the absence of a dirigiste state has meant a higher degree of flexibility in restructuring exercises, as well as a lesser degree of dependence on state patronage for economic success.

Finally, in all three societies, individual businesses and business associations now see increasingly more sense in orienting their business strategy towards government because continued economic uncertainty and increased economic competition in world markets makes them more dependent on government aid. But, at the same time, in conditions of limited growth government intervention sometimes means action which favours one industry, region or enterprise over another and which cannot satisfy the interests of both capital and labour at the same time. Whereas in past decades, state intervention in industry was often motivated by both economic goals and social considerations the latter are now receiving an increasingly lower priority. This latter conflict of interests and the role of the state in managing it will be explored in the following section.

NOTES

1. For an overview of the high tech industries, see Stoffaës (1986).
2. Since 1982, nearly 50 per cent of large-scale industry has been held in public ownership (Stoffaës, 1986: 42), and 80 per cent of credit has been available for steering to state agencies (Auer et al., 1983: 125).
3. In 1986–87 the Conservative government sold off 13 state-owned enterprises (*The Economist* 2 March)
4. The big banks own considerable share capital in the large corporations and also act as proxy voters for customers' shares. They are well represented on supervisory boards. In the late 1970s the banks voted 70 per cent of the shares of the 425 largest firms in Germany, accounting for three-quarters of the value of all the shares on the stock exchange. 318 of the top 400 companies had two bank representatives on their supervisory boards (Medley, 1981: 48, quoted by Hall, 1986: 235). Inter-corporate integration is also promoted by mutual share holding and representation on supervisory boards, particularly in relation to firms who are major customers or suppliers.
5. In the early 1980s publicly-owned enterprises employed around 8 per cent of all employees (Claessens et al., 1981: 276), and they are expected to operate according to the same criteria of profitability as are privately owned firms.

11 Business and the State: Employment Policy

Employment policy embraces a large variety of measures which, by either influencing the supply or the demand for labour, determine the quantity and quality of employment available at a given time or, conversely, the level of unemployment. The nature of employment policy also has an effect on the degree of ease with which adjustments on the labour market can be achieved. Both the quantity and quality of employment can be determined either at the governmental level or at the level of the firm. It is not clear to what extent employment policy is shaped by the state and to what extent the state merely sanctions developments which are already pursued at the microeconomic level.

Policy-making and outcomes occur within a larger framework of social and economic development which, in each society, is shaped by the strength of the two main parties in the employment relationship – capital and labour, as well as by the role of the state. During the last decade or so, a fundamental change has occurred in this social and economic framework, and the impact of this change on policy will be traced out in this chapter. Sengenberger (1984b) has described this changing framework in terms of two models of development – welfare capitalism and 'free market' capitalism. (Sengenberger applies these models only to Germany but they can be adapted to fit the other two societies.)

WELFARE CAPITALISM

The first model which is termed 'socially controlled welfare capitalism' prevailed during the period of the post-war economic boom, particularly in the 1960s and the first half of the 1970s. In this model state intervention serves to curtail the free working of the market in order to moderate or cancel out its more adverse effects on labour. The state tries to balance the interests of capital and labour, and labour is included, to a greater or lesser degree, in this bargaining process. Involvement and cooperation of labour at the macro- or governmental

level, i.e. corporatist or tripartite decision-making, has been characteristic of Germany and Britain but not of France. But in all three societies,
policy-making on issues of employment and welfare has been mindful of
the power of organized labour during a period of economic expansion
and labour shortage, and policies were devised with the interests of
labour in mind.

Labour has achieved a rising standard of living and a reduction of the
risks to health, safety and income and employment security associated
with the production process. A standard employment relationship, i.e. a
stable, socially secured, full-time employment became the norm. In
cases where the capacity to labour was jeopardized through accident, ill-
health, maternity, loss of employment or old age, adequate compensation was assured. Capital, in return, secured from labour a degree of
active cooperation or, at least, acquiescence in its effort to ensure
continuous production as well as raise productivity and modernize the
productive process, although British capital was much less successful in
this latter respect than its German and French counterparts. Many of
the agreements made between capital and labour took the form of legal
or collective agreements.

Such active and protective employment and social policies have had
the effect of curbing competition in the labour market. Workers who, if
temporarily unemployed, are assured of a reasonable income replacement level and/or of easy re-entry into employment, are less likely to
accept employment with conditions inferior to their last jobs. The
resulting lack of competition for jobs prevents the downward adjustment of terms and conditions of employment, e.g. wage cuts or insecure
employment. Such lack of worker competition, it is further argued,
leads to employment rigidity. Employers have found it difficult to adjust
the quantity and, to a lesser degree, the quality of labour supply to their
changing demand situation. Rigidity also extended to methods and
levels of wage payments.

Whereas qualitative adjustment of labour, i.e. the adjustment of the
degree and kind of skill to the changing requirements of production,
occurs mainly on internal labour markets, quantitative adjustment, i.e.
the increase or decrease of the number of employed in accordance with
changes in the level of demand, is effected on external labour markets.
Factors which affect the degree of labour market rigidity are manifold and
range from labour costs (wages and social costs) to conditions of employment (particularly, the degree of job security), work practices and patterns, government regulations, training practices and the extent and kind
of labour mobility. Different societies display different balances between
internal and external rigidities and in the factors which generate them.

LABOUR MARKET RIGIDITIES DURING THE 1970S: THE NATIONAL PATTERNS

During the 1960s and 1970s, protective legislation and collective agreements greatly increased employment rights in all three European societies and hence the quantitative rigidity of labour. A standard employment relationship with fixed and uniform working hours and working times became the norm. But the degree to which labour had become a fixed factor of production varied considerably between the three societies as did the balance between external and internal rigidity. External rigidity was the least developed in Britain and probably the most in France (Marsden 1987: 192; *Problèmes Economiques*, 1946, October 1985), although Germany did not come far behind France, if at all.

The strong dependence on internal promotion in France made French employees particularly concerned with job security (Marsden, 1987: 190). A national agreement regulating redundancy procedure was negotiated in 1969. This was supplemented by a further agreement in 1974 and by legislation in 1973 and 1975. All these provisions subjected employers to both internal control over collective redundancies by worker representative bodies and to external pressure by Labour Market Inspectorates, as well as obliging them to work out alternative solutions. The overall effect was that both French employers and state industrial policy became oriented towards the avoidance of large-scale redundancies (Laroque, 1984: 219). Part-time employment was under-developed – only 7.5 per cent of the employed population worked part-time in 1975 (Marchand, 1987: 112) – and rigidly regulated. Temporary employment was already established but was hedged in by regulations.

In Germany, the 1972 revision of the Works Constitution Act had very similar effects on employment security. The powers of consultation and co-determination in the area of hiring and firing, conferred on the works council and the obligation on employers to work out a Social Plan in the event of collective redundancies, also caused German managements to develop long-term manpower planning which circumvented the necessity for redundancies. Non-standard forms of employment such as part-time and temporary work were not prominent. The part-time quota in the 1970s was between 10 and 12 per cent (Fuchs, 1988: 15, Table 5). As in Britain, part-time workers had less favourable conditions and could be employed quite flexibly but their much lesser weight in the labour force, and particularly in industry, did not make them a significant source of flexibility. Insufficient regional mobility was maintained by the system of centralized pay bargaining which prevented the development of large regional wage differences (Bosch, 1988: 178, 182).

In Britain, too, individual and collective employment rights were protected by legislation (Redundancy Payments Act 1965; Employment Protection Act 1978). But the lack of negotiation between managements and unions in this area meant that in practice employers had relatively little problem in achieving redundancies and resorted to this measure much more freely than their continental counterparts. The absence of regulations for a Social Plan, laying down redeployment and retraining obligations, also made redundancies cheaper for them. Whereas French and German workers in the core sectors of industry were virtually ensured of employment security, British workers were at best sure of a reasonable compensation for their loss of employment (e.g. Edwards, 1987: 203, 208). Greater external labour market flexibility in Britain was also guaranteed by a higher incidence[1] and lesser degree of state regulation of the use of part-time and female labour (e.g. Gregory, 1988; Hantrais, 1988) and by a well-established tradition of using temporary labour. Hakim (1987b: 555) dates the trend towards hiring part-time labour as starting in the 1960s and intensifying greatly in the 1970s, and of hiring temporary workers in the early 1950s. Lastly, the relatively high degree of overtime working has also created numerical flexibility. But this greater degree of manoeuvring room for British employers did not ensure greater geographical mobility of labour towards higher-value industries (Marsden, 1987: 180). Excessive rigidities in the housing market (a combination of an inflexible council housing system and large regional discrepancies in house prices), in pension schemes and inadequate training efforts have inhibited such mobility.

Rigidity of external labour markets in Germany was counterbalanced by flexible internal markets. In Britain, in contrast, internal flexibility has been lacking, and in French enterprises an ambiguous in-between situation has prevailed. In Germany, after 1974/75, managements were able to obtain a relatively free hand over internal redeployment of labour and also greatly stepped up further training (Bosch, 1988: 180). In Britain managements were greatly constrained in this respect (see Chapter 7). French managements also enjoyed considerable freedom in the area of redeployment (Marsden, 1987: 202) but, according to Maurice et al. (1986b), the cumbersome French system of job classification and the relatively low level of skill of the labour force did not gain management the same degree of internal flexibility as was enjoyed by their German counterparts.

Pay rigidities have also been pronounced but took different forms in the three societies. Although the British system of decentralized pay bargaining is designed to give employers flexibility, in practice it has not always had this effect. British employers have found it very difficult to keep wage levels below those of productivity, and to differentiate pay to reward merit or induce occupational mobility. The practice of Wages Councils to fix minimum conditions in many industries and to peg the wages of young people close to those of adults has created further rigidities.

The French payment system, with its emphasis on seniority and its indexation of wages to prices, has shared many of the British rigidities, and, in addition, widespread industry-level pay bargaining has also restricted the manoeuvring space of individual employers (Schwab, 1987). French employers have also been disadvantaged in comparison with those in Germany, Britain and non-European countries by relatively high social charges as a proportion of labour costs (Laroque, 1984: 177).[2]

The German system of pay determination has been more successful in differentiating levels of pay between skill group and in preventing wage inflation. But its focus on industry-level bargaining has placed restrictions on individual employers, particularly those in SMEs.

In the 1960s and early 1970s, all these labour market and pay rigidities were not felt to be critical. Greater market stability did not produce constant fluctuation in demand, and minor changes could be handled by easy recourse to one source of more flexible labour – immigrants – who, particularly in Germany and France, could be attracted as needed.[3] In Britain, in addition, part-time women workers have also been a source of flexible labour. In any case, the more buoyant economies of that period could more easily absorb disadvantages flowing from an inflexible labour supply and payment system. Also the lesser degree of competition on world markets made the negative effects of employment rigidity less obvious.

The model of socially controlled welfare capitalism, to recapitulate, thus resulted in full employment, rising standards of employment conditions and of living, a comprehensive system of welfare provisions and the participation of labour both in the determination of employment conditions and of standards of welfare. The existence of full employment is not a natural consequence of a capitalist market economy but requires constant intervention, both at the level of the economy and in the working of the labour market. Consequently, the role of the state became considerably enlarged during this period. Although both macro-economic and labour market policy differed in detail between Britain, France and Germany (for details of the former see Hall, 1986: Chapter 9), it is nevertheless the case that postwar development in all three societies was characterized by the adoption of this model in most or all of its elements. It remained in place until around the middle 1970s and then began to crumble more or less quickly in these societies, to give way to the gradual emergence of a new model of social and economic development – market capitalism.

MARKET CAPITALISM

Around 1975, the general deterioration of economic development and the growing uncertainty and instability on world product markets (see Chapter 7) brought about new requirements in the utilization of labour, as well as mass unemployment. The ensuing loss of numerical and organizational strength of organized labour resulted in a decisive shift in the balance of power between capital and labour. This shift was accompanied by an ideological reorientation, both at the level of the state and among employers. A model of 'free market capitalism', advocating managerial freedom in the use of capital and labour, came to the fore. The model demanded the dismantling of any restraint on the free working of the market, exercised both by organized labour and by the state.

Withdrawal of the state from the economic sphere became the new orthodoxy. Both an active employment and welfare policy became regarded as dysfunctional to the efficient working of the market. The new model postulated that the overcoming of economic crisis requires a more selective promotion of economic growth, some unemployment, a lowering of costs and a general deregulation of the economy in order to facilitate and increase investment and profits and a restructuring of the economy. The restoration of worker competition for employment, and the increased flexibility of labour implied by it, is seen as an important means to this end. The provision of a comprehensive system of social welfare was to be replaced by greater individual and family self-help and collective action was to give way to the development of individual initiative and entiepreneurial spirit.

This reorientation at the ideological level was accompanied and, indeed, facilitated by the deepening of economic recession and the growth of unemployment. Unemployment began to rise significantly around 1975 and accelerated further in the early 1980s. By 1984 it had reached 7.1 per cent in Germany, 9.7 per cent in France and 11.7 per cent in Britain (*Faits et Chiffres 1987*). In both Britain and France youth unemployment was much higher than unemployment in general, and long-term unemployment was also much more developed in Britain and France than in Germany. As unemployment expenditure (both to create employment and to compensate for the loss of it) rose to alarming proportions, the new labour flexibility drive became legitimized not only for its promotion of economic adjustment and growth but also for its positive effect on employment-creation. This faced organized labour with the dilemma of having to contemplate a deterioration in the quality of employment in exchange for a decrease in unemployment. Deep divisions began to separate employed from unemployed labour.

The shift from the old to the new model of capitalism can be observed in many areas, but it is important to distinguish between proclaimed ideologies and policy goals and actually achieved results in the areas of employment and welfare. The following section will examine the extent of change achieved in labour market policy. It will assess the trend towards flexibility of labour deployment in its diverse manifestations and attempt to evaluate the impact of the new flexibility drive, both on economic competitiveness and on the level of unemployment and the quality of employment. It is notable that in all three societies actual practice in the field of employment has come nowhere near a full realization of 'free market capitalism' and that, on the whole, neither politicians nor managers are intent on the full dismantling of the rights which labour had acquired in the postwar period (Jeammeaud and Friant, 1987; Kern and Schumann, 1989). Many managers are aware that the maintenance of internal flexibility depends on a satisfactory degree of employment security.

THE FLEXIBILITY THESIS

Organized labour has tried to defend the maintenance of achieved levels and structures of wages, employment security and other existing job and employment rights. Employers, in contrast, have begun to demand greater freedom to vary employment conditions in accordance with variations in the quantity and quality of demand. They have also tried to achieve a downward adjustment of both wage and social costs, declaring that wages are a cost which prejudices external competitiveness. There have been calls for a differentiation of wage payments according to the financial situation of the firm and/or individual productivity, as well as demands to abandon or weaken statutory protection of minimum wage levels (Boyer, 1987: 4). Individualization of pay has become the new watchword.

This new employment strategy is said to have become expressed in the intensification of dualism or dual employment structures, based on the distinction between a core and a peripheral labour force (Laroque, 1984; IMS 1986). This segmentation of labour markets thus may run through individual firms, leading to the creation of 'the flexible firm' (IMS, 1986). Workers in the core labour force are, in the main, able to maintain a standard employment relationship whereas workers on the periphery are forced to accept individualized employment contracts which eliminate employment security and depress levels of benefits and/or wages. Consequently employers can cope with uncertainty and increased risks by attracting or expelling peripheral workers in accordance with fluctuations in demand as well as reduce the costs of hiring. An additional way of shifting the burden of risk has been sought by an increase in subcontracting. The decentralization of production to smaller units implied by subcontracting has, in turn, brought a further deterioration in the conditions of employment for those employed in smaller firms.

THE TREND TOWARDS FLEXIBILITY: THE EVIDENCE

While a certain amount of dualism has long been present in the labour markets of the three European societies, during the last decade or so this has both increased in scope and has assumed new manifestations. This development started much earlier and is more advanced in Britain and France, whereas in Germany a decisive change of policy was only signalled in 1985, and institutional impediments to the development of dualism have remained stronger. It is, however, difficult to make any precise quantitative comparisons between the three countries as non-standard forms of employment are not always defined and measured in the same way nor do available data always cover comparable samples or periods. The focus in the following will be mainly on external or numerical flexibility and on pay flexibility as internal functional flexibility has already been considered in Chapter 7. The main forms of gaining numerical flexibility considered will be the following: reductions of employment security; growth of temporary and fixed-term working; increases in geographical/occupational/job mobility; part-time work which permits flexible deployment[4] and the use of youth training schemes.[5]

France

In France, the different forms of employment are clearly defined by law, and data to measure trends have been systematically collected. The trend towards employment flexibility began in 1976–81 (Marchand, 1987: 93; Boyer, 1987: 2), was interrupted by the temporary return to welfare capitalism under the socialist government, and then resumed again in 1986 under a Conservative government. Both the two principal forms of flexible employment, fixed-term (FTE) and temporary employment (TE),[6] were already well established before 1981 (Laroque, 1984: 200–1; Bernard, 1987: 10). They were perceived to be so divisive of the working class that the socialist government felt obliged to take up the battle against precarious forms of employment (Laroque, 1984: 199). Decentralization of production to smaller production units and to less unionized geographical areas was also well under way in the 1970s (Berger, 1980). But part-time work was still underdeveloped and, in its conditions of employment, could not be considered precarious. Payment rigidities were not yet under attack.

The election of a socialist government in 1981 temporarily arrested the trend towards flexible employment but did not reverse it. Despite deteriorating economic conditions, the government tried to fulfil its electoral promises to the working class. Attempts were made to place restrictions on the use of precarious forms of employment, to reduce their negative consequences for employees, to raise levels of income and social benefits for the lower income groups, to strengthen the role of enterprise representative bodies in the area of employment and, above all, to bring down unemployment.

The strong rules regulating redundancy remained unchanged. Although 1984 ordinances decreased the level of unemployment benefit, there occurred a strengthening of employers' obligation to consult and negotiate with their workforces on redundancy and other forms of precarious employment (see Chapter 9). The significant enlargement of the public sector also enhanced employment security. Legislation passed in 1982 restricted the recourse to precarious employment contracts and improved the social situation of affected workers (Caire, 1986: 728). Consequently, these forms of employment became more cumbersome and costly for employers to use, but did not greatly decline in importance. In 1985, the majority of new entries into, and exits from, the labour force were on FT contracts. Thirty-seven per cent of job-seekers, registered with the national employment agency, were unemployed due to the termination of a FT contract, as compared with only 17 per cent in 1976 (Bernard, 1987: 8).

The removal in 1982 of legislative barriers to the flexible use of part-time labour led to an increase in part-time work. But, in contrast to the situation in Britain, it did not become a cheap alternative to full-time work, nor did French employers gain the same wide scope for varying work time as their British counterparts (Gregory, 1988: 3, 6).

The movement towards greater wages flexibility also started in the early 1980s (Schwab, 1987: 25–7). Although it was still rare in the early 1980s for employers totally to abandon a *general* pay increase for the non-cadre labour force, there occurred a significant increase of individualized payment schemes. More individualized determination of bonus payments for cadres also increased significantly (ibid.).

The Conservative government which came to power in 1986 was more inclined to accede to employers' demands for greater flexibility and, by various measures, intensified the move towards flexible and insecure employment. Two laws passed in July 1985 and 1986 relaxed the restrictions on the use of precarious employment contracts and extended their scope. Precarious employment contracts are still only used for a small minority of the labour force. In 1986, 4.8 per cent of employed outside the state sector had temporary, FT or training contracts (Marchand, 1987: 93–4). But statistics show a strong growth of this form of employment in recent years, particularly among new, young and unskilled entrants to the labour force (ibid.). In 1986, 63 per cent of new entrants were given FT contracts and only 24 per cent started a new job on standard contracts (Bernard, 1987: 8).

Part-time employment, although risen to 11.8 per cent of all employment by 1986 (Marchand, 1987: 112), was still at a low level by European standards. But a 1986 Ordinance legitimated a new form of part-time work – intermittent work. This is based on an employment contract of unspecified duration which provides for regular or irregular periods of not working (*Social Europe*, 2, 1987).

Formulas for short, paid training periods among the young – another measure which gains employers flexibility as well as considerably reducing their costs – also multiplied during the 1980s. A scheme started in 1986, for example, called *Formation en Alternance*, enabled employers to take on young people for short spells (up to six months) without an employment contract. They had to contribute towards their pay only between 17 and 27 per cent of the national minimum wage (SMIC), as well as being exempt from paying social costs (Bernard, 1987: 12). There are signs that employers are using this scheme instead of FT contracts (ibid.).

A 1986 law also eased the constraints on making redundancies in response to employers' claims that they had led to overemployment and a reluctance to enlarge their core labour force. Employers are now no longer obliged to justify economic redundancies to local labour market authorities. Bernard (1987: 14) suggests that this legislation increased the volume of redundancies in the short term through the shedding of surplus manpower but is less certain about long-term effects. Employment security has also been decreased by the privatization offensive of the Conservative government (Jeammeaud and Friant, 1987: 215). To sum up the French situation on employment flexibility, the 1976–86 period witnessed a significant, though still moderate, growth in both numerical and pay flexibility and in employee insecurity. Although the socialist government managed to slow down the growth of insecure and poorly paid employment, it could not reverse the trend. The attack on employment rigidity has proceeded on many different fronts and has affected the labour force very unevenly. Although the progress towards flexibility was still relatively moderate by 1986 and no attack on the enterprise system of worker representation had occurred, the foundations for further growth have been laid. Throughout the 1976–86 period, the state assumed a prominent interventionist role, responding to pressures from different social constituencies.

Britain

A study of flexibility trends in Britain is made difficult by the more imprecise definitions of employment forms, different forms of measurement and by a lack of consistent longitudinal data. Consequently, there is disagreement in the literature on actual trends.

Governmental attacks on labour market rigidities during the 1980s took a variety of forms which differed in several respects from those in France. Legislative activity has been less developed and indirect attacks more pronounced. In view of the already relatively well developed degree of external flexibility (see pp. 274f) there has not been the same determined push towards introducing/increasing precarious forms of employment as in France and Germany, although both the government (1985 White Paper on Employment) and the employers (CBI and Institute of Directors) have argued in favour of flexible patterns (Hakim, 1987c: 550).

Hakim (ibid.: 550–2) put the size of the flexible workforce (FW) in 1986 as being as high as one third the total workforce (35 per cent) and identifies a growth of 5 per cent during the 1980s, particularly in 1983–85. She arrives at this high proportion by including in the FW not only temporary workers (one fifth of the FW) but also part-timers (one half of the FW). Although there is a good deal of justification, from the employer's point of view, in considering part-timers in Britain as flexible workers this applies only to a certain proportion. A detailed analysis by Dale and Barnford (1988b: 19, 22) makes clear that permanent part-timers are the least likely category of employed to work variable hours although a high proportion (46 per cent in 1984) fell outside the employment protection legislation. Hence, in the context of the flexibility debate, Hakim's estimate is too high. A more detailed analysis of the various flexibility drives and their impact on different categories of workers is in order.

One of the most important changes in Britain has been a significant reduction of the number of employees eligible for employment protection. Legislation in 1980 and 1985 increased the period of continuous employment necessary to come under the scope of the Employment Protection Act from six months to two years. This has provided employers with a considerably enlarged margin to adapt their labour forces without financial penalties. Additional numerical flexibility is guaranteed by the high proportion – 23 per cent in 1987 (Hakim, 1987b) – of part-timers in the LF who, in Britain, can be deployed more flexibly than in France both in terms of hours and times worked (Gregory, 1988). Although this is not a new phenomenon, the 1980s, (1981–87) still witnessed a moderate growth of 2 per cent (Hakim, 1987b: 555, Table 7).

The available evidence on the two principal forms of flexible employment, FT and temporary working, is ambiguous. As no legal definition exists of either form of employment and a difference between the two is not always made [7] data are derived from subjective evaluations of employment status by either employees or employers. The only regular yearly survey, the Labour Force Survey (LFS), provides genuinely comparable data only from 1983 onwards.

In 1986, according to Hakim's analysis of the LFS, temporary workers constituted 6 per cent of the employed population or 7 per cent, if the large proportion of young workers on training schemes[8] is included (Hakim, 1987c: 557). Such an inclusion, I believe, is justified because the majority of such workers regard themselves, and are regarded, as temporary workers. Furthermore, as evidence from France suggests (Bernard, 1987: 12), employers tend to substitute workers on training schemes for the more expensive adult temporary workers. Cockburn (1987: 5, 21) suggests that British YTS trainees, who are both cheap and unprotected, are frequently taken on by employers in place of workers on a proper wage. Meager (1986: 8), drawing his data from an employers' survey in various sectors, puts the proportion of temporary workers in 1984 at 7.5 per cent. Some studies (Casey, 1987: 74; Hakim, 1987b) suggest that temporary working has been common for a long time and has occurred for reasons other than those connected with the idea of 'the flexible firm'.

Conclusions differ about trends in temporary working during the 1980s.[9] But the balance of evidence is that, whether looking at employers' or employees' surveys in the 1980s, and particularly between 1983–85 and 1986 and 1987 (King, 1988: 239), there was a small increase in the proportion of temporary workers, narrowly defined. Moreover, employers' surveys suggest further increases up to 1990 (Hakim, 1987b: 558; Meager, 1986: 218). Although many employers still engage temporary workers for traditional reasons, a significant proportion (44 per cent in Meager's survey), particularly of larger employers in the manufacturing sector, now justify such engagement in terms of the 'flexible firm' thesis (Meager, 1986: 12–14). Meager (1986: 9) found a large proportion of users of temporary workers to be in industry. Inclusion of the large proportion of workers on training schemes in the category of temporary workers would, of course, greatly inflate it.

It is, however, clear from several surveys (Dale and Bamford, 1988 a and b; Meager, 1986: King, 1988) that temporary workers are very heterogeneous in terms of sex, age, marital status, qualifications and occupation,[10] and that a majority have adopted 'temporary' status by choice and should not be considered disadvantaged workers (Hakim, 1987b; Casey, 1987; King, 1988). On the other hand, however, a large proportion of temporary workers clearly *are* disadvantaged as they do not get the same fringe benefits as permanent workers, (*Incomes Data Services*, 406, 1988) and in some industries they also receive lower rates of pay (Casey, 1987: 73).

The growth in temporary working is often linked to an increase in subcontracting to smaller, less unionized forms. Subcontracting is seen as another employer strategy to reduce risk and increase flexibility (IMS, 1986). But most data on the *growth* in subcontracting show that actual trends do not measure up to the importance which this phenomenon is accorded in the 'flexibility' literature, although there may have been selective increases in some sectors, e.g. in engineering. (See the discussion of this in Pollert 1988: 289–90.) The 1987 ACAS survey, however, noted a significant increase in subcontracting during the preceding three years from an already extremely high base (ACAS 1988: 12).

The relatively modest increase in temporary workers in Britain can be explained in two ways: First, the number of flexible workers (counting both temporary workers and a proportion of the part-time labour force) has long been more sizeable in Britain than in the other two societies. Second, there is a relatively large proportion of unprotected workers, i.e. all full-time workers who have been in the same employment for less than two years and all part-timers, working either less than eight hours per week or working eight–sixteen hours and having been with their current employer for less than five years. Thus, in 1984, 46 per cent of 'permanent' part-timers fell outside the employment protection legislation

(Dale and Bamford, 1988b: 22). All these circumstances greatly reduce the need to issue fixed-term contracts. As Casey (1987: 72) points out, many employers find such contracts not only unnecessary but also too restrictive.

Yet another attack on employment rigidity during the 1980s consists of government measures, designed to remove the obstacles to geographical, occupational and job mobility. Attempts in this direction include the encouragement of the private rented sector at the expense of public housing, the Social Security Law 1985 to make pension rights more easily transferable between firms and increased further training programmes. It is difficult to assess the full effect of these measures but continuing large discrepancies in regional rates of unemployment suggest relatively little progress in regional/occupational mobility.

The achievement of greater pay flexibility has been a very prominent government goal during the 1980s. High unemployment in general and youth unemployment in particular, it has been claimed, is to a large extent due to inflated wage claims. Both the reduction of union power (see Chapter 8) and of the competencies of Wages Councils in 1985, as well as the low wages of YTS trainees, must be seen as responses in pursuit of this goal. Since 1985 the 26 Wages Councils in low-pay industries can no longer fix minimum wages for workers under 21, nor do they any longer have power of decision over conditions of employment. The effects of these measures cannot easily be distinguished from those of other influences, such as unemployment itself. Santini (1987: 2) suggests that, because wages councils affect only around 10 per cent of the total labour force and a much smaller proportion of employed in industry, the curtailment of their functions cannot have been very effective. The reduction of union power, it is suggested, has also had surprisingly little effect on wage settlements. Although there is evidence of greater union moderation and more willingness to match pay rises to productivity increases in some industries and firms, wage settlements are still mostly unrelated to growth in output, enterprise financial performance or other such measures (Millward and Stevens, 1986). The positive impact of decentralized pay bargaining and of multi-unionism on real wage rises has not been cancelled out by the above measures, and the management practice of buying workers' acceptance of new technology and redundancies with pay rises are also responsible for wage increases above those of productivity. On the other hand, however, the proportion of workers not covered by union agreements – particularly those on YTS schemes and many part-timers – has grown during the 1980s and must have increased payment flexibility at the bottom of pay scales.

Germany

During the first half of the 1980s dualism has remained much less developed than in Britain and France. The relatively low proportion of workers with 'everyman' qualifications (Sengenberger, 1978) meant that occupational and internal labour markets were dominant and that there was less scope for the development of peripheral labour forces. Internal labour markets have, however, become more open to entrants from occupational markets, as indicated by the growing substitution of skilled workers for un- or semi-skilled ones (Bosch, 1988: 178). Although German commentators (e.g. Kern and Schumann, 1989: 25f) connect the growth in long-term unemployment,[11] together with the upskilling offensives in, and closures of, internal labour markets to the non-skilled, with a growing and more rigidly set segmentation of the labour force, this has remained considerably less pronounced than in the other two societies. (See figures on long-term unemployment on P.291.)

Except for the growing unemployment, the employment situation in the early 1980s did not fundamentally differ from that in the 1970s. The relatively high degree of employment security contributed to the fact that full-time employment, with a standard working week, remained the norm, much more than elsewhere (Streeck, 1987a: 17). Thus, in the mid-1980s, the average length of employment in Germany was second only to that in Japan, and adjustment of employment in reaction to changes in output took longer than anywhere else, excepting only Japan (OECD statistics quoted by Streeck, 1987a: 19). The high value put on functional flexibility by German employers and the awareness that the latter depends on a reasonable degree of employment security, also preserved stability. The lower degree of youth unemployment and strong commitment to three-year apprenticeship training also meant that special short-term training schemes could not become the prominent source of flexible, precarious employment they became in Britain and France. The part-time[12] quota remained relatively low – between 11 and 13 per cent during the first half of the 1980s (Fuchs, 1988: 15, Table 5), and the amount of fixed-term or temporary employment stayed below the British and French levels up to 1985 (Bosch, 1988: 184).

Although the flexibility debate also preoccupied German employers in the early 1980s, significant change in this field emerged only in 1985 when the Employment Promotion Act (EPA) was passed. This Act, introduced in response to employer demands, constituted a radical attack on employment rigidity on many fronts and also aimed to bring down unemployment. It was particularly designed to reduce the risk for small firms of taking on new employees. An evaluation of its impact has to be careful to distinguish intended from actual effects. The EPA tried to increase part-time employment by making it slightly more equal to the full-time variety and by legally regulating work sharing. The Act regulated and made it easier to issue fixed-term contracts if these resulted in the employment of unemployed or the retention of apprentices (*Social Europe* 1, 1985: 78). The period for loan work was extended from 3 to 6 months,[13] and 'work on call' became legally regulated. Lastly, employment protection was lowered by raising the threshold at which firms were obliged to establish a Social Plan – a measure with a limited impact calculated to benefit smaller firms. Thus the Act generally facilitates the reduction of stable and secure employment although, except for the change of rules on the establishment of Social Plans, it does not attempt to regulate employment itself.

It is too short a period since the introduction of the Act to assess its effects in all its aspects, and evaluations for some areas only are available. Although the Act legitimated numerical flexibility and put it firmly on the German agenda it has so far not radically altered existing employment practice. Medium-sized employers, who have a strong relative weight in the FRG, tend to equate numerical flexibility with general instability and have remained wary of it (Fuchs, 1988: 25–7). The biggest impact appears to have been in the area of fixed-term employment which has greatly increased since the Act and, according to an article in the academic journal of the DGB (Bosch, 1988: 186), stood at 8.5 per cent of total employment in 1986. This development, in turn, is linked to a weakening of works councils in the area of employment regulation (ibid.). The same author also detects an increase in loan work and subcontracting but provides no statistics to document such trends. In the area of part-time employment, in contrast, the Act has had very little impact and has made it more expensive and less flexible, in as far as trade unions in several industries have responded by including part-timers in wage bargaining agreements (Fuchs, 1988: 25). The development of part-time work has stagnated since the Act, particularly in the private sector. For women, the increase in full-time employment was even greater than that in part-time employment (Fuchs, 1988: 13f).

Pay rigidities, particularly the insignificant degree of variation between regions and sizes of firms,[14] have also come under attack, and, as in France, the individualization of pay has been extensively debated during the 1980s. Attempts to obtain differential pay settlements in crisis enterprises or industries have been noted during the 1980s (Streeck, 1984b). But the continued practice of industry-level bargaining has so far prevented significant changes in this direction. The system of pay bargaining retains some credit for its effect of keeping real wages aligned with levels of productivity and for making job mobility easy. Nevertheless, enterprise bargaining is said to have assumed increased importance in recent years.

THE IMPACT OF THE FLEXIBILITY DRIVE

To sum up, the move to 'free market' capitalism in Britain, Germany and France has entailed considerable efforts by both employers and the state to loosen up labour markets and to increase employment flexibility. Some of the flexibility trends were already underway in the 1970s, particularly in Britain and, to a lesser extent, France, and thus do not constitute a totally new phenomenon. In France and, more so, in Germany, a sustained attack on employment rigidity occurred only from the middle 1980s onwards. In none of the three societies has flexible employment increased dramatically, and everywhere the peripheral labour force has remained a minority. But the trend towards flexible employment does, nevertheless, constitute a notable new phenomenon. It is qualitatively different from previous employment practices because the attack on rigidity has occurred on so many fronts and has led to the simultaneous emergence of a large variety of forms of labour market flexibility. At the same time, already existing firms of precarious employment have, in the process, acquired a more legitimate position in the arsenal of labour market policy measures.

The flexibility drive has affected the labour force very unevenly. An increase in precarious forms of employment has been much stronger in the service than in the industrial sector of the European economics and has had a differential impact on different socio-economic groups. In all three societies precarious forms of employment have affected particularly the young of both sexes and also married women over 25 years of age. The latter group is marginalized particularly strongly in Britain (Dale and Bamford, 1988b) where largely female, temporary part-time workers on variable hours – the most disadvantaged group among the employed – form a substantial part of the labour force. British male workers over 25 years of age, in contrast, have hardly been exposed to the 'flexibility drive' (ibid.).

The trends towards increased external and pay flexibility outlined above have been initiated by both employers and the state with two basic goals in mind: the increase of business competitiveness in international markets and the lowering of the level of unemployment. Whether or not these goals have been achieved is an extremely difficult question to answer as the attainment of both is affected by a multitude of other factors besides greater labour flexibility. Consequently only tentative and very general conclusions can be drawn.

Competitiveness of European manufacturing enterprises on world markets, it has been argued in Chapter 7, is increasingly influenced by a firm's ability to offer high-quality products, and to adapt production swiftly to changes in demand, and only secondarily by the competitive pricing of products. A high degree of numerical and pay flexibility, while favourable to the latter, is not likely to enhance a firm's capacity in the former respect. On the contrary, an excessive pursuit of external flexibility will be incompatible with the retention of a highly skilled labour force and the achievement of functional flexibility. Functional flexibility can only be maintained in the context of a reasonable degree of employment stability and security (OECD, 1986c).

Unemployment levels have developed differently in the three societies during the middle 1980s. Whereas unemployment has been considerably reduced in Britain and slightly in Germany, in France it has increased steadily during that period.[15] Although it might be tempting to argue that these changes have been due to the differential degrees of labour market flexibility achieved in the three societies, such a claim would be difficult to substantiate. Numerous other factors, such as the general economic climate, macroeconomic policy, demographic trends[16] and policies, stimulating the demand for, or reducing the supply of, labour also affect the level of unemployment, and it is impossible to separate their effect from that of the flexibility offensive. The pronouncements by politicians in all three societies that legislative and other flexibility measures have been successful in creating employment must, therefore, be regarded with scepticism. It is highly unlikely that, by themselves, these measures will be able to have a substantial effect, let alone solve the problem of unemployment. (For an analysis of the employment effect of the German Employment Promotion Act, see Adamy, 1987.)

In all three societies, the most prominent policy instrument to reduce unemployment has been a reduction of the supply of labour. All three societies, but particularly Britain and France, have taken substantial proportions of young unemployed off the register by establishing youth training schemes on a large scale. Germany and France, in addition, have tried to tackle the problem by a reduction of hours worked during the week, the year and over the whole working life. Numerous state-sponsored initiatives to shorten the working week, lengthen paid holidays and introduce early retirement schemes are described in the literature.[17] These solidary approaches to the problem of unemployment have been favoured by the union movements which have been extremely concerned about the flexibility drives. Although employers have also benefited from some of the measures to reduce working time, particularly from the 'early retirement' schemes, they are not likely to recognize them as alternatives to the introduction of flexible employment. The remaining high levels of unemployment will ensure that the general complexion of employment policy during the late 1980s and early 1990s will continue to be shaped predominantly by employers' needs.

NOTES

1. The discrepantly high incidence of part-time work in Britain is due to the fact that there is a relatively high threshold at which social insurance is payable. This encourages employers in low-income sectors to create part-time jobs (*Problèmes Economiques*, 1946, October 1985: 14).
2. In 1975 social charges amounted to 18 per cent of labour costs in France, as compared with 15 per cent in Germany and 12 per cent in Britain (Marsden, 1987: 205).
3. The proportion of the labour force, described as immigrant, foreign or ethnic minority, was between 7 and 8.5 per cent in 1980 in the three societies. Although their economic status was similar, in Germany and France they had no political rights and only conditional citizenship rights.
4. Part-time work which gives employers the freedom to vary hours worked and working times must be considered an important form of flexible working.
5. Although participation *may* lead to permanent employment it is, by its very nature, governed by a fixed-term contract and has been widely used to fulfil the need for cheap and temporary labour.
6. Temporary employment in France differs from fixed-term employment in that the employment contract binds the worker to the temporary work agency rather than the firm in which he/she works. In the 1970s these two contracts were regulated by separate legislation, but in the 1980s they became subject to the same legal regulations. Temporary work received an almost 20-fold increase between 1962 and 1981 (Statistics from UNIDEC, quoted by Bernard, 1987: 10).
7. In contrast to the situation in France, there exists no legal time limit to distinguish FT and temporary working from permanent working. Consequently, the distinction is made informally, according to local requirements, between employers, employees and unions (Meager, 1986: 8). A large proportion of temporary workers stay with the same employer for years (King, 1988: 246). Some surveys (e.g. the LFS since 1983) distinguish between casual/seasonal/temporary work and FT work although the term 'temporary' is often applied to both forms in the literature. Whereas the LFS gets its data from household interviews of employees, most other surveys have consulted employers.
8. According to the *Labour Market Quarterly Report* (September 1987: 8), such workers constituted 28 per cent of all employed in 1987.
9. Whereas Meager (1986: 9), Hakim (1987b: 557), King (1988: 239) and the CBI 1985 survey pinpointed a slight increase during the 1980s, particularly since 1983, the WIRS (Millward and Stevens 1986) and Casey (1987: 74) saw no or hardly any increases in temporary working.
10. Fixed-term or -task employees are more likely to be technical or professional workers who are in a position to negotiate favourable employment conditions or rates of pay, but these are a minority among temporary workers – 25 per cent of temporary workers in 1986 were FT workers (King, 1988: 239).

11. Between 1981 and 1985 the proportion of long-term (more than one year) unemployed increased from 0.8 per cent to 2.7 per cent of wage earners (Streeck, 1987a: 19).
12. Statistics on part-time work in Germany, counting also 'work-on-call' and jobsharing, in comparative terms tend to include more workers in this category than other European societies (Fuchs, 1988: 13).
13. Loan work was already well established before the Act (Zachert, 1986: 378).
14. Average wages in small and medium-sized enterprises are closer to those in large ones than in other societies with a prominent SME sector (Bosch, 1988: 181).
15. In 1987, France not only had the highest level of unemployment in general but also the highest proportion (around 47 per cent) of long-term unemployed. Britain now occupies a middle position in both respects, and Germany still has the best record (*The Economist*, 10–16 October 1987: 111). Youth unemployment, too, is significantly lower in Germany than in the other two societies. In 1986, youth unemployment, as a proportion of all unemployment, was 35.6, 33.2 and 22.9 per cent in Britain, France and Germany, respectively (*CEDEFOP News*, 2, 1986).
16. In France, the rise in unemployment has been exacerbated by the strong growth of the active population since 1975 which is expected to continue into the next century (Marchand, 1987: 84).
17. Mouriaux and Mouriaux (1984); Webber and Nass (1984); Elbaum (1987); Moon (1984); Laroque (1984).

Conclusions

The foregoing chapters have each examined comparatively one important aspect of the organization of an industrial enterprise and together
have conveyed a picture of what it means to run a firm the German,
British or French way. Every chapter has shown the strength of national
specificity in the arrangements for managing and working in a manufacturing enterprise. Although the three economies and the business
organizations which constitute them are, at present, being confronted
with similar problems and opportunities management, labour and the
state in each society continue to interact in nationally distinctive ways to
cope with these challenges. Cultural specificity, expressed in, and
reinforced by, different institutional frameworks has withstood the
strong pressures towards uniformity, exerted by advanced industrialism
and an increasingly more global capitalist economic system. These
institutional structures, created by complex historical processes, varying
in length between several centuries and a few decades, influence social
actors and are, in turn, shaped and perpetuated by them. The organization
of a business enterprise, and the management and working practices
which are part of it, have been created in a complex process of interaction between different institutional structures which mutually reinforce each other. Hence, as has been pointed out by the proponents
of the 'societal effect' approach, it is difficult to isolate discrete factors
which have been crucial in determining each national syndrome. Instead
of positing a linear cause–effect pattern it is more appropriate to speak
of a circular one of continual mutual interaction. A detailed investigation of the historical processes which have shaped the national patterns
– a task of considerable complexity – has been beyond the scope of this
study. The focus throughout has been predominantly on their present
manifestations and, particularly, on the processes of interaction between the various institutional structures and their impact on organizational behaviour.

Each of the national syndromes of industrial organization was created
in response to certain historic, economic and political pressures and
opportunities and constituted an appropriate and hence efficient response at that time in history. Although the three national patterns have

adapted to changing external circumstances they have displayed a differential capacity to accommodate to, and cope with, the far-reaching economic transformations of the postwar period and, particularly, of the late 1970s and 1980s. All through this period the German pattern of industrial organization, although not without problems, has displayed a greater degree of efficiency than the other two. The French pattern proved to be effective during the expansionary earlier postwar decades but has been seen as less satisfactory in more recent time. The inadequacies of British industrial organization were partially veiled by the postwar boom but have since become glaringly obvious to large sections of British society. Despite some modest improvements in industrial performance in recent years, the urgent need to change is now acknowledged by politicians of both the left and the right as well as by professional analysts of the industrial scene and its more reflective and farsighted practitioners, and a greater willingness to do so is discernible. At the same time, there is a realization that the recognition of shortcomings and the mere exhortation to adopt new attitudes and orientations is insufficient. Cultural orientations cannot be changed unless institutional structures are adapted to foster and support changed norms and values.

The issue of whether industrial change can only occur *within* the already established mould or whether this mould can be broken by inserting into it new elements, borrowed from foreign practice, is a very complex one. The problem of cultural borrowing needs to be discussed first in the general theoretical terms, spelled out above. In a second step, it will be reviewed in the context of the particular problems, presented by British society.

The theoretical discussion of the transfer of elements of industrial culture/institutions from one society to another, situated within the 'societal effects' paradigm, broadly interpreted, has been characterized both by a recognition of the highly problematic nature of such borrowing and hence some scepticism about the success of cultural transplants and by a pragmatic willingness to nevertheless contemplate it. (See, for example, Lawrence, 1980: 176; and Sorge and Warner, 1986: 203.)

The problems are broadly of two kinds which are, to some extent, interrelated. The first can be described as consisting of the fact that industrial culture/institutions have long historical roots and that the resulting patterns are, therefore, so deep-seated in national consciousness and practice that they cannot be uprooted without destroying the whole fabric. There is a suggestion that the longer the roots the more insurmountable becomes the problem of change (e.g. Fox, 1983; Hall, 1986). Although there is strong evidence to support the suggestion that social inertia and resistance to change increases in proportion to the length of the period of social stability, few social scientists are prepared to accept the implied total structural determinism of this analysis. It cannot be denied, to paraphrase Marx, that circumstances transmitted from the past constitute powerful limitations on present endeavours to change society but, equally, it must be borne in mind that people make their own history. There is, however, more widespread acceptance of the claim that a strong lever, such as presented by national crises, is needed to loosen these long-established cultural roots.

A second formidable problem to the social engineering of industrial change is presented by the tightly interwoven pattern of institutional structures and cultural values and the interaction between the various elements. Questions such as where does one break into the circle and which elements are more decisive than others in shaping the whole pattern have to be confronted. Scientific answers to these questions are impossible and only intuitive, informed guesses can be made. The problem could be avoided if the whole syndrome were to be imported but, in practice, this is not a feasible solution. In view of these grave difficulties, it is not surprising that some social scientists abandon the idea of cultural borrowing altogether. But actual practice has shown that, despite these problems, such transfers have nevertheless frequently been attempted, although with varying success. If borrowing becomes too piecemeal and occurs without recognition of the wider context from which elements have been severed or in which they will have to be implanted, failure or a low rate of success becomes inevitable. But, at the same time, if borrowing remains confined to only such institutional arrangements which go comfortably *with* the cultural grain of the receiving society, the vicious circle might never be broken. It is clear then that the borrowing process has to be handled very judiciously and with great sensitivity both for the donor and the recipient culture.

Recent historical examples of both fairly piecemeal copying of mere management techniques and of more radical transfer of whole industrial structures can be found both in our three European societies and in a world industrial context. Hofstede (1980) cites the instructive example of a transfer of the American management technique of 'Management by Objectives' (MBO) shaped by American values, to both Germany and France. In Germany MBO became very popular. It was adapted to native values and structures, particularly to those of co-determination, and became transformed into 'Management by Joint Objectives' (*Führung durch Zielvereinbarung*), with a strong emphasis on team work. In France, in contrast, where it was also introduced to democratize organizational relations (as *Direction Participative par Objectifs*

– DPPO), the technique sat uneasily with established highly personalized authority relations and remained an empty slogan (ibid.). A similar lack of success was experienced by French business organizations with a bolder structural reform of the industrial relations system – the introduction of works committees, modelled on the German works councils – to achieve greater industrial democracy. Not only did this innovation go against the established grain of French industrial culture but it was imposed by the state on employers who did not see the necessity for democratization. But the French works committees have not been a complete failure and have, over time, gradually brought the two sides of industry closer together, even if the original ideal still eludes them. This example illustrates that, over time, structural changes can, to some extent, remould attitudes and behaviour. This is more clearly demonstrated by the adoption of co-determination in Germany. German management before and immediately after World War II was known to be either paternalist or authoritarian, and the idea of co-determination did not fit comfortably into existing management–worker relations. Over the postwar period, however, the institution of co-determination has done much to democratize these relations and to educate management to the effectiveness of a more democratic style.

An equally striking success has been the transformation of the German system of trade union organization, introduced after World War II under the supervision of the Western allies, particularly of the British. The established system of competitive unionism, based on union membership according to ideological orientation (*Richtungsgewerkschaften*), was replaced by a unified system of industrial unions (*Einheitsgewerkschaften*) which fundamentally changed trade union organization (see Chapter 8). An important precondition for the successful implantation of this organizational innovation was the involvement of the unions in this change and also their experience of political defeat by the Fascist state, attributed partly to the failing of their old system of organization. If we move outside Europe, Japan is often cited (e.g. Dore, 1973; Trevor, 1985) as the prime example of a society which has extensively borrowed techniques and structural arrangements from older industrialized societies and successfully adapted them to its own industrial purposes.

This short overview of the theoretical problems of borrowing elements from other industrial cultures has made clear the limitations of a social scientific approach. But because such borrowing has nevertheless been frequently attempted in practice and has sometimes been very successful, an improved interpretative understanding of the complex industrial structures of our own and other industrial countries will be of value in guiding this process of cultural/institutional transplant.

It may be objected, however, that younger industrial countries, like Japan and Germany, which have, furthermore, been able to start with a clean slate after total defeat in WWII, do not face the same problems in this borrowing process, as are experienced by an old and stable industrial nation like Britain. The following lucid formulation of this objection by Fox (1983: 6, 8) is representative of the reservations and qualms of many other distinguished analysts of this problem. Fox points to nearly 300 years of political stability in Britain and to

> the massive and stubborn resistances that are encountered by attempts to transform basic, long-standing responses of large numbers of people in their everyday behaviour; by attempts to preserve institutional dispositions and tendencies that have been shaped over a long period; or by attempts to repudiate expectations that have likewise been generated by persistent historical continuities.

Fox, however, does not totally repudiate the possibility of change in the organization of British manufacturing organizations but raises the question of whether the costs of change will not outweigh the benefits. Only a decade ago most people would have shared Fox's expression of qualms. Since then, however, economic and political change have transformed the context in which reform is contemplated and with it public opinion about it. Three developments in this respect are of note.

Industrial decline during the late 1970s and early 1980s, expressed in an alarming reduction of industrial capacity and employment and in a further loss of competitiveness on world markets for manufactured goods, has led to a widespread feeling that Britain is now faced with a national crisis. It is believed that, unless remedial action is taken, decline will proceed to a point where Britain's future as an industrial nation is jeopardized. Thus, in the most diverse circles, there has arisen the conviction that the costs of inertia have now become higher than the costs of fundamental change. Industrial crisis has become a catalyst of change which, although not in the league of political revolution or total war, has nevertheless assumed a powerful impetus. Change is now welcomed by both the political left (see the new Labour Party manifesto on industrial relations) and right, by politicians, industrialists and employees, as well as by some unions.

This conviction that change of industrial structures and attitudes is now unavoidable has also been based on a pragmatic recognition that, if it is not initiated by the main political actors – employers, unions and the state – or by individual, more adventurous or determined firms, then it will be imposed from outside through the colonization of British industry by foreign-owned firms through joint ventures and takeovers.

The activity in this respect of the Japanese, believed to favour structural arrangements and value orientations deviating strongly from British practice and inclination, has received particularly wide publicity. Although the number of firms partly or wholly Japanese-owned is not yet very large, their influence has already been out of proportion to their numerical weight. As British firms have to collaborate with, and more directly compete against, Japanese firms, their superior efficiency and results force a serious consideration of their practices on British firms even outside their direct influence. Their impact on industrial relations, as recently outlined by Bassett (1986) and also demonstrated by events, e.g. the Ford withdrawal from a proposed electronics plant in Scotland, has gone beyond these firms and is forcing the adoption of change on the part of British unions. The Japanese impact on management organization and methods has also been considerable (e.g. Trevor, 1985). These developments have thus further highlighted the inevitability of industrial change and have raised determination in some quarters to initiate it while there is still an opportunity to adopt British-chosen organizational solutions, rather than be forced to accept imposed changes, perceived to be alien to British sensibilities.

Lastly, the contemplation of industrial reform now occurs in a political environment which is more conducive to its achievement than has been the case in the past. As Fox (1983: 29) points out, in the past British governments and state agencies have not seen it as their role to mobilize and stimulate industrial strength, and they moved mostly in response to pressures from organized interests. The Thatcher government still claims a non-interventionist role for the state but has, in fact, actively intervened on many occasions to rekindle industrial competitiveness. It has not been afraid to confront organized interests and has generally adopted a more proactive stance than its predecessors. Although state intervention has not and probably cannot by itself achieve the regeneration of manufacturing industry it has created a more supportive environment for innovative industrial firms which want to make radical changes to their organizational practices.

The necessary transformations of British industrial structures and practices need to be initiated or powerfully stimulated by the state, at least in the initial phase, as the capacity for change of both unions and employers' associations is too weak. Such intervention should not interfere directly in the running of individual firms but should provide a much stronger general framework in such areas as education and training, research and development and industrial relations which would, at the same time, seek to stimulate the involvement of individual firms in these areas. Change should be introduced in such a way that it secures widespread acceptance. Although acceptance cannot always be gained if powerful interests are offended, a greater effort to balance the costs to affected groups with some benefits would be advisable.

What lessons, then, can be derived from a comparative study of business organization in Europe and what particular changes are advisable in the British context? It is clear that Britain is more likely to look to the German than the French example. Not only has German business organization proved to secure better business results, but practices in many areas are also more compatible with British value-orientations than are French ones (see the discussion of value compatibility by Hofstede, 1980, Chapter 9). This concluding chapter can do no more than make broad suggestions on how British firms might benefit from studying the practices of their German competitors. It is not implied that features of German business organization should be slavishly copied. No doubt they would be adapted to what is possible and acceptable in the British context.

The strengths of German manufacturing enterprises are widely seen to emanate from two core institutional complexes – the system of vocational education and training and the system of industrial relations. The first not only creates high levels of technical skill throughout the industrial enterprise but also engenders a homogeneity of skills at all levels of the hierarchy, as well as fostering certain orientations to the work task and the work community. These characteristics, in turn, structure organizational relations, influence communication and cooperation along both horizontal and vertical lines and encourage labour deployment in accordance with the principle of responsible autonomy. The craft ethos permeates the whole of the organization and creates a common focus and identity for management and production workers, although not necessarily a community of interests. The cooperative works culture, fostered by the training system, is further reinforced by the system of industrial relations, particularly by the works council. The autonomy and responsibility encouraged by the organization of work is paralleled and enhanced by the participative industrial relations style, flowing from the system of co-determination. Finally, such a task orientation and cooperative stance is not only found in the many small to medium-sized artisanal (*Handwerk*) enterprises but they have permeated also large-scale volume production, and the 'industrial' elements of the latter have been taken on board by the smaller enterprises.[1] Smaller and large enterprises have, from the beginning of industrialization, coexisted in Germany and have benefited from extensive cross-fertilization.

These pervasive linkages have been lacking in British manufacturing industry although a move away from large industrial units has gained momentum from the late 1970s onwards. A more cooperative organizational climate and a developed production orientation can also be found in many smaller British enterprises (see Bessant and Grunt, 1985), and a few of the foremost larger companies have also developed a highly individualistic style, similar to that found in Germany (see Goldsmith and Clutterbuck, 1984). But in Britain the organizational features outlined above remain the exception rather than the rule. They are fostered by individual, highly motivated managers and are not supported by the societal institutional framework.

To achieve more widespread change in organizational structures and behaviour a new approach to the system of skill development needs to be adopted. Not only will initial and further VET have to become more extensive both among workers and managerial staff but they also have to be organized in a more integrated manner. Skill development at the higher levels has to build on that at lower levels, and shopfloor workers have to be given more opportunities to use vocational training for advancement to higher levels of the organizational hierarchy. Although the increased recruitment of graduates into staff and line positions is to be welcomed more effort has to be put into closing the skill and communication gap between works and staff. The old British apprenticeship system fulfilled this function to a certain extent, and the gradual phasing out of this system, for all its faults, has also swept away its more positive contributions. The new training system, developed by the MSC, has the virtue of making training more widely available and of raising the skill floor for a large section of manual workers. But it is unlikely, in its present form, to develop a 'craft' orientation, nor will it enhance the homogeneity of skill within the manufacturing enterprise. The training effort by the MSC will also have to be supplemented to a larger extent by enterprises themselves, and a compulsory levy-grant system may have to be introduced to overcome employers' reluctance or passivity in this sphere. The German example shows that investment in training has given employers ample returns in terms of worker productivity and commitment to quality production. Such greater commitment is, however, also secured by the greater employment security negotiated by German workers.

Recent changes of the British system of industrial relations have already gone much further than in the area of vocational training. But the efforts exerted both through legislation and more individualized negotiation, although in many cases very necessary, have concentrated too one sidedly on destroying old structures and practices and have not replaced them with new ones, which might be beneficial to both sides of industry. It might be possible to achieve such mutually beneficial results by the introduction into the British system of industrial relations of a body akin to the German works council. The growing popularity among both managements and workforces of consultative committees in recent years (Millward and Stevens, 1986) indicates that a move away from adversarial forms of communication is already occuring. A study of existing works councils in a few British companies, such as Bulmers and Cadbury-Schweppes, would shed further light on feasible approaches in the British context.

Although many British unions and employers have been opposed to the idea of the works council in the past, changed conditions, particularly the greater need for a more committed and responsible work force (see Chapter 7), might make them more acceptable to employers at the present time. Unions and workers, it was shown in Chapter 9, can also derive substantial advantages from agreements negotiated through the works council, but the unions would, no doubt, also have to be prepared for some loss of direct influence. Although it is not intended to prescribe what features of the German system of co-determination should be adopted a clear division of competencies between works councils and unions is considered to be indispensable. It is unlikely that effective change could be accomplished without some short-term costs to the existing trade union system. A greater professionalization of representative bodies, along with a raising of education and skill levels, would also be necessary for workers to make full use of the co-decision rights conferred by the works council.

Many readers will, no doubt, remain sceptical about the possibility of changing British industrial organization through the implant of elements borrowed from another culture. They might nevertheless value the comparative study of European business organizations because it conveys a superior understanding of the peculiar characteristics of potential customers, competitors, collaborators, partners in joint ventures or colleagues in multinational organizations. The emergence of a genuinely common European market in 1992 will no doubt bring about an increase in such cross-national contacts. In joint ventures and multinational organizations knowledge of French or German cultural/institutional specificity will influence top management to either make allowances for the latter or to provide extra training to familiarize foreign nationals with British practices and expectations. Collaborative contacts are more likely to be fruitful if there is a clear understanding on both sides of mutual strengths and limitations. Further research in this area of European joint-ownership, collaboration or other forms of business ties would be a fruitful area of investigation, particularly in view of the forthcoming greater opening of national markets.

The coverage in this book of a wide spectrum of aspects of business organization and their comparative analysis have made it evident that some aspects are, as yet, underresearched and would benefit from further comparative study. Whereas the literature on work organization on the shopfloor has been growing in recent decades there is still very little information about the way management at various levels of the hierarchy carry out their tasks and how they relate to each other and to staff in scientific/technical positions. More particularly, a comparative study of the management of technological/organizational change at the present time would be of particular interest. In the British context, studies of firms which have initiated successful organizational change and have built, and gained acceptance for, an enterprise culture which goes against the grain of the wider societal culture, would throw much needed light on problems and opportunities of industrial transformation.

NOTES

1. I am indebted to Arndt Sorge, of the WZB, for this point.

Bibliography

ACAS (1988), *Labour Flexibility in Britain. The 1987 ACAS Survey*, Occasional Paper 41, London: ACAS.

Adams, W. J. and Stoffaës, C. (eds) (1986), *French Industrial Policy*, Washington D.C.: The Brookings Institution.

Adamy, W. (1987), 'Beschäftigungsförderungsgesetz – Brücke zu Arbeit oder zu Arbeitslosigkeit?', *Soziale Sicherheit* 6.

Ahlström, G. (1982), *Engineers and Industrial Growth*, London: Croom Helm.

Altmann, N., Binkelmann P. Düll, K. and Stück, H. (1982) *Grenzen neuer Arbeitsformon*, Frankfurt: Campus.

Armstrong, P. (1987), 'Engineers, Management and Trust', *Work, Employment and Society*, 4: 421–40.

Atkinson, J. (1985), 'The Changing Corporation', D. Clutterbuck (ed.), *New Patterns of Work*, Aldershot: Gower.

Auer, P., Penth, B. and Tergeist, P. (eds) (1983), *Arbeitspolitische Reformen in Industriestaaten*, Frankfurt: Campus.

Aujac, H. (1986), 'An Introduction to French Industrial Policy', W. J. Adams and C. Stoffaës (eds), *French Industrial Policy*, Washington D.C.: The Brookings Institution.

Balassa, B. (1986), 'Selective versus General Economic Policy in Postwar France', W. J. Adams and C. Stoffaës (eds), *French Industrial Policy*, Washington D.C.: The Brookings Institution.

Banham, J. (1988), 'An Era of Investment in Manufacturing: Maintaining the Momentum of the Economic Recovery', *Policy Studies*, 8, 4: 23–8.

Barker, K., Britton, A. and Major R. (1984), 'Macroeconomic Policy in France and Britain', *National Institute Economic Review*, 110, November 1984: 68–84.

Basset, P. (1986), *Strike-Free: New Industrial Relations in Britain*, London: Macmillan.

Beechey, V. and Perkins, T. (1987), *A Matter of Hours. Women. Part-time Work and the Labour Market*, Cambridge: Polity Press.

Bellon, B. (1985), 'Strengths and Weaknesses of French Industry', S. Zukin (ed.), *Industrial Policy. Business and Politics in the United States and France*, New York: Praeger.

Berger, S. (1980), 'The Traditional Sector in France and Italy', S. Berger and M. Piore (eds), *Dualism and Discontinuity in Industrial Societies*, Cambridge: Cambridge University Press.

Berghahn, V. R. (1985), *Unternehmer und Politik in der Bundesrepublik*, Frankfurt: Suhrkamp.

Berghahn, V. R. and Karsten, D. (1987), *Industrial Relations in West Germany*, London: Berg Publishers.

Bernard, M. P. (1987), 'L'ajustement des effectifs', *Les Cahiers Français*. Special issue on 'La flexibilité du travail', 231: 7–14.

Berry, M. (1988), 'Taylor et les robots', *Pour Une Automatisation Raisonnable de l'Industrie*, Special Issue of *Annales des Mines*, January 1988, Paris.

Bessant, J. R. and Grunt, M. (1985), *Management and Manufacturing Innovation in the United Kingdom and West Germany*, Aldershot: Gower.

Blackaby, F. (ed.), (1979), *De-Industrialisation* London: Heinemann.

Bolte, K. M. and Hradil, S. (1984), *Soziale Ungleichheit in der Bundesrepublik Deutschland*, Opladen: Leske und Budrich.

Borgaes, H. U. (1985), 'Das neue Recht der Leiharbeit;, R. Wahsner et al. (eds), *'Heuern und Feuern' – Arbeitsrecht nach der Wende*, Hamburg.

Bosch, G. (1988), 'Der bundesdeutsche Arbeitsmarkt im internationalen Vergleich; "Eurosklerose oder Modell Deutschland"'?, *WSI Mitteilungen*, 3: 176–85.

Boyer, R. (1987), 'Crise et flexibilité' *Les Cahiers Français*. Special issue on 'La flexibilité du travail', 231: 2–6.

Brady, T. (1984), *New Technology and Skills in British Industry*, A Report for the Manpower Services Commission, Science Policy Research Unit.

Brannen, P. (1983), *Authority and Participation in Industry*, London: Batsford.

Braverman, H. (1974), *Labour and Monopoly Capital*, New York: Monthly Review Press.

Brossard, M. and Maurice, M. (1976), 'Is there a Universal Model of Organizational Structure?', *International Studies of Management and Organization*, 6: 11–45.

Brown, W. (ed.), (1981), *The Changing Contours of British Industrial Relations*, Oxford: Basil Blackwell.

Brumlop, E. and Jürgens, U. (1986), 'Rationalisation and Industrial Relations: A Case Study of Volkswagen', O. Jacobi et al. (eds), *Technological Change, Rationalisation and Industrial Relations*, London/Sydney: Croom Helm.

Buchanan, D. A. and Huczynski, A. A. (1985), *Organizational Behaviour*, Prentice-Hall International.

Budde, A., Child, J., Francis, A. and Kieser, A. (1982), 'Corporate Goals, Managerial Objectives, and Organizational Structures in British and West German Companies', *Organization Studies*, 3/1: 1–32.

Bunel, J. and Saglio, J. (1984), 'Employers' Associations in France', J. P. Windmüller and A. Gladstone (eds), *Employers' Associations and Industrial Relations. A Comparative Study*, Oxford: Clarendon Press.

Bunn, R. F. (1984), 'Employers' Associations in the Federal Republic of Germany', J. P. Windmüller and A. Gladstone (eds), *Employers' Associations and Industrial Relations. A Comparative Study*, Oxford: Clarendon Press.

Caire, G. (1984), 'Recent Trends in Collective Bargaining in France', *International Labour Review*, 123, 6: 723–42.

Casey, B. (1987), 'The extent and nature of temporary employment in Great Britain', *Policy Studies*, 8, 1: 64–75.

Cawson, A., Holmes, P. and Stevens, A. (1987), 'The Interaction between Firms and State in France: The Telecommunications and Consumer Electronics Sectors', S. Wilks and M. Wright (eds), *Comparative Government and Industry Relations*, Oxford: Oxford University Press.

CEDEFOP (1983), *New Perspectives on Continuing Education and Training in the European Community*, Berlin.

CEDEFOP (1984), *Vocational Training Systems in the Member States of the European Community*, Luxembourg.

CEDEFOP (1987), *The Role of the Social Partners in Vocational Training and Further Training in the FRG*, Report prepared by W. Streeck, J. Hilbert, K. H. van Kevelaer, F. Maier and H. Weber, Berlin and Bielefield.

A Challenge to Complacency. Changing Attitudes to Training, (1985). A Report to the MSC and NEDO by Coopers and Lybrand.

Child, J. (1969), *The Business Enterprise in Modern Industrial Society*, London: Collier-Macmillan.

Child, J. and Kieser, A. (1979), 'Organization and Managerial Roles in British and West German Companies: An Examination of the Culture-Free Thesis', C. J. Lammers and D. J. Hickson (eds), *Organizations Alike and Unlike*, London: Routledge and Kegan Paul.

Child, J. (1981), 'Culture, Contingency and Capitalism in the Cross-National Study of Organizations', *Research in Organizational Behaviour*, Vol. 3, ed. B. M. Staw and L. L. Cumings.

Child, J. (1984), *Organization. A Guide to Problems and Practice*, (2nd edn), London: Harper and Row.

Child, J. and Partridge, B. (1982), *Lost Managers: Supervisors in Industry and Society*, Cambridge: Cambridge University Press.

Child, J. and Tayeb, M. (1982–83), 'Theoretical Perspectives in Cross-National Organizational Research', *International Studies of Management and Organization*, Winter 1982–83, XII, 4: 23f.

Christie, I. (1988), 'Research and Development Policy: The Great Debate', *Policy Studies*, 8, 4: 11–22.

Claessens, D., Klönne, A. and Tschoepe, A. (1981), *Sozialkunde der Bundesrepublik Deutschland*, Düsseldorf/Köln: Diederichs.

Clark, J. (1985), 'Die Gewerkschaftsgesetzgebung 1979 bis 1984 und ihre Folgen für die Politik der Gewerkschaften', O. Jacobi and H. Kastendieck (eds), *Staat und Industrielle Beziehungen in Grossbritannien*, Frankfurt: Campus.

Clegg, H. A. (1983), *The Changing System of Industrial Relations in Great Britain*, Oxford: Basil Blackwell.

Cockburn, C. (1987), *Two-Track Training*, London: Macmillan.

Constable, J. and McCormick, R. (1987), *The Making of British Managers*, Sponsored by BIM/CBI.

Coombs, R., Saviotti, P. and Walsh, V. (1987), *Economics and Technological Change*, London: Macmillan.

Coriat, B. (1984), 'Labour and Capital in the Crisis: France 1966–82', M. Kesselman and G. Groux (eds), *The French Workers' Movement*, London: Allen and Unwin.

Cox, A. (ed.) (1986), *State, Finance and Industry: A Comparative Analysis*, Brighton: Wheatsheaf Books.

Cross, M. (1985), 'Flexible Manning', D. Clutterbuck (ed.), *New Patterns of Work*, Aldershot: Gower.

Crouch, C. (1979), 'Industrial Relations in Western Europe: Patterns of Change', W. Matthes (ed.), *Sozialer Wandel in Westeuropa*, Frankfurt: Campus.

Dale, A. and Bamford, C. L. (1988a), 'Temporary Workers: Case for Concern or Complacency?' *Work, Employment and Society*, 2, 2: 191–209.

Dale, A. and Bamford, C. (1988b), *Flexibility and the Peripheral Work-Force*, Department of Sociology, University of Surrey, June.

Daly, A., Hitchens, P. and Wagner, K. (1985), 'Productivity, Machinery and

Skills in a Sample of British and German Manufacturing Plants', *National Institute Economic Review*, 111, February: 48–61.

Daniel, W. (1987), *Workplace Industrial Relations and Technical Change*, London: Frances Pinter.

Daniel, W. W. and Millward, N. (1983), *Workplace Industrial Relations in Britain*, London: Heinemann.

Davis, L. E. (1979), 'Job Design: Historical Overview', L. E. Davis and J. C. Taylor (eds), *Design of Jobs*, (2nd edn), Goodyear Publishing Company: Santa Monica.

Davis, L. E. and Taylor, J. C. (1979), *Design of Jobs*, (2nd edn), Goodyear Publishing Company: Santa Monica.

Delamotte, Y. (1979), 'France', ILO (ed.), *New Forms of Work Organisation*, Geneva: ILO.

Delamotte, Y. (1986), *Les Cadres des Entreprises Dans une Monde en Mutation*, Geneva: ILO.

Diefenbacher, H., Kissler, L., Nutzinger, H.-G. and Teichert, V. (1984), *Mitbestimmung: Norm und Wirklichkeit. (Fallstudie aus einem Grossbetrieb der Automobilindustrie)*, Frankfurt: Campus.

Dore, R. (1973), *British Factory – Japanese Factory. The Origins of National Diversity in Industrial Relations*, London: Allen and Unwin.

Dore, R. (1986), *Flexible Rigidities*, London: Athlone Press.

Dräger, C. (1982), 'Das Betriebsverfassungsgesetz von 1972 aus der Sicht des Eigentümer-Unternehmers', M. Lezius (ed.), *10 Jahre Betriebsverfassungsgesetz 1972*, Spardorf: R. F. Wilfer.

Drexel, I. (1985), 'Neue Produktionsstrukturen auf Italienisch?', *Soziale Welt*, 2: 106–27.

Drexel, I. and Nuber, C. (1979), *Qualifizierung für Industriearbeit im Umbruch*, Frankfurt: Campus.

Dubois, P. (1981), 'Workers' Control over the Organization of Work: French and English Maintenance Workers in Mass Production Industry', *Organization Studies*, 2: 347–60.

Dubois, P. (1984), 'The Strike in France', M. Kesselman and G. Groux (eds), *The French Workers' Movement*, London: Allen and Unwin.

Dubois, P. (1986), 'Fifteen Years of New Forms of Work Organisation in France', P. Grootings et al. (eds), *New Forms of Work Organization and the Social and Economic Environment*, Budapest: Statistical Publishing House.

Duchêne, F. and Shepherd, G. (1987), *Managing Industrial Change in Western Europe*, London/New York: Frances Pinter.

Düll, K. (1984), 'Ein deutsch–französischer Beitrag über Arbeitsbedingungen und veränderte Formen der Nutzung von Arbeitskraft', K. Düll (ed.), *Industriearbeit in Frankreich*, Frankfurt: Campus.

Düll, K. (1985), 'Gesellschaftliche Modernisierungspolitik durch "neue Produktionskonzepte"?', *WSI Mitteilungen*, 3: 141–5.

Dyas, G. P. and Thanheiser, H. (1976), *The Emerging European Enterprise. Strategy and Structure in French and German Industry*, London: Macmillan.

Dyson, K. (1986), 'The State, Banks and Industry: The West German Case', A. Cox (ed.), *The State, Finance and Industry*, Brighton: Wheatsheaf Books.

Edwards, P. K. (1987), *Managing the Factory*, Oxford: Basil Blackwell.

Elbaum, M. (1987), 'Les Politiques de l'Emploi depuis Trente Ans', INSEE, *Données Sociales*, Paris.

Equal Opportunities Commission (1986), *Women and Men in Britain*, London: HMSO.

Erbes-Séguin, S. (1984), 'Trade Unions, Employers and the State: Towards a New Relationship?', M. Kesselman and G. Groux (eds), *The French Workers' Movement*, London: Allen and Unwin.

Esser, J. and Fach, W. (1983), '"Social Market" and Modernization Policy: West Germany', K. Dyson and S. Wilks (eds), *Industrial Crisis*, London: Martin Robertson.

European Foundation for the Improvement of Living and Working Conditions, (1978), *New Forms of Work Organisation in the European Community. United Kingdom*, Dublin.

Eyraud, F. and Tchobanian, R. (1985), 'The Auroux Reforms and Company Level Industrial Relations in France', *British Journal of Industrial Relations*, 23, 2: 241–58.

Eyraud, F. and Rychener, F. (1986), 'A Societal Analysis of New Technologies', P. Grootings (ed.), *Technology and Work. East–West Comparison*, London: Croom Helm.

Fidler, J. (1981), *The British Business Elite. Its Attitudes to Class, Status and Power*, London: Routledge and Kegan Paul.

Finlay, P. (1981), 'Overmanning: Germany vs. Britain', *Management Today*, August: 43–7.

Fores, M. and Glover, I. (eds) (1978), *Manufacturing and Management*, London: HMSO.

Fox, A. (1974), *Beyond Contract: Work, Power and Trust Relations*, London: Faber and Faber.

Fox, A. (1983), 'British Management and Industrial Relations: The Social Origins of a System', M. J. Earl (ed.), *Perspectives on Management*, Oxford: Oxford University Press.

Freeman, C. (1979), 'Technical Innovation and British Trade Performance', F. Blackaby (ed.), *De-Industrialization*, London: Heinemann.

Freyssenet, M. (1984), 'La requalification des opérateurs et la forme sociale actuelle d'automatisation', *Sociologie Du Travail*, 4: 422–34.

Friedman, A. (1977), *Industry and Labour. Class Struggle at Work and Monopoly Capitalism*, London: Macmillan.

Fuchs, G. (1988), 'Labour Market and Employment Policies in the Eighties. The Case of the FRG', Paper presented at the Aston/UMIST 'Labour Process' Conference in Birmingham.

Fürstenberg, F. (1984), 'Recent Trends in Collective Bargaining in the Federal Republic of Germany', *International Labour Review*, 123, 5: 615–30.

Gallie, D. (1978), *In Search of the New Working Class. Automation and Social Integration Within the Capitalist Enterprise*, Cambridge: Cambridge University Press.

Gallie, D. (1983), *Social Inequality and Class Radicalism in France and Britain*, Cambridge: Cambridge University Press.

Gamble, A. (1985), *Britain in Decline*, (2nd edn), London: Macmillan.

Gaudier, M. (1987), *Labour Market Flexibility: A Magic Wand or the Foundation of a New Industrial Society? A Bibliographic Essay*, Geneva: Institut International d'Etudes Sociales.

Gerstl, J. C. and Hutton, S. P. (1966), *Engineers: The Anatomy of a Profession*, London: Tavistock Publications.

Gill, C. (1985), *Work, Unemployment and the New Technology*, Cambridge: Polity Press.

Glover, I. and Kelly, M. P. (1987), *Engineers in Britain. A Sociological Study of the Engineering Dimension*, London: Allen and Unwin.

Glover, I. (1978), 'Executive Career Patterns: Britain, France, Germany, and Sweden', M. Fores and I. Glover (eds), *Manufacturing and Management*, London: HMSO.

Goldsmith, W. and Clutterbuck, D. (1984), *The Winning Streak. Britain's Top Companies Reveal their Formulas for Success*, London: Weidenfeld and Nicolson.

Grant, W. (with Sargent J.) (1987), *Business and Politics in Britain*, London: Macmillan.

Green, D. (1986), 'The State, Finance and Industry in France', A. Cox (ed.), *The State, Finance and Industry*, Brighton: Wheatsheaf Books.

Green, D. (1983), 'Strategic Management and the State: France', K. Dyson and St Wilks (eds), *Industrial Crisis*, London: Martin Robertson.

Gregory, A. (1988), 'Part-time Work in Large-Scale Grocery Retailing – Flexibility for Whom?', Paper presented at the Aston/UMIST 'Labour Process' Conference in Birmingham.

Grünberg, L. (1986), 'Workplace Relations in the Economic Crisis: A Comparison of a British and a French Automobile Plant', *Sociology*, 20, 4: 503–31.

Grünwald, W. and Lilge, H.-G. (1981), 'Change of Leadership Style in German Enterprises: From Authoritative to Participative Leadership?', G. Dlugos, K. Weiermair and W. Dorow (eds), *Management Under Differing Value Systems – Political, Social and Economical Perspectives in a Changing World*, Berlin: Walter de Gruyter.

Hakim, C. (1987a), 'Homeworking in Britain', *Employment Gazette*, February: 92–104.

Hakim, C. (1987b), 'Homeworking in Britain', *Employment Gazette*, April: 218f.

Hakim, C. (1987c), 'Trends in the Flexible Workforce', *Employment Gazette*, November: 549–61.

Hall, P. (1986), *Governing the Economy. The Politics of State Intervention in Britain and France*, Cambridge: Polity Press.

Hantrais, L. (1988), 'Restructuring Work Time: International Issues and Perspectives', Paper presented at the Aston/UMIST 'Labour Process' Conference in Birmingham.

Hantrais, L. (1982), *Contemporary French Society*, London: Macmillan.

Harris, R. (1987), *Power and Powerlessness in Industry*, London: Tavistock.

Hartmann, G., Nicholas, I. J., Sorge, A. and Warner, M. (1984), 'Consequences of CNC Technology: A Study of British and West German Manufacturing Firms', M. Warner (ed.), *Microprocessors, Manpower and Society*, London: Gower.

Hayward, J. (1986), *The State and the Market Economy. Industrial Patriotism and State Intervention in France*, Brighton: Harvester Press.

Heizman, J. (1984), 'Work Structuring in Automated Manufacturing Systems Exemplified by Use of Industrial Robots for Body Shell Assembly', T. Martin (ed.), *Design of Work in Automated Manufacturing Systems*, Oxford: Pergamon Press.

Herz, T. (1983), *Klassen, Schichten, Mobilität*, Stuttgart: Teubner.

Herzberg, F. (1976), *The Managerial Choice*, Homewood/Illinois.
Hickson, D. J., Pugh, D. S. and Pheysey, D. (1969), 'Operations Technology and Organisation Structure: An Empirical Reappraisal', *Administrative Science Quarterly*, 14: 378–97.
Hickson, D. J., McMillan, C. J., Azumi, K. and Horvath, D. (1979), 'Grounds for Comparative Organization Theory: Quicksands or Hard Core?', C. J. Lammers and D. J. Hickson (eds), *Organizations Alike and Unlike*, London: Routledge and Kegan Paul.
Hofstede, G. (1979), 'Hierarchical Power Distance in Forty Countries', C. J. Lammers and D. J. Hickson (eds), *Organizations Alike and Unlike. International and Interinstitutional Studies in the Sociology of Organization*, London: Routledge and Kegan Paul.
Hofstede, G. (1980), *Culture's Consequences. International Differences in Work-Related Values*, London: Sage.
Horn, E.-J. (1982), *Management of Industrial Change in the Federal Republic of Germany*, Sussex European Papers No. 13, Brighton: Sussex European Research Centre.
Horovitz, J. (1980), *Top Management Control in Europe*, New York: St Martin's Press.
Horvath, D., Azumi, K., Hickson, D. J. and McMillan, C. J. (1981), 'Bureaucratic Structures in Cross-National Perspective: A Study of British, Japanese, and Swedish Firms', G. Dlugos, K. Weiermair, and W. Dorow (eds), *Management Under Differing Value Systems*, Berlin: Walter de Gruyter.
Hough, J. R. (1981), 'France', E. O. Smith (ed.), *Trade Unions in the Developed Economies*, London: Croom Helm.
Howarth, J. (1982), 'The French Communist Party and "Class Alliances"', D. S. Bell (ed.), *Contemporary French Political Parties*, London: Croom Helm
Hyman, R. (1984), *Strikes*, (3rd edn), London: Fontana.
Industrial Democracy in Europe (IDE) Research Group (1981a), *European Industrial Relations*, Oxford: Oxford University Press.
Industrial Democracy in Europe (IDE) Research Group (1981b), 'Industrial Democracy in Europe', *Organisation Studies*, 2, 2: 113–29.
Information Technology (IT) Skills Shortages Committee (1985), *Second Report: Changing Technology, Changing Skills*, London: Dept of Trade and Industry.
ILO, (1979), *New Forms of Work Organisation*, Geneva: ILO.
Institute of Manpower Studies (IMS) (1984), *Competence and Competition – Training and Education in the FRG*, Report for the NEDO and the MSC, London: IMS.
Institute of Manpower Studies (IMS) (1986a), *Changing Working Patterns*, A Report for the National Economic Development Office in Association with the Department of Employment, London: IMS.
Institute of Manpower Studies (IMS) (1986b), *UK Occupation and Employment Trends to 1990*, A. Rajan and R. Pearson (eds), London: Butterworth.
d'Iribarne, A. and Lutz, B. (1983), 'Work Organization in Flexible Manufacturing Systems – First Findings from International Comparisons', T. Martin (ed.), *Design of Work in Automated Manufacturing Systems*, Oxford: Pergamon Press.
Jacobi. O. (1985), 'Ökonomische Schwäche und fragmentierte Kollektivbeziehungen – Zum Problem des "vicious circle"', O. Jacobi and H. Kastendieck (eds), *Staat und Industrielle Beziehungen in Grossbritannien*, Frankfurt: Campus.

Jacobs, E., Orwell, St, Paterson, P. and Weltz, F. (1978), *The Approach to Industrial Change in Britain and Germany. A Comparative Study of Workplace Relations and Manpower Policies*, London: Anglo-German Foundation.

Jamieson, I. (1982–83), 'The Concept of Culture and Its Relevance for an Analysis of Business Enterprise in Different Societies', *International Studies of Management and Organisation*, Winter 1982–83, XII, 4: 71f.

Jeammeaud, A. and Friant, M. L. (1987), 'Liberalisierung von Arbeitsmarkt und Arbeitsrecht in Frankreich', *WSI Mitteilungen*, 4: 213–18.

Jenkins, D. (1981), 'Work Reform in France', Work Research Unit Occasional Paper, 15, January.

Jones, B. (1988), 'Work and Flexible Automation in Britain: A Review of Developments and Possibilities', *Work, Employment and Society*, 2, 4: 451–86.

Jürgens, U., Dohse, K. and Malsch, T. (1986), 'New Production Concepts in West German Car Plants', S. Tolliday and J. Zeitlin (eds), *The Automobile Industry and its Workers*, Cambridge: Polity Press.

Kern, H. and Schumann, M. (1970), *Industriearbeit und Arbeiterbewusstsein*, 2 Volumes, Frankfurt: Campus.

Kern, H. and Schumann, M. (1984a), 'Neue Produktionskonzepte haben Chancen', *Soziale Welt*, 35, 1–2: 146–58.

Kern, H. and Schumann, M. (1984b), *Das Ende der Arbeitsteilung? Rationalisierung in der industriellen Produktion*, Munich: Verlag C. H. Beck.

Kern, H. and Schumann, M. (1989). 'New Concepts of Production in German Plants', P. J. Katzenstein (ed.), *The Third West German Republic: forthcoming*.

Kerr, C., Dunlop, J. T., Harbison, F. H. and Myers, C. A. (1960), *Industrialism and Industrial Man*, London: Heinemann.

Kesselman, M. (1984), 'Conclusion', M. Kesselman and G. Groux (eds), *The French Workers' Movement: Economic Crisis and Political Change*, London: Allen and Unwin.

Kesselman, M. and Groux, G. (eds) (1984), *The French Workers' Movement*, London: Allen and Unwin.

King, S. (1988), 'Temporary Workers in Britain. Findings from the 1986 Labour Force Survey', *Employment Gazette*, April: 238f.

Kotthoff, H. (1981), *Betriebsräte and Betriebliche Herrschaft*, Frankfurt: Campus.

Landes, D. (1969), *The Unbound Prometheus. Technological Change and Industrial Development*, Cambridge: Cambridge University Press.

Lane, T. (1987), 'Unions: Fit for Active Service?', *Marxism Today*, February: 20f.

Laroque, M. (1984), *Politiques Sociales dans la France Contemporaine*, Paris: Les Editions S.T.H.

Lawrence, P. (1980), *Managers and Management in West Germany*, London: Croom Helm.

Lawrence, P. (1982), *Personnel Management in West Germany: Portrait of a Function*, Research Paper, Dept of Management Studies, University of Loughborough.

Lawrence, P. (1984), *Management in Action*, London: Routledge and Kegan Paul.

Lawrence, P. (1988), 'In Another Country', A. Bryman (ed.), *Doing Research in Organizations*, London: Routledge.

Lee, G. (1981), *Who Gets to the Top*, Aldershot: Gower.

Lee, G. (1986), *Information Technology and the Engineer: Professional Powerholders or Technicians to the Powerful?*, Research Paper, ESRC Work Organization Research Centre, Aston University.

Levy-Leboyer, M. (1980), 'The Large Corporation in Modern France', A. D. Chandler and H. Daems (eds), *Managerial Hierarchies*, Cambridge, Mass.: Harvard University Press.

Lezius, M. (ed.) (1982), *10 Jahre Betriebsverfassungsgesetz 1972, Gelungene Partnerschaft – Utopie oder Wirklichkeit?*, Spardorf: R.F. Wilfer

Lisle-Williams, M. (1986), 'The State, Finance and Industry in Britain', A. Cox (ed.), *State, Finance and Industry*, Brighton: Wheatsheaf Press.

Littek, W. and Heisig, U. (1986), 'Rationalisierung von Arbeit als Aushandlungsprozess', *Soziale Welt*, 37, 2/3.

Littler, C. (1982), *The Development of the Labour Process in Capitalist Societies*, London: Heinemann.

Littler, C. and Salaman, G. (1984), *Class at Work. The Design, Allocation and Control of Jobs*, London: Batsford.

Lorino, P. (1985), 'French Industrial Policy and U.S. Industry', S. Zukin (ed.), *Industrial Policy*, New York: Praeger.

Lupri. E. (1970), 'Gesellschaftliche Differenzierung und familiale Autorität', G. Lüschen and E. Lupri (eds), *Soziologie der Familie*, Special Issue (14) of *Köllner Zeitschrift Für Soziologie und Sozialpsychologie*, Opladen.

Lutz, B. (1981), 'Education and Employment: Contrasting Evidence from France and the Federal Republic of Germany', *European Journal of Education*, 16: 73–86.

Lutz, B. and Schultz-Wild, R. (1983), 'Tendenzen und Faktoren des Wandels der Arbeitswelt bei fortschreitender Automatisierung', *ZWE*, 78.

Maier, C. S. (1970), 'Between Taylorism and Technocracy: European ideologies and the vision of industrial productivity in the 1920s', *The Journal of Contemporary History*, 5, 2: 27–62.

Maitland, I. (1983), *The Causes of Industrial Disorder. A Comparison of a British and a German Factory*, London: Routledge and Kegan Paul.

Mangham, I. L. and Silver, M. S. (1986), *Management Training – Context and Practice*, ESRC and DTI, School of Management: University of Bath.

Mant, A. (1978), 'Authority and Task in Manufacturing Operations of Multi-National Firms', M. Fores and I. Glover (eds), *Manufacturing and Management*, London: HMSO.

Marceau, J. (1977), *Class and Status in France. Economic Change and Social Immobility 1945–75*, Oxford: Clarendon Press.

Marchand, O. (1987), 'Population Active, Emploi, Chômage: Données de Cadrage', *Données Sociales* : 84–94.

Marsden, D. (1978), *Industrial Democracy and Industrial Control in West Germany, France and Great Britain*, Dept. of Employment Research Paper No. 4, London.

Marsden, D. (1987), 'Collective Bargaining and Industrial Adjustment in Britain, France, Italy and West Germany', F. Duchêne and G. Shepherd (eds), *Managing Industrial Change in Western Europe*, London/N.Y. : Frances Pinter.

Maurice, M. and Sellier, F. (1979), 'Societal Analysis of Industrial Relations: A Comparison Between France and West Germany', *British Journal of Industrial Relations*, 17, 3: 322–36.

Maurice, M., Sellier, F. and Silvestre, J.-J. (1977), *Production de la Hierarchie Dans L'Entreprise. Recherche D'Un Effet Sociétal*, Aix-en Provence: LEST.

Maurice, M., Sellier, F. and Silvestre, J.-J. (1986a), *The Social Foundations of Industrial Power*, London: MIT Press.

Maurice, M., Eyraud, F., d'Iribarne, A. and Rychener, F. (1986b), *Des Entreprises en Mutation dans la Crise*. Research Report. Aix-en-Provence: LEST.

Maurice, M., Sorge, A. and Warner, M. (1980), 'Societal Differences in Organising Manufacturing Units', *Organization Studies*, 1: 63–91.

Mauritz, W., '10 Jahre Betriebsverfassungsgesetz aus der Sicht des Eigentümer-Unternehmers', M. Lezius (ed.), *10 Jahre Betriebsverfassungsgesetz 1972*, Spardorf: R. F. Wilfer.

May, B. (1974), *Social, Educational and Professional Background of German Management*, Unpublished Research Report.

Mayes, D. G. (1987), 'Does Manufacturing Matter?', *National Institute Economic Review*, 122, 4: 47–58.

Meager, N. (1986), 'Temporary Work in Britain', *Employment Gazette*, January: 7–15.

Mendius, H. G., Sengenberger, W. and Weimer, S. (1987), *Arbeitskräfteprobleme und Humanisierungspotentiale in Kleinbetrieben*, Frankfurt: Campus.

Merkle, J. (1980), *Management and Ideology. The Legacy of the International Scientific Management Movement*, Berkeley, Los Angeles, London: University of California Press.

Millar, J. A. (1974), *British Management vs. German Management*, Aldershot: Gower.

Mills, G. (1985), *On the Board*, London: Allen and Unwin.

Millward, N. and Stevens, M. (1986), *British Workplace Industrial Relations 1980–1984*, The DE/ESRC/PSI/ACAS Surveys, Aldershot: Gower.

Mintzberg, H. (1973), *The Nature of Managerial Work*, New York: Harper and Row.

Mitbestimmungskommission (The Biedenkopf Report) (1970), *Mitbestimmung im Unternehmen*, Stuttgart: Kohlhammer.

Moon, J. (1984), 'The Reponses of British Governments to Unemployment', J. Richardson and R. Henning (eds), *Unemployment. Policy Responses of Western Democracies*, London: Sage.

Mooser, J. (1984), *Arbeiterleben in Deutschland 1900–1970*, Frankfurt: Suhrkamp.

Mouriaux, M.-F. and Mouriaux, R. (1984), 'Unemployment Policy in France, 1976–82', J. Richardson and R. Henning (eds), *Unemployment. Policy Responses of Western Democracies*, London: Sage.

Müller-Jentsch, W. (1986), *Soziologie der industriellen Beziehungen*, Frankfurt: Campus.

Naujoks, W. and Kayser, G. (1983), *Mittelstand 1983: Lage im Wettbewerb und betriebswirtschaftliche Praxis*, Göttingen: Verlag Otto Schwartz.

NEDO, (1981), *Tool Making. A Comparison of UK and West German Companies*, Gauge and Tool Sector Working Party, London: NEDO.

NEDO, (1987), *The Making of Managers*, Report on behalf of the MSC, NEDC, and BIM, London: NEDO.

New, C. C. and Myers, A. (1986), *Managing Manufacturing Operations in the UK 1975–1985*, London: Institute of Manpower Studies.

Nichols, T. (1986), *The British Worker Question*, London: Routledge and Kegan Paul.

Noelle-Neumann, E. (1981), *The Germans. Public Opinion Polls, 1967–80*, Westport, Conn.: Greenwood Press.

Northcott, J., Rogers, P., Knetsch, W. and de Lestapis, B. (1985), *Microelectronics in Industry. An International Comparison: Britain, Germany, France*, London: Policy Studies Institute.

OECD (1986a), *OECD Economic Surveys 1985/86, Germany*, Paris: OECD.

OECD (1986b), *OECD Economic Surveys 1985/86, United Kingdom*, Paris: OECD.

OECD (1986c), *Labour Market Flexibility*. Report by a high-level group of experts to the Secretary-General, Paris: OECD.

Oechslin, J.-J. (1987), 'Training and the business world: the French experience', *International Labour Review*, 126, 6: 653–67.

Patel, P. and Pavitt, K. (1987), 'The Elements of British Technological Competitiveness', *National Institute Economic Review*, 122, 4: 72–83.

Peacock, A. (in collaboration with Bob Grant) (1980), *Structural Economic Policies in West Germany and the United Kingdom*, London: Anglo-German Foundation for the Study of Industrial Society.

Perrin-Pelletier, F. (1986), 'Industrial Policy and the Automobile Industry', W. J. Adams and C. Stoffaës (eds), *French Industrial Policy*.

Perrow, C. (1970), *Organisational Analysis: A Sociological View*, London: Tavistock Publications.

Piore, M. J. and Sabel, C. (1984), *The Second Industrial Divide*, New York: Basic Books.

Piotet, F. (1984), 'Automation and Working Conditions in France', F. Butera and J. Thurman (eds), *Automation and Work Design*, ILO Study, Amsterdam/New York/Oxford: North-Holland.

Pollert, A. (1988), 'The "Flexible Firm". Fixation or Fact?', *Work, Employment and Society*, 2, 3: 281–316.

Poole, M. (1986), *Towards a New Industrial Democracy. Workers' Participation in Industry*. London: Routledge and Kegan Paul.

Prais, S. J. (1981a), *Productivity and Industrial Structure: A Statistical Study of Manufacturing Industry in Britain, Germany and the US*, Cambridge: Cambridge University Press.

Prais, S. J. (1981b), 'Vocational Qualifications of the Labour Force in Britain and Germany', *National Institute Economic Review*, 98: 47–59.

Prais, S. J. and Wagner, K. (1985), 'Schooling Standards in England and Germany: Some Summary Comparisons, Bearing on Economic Performance', *National Institute Economic Review*, 112 (2): 53–72.

Pratten, C. F. (1976), *Labour Productivity Differentials Within International Companies*, Cambridge: Cambridge University Press.

Przeworski. A. and Teune, H. (1970), *The Logic of Comparative Enquiry*, New York: Wiley.

Pugh, D. S. and Hickson, D. J. (1968), 'The Comparative Study of Organizations', D. Pym (ed.), *Industrial Society*, Harmondsworth: Penguin Books.

Purcell, J. and Sisson, K. (1983), 'Strategies and Practices in the Management of Industrial Relations', G. Bain (ed.), *Industrial Relations in Britain*, Oxford: Basil Blackwell.

Roberts, J. (1986), 'Apprenticeships in West Germany', *Employment Gazette*, March–April: 109–15.

Roberts, K. H. (1970), 'On Looking at an Elephant: An Evaluation of Cross-Cultural Research Related to Organizations', *Psychological Bulletin*, 74: 327–50.

Rose, M. (1985), 'Universalism, Culturalism and the Aix Group', European Sociological Review, I, 1: 65–83.

Roy, A. D. (1982), 'Labour Productivity in 1980: An International Comparison', *National Institute Economic Review*, 101, August.

Rudolph, J. (1987), 'Das englische Produktivitätswunder', *Frankfurter Allgemeine Zeitung*, 19 August 1987.

Ruffier, J. (1984), 'Eine Typologic Organisatorischer Veränderungen in Französischen Betrieben', K. Düll (ed.), *Industriearbeit in Frankreich*, Frankfurt: Campus.

Sabel, C. (1982), *Work and Politics*, Cambridge: Cambridge University Press.

Säcker, F.-J. (1981), 'The German Model of Co-Determination: Programmatic Perspectives, Confrontative Issues, and Prospective Developments', G. Dlugos, K. Weiermair and W. Dorow (eds), *Management under Differing Value Systems*, Berlin: Walter de Gruyter.

Santini, J.-J. (1987), 'La flexibilité en Grande Bretagne', *Les Cahiers Français*, 231. Les Notices 8.

Saunders, C. and Marsden, P. (1981), *Pay Inequalities in the European Community*, London: Butterworth.

Savall, F. (1976), *Work and People*, Oxford: Clarendon Press.

Scarborough, H. (1986), 'The Politics of Technological Change at British Leyland', O. Jacobi et al. (eds), *Technological Change, Rationalisation and Industrial Relations*, London/Sydney: Croom Helm.

Schwab, L. (1987), 'L'individualisation des salairies', *Les Cahiers Français*, Special issue on 'La flexibilité du travail', 231: 25–9.

Scott, J. (1985), *Corporations, Classes and Capitalism*, (2nd edn), London: Hutchinson.

Sengenberger, W. (1984a), 'Vocational Worker Training, Labour Market Structure, and Industrial Relations in West Germany', *The Keizai Gaku, Annual Report of the Economic Society, Tohoku University*, 46, 2: 23–37.

Sengenberger, W. (1984b), 'West German Employment Policy: Restoring Worker Competition', *Industrial Relations*, 23, 3: 323–43.

Sengenberger, W. (ed.), (1978), *Der gespaltene Arbeitsmarkt*, Frankfurt: Campus.

Sharp, M. (ed.) (1985), *Europe and the New Technologies*, London: Frances Pinter.

Smith, W. R. (1984), 'Dynamics of Plural Unionism in France', *British Journal of Industrial Relations*, 22, 1: 15–33.

Sorge, A. and Streeck, W. (1987), *Industrial Relations and Technical Change: The Case for an Extended Perspective*, Discussion Paper, Research Unit Labour Market and Employment, Wissenschaftszentrum Berlin. Published, in R. Hyman and W. Streeck (eds), *New Technology and Industrial Relations*, Oxford: Basil Blackwell, 1988.

Sorge, A. and Warner, M. (1980), 'Manpower Training, Manufacturing Organization and Workplace Relations in Great Britain and West Germany', *British Journal of Industrial Relations*, 18: 318–33.

Sorge, A. and Warner, M. (1986), *Comparative Factory Organization. An Anglo-German Comparison of Management and Manpower in Manufacturing*, WZB Publications, Gower.

Soulage, B. (1985), 'Industrial Priorities in the Current French Plan', Sh. Zukin (ed.), *Industrial Policy*, New York: Praeger.

Stähle, W. H. (1979), 'Federal Republic of Germany', ILO (ed.), *New Forms of Work Organisation*, Geneva: ILO.

Stocks, M. (1983), *West Germany: A Structural Forecast to 1990*, Special Report No. 147, The Economist Intelligence Unit, London.

Stoffaës, C. (1986), 'Industrial Policy in the High-Technology Industries', W. J. Adams and C. Stoffaës (eds), *French Industrial Policy*, Washington D.C.: The Brookings Institution.

Storey, D. J. (1982), *Entrepreneurship and the New Firm*, London: Croom Helm.

Streeck, W. (1984a), *Industrial Relations in West Germany. A Case Study of the Car Industry*, London: Heinemann.

Streeck, W. (1984c), 'Co-Determination: The Fourth Decade', B. Wilpert and A. Sorge (eds), *International Perspectives on Organizational Democracy*, Chichester: John Wiley.

Streeck, W. (1987a), 'Industrial Relations in West Germany: Agenda for Change', Discussion Paper. Research Unit Labour Market and Employment Wissenschaftszentrum, Berlin.

Streeck, W. (1987b), 'The Uncertainties of Management in the Management of Uncertainty: Employers, Labour Relations and Industrial Adjustment in the 1980s', *Work, Employment and Society*, 1, 3: 281–309.

Syzman, J. (1983), *Governments, Markets and Growth*, Oxford: Martin Robertson.

Telesis, (1986), *Competing for Prosperity. Business Strategies and Industrial Policies in Modern France*, Research Report by B. Déchéry for the Policy Studies Institute, London.

Tolliday, St and Zeitlin, J. (eds) (1986), *The Automobile Industry and its Workers*, Polity Press: Cambridge.

Torrington, D. (1978), *Comparative Industrial Relations in Europe*, Associated Business Programmes.

Trevor, M. (1985), *Japanese Industrial Knowledge. Can It Help British Industry?*, Aldershot: Gower.

Turnbull, P. W. and Cunningham, M. T. (eds) (1981), *International Marketing and Purchasing*, London: Macmillan.

Vickerstaff, S. (1985), 'Industrial Training in Britain: the Dilemmas of a Neo-Corporatist Policy', A. Cawson (ed.), *Organized Interests and the State*, London/Beverly Hills/New Delhi: Sage Publications.

Vickery, L. (1986), 'France', P. Burns and J. Dewhurst (eds), *Small Business in Europe*, London: Macmillan.

Vogl. F. (1973), *German Business after the Economic Miracle*, London: Macmillan.

Volz, J. (1983), *Vocational Training and Job Creation Schemes in France*, Berlin: CEDEFOP.

Walsh, K. (1982), 'An Analysis of Strikes in Four EEC Countries', *Industrial Relations Journal*, 13, 4, Winter: 65–72.

Webber, D. and Nass, G. (1984), 'Employment Policy in West Germany', J.

Richardson and R. Henning (eds), *Unemployment. Policy Responses of Western Democracies*, London: Sage.

Weber, W. (1982), 'Der Einfluss des Betriebsverfassungsgesetzes 1972', M. Lezius (ed.), *10 Jahre Betriebsverfassungsgesetz 1972*, Spardorf: R. F. Wilfer.

Weiermair, K. (1986), *Industrial Training Systems in Japan and West Germany*, Unpublished Research Report, 1, Toronto.

Weltz, F. (1978), *Introduction of New Technologies, Employment Policies and Industrial Relations*, London: Anglo-German Foundation.

Whalley, P. (1986), *The Social Production of Technical Work*, London: Macmillan.

Whitley, R., Alan, T. and Marceau, J. (1981), *Master of Business. The Making of a New Elite?*, London: Tavistock.

Wiener, M. J. (1981), *English Culture in the Decline of the Industrial Spirit, 1850–1980*, Cambridge: Cambridge University Press.

Wilks St (1983), 'Liberal State and Party Competition: Britain', K. Dyson and St Wilks (eds), *Industrial Crisis*, London: Martin Robertson.

Wilks, St and Wright, M. (eds) (1987), *Comparative Government and Industry Relations*, Oxford: Clarendon Press.

Willman, P. (1986), *Technological Change, Collective Bargaining and Industrial Efficiency*, Oxford: Clarendon Press.

Wilpert, B. and Rayley, J. (1983), *Anspruch und Wirklichkeit der Mitbestimmung*, Frankfurt: Campus.

Wilson, G. K. (1985), *Business and Politics – A Comparative Introduction*, London: Macmillan.

Windmüller, J. P. and Gladstone, A. (1984), *Employers Associations and Industrial Relations. A Comparative Study*, Oxford: Clarendon Press.

Wood, S. (1982), *The Degradation of Work? Skill, Deskilling and the Labour Process*, London: Hutchinson.

Wood, S. and Kelly, J. (1982), 'Taylorism, Responsible Autonomy and Management Strategy', in S. Wood (ed.), *The Degradation of Work? Skill, Deskilling and the Labour Process*, London: Hutchinson.

Zachert, U. (1986), 'Ein Jahr "Beschäftigungsförderungsgesetz" – eine erste Bilanz', *WSI Mitteilungen*, 5: 377–80.

Zukin, Sh. (ed.), *Industrial Policy*, New York: Praeger.

Zürn, P. (1985), *Vom Geist und Stil des Hauses. Unternehmenskultur in Deutschland*, Verlag Moderne Industrie.

Index